TECHNICAL READOUT:™

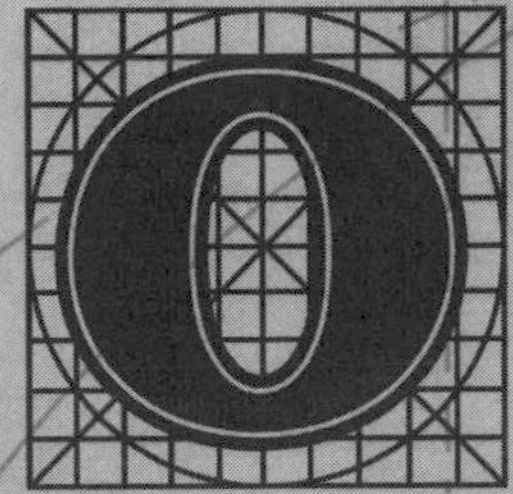

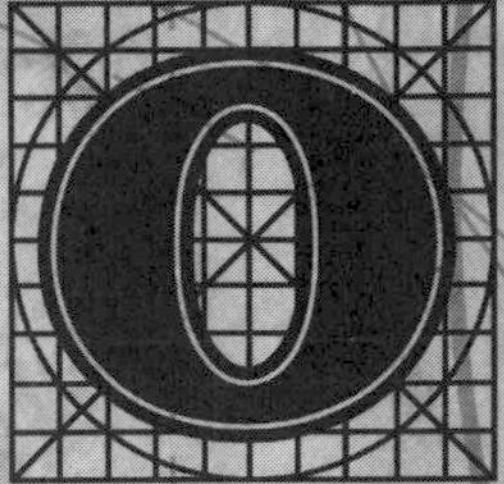

• FASA CORPORATION •

TABLE OF CONTENTS

CREDITS

Design
Randall N. Bills
Dan "Flake" Grendell
Chris Hartford
Bryan Nystul

Writing
Herbert Beas
Randall N. Bills
Hugh Browne
Loren L. Coleman
Dan "Flake" Grendell
Chris Hartford
Christopher Hussey
Patrick Kirkland
Bryan Nystul
Christoffer "Bones" Trossen

Product Development
Randall N. Bills
Bryan Nystul

Product Editing
Tara Gallagher
Sharon Tuner Mulvihill
Diane Piron-Gelman

BattleTech Line Developer
Bryan Nystul

Editorial Staff
Editorial Director
Donna Ippolito
Managing Editor
Sharon Tuner Mulvihill
Associate Editors
Diane Piron-Gelman
Robert Boyle
Tara Gallagher

Production Staff
Art Director
Jim Nelson
Cover Art
Doug Chaffee
Graphic Design
Jim Nelson and John Bridegroom
Illustrations
Doug Chaffee
Kevin Long
Mathew Plog
Brian Snoddy
Franz Vohwinkel
Original Nova Cat Graphic Creation
Lex Story
Layout
John Bridegroom

Playtesters
Randall N. Bills, David Briedis, Frank Crull, Dan "Flake" Grendell, Craig Gulledge, Chris Hartford, Lewis Helfer, James Lillian, Luke Miller, Bryan Nystul, Richard Raisley, Chris Raisley. *Austin Playtest Group*: Charles Bellamy, Chris Chapa, Marty Davis, Mitchel Elstrom, Kevin Hambel, Cody Hammock, Greg Hazel, Clint Hill, Robby Houser, Robert Koefed, Adam Parker, Jeff Webb. *Group W*: Andrew Bethke, James W. Moorman, Jr., Robert G. Kranker, Edward C. Witzlib. *The Singapore Longshoremen*: Harry Andrew Collis, Tom Evans, John Kielman, Andy Lichey, Frank Lutovsky, Derek Manchester, Nicholas Marsala, Rick Remer, Rick Seidl, Chris Smith, Christoffer "Bones" Trossen. *Steel City MechWarriors*: Dave Barton, Jeff Boggess, Rich Cencarik, Bob Cook, Rich Darr, Jeff George, Brian Golightly, Scott Jamison, Christopher Keegel, Stephen Kuhn, Josh Shaffer, Ed Suchacek, Stephen Watts. *Wounds Unlimited*: Dave Carlson, Christopher Hussey, Shayne Schelinder, Paul D. Thompson.

Published by FASA Corporation
1100 W. Cermak Road • Suite B305
Chicago, IL 60608

FASA Corporation can be reached on America OnLine (E. Mail—FASAInfo (General Information, Shadowrun, BattleTech) or FASA Art (Art Comments)) in the Online Gaming area (Keyword "Gaming"). Via InterNet use <AOL Account Name>@AOL.COM, but please, no list or server subscriptions. Thanks!

Visit our World Wide Web site at http://www.FASA.com

INCOMING MESSAGE

SEND

SAVE

CANCEL

DELETE

It is ironic that in their rabid desire to conquer us and forge a new Star League, the Clans forced the Inner Sphere to create the only thing that could save us—a new Star League. With the stroke of a pen, the Great House leaders achieved what they had failed to accomplish through force of arms. The combined might of the Inner Sphere—united under the banner of the Star League—moved like a whirlwind into the Smoke Jaguar occupation zone, sweeping the Jaguar forces before them. In four short months, they reclaimed what most had thought lost forever: forty-four worlds occupied by the Clans. Hoping to deal the final blow to the already wounded Jaguars, Archon-Prince Victor Steiner-Davion, along with Precentor Martial Anastasius Focht and many others, led a multinational force in a far-ranging strike against Clan Smoke Jaguar's homeworld, Huntress.

More than a year has passed since their departure, but my calculations indicate that the task force should already be returning to the Inner Sphere. I can conceive of no other outcome but that they will return.

All has not been quiet in their absence. The Inner Sphere united to annihilate an entire Clan, but the Star League alliance is troubled at best. First Lord Sun-Tzu Liao is using his position to expand his realm. Tension brewing between the Federated Commonwealth and Lyran Alliance seems certain to erupt into a full-scale war between two of the most powerful Houses in the Inner Sphere. In addition, four Clans still hold more than one hundred fifty worlds. All of this has spurred the military designers and manufacturers of the Inner Sphere to new heights of innovation. In my 3058 report, I noted that the Draconis Combine had begun to field its own OmniMechs. As you will note in this latest report, all the Houses save the Federated Commonwealth are currently constructing and fielding OmniMechs. (House Davion's lack of progress in this area must be attributed to Prince Victor's preoccupation with the Clans and recent absence.) Perhaps even more startling is the abundance of new weapon systems appearing in Inner Sphere 'Mechs and vehicles. Though most of this technology has been re-engineered from captured Clan technology, several weapon systems are unique to the Inner Sphere, attesting to the drive and ingenuity of Inner Sphere scientists.

Many are proclaiming that the resurrected Star League will bring back the prosperity and peace of days gone by, but I have my doubts. With the Inner Sphere (and Clans) producing more 'Mechs and introducing new technologies for military use faster than ever before, I can only assume that continued war will result.

As always, I wish to thank the legions of ComStar personnel whose observations and painstaking research make up this report. All our efforts would be in vain without their aid. Additionally, I pray for a speedy return of our forces. All I can do is entrust this report to our Explorer Corps, and hope that their HPG transmission will find my good friend Pascal and our Precentor Martial in good health and on their way home.

—Merle Jimmus
Demi-Precentor VII-Sigma
ComStar Archives, Terra
1 November 3060

INTRODUCTION

INCOMING MESSAGE

SEND

SAVE

CANCEL

DELETE

Per the order of the Precentor Martial, I have compiled a report of the current military hardware that has become available to both the Clans and Inner Sphere forces since our last report.

My team and I have spent countless hours decoding a wealth of captured Smoke Jaguar military files. Though many of the files were corrupted, we have successfully pieced together our first look at Clan military documentation. Production facilities, structural components, weapon series—all have finally fallen into our hands. Additionally, we have information on many of the second-line 'Mechs that have not yet been seen in the Inner Sphere, as well as Clan vehicles. We have also painstakingly compiled as much information as possible about the new ProtoMechs fielded against Task Force Serpent by the Smoke Jaguars. I personally doubt we will ever field Inner Sphere ProtoMechs. First, the enhanced imaging (EI) technology required to pilot a ProtoMech is proving extremely difficult to duplicate. Second, and perhaps more important, are the psychological requirements of the ProtoMechs: invasive surgery for the EI implants, plus complete sensory deprivation and total personality submersion when piloting the ProtoMechs. Clansmen, who are born and raised warriors, can easily adapt to such extreme conditions. Most Inner Sphere warriors would simply not submit to or survive that type of trauma. This knowledge remains valuable, however; for though the Smoke Jaguars are no more, the other Clans are most likely already involved in Trials of Possession for this new technology, and ProtoMechs will surely soon appear in their toumans.

I recently received a report from Demi-Precentor Merle Jimmus—transmitted to our convoy by the Explorer Corps via our HPG system—on the current status of the Inner Sphere, which I have included in this report. I have always considered Jimmus remarkably gifted at reading and extrapolating from current events in the Inner Sphere; we should heed his warnings, so that we are not surprised at the state of affairs when we return home.

Finally, I must humbly thank the Precentor Martial for all his support and assistance. That my work has been of some use to our forces and our Inner Sphere allies is of great comfort to me. Additionally, I humbly thank the Precentor Martial for thinking me worthy of promotion to the rank of Precentor. I pray that this report is worthy of my new station.

—Jared Pascal
Precentor I-Omega
Deep Periphery
7 December 3060

INNER SPHERE VEHICLES

In the past three decades, the Inner Sphere has experienced a renaissance of new technology. Following the end of the Fourth Succession War and the War of 3039, BattleMechs across the Inner Sphere began carrying technology unseen in the Inner Sphere for centuries. Because the BattleMech had been the king of the battlefield for most of the Succession Wars, little emphasis was placed on developing new technologies for conventional vehicles.

When the Clans invaded, they did not field conventional vehicles in their front-line units. The Inner Sphere manufacturers' natural response was to concentrate their research efforts on further improving BattleMech technology, allowing vehicle developments to continue to decline. When it became clear that effective use of combined-arms units could make a difference against the invading forces, as dramatically demonstrated in ComStar's victory over the Clans on Tukayyid, a vehicle arms race ensued. Militaries throughout the Inner Sphere began upgrading existing designs and constructing new ones. In my 3058 document, I reported that it was still too soon to tell whether upgraded vehicles would play a major part in halting the Clan invaders. I can now confidently declare that vehicles played a significant role in the recent fall of the Smoke Jaguars. When the multi-House Star League force fell on the Smoke Jaguar occupation zone, they deployed eighty BattleMech line regiments along with two hundred support regiments. The well-planned implementation of combined-arms tactics greatly aided in the Jaguars' swift defeat. It is also true, however, that the combined-arms units succeeded against the Clans in large part because the Clans generally do not use such strategies themselves.

Though the Inner Sphere created and fielded a wide array of new vehicle designs against the Smoke Jaguars, the frenzied pace of development has lessened as the threat of the Clans has waned. You will note in this report that although better construction techniques and new technologies are being incorporated into conventional vehicles—even Omni technology has begun to appear on vehicles—fewer new designs are rolling off Inner Sphere assembly lines. Whether or not this portends a repeated decline in vehicle use in the years to come must remain the subject of speculation. For now, however, conventional vehicles have certainly assured themselves a place on the battlefield.

—Igarashi Miya
Precentor VIII-Lambda/Omega
ComStar Archives, Terra
18 October 3060

Type: **Flatbed Truck**
Mass: 10 tons
Movement Type: Wheeled
Power Plant: Generic 30 Internal Combustion
Cruising Speed: 54 kph
Flank Speed: 86 kph
Armor: Lightweight steel body panels
Armament: None standard
Communications System: Various
Targeting and Tracking System: None standard

Overview

This standard flatbed truck is used for small-scale cargo transport on planets throughout the Inner Sphere. The spacious armored cab carries the driver and six tons of cargo, and the flatbed trailer can accommodate up to ten more tons of unprotected cargo. Loading the trailer to full capacity significantly reduces the vehicle's speed.

Variants

Though the standard version of the truck is unarmed, in war zones such as the Chaos March or on the Clan front, some trucks mount defensive weapons. The simplest and most common variant sacrifices one-third of the internal cargo space for a forward-firing SRM-2 launcher and fifty reloads. Other variants represent attempts to beef up the truck's poor armor plating; these efforts rarely succeed, because the truck's frame is not designed to support heavy armor.

Type: **BattleMech Recovery Vehicle**
Mass: 50 tons
Movement Type: Wheeled
Power Plant: Generic 280 Internal Combustion
Cruising Speed: 65 kph
Flank Speed: 97 kph
Armor: Lightweight steel panels
Armament: None
Communications System: Various
Targeting and Tracking System: None

Overview

The BattleMech recovery vehicle is used by every military in the Inner Sphere for scavenging and salvage operations on the battlefield. Its single-drum winch, containing a 2cm cross-braided diamond monofilament cable, produces enough power to pull up to 60 tons of BattleMech onto the vehicle's flatbed. Eighteen large tires distribute the cargo weight evenly along the length of the vehicle. Its massive internal combustion engine generates enough horsepower to allow even a fully loaded recovery vehicle to reach top speeds of 54 kph.

Type: **Heavy BattleMech Recovery Vehicle**
Mass: 70 tons
Movement Type: Wheeled
Power Plant: Generic 260 Internal Combustion
Cruising Speed: 43 kph
Flank Speed: 65 kph
Armor: Various
Armament: None
Communications System: Various
Targeting and Tracking System: None

Overview

Though seen less frequently than the standard BattleMech recovery vehicle, every military in the Inner Sphere also fields the heavy BattleMech recovery vehicle. Considerably larger than the standard version, the heavy version can load and haul up to 100 tons, allowing it to carry any BattleMech currently produced. Designed to move fairly slowly, the heavy BattleMech recovery vehicle virtually crawls at 32 kph when loaded with any 'Mech weighing more than 30 tons. To counter that disadvantage in the field and protect the vehicle's crew, it carries significantly more armor than the standard version of the recovery vehicle.

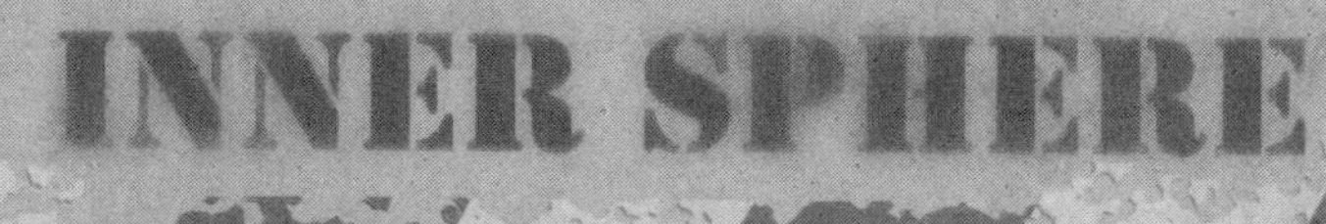

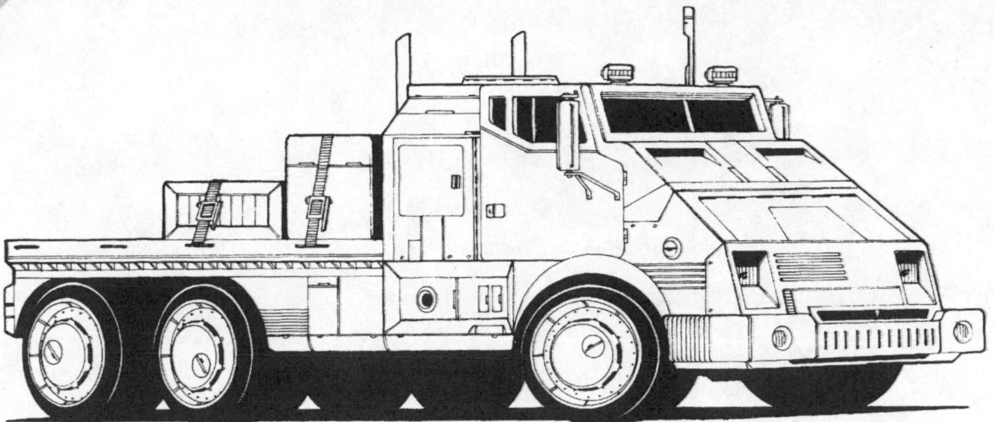

Type: **Flatbed Truck**
Technology Base: Inner Sphere
Movement Type: Wheeled
Tonnage: 10
Battle Value: 9

Equipment		**Mass**
Internal Structure:		1
Engine:	30	2
Type:	ICE	
Cruising MP:	5	
Flank MP:	8	
Heat Sinks:	0	0
Control Equipment:		0.5
Lift Equipment:		0
Power Amplifier:		0
Turret:		0
Armor Factor:	8	0.5
	Armor Value	
Front	2	
R/L Side	2/2	
Rear	2	

Weapons and Ammo	**Location**	**Tonnage**
Cargo	Body	6

BATTLEFORCE 2

MP	**Damage PB/M/L**	**Overheat**	**Class**
5w	—/—/—	—	L

Armor/Structure	**Point Value**	**Specials**
—/1	0.5	tran6

Type: **BattleMech Recovery Vehicle**
Technology Base: Inner Sphere
Movement Type: Wheeled
Tonnage: 50
Battle Value: 16

Equipment		**Mass**
Internal Structure:		5
Engine:	280	32
Type:	ICE	
Cruising MP:	6	
Flank MP:	9	
Heat Sinks:	0	0
Control Equipment:		2.5
Lift Equipment:		0
Power Amplifier:		0
Turret:		0
Armor Factor:	8	.5
	Armor Value	
Front	2	
R/L Side	2/2	
Rear	2	

Weapons and Ammo	**Location**	**Tonnage**
Cargo	Body	10

BATTLEFORCE 2

MP	**Damage PB/M/L**	**Overheat**	**Class**
6w	—/—/—	—	M

Armor/Structure	**Point Value**	**Specials**
—/1	.5	tran10

Type: **Heavy BattleMech Recovery Vehicle**
Technology Base: Inner Sphere
Movement Type: Wheeled
Tonnage: 70
Battle Value: 45

Equipment		**Mass**
Internal Structure:		7
Engine:	260	27
Type:	ICE	
Cruising MP:	4	
Flank MP:	6	
Heat Sinks:	0	0
Control Equipment:		3.5
Lift Equipment:		0
Power Amplifier:		0
Turret:		0
Armor Factor:	40	2.5
	Armor Value	
Front	10	
R/L Side	10/10	
Rear	10	

Weapons and Ammo	**Location**	**Tonnage**
Cargo	Body	30

BATTLEFORCE 2

MP	**Damage PB/M/L**	**Overheat**	**Class**
4w	—/—/—	—	H

Armor/Structure	**Point Value**	**Specials**
—/2	.5	tran30

MANTIS LIGHT ATTACK VTOL

Mass: 15 tons
Movement Type: VTOL
Power Plant: Galas 70 Micro-Fusion
Cruising Speed: 119 kph
Maximum Speed: 184 kph
Armor: Star Slab/3

Armament: 5 Diverse Optics Sunbeam Extended Range Small Lasers
Manufacturer: Michaelson Heavy Industries
Primary Factory: Ruchbah
Communications System: Garret Supremesound
Targeting and Tracking System: Garret D2j

Overview

Still undergoing field testing at Michaelson Heavy Industries' live-fire range on Ruchbah, the production of the Mantis Light Attack VTOL is a direct result of Michaelson's successful contract with Imperator Automatic Weaponry of Atreus. The ease with which Michaclson obtained permission through the Free Worlds League to purchase light Gauss rifles for their Hawk Moth gunship in turn sparked the company's interest in the new extended-range lasers sold by Diverse Optics. As with Imperator, Diverse Optics readily agreed to sell its new weaponry to the factory—though with the stipulation that the first production run would ship to the Free Worlds League (at a considerably reduced price)—and the Mantis was born.

Capabilities

The design specifications for the Mantis called for a helicopter of surpassing speed that could deliver a fusillade of laser fire while surviving significant damage from ground- and air-based weapons fire. The Mantis achieves these goals with fluid grace.

With a maximum speed of nearly 185 kph, the Mantis can outdistance most other vehicles and BattleMechs on the battlefield. This agility and speed allows it to dart in to attack, then quickly retreat to safety. Its five extended-range Diverse Optics small lasers give it a devastating amount of firepower for a vehicle of its size—almost twice the firepower of most helicopters twice its weight.

Finally, as with most Michaelson Heavy Industries helicopters, the Mantis can survive a direct hit to the nose from a Clan extended-range particle projector cannon—a feat that many ground vehicles cannot claim.

Deployment

The Mantis Light Attack VTOL is still in the prototype stage, but the presence of a steady stream of strong, viable helicopter designs lifting off of Michaelson's production lines—the Sprint Scout helicopter, Yellow Jacket gunship, Cavalry Attack helicopter and Hawk Moth gunship—automatically generates strong interest in their newest design.

MANTIS LIGHT ATTACK VTOL

Type: **Mantis Light Attack VTOL**
Technology Base: Inner Sphere
Movement Type: VTOL
Tonnage: 15 tons
Battle Value: 546

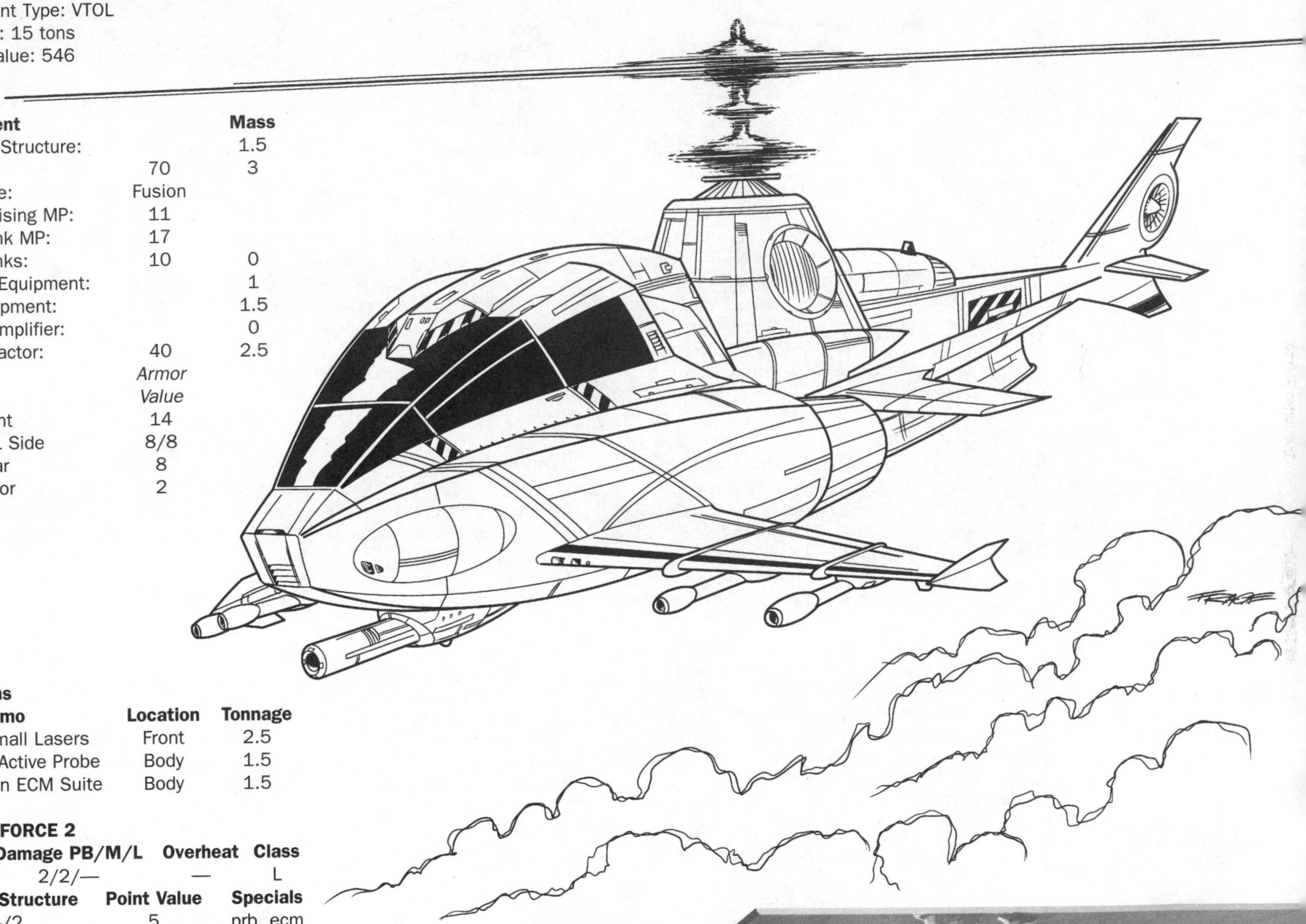

Equipment		**Mass**
Internal Structure:		1.5
Engine:	70	3
Type:	Fusion	
Cruising MP:	11	
Flank MP:	17	
Heat Sinks:	10	0
Control Equipment:		1
Lift Equipment:		1.5
Power Amplifier:		0
Armor Factor:	40	2.5
	Armor Value	
Front	14	
R/L Side	8/8	
Rear	8	
Rotor	2	

Weapons and Ammo	**Location**	**Tonnage**
5 ER Small Lasers	Front	2.5
Beagle Active Probe	Body	1.5
Guardian ECM Suite	Body	1.5

BATTLEFORCE 2

MP	**Damage PB/M/L**	**Overheat**	**Class**
11v	2/2/—	—	L

Armor/Structure	**Point Value**	**Specials**
—/2	5	prb, ecm

HEAVY ARMORED PERSONNEL CARRIERS

Mass: 20 tons
Movement Type: Hover, Tracked and Wheeled
Power Plant:
Hover: Type 75 Internal Combustion
Tracked/Wheeled: Type 100 Internal Combustion

Cruising Speed
Hover: 86 kph
Tracked: 54 kph
Wheeled: 65 kph
Flank Speed
Hover: 130 kph
Tracked: 86 kph
Wheeled: 97 kph

Armor: Standard
Armament: 2 Machine Guns
Manufacturer: Various
Communications System: Various
Targeting and Tracking System: Various

Overview

Armies have used armored personnel carriers (APCs) for centuries to transport troops to the front lines. The models described here are the largest dedicated APCs in modern use, with enough cargo area to carry two platoons of standard infantry or a single platoon of motorized or jump-pack equipped troops.

Capabilities

The more common 10-ton APCs, though marginally faster than the heavy models, can carry only a single squad of infantry. In order for an entire platoon to be deployed at a target location, a single platoon must be spread across a lance of four APCs, forcing the APCs to stay in tight formation for the insertion.

The heavy models, twice as large as standard APCs, each are designed to carry two full platoons of foot troopers along with their gear. This improved capacity, in addition to more substantial armor protection, makes heavy APCs the preference of commanders who can obtain them.

Though the front armor on these vehicles offers excellent protection, the design of the rear-mounted assault ramp where troops disembark prevents these vehicles from carrying heavy rear armor. Because APCs also lack turrets for their front-mounted machine guns, they are particularly vulnerable to flanking attacks from the rear. Most APCs, however, can successfully unload their troops before an enemy can position itself for a rear attack.

Deployment

Most militaries throughout the Inner Sphere use heavy APCs. They are most commonly seen in mobile forces that include large infantry contingents, such as Federated Commonwealth Regimental Combat Teams.

Variants

The most common variants of these vehicles replace cargo space with additional weaponry, usually an SRM-4 launcher or even a single LRM-5 launcher. When deployed in urban areas against heavy infantry opposition, these vehicles mount additional machine guns.

Type: **Heavy Hover APC**
Technology Base: Inner Sphere
Movement Type: Hover
Tonnage: 20
Battle Value: 70

Equipment		**Mass**
Internal Structure:		2
Engine:	75	4
Type:	ICE	
Cruising MP:	8	
Flank MP:	12	
Heat Sinks:	0	0
Control Equipment:		1
Lift Equipment:		2
Power Amplifier:		0
Turret:		0
Armor Factor:	56	3.5
	Armor Value	
Front	20	
R/L Side	13/13	
Rear	10	

Weapons and Ammo	**Location**	**Tonnage**
2 Machine Guns	Front	1
Ammo (MG) 100	Body	.5
Infantry	Body	6

Type: **Heavy Tracked APC**
Technology Base: Inner Sphere
Movement Type: Tracked
Tonnage: 20
Battle Value: 77

Equipment		**Mass**
Internal Structure:		2
Engine:	100	6
Type:	ICE	
Cruising MP:	5	
Flank MP:	8	
Heat Sinks:	0	0
Control Equipment:		1
Lift Equipment:		0
Power Amplifier:		0
Turret:		0
Armor Factor:	56	3.5
	Armor Value	
Front	20	
R/L Side	13/13	
Rear	10	

Weapons and Ammo	**Location**	**Tonnage**
2 Machine Guns	Front	1
Ammo (MG) 100	Body	.5
Infantry	Body	6

Type: **Heavy Wheeled APC**
Technology Base: Inner Sphere
Movement Type: Wheeled
Tonnage: 20
Battle Value: 70

Equipment		**Mass**
Internal Structure:		2
Engine:	100	6
Type:	ICE	
Cruising MP:	6	
Flank MP:	9	
Heat Sinks:	0	0
Control Equipment:		1
Lift Equipment:		0
Power Amplifier:		0
Turret:		0
Armor Factor:	56	3.5
	Armor Value	
Front	20	
R/L Side	13/13	
Rear	10	

Weapons and Ammo	**Location**	**Tonnage**
2 Machine Guns	Front	1
Ammo (MG) 100	Body	.5
Infantry	Body	6

BATTLEFORCE 2

Type: Heavy Hover APC

MP	**Damage PB/M/L**	**Overheat**	**Class**
8h	—/—/—	—	L
Armor/Structure	**Point Value**	**Specials**	
—/2	1	tran6	

Type: Heavy Tracked APC

MP	**Damage PB/M/L**	**Overheat**	**Class**
5t	—/—/—	—	L
Armor/Structure	**Point Value**	**Specials**	
—/2	1	tran6	

Type: Heavy Wheeled APC

MP	**Damage PB/M/L**	**Overheat**	**Class**
6w	—/—/—	—	L
Armor/Structure	**Point Value**	**Specials**	
—/2	1	tran6	

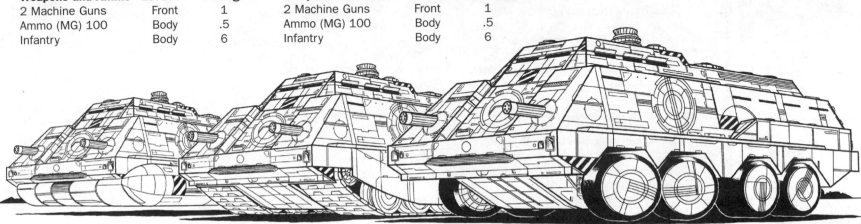

HAWK MOTH GUNSHIP

Mass: 25 tons
Movement Type: VTOL
Power Plant: Michaelson 60 Internal Combustion
Cruising Speed: 86 kph
Maximum Speed: 130 kph
Armor: StarSlab 5 Ferro-Fibrous

Armament: 1 Imperator Light Gauss Rifle
Manufacturer: Michaelson Heavy Industries
Primary Factory: Ruchbah
Communications System: Garret Supremesound
Targeting and Tracking System: Garret D2j

Overview

In 3058, Michaelson Heavy Industries unveiled a revolutionary new type of VTOL: the Yellow Jacket gunship. Throwing aside conventional wisdom, which dictated that VTOLs should mount numerous small-caliber weapons, the Yellow Jacket mounted a single weapon—a massive Gauss rifle. The logic behind this vehicle was that the incredible firepower and long range of the Gauss rifle, combined with the natural agility of a VTOL, could combine to produce a deadly firing platform. The Yellow Jacket's spectacular successes against Clan Smoke Jaguar during Operation Bulldog validated this design and made it one of the most sought-after VTOLs on the field today.

With such success supporting their efforts, it was only natural that the design team at Michaelson Heavy Industries would take the opportunity to experiment with the new light Gauss rifle produced by Imperator Automatic Weaponry of Atreus in the Free Worlds League. Imperator proved quite willing to sell the new weapon to Michaelson, their only stipulation for the sale being a contract under which Michaelson would ship the first Hawk Moths off the production line to the Free Worlds League. Because the new, lighter gunship was based on an already proven model, Michaelson's team enjoyed the luxury of taking numerous design shortcuts, and so production is already underway.

Capabilities

Like the Yellow Jacket gunship, the Hawk Moth gunship is built around a single weapon, the new light Gauss rifle. Though the light Gauss offers considerably less firepower than the standard Gauss, its increased range makes it one of the farthest-firing weapons among both the Inner Sphere and Clans, able to strike at a staggering 750 meters. Additionally, the light Gauss carries twice as much ammo as the standard rifle for the same weight—an important selling point, especially considering that one of the first Yellow Jacket variants stripped off a ton of armor to add more ammo. The primary design mounts two tons of ammo for the light Gauss, giving the vehicle unmatched staying power on the battlefield.

Another significant feature is the Hawk Moth's maximum speed of 130 kph, a significant jump from the much slower 97 kph maximum of the Yellow Jacket. This additional speed and maneuverability proved in field tests to significantly increase the Hawk Moth's survivability.

Opponents of the design cite its relative lack of armor as a serious liability, especially when compared to the Yellow Jacket or even the Cavalry Attack helicopter, both of which can survive a direct hit by a Clan particle projector cannon.

Deployment

The first production run of the Hawk Moth, per the contract between Imperator and Michaelson, was shipped in its entirety to the Free Worlds League, where it has been assigned to several regiments of the Free Worlds Legionnaires. However, much to Michaelson's pleasure, every military in the Inner Sphere has already placed orders for this new design.

Variants

The only Hawk Moth variant, which is currently being field tested, sheds a ton of ammo and adds armor, increasing the VTOL's protection by almost 80 percent.

HAWK MOTH GUNSHIP

Type: **Hawk Moth Gunship**
Technology Base: Inner Sphere
Movement Type: VTOL
Tonnage: 25 tons
Battle Value: 734

Equipment		Mass
Internal Structure:		2.5
Engine:	60	3
Type:	ICE	
Cruising MP:	8	
Flank MP:	12	
Heat Sinks:	0	0
Control Equipment:		1.5
Lift Equipment:		2.5
Power Amplifier:		0
Armor Factor:	27	1.5

	Armor Value
Front	9
R/L Side	6/6
Rear	4
Rotor	2

Weapons and Ammo	Location	Tonnage
Light Gauss Rifle	Front	12
Ammo (Light Gauss) 32	Body	2

BATTLEFORCE 2

MP	Damage PB/M/L	Overheat	Class
8v	1/1/1	—	L

Armor/Structure	Point Value	Specials
—/1	7	

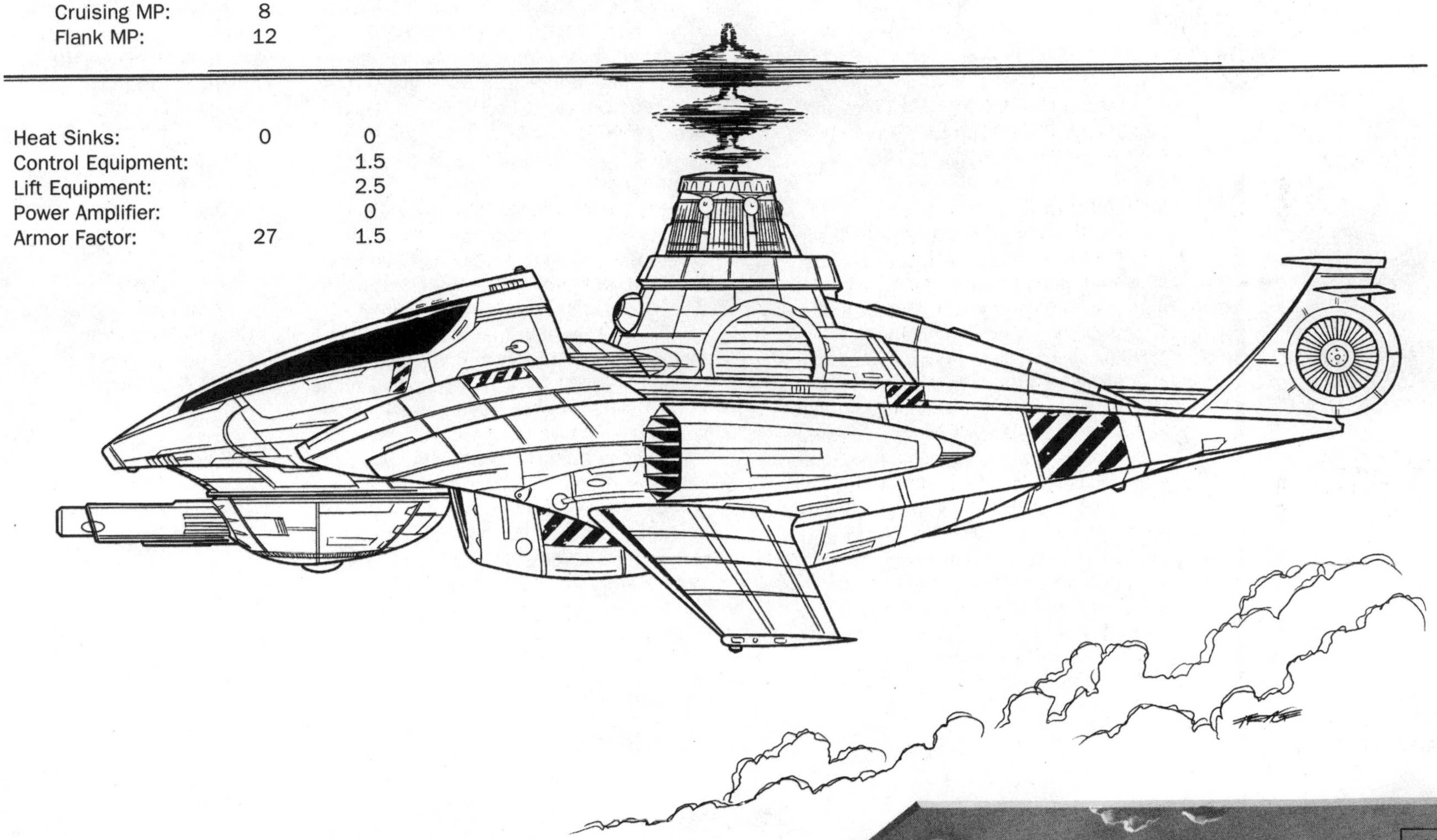

PINTO ATTACK VTOL

Mass: 30 tons
Movement Type: VTOL
Power Plant: Robinson 160 Fuse-Pak
Cruising Speed: 108 kph
Maximum Speed: 162 kph
Armor: Krupp Draco-100 Ferro-Fibrous

Armament:
3 Blankenburg Technologies Medium Lasers
1 Magna Longbow-5 Long-Range Missile System with Artemis IV FCS
Manufacturer: Krupp Armament Works
Primary Factory: Bochum, Terra

Communications System:
Marshall Long-Talk
Targeting and Tracking System:
GPT Multi-Track

Overview

Krupp Armament Works' Pinto first entered service in 3055 as an assault VTOL. Currently, both Com Guard and Explorer Corps forces use the swift, well-protected rotor-blade craft as an attack VTOL.

Capabilities

The Pinto is powered by a Robinson 160 Fuse-Pak power plant and features Krupp Armament's new Draco-100 ferro-fibrous armor plating. The Pinto's firepower is provided by three Blankenburg Technologies medium lasers mounted in a chin turret located immediately forward of the cockpit, and a forward-firing, Artemis-equipped Magna LRM-5 system situated in a belly mount. The lasers provide the Pinto with excellent close-range firepower, while the missiles enable the Pinto to engage other units without exposing itself to medium- and short-range return fire.

A small, 1-ton cargo hold is immediately behind the cockpit. Many Pintos use the cargo space to ferry squads of conventional infantry or additional electronics.

The Pinto can also be transported and stored quite easily. The VTOL's rotors dismantle in less than five minutes, allowing Pintos to be stored in conventional vehicle or cargo bays as well as in the dedicated aerospace bays other VTOLs require.

Deployment

Pintos are employed by several Com Guard divisions, most notably the 388th (White Banshees) and 82nd (Web Cutters). A number of Pintos were also deployed with the 201st Division on Terra, but these machines were destroyed along with the rest of the 201st in Operation Odysseus during the fall of Terra in 3058. The Explorer Corps makes extensive use of the Pinto, as both a gunship and a light utility transport.

Despite Com Guard attempts to sabotage Krupp's Bochum plant, intelligence analysts believe that the Word of Blake is producing Pintos at the plant for its own use, a supposition supported by the fact that several Pintos have been spotted serving with the Word of Blake Fourth Division (Blake's Boldest).

Type: **Pinto Attack VTOL**
Technology Base: Inner Sphere
Movement Type: VTOL
Tonnage: 30 tons
Battle Value: 980

Equipment		**Mass**
Internal Structure:		3
Engine:	160	9
Type:	Fusion	
Cruising MP:	10	
Flank MP:	15	
Heat Sinks:	10	0
Control Equipment:		1.5
Lift Equipment:		3
Power Amplifier:		0
Armor Factor:	72	4
	Armor Value	
Front	20	
R/L Side	18/18	
Rear	14	
Rotor	2	

PINTO ATTACK VTOL

Weapons and Ammo	Location	Tonnage
3 Med. Lasers	Front	3
LRM 5	Front	2
Artemis IV FCS	Front	1
Ammo (LRM) 24	Body	1
Beagle Active Probe	Front	1.5
Cargo (Infantry)	Body	1

BATTLEFORCE 2

MP	Damage PB/M/L	Overheat	Class
10v	2/2/—	—	L

Armor/Structure	Point Value	Specials
—/3	10	prb, tran1

411 7.

Chrisplee '96

CHEVALIER LIGHT TANK

Mass: 35 tons
Movement Type: Wheeled
Power Plant: RT 190
Cruising Speed: 65 kph
Maximum Speed: 97 kph
Armor: Chobham Max-Tec

Armament:
1 Blankenburg Extended Range Large Laser
2 Zone-Tone Streak-2 SRM Launchers
Manufacturer: Millennium Industries
Primary Factory: Azania, Terra

Communications System: Dec-10 Whisperer
Targeting and Tracking System: Blankenburg Trooper

Overview

Cannibalized for their sophisticated weapons systems, the number of Star League-designed Chevaliers dwindled steadily during the Succession Wars. In fact, at the time of the Clan invasion, fewer than a dozen Chevaliers served among all the Successor State militaries.

Only one manufacturer—Millennium Industries of Terra—continued to produce the Chevalier according to its original specifications. Though the armies of the Draconis Combine and Federated Commonwealth possess a few Chevaliers, most of Millennium's output was purchased by the Com Guard prior to the Word of Blake invasion of Terra.

Capabilities

The Chevalier is a well-designed, versatile tank capable of performing for extended periods between maintenance and resupply stops.

The Chevalier's six and a half tons of Chobham Max-Tec armor provide it with remarkable protection for a light tank. A turret-mounted extended-range large laser serves as the tank's primary weapon, while a pair of forward-firing Streak-2 short-range missile launchers provide additional firepower up to 300 meters. Though this weapon mix leaves the Chevalier with less firepower than many contemporary light-tank designs, the large laser enables the Chevalier to operate for long periods without stopping to replenish ammunition.

The Chevalier's laser and eight-wheeled locomotive system are powered by a massive RT 190 fusion plant that constitutes a third of the Chevalier's mass. The RT 190 enables the Chevalier to reach a top speed of 97 kph—considerably slower than hovercraft of comparable mass, but quite respectable for a wheeled or tracked vehicle.

The main weakness in the Chevalier's design is the tank's cramped crew quarters. This space contains barely enough room for the vehicle's three crew members, let alone food and other supplies.

Deployment

Originally designed as a fast reconnaissance tank, the Chevalier has been superseded by a host of new vehicles armed with sophisticated electronics systems. However, the Com Guard continues to employ impressive numbers of Chevaliers for reconnaissance and among screening forces, and many serve with rear-echelon units in a wide variety of roles. Despite the inherent limitations of the tank's wheeled drive system, the Explorer Corps commonly uses Com Guard Chevaliers as planetary rovers, deploying them with garrison forces.

Variants

A number of Chevalier variants serve with the Com Guard and Explorer Corps. Most of these versions feature less armor and increased speed or expanded weapon arrays. One variant, employed by the Com Guard's Thirty-first Division (The Lost Boys) uses four and a half tons of armor and a single Streak launcher, and boasts a top speed of 119 kph. Another variant, used by many Explorer Corps units, carries four tons of armor, a Beagle active probe and a Sperry-Browning machine gun with half a ton of ammunition.

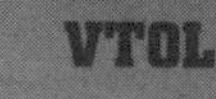

CHEVALIER LIGHT TANK

Type: **Chevalier Light Tank**
Technology Base: Inner Sphere
Movement Type: Wheeled
Tonnage: 35 tons
Battle Value: 444

Equipment		**Mass**
Internal Structure:		3.5
Engine	190	11.5
Type	Fusion	
Cruising MP:	6	
Flank MP:	9	
Heat Sinks:	12	2
Control Equipment:		2
Power Amplifier:		0
Turret:		.5
Armor Factor:	104	6.5
	Armor Value	
Front	26	
R/L Side	20/20	
Rear	16	
Turret	22	

Weapons and Ammo	**Location**	**Tonnage**
ER Large Laser	Turret	5
2 Streak SRM 2	Front	3
Ammo (Streak) 50	Body	1

BATTLEFORCE 2

MP	**Damage PB/M/L**	**Overheat**	**Class**
6w	2/2/1	—	L
Armor/Structure	**Point Value**	**Specials**	
—/4	4		

GLADIUS MEDIUM HOVER TANK

Mass: 40 tons
Movement Type: Hover
Power Plant: Omni 145 ICE
Cruising Speed: 86 kph
Flank Speed: 130 kph
Armor: Marian Arms Standard

Armament: 1 Pontiac 50 Autocannon
Manufacturer: Marian Arms, Inc.
Primary Factory: Alphard
Communications System: Garret T10B
Targeting and Tracking System: O/P 911

Overview

Bandit kings have always prized hovercraft for those vehicles' excellent hit-and-run capabilities and affordability. Seeking a more flexible alternative to the venerable Saladin Assault hovertank, Imperator Marius O'Reilly of the Periphery's Marian Hegemony commissioned the Gladius in 3042. All of the new hovertank's components were manufactured on the Marian capitol of Alphard, with the exception of the tank's armament. In a groundbreaking trade agreement, the Hegemony acquired a supply of the Pontiac 50 autocannon from the Taurian Concordat in exchange for 25 percent of the tanks equipped with the weapon.

By the time Caesar Sean O'Reilly, Marius's son, assumed control of the Hegemony, the Marian Legions were armed with more than a hundred of the quick and effective new vehicles. Protector Thomas Calderon of the Taurian Concordat was pleased with his end of the deal as well, and stationed his Gladius units along the Federated Commonwealth border in anticipation of an attack by that realm. The Commonwealth attack never materialized, but Gladius units did prove instrumental in the Hegemony's conquest of the Lothian League.

Capabilities

Named for the sword of the Roman legions, the Gladius is a simple but effective machine. Constructed of readily available components and time-tested electronics, the tank rarely breaks down and is easy to repair. Though the Gladius is not notably fast, it is capable of executing high-speed flanking maneuvers over difficult terrain and over water. With three times more armor than the Saladin, the Gladius can take a significant amount of punishment, especially to its front.

The only apparent flaw in this otherwise excellent vehicle design is the Gladius's lack of a weapon turret. The Pontiac 50's range and power make it a good choice for a one-gun tank, but without a turret the autocannon can fire only at targets directly in front of the hovertank. Generally, the hovertank's impressive mobility enables Gladius crews to target enemies effectively despite this drawback, but more than one retreating Gladius crew has died because of their tank's inability to fire on and discourage pursuers. The Gladius's fixed-cannon configuration does offer some advantages, however. The cannon is mounted deep in the interior of the tank's chassis, which protects it from battle damage, and the weight savings provided by the turretless design enables the Gladius to carry a generous amount of heavy armor.

Deployment

Gladius units are stationed only in the Marian Hegemony and the Taurian Concordat. Currently, the Hegemony fields only about half as many Gladiuses as the Concordat, an imbalance created by the Hegemony's losses during the Lothian campaign. As soon as Jeffrey Calderon cut off Taurian relations with the Hegemony, manufacture of the Gladius ground to a halt, and until a suitable replacement for the Pontiac 50 can be found, no new units will be produced.

GLADIUS MEDIUM HOVER TANK

Type: **Gladius Medium Hover tank**
Technology Base: Inner Sphere
Movement Type: Hover
Tonnage: 40
Battle Value: 378

Equipment		**Mass**
Internal Structure:		4
Engine:	145	10
Type:	ICE	
Cruising MP:	8	
Flank MP:	12	
Heat Sinks:	0	0
Control Equipment:		2
Lift Equipment:		4
Power Amplifier:		0
Turret:		0
Armor Factor:	96	6
	Armor Value	
Front	30	
R/L Side	24/24	
Rear	18	

Weapons and Ammo	**Location**	**Tonnage**
AC/10	Front	12
Ammo (AC) 20	Body	2

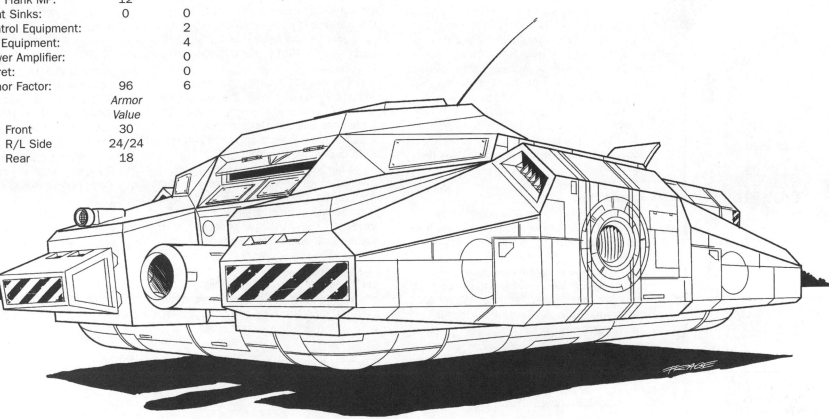

BATTLEFORCE 2

MP	**Damage PB/M/L**	**Overheat**	**Class**
8h	1/1/—	—	M

Armor/Structure	**Point Value**	**Specials**
—/4	4	

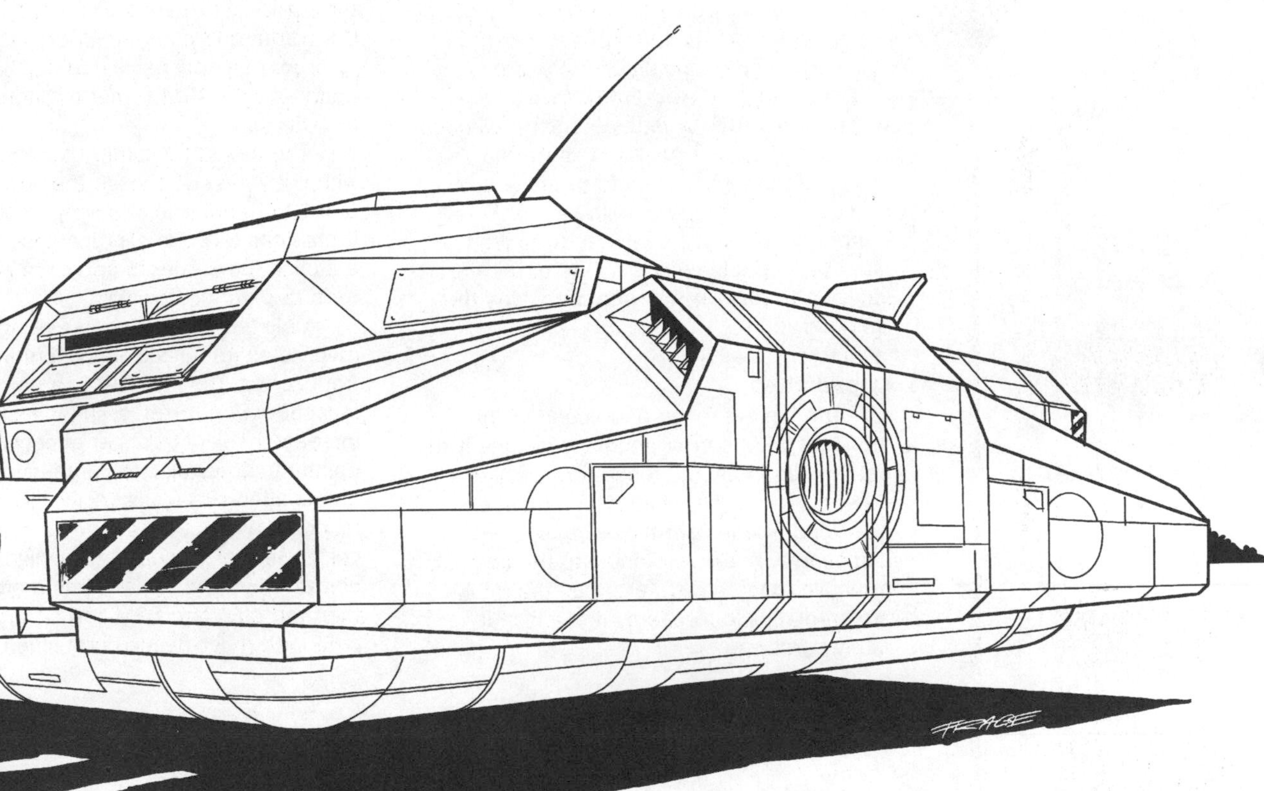

LIGHT SRM CARRIER

Mass: 40 tons
Movement Type: Wheeled
Power Plant: InterComBust 140
Cruising Speed: 43 kph
Flank Speed: 65 kph
Armor: Standard

Armament: 5 Shannon Six-Shooter SRM Launchers
Manufacturer: Pinard Protectorates Limited
Primary Factory: Perdition
Communications System: Communicator
Targeting and Tracking System: FireScan with IndirecTrack

Overview

While the Inner Sphere continues to produce a plethora of new 'Mechs and vehicles using upgraded technology, the Periphery states, generally lacking in advanced technology, have investigated other avenues for increasing their military might. Rather than pay the high costs of designing and producing entirely new vehicles, the Periphery states have chosen to upgrade older but reliable vehicles. One of the first vehicles to receive this treatment was the SRM carrier.

Capabilities

The limited range and speed of the standard SRM carrier generally confine it to battlefields in cities, dense forests and other close terrain. Military commanders also tend to consider these units disposable, because closing to the carrier's effective range always exposes the thinly armored vehicle to enemy fire, which it rarely survives.

Pinard Protectorates Limited on Perdition in the Taurian Concordat—already the main vehicle supplier for the Taurian Concordat and other Periphery realms—incorporated several new features in the updated light SRM carrier to address these drawbacks.

The new SRM carrier has a smaller, wheeled chassis. Though the new chassis restricts the unit to relatively smooth terrain, it provides a 33 percent increase in speed, enabling the carrier to approach and retreat from targets more rapidly.

Unlike the standard carrier, which mounts all its missile launchers in a static front facing, the light SRM carrier mounts its launchers in a turret, giving it vastly increased ability to target enemy units. The updated carrier also features increased ammunition-storage capacity, giving each launcher an increased number of volleys. To complete the new design, the light SRM carrier mounts a ton and half more armor than the standard SRM carrier, providing the crew with much-needed protection.

Deployment

Because the light SRM carrier is produced with commonly available parts, its service and repair is cheap and easy, making it a perfect support unit for any planetary militia. Every major Periphery realm (and most lesser Periphery states) has already produced and purchased massive quantities of this new design. The willingness of the Taurian Concordat to sell this design to any interested Periphery realm eloquently supports the Protector's oft-repeated statement that to survive, the Periphery must stand united against the Inner Sphere Houses.

LIGHT SRM CARRIER

Type: **Light SRM Carrier**
Technology Base: Inner Sphere
Movement Type: Wheeled
Tonnage: 40
Battle Value: 423

Weapons and Ammo	**Location**	**Tonnage**
5 SRM 6	Turret	15
Ammo (SRM) 45	Body	3

BATTLEFORCE 2

MP	**Damage PB/M/L**	**Overheat**	**Class**
4w	3/3/—	—	M

Armor/Structure	**Point Value**	**Specials**
—/3	4	

Equipment		**Mass**
Internal Structure:		4
Engine:	140	10
Type:	ICE	
Cruising MP:	4	
Flank MP:	6	
Heat Sinks:	0	0
Control Equipment:		2
Lift Equipment:		0
Power Amplifier:		0
Turret:		1.5
Armor Factor:	72	4.5
	Armor Value	
Front	16	
R/L Side	14/14	
Rear	12	
Turret	16	

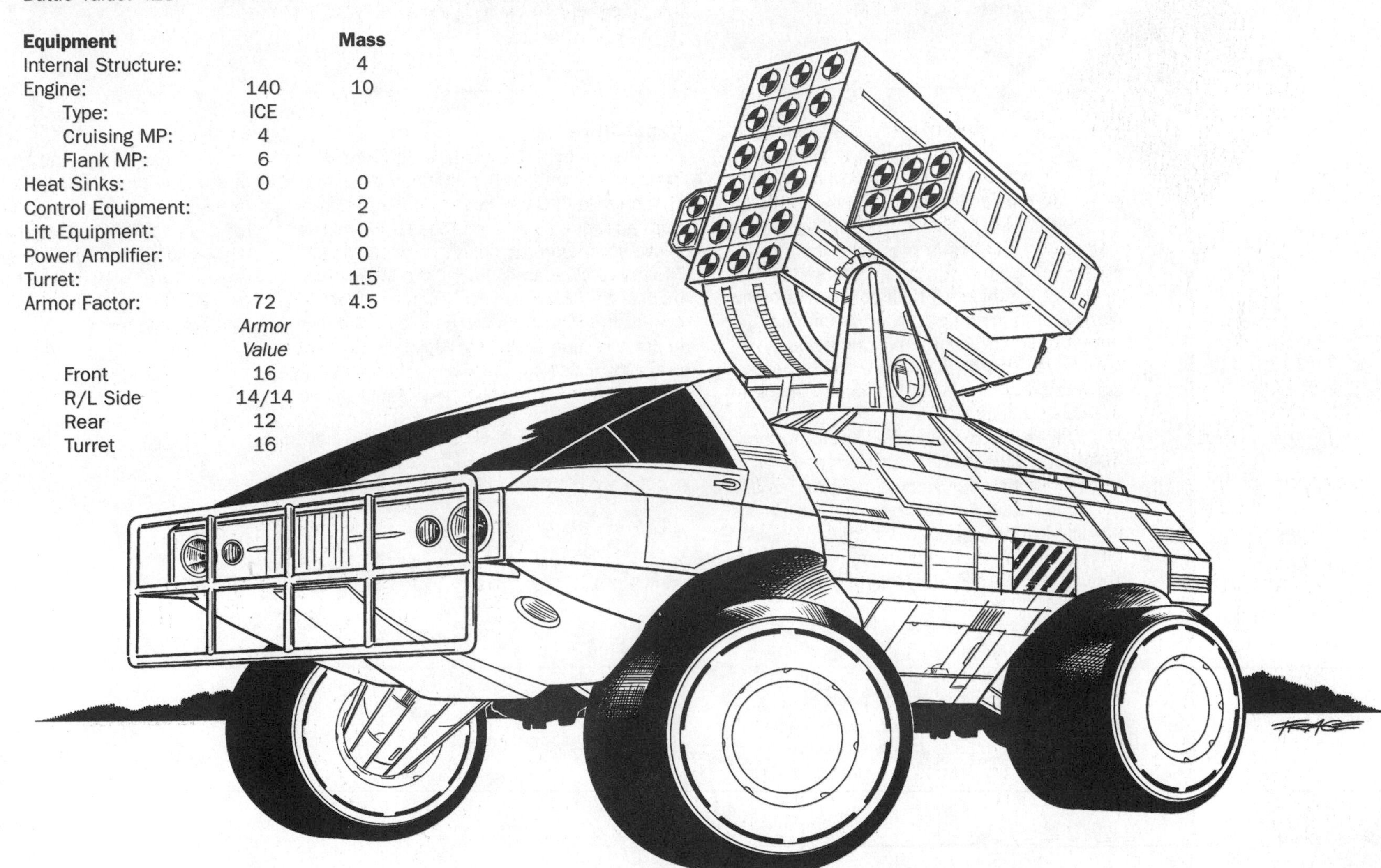

MYRMIDON MEDIUM TANK

Mass: 40 tons
Movement Type: Tracked
Power Plant: Nissan 200 Fusion Engine
Cruising Speed: 54 kph
Flank Speed: 86 kph
Armor: ArcShield Maxi II

Armament: 1 Parti-Kill Heavy Cannon
1 SureShot Mk VI SRM Launcher
Manufacturer: New Earth Trading Company
Primary Factory: New Earth
Communications System: OP/R Janxiir
Targeting and Tracking System: TargiTrack 717

Overview

In response to the Clan war effort and increasing tensions in the Federated Commonwealth's Sarna March, New Earth Trading Company has begun producing the Myrmidon. Named for the defenders of ancient Troy, this new tank possesses many components in common with its famous parent design, TechniCorp's venerable Manticore. This design choice allowed easy conversion of existing NETC factory space to the new production line.

The choice to shift construction to the 40-ton Myrmidon was a business decision, rather than one motivated by tactical needs. The Clan war and the sporadic conflict in the so-called Chaos March have created a vast market for cheap, reliable armored vehicles. Though the Myrmidon is expensive for a tank, it is quite inexpensive compared to BattleMechs of similar capabilities. The main reason for the shift in production was that the smaller 200-rated fusion engine made the Myrmidon considerably cheaper to produce than the Manticore, even though the Myrmidon mounts nearly as much firepower as the Manticore—making it a more attractive buy.

Capabilities

The focus of the Myrmidon's firepower is its turret-mounted Parti-Kill heavy cannon. This reliable PPC can destroy enemy units from a great distance, and the tank's speed allows it to keep the enemy at arm's length. To survive close encounters, the Myrmidon mounts an SRM-6 rack on the turret, right next to the PPC. Both weapons can be fired in any direction, giving the Myrmidon tactical flexibility. Excellent armor protection on all sides rounds out the Myrmidon's impressive capabilities.

Deployment

Still new to the battlefield, most of the Myrmidons produced so far have been sold to the Lyran Alliance to fortify its border with the Clans. The remainder have been sold to various independent armies operating in the Chaos March, where they have performed very well in a number of skirmishes with Liao gucrrilla forces.

MYRMIDON MEDIUM TANK

Type: **Myrmidon Medium Tank**
Technology Base: Inner Sphere
Movement Type: Tracked
Tonnage: 40
Battle Value: 492

Equipment		**Mass**
Internal Structure:		4
Engine:	200	13
Type:	Fusion	
Cruising MP:	5	
Flank MP:	8	
Heat Sinks:	10	0
Control Equipment:		2
Lift Equipment:		0
Power Amplifier:		0
Turret:		1
Armor Factor:	144	9

	Armor Value
Front	35
R/L Side	25/25
Rear	24
Turret	35

Weapons and Ammo	**Location**	**Tonnage**
PPC	Turret	7
SRM 6	Turret	3
Ammo (SRM) 15	Body	1

BATTLEFORCE 2

MP	**Damage PB/M/L**	**Overheat**	**Class**
4t	2/2/1	—	M

Armor/Structure	**Point Value**	**Specials**
—/5	5	

HEAVY LRM CARRIER

Mass: 80 tons
Movement Type: Tracked
Power Plant: InterComBust 160
Cruising Speed: 22 kph
Flank Speed: 32 kph
Armor: Standard
Armament: 4 Delta Dart LRM-20 Launchers

Manufacturer: Majesty Metals and Manufacturing
Primary Factory: Dunianshire, Canopus IV
Communications System: Communicator
Targeting and Tracking System: FireScan with IndirecTrack

Overview

When Pinard Protectorates Limited of the Taurian Concordat announced its plans to create a new "lighter" SRM carrier, the Magestrix Command Center of the Magistracy of Canopus petitioned Magestrix Emma Centrella to begin a similar project with the reliable LRM carrier. Not only would this provide the Magistracy Armed Forces with a new and powerful vehicle, but it also represented an astute political move; it demonstrated the Canopians' strength and their willingness to aid other Periphery realms by selling them the new vehicle. Magestrix Centrella saw the wisdom in such actions and immediately authorized the project.

Capabilities

To improve the LRM carrier, the designers chose to convert the design to a larger and slower "crawler" configuration. This heavier design sacrificed 60 percent of the original carrier's speed, but the designers compensated by adding a significant amount of additional armor for crew protection, as well as more firepower. Initial field testing proved these additions to be a very satisfactory tradeoff.

The smaller internal combustion engine provides room to mount an additional LRM-20 rack, which enables the heavy LRM carrier to launch eighty missiles in a single salvo—considerably more missile firepower than any other Inner Sphere vehicle or 'Mech. The updated design also carries twice as much ammunition as the original, allowing for longer sustained barrages.

Like the light SRM carrier, the new heavy LRM carrier mounts all of its weaponry in a turret. This allows the ponderous vehicle to track targets on multiple fronts and is especially effective against targets approaching or passing close to the carrier.

The design also features additional armor plating on the front of the vehicle, but this only marginally improves the LRM carrier's life span.

Deployment

The heavy LRM carrier began rolling off of the assembly lines only months after the light SRM carrier. This timing allowed Majesty Metals and Manufacturing and Pinard Protectorates Limited—with the blessing of Magestrix Centrella and President Calderon—to launch a propaganda campaign featuring the two vehicles working together in the New Colony Region to defend against Inner Sphere predations.

Sales of both vehicles have soared, boosted by the promise of easy repair and maintenance, as well as the clever ad campaign. To keep up with demand, Majesty Metals and Manufacturing has already begun to retool its plant on Canopus IV to produce the heavy LRM carrier.

Nearly every militia in the Periphery currently fields the heavy LRM carrier.

Type: **Heavy LRM Carrier**
Technology Base: Inner Sphere
Movement Type: Tracked
Tonnage: 80
Battle Value: 769

Equipment		**Mass**
Internal Structure:		8
Engine:	160	12
Type:	ICE	
Cruising MP:	2	
Flank MP:	3	
Heat Sinks:	0	0
Control Equipment:		4
Lift Equipment:		0
Power Amplifier:		0
Turret:		4
Armor Factor:	64	4
	Armor Value	
Front	14	
R/L Side	12/12	
Rear	12	
Turret	14	

Weapons and Ammo	**Location**	**Tonnage**
4 LRM 20	Turret	40
Ammo (LRM) 48	Body	8

BATTLEFORCE 2

MP	**Damage PB/M/L**	**Overheat**	**Class**
2t	2/5/5	—	A

Armor/Structure	**Point Value**	**Specials**
—/3	8	if

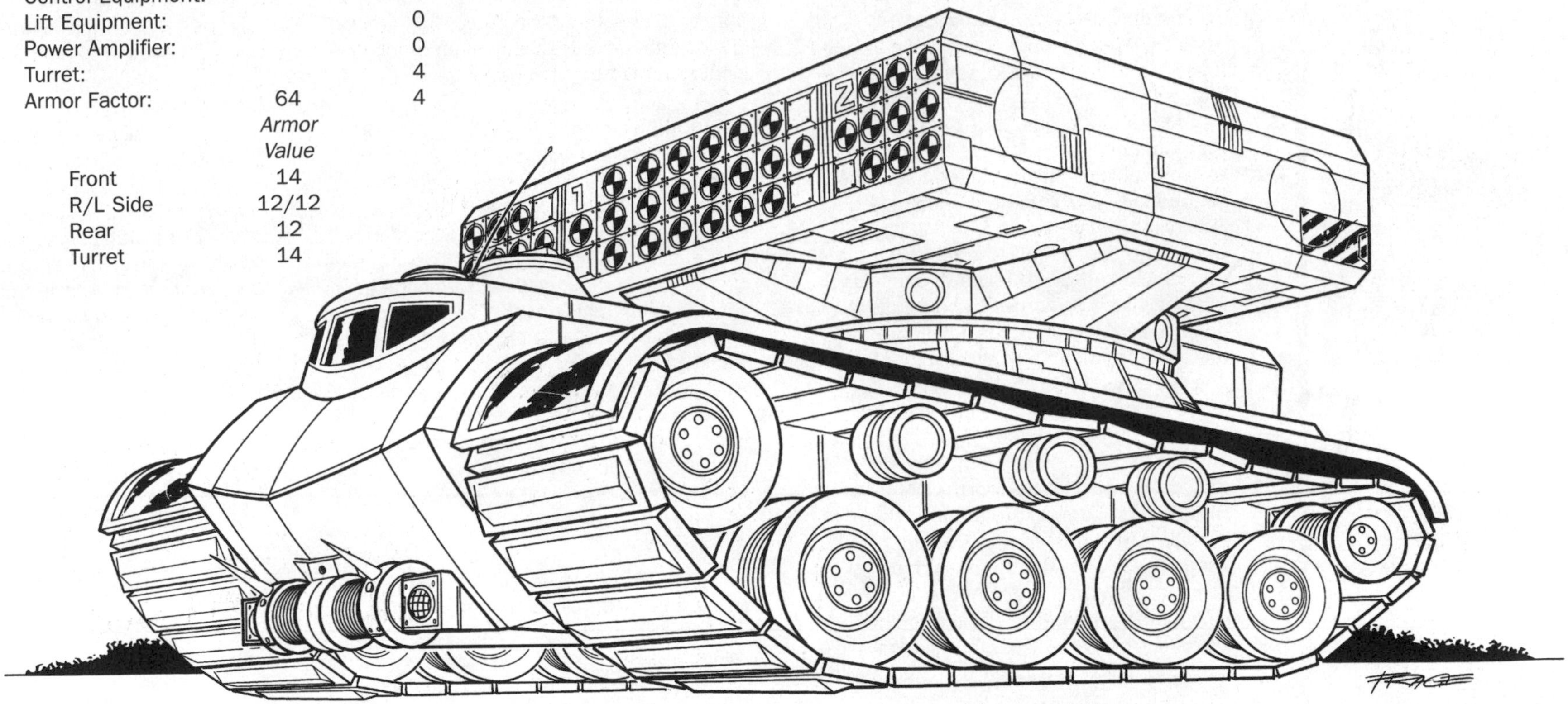

SCHILTRON

Mass: 80 tons
Movement Type: Wheeled
Power Plant: 220 DAV Fusion
Cruising Speed: 32 kph
Flank Speed: 54 kph
Armor: Protec 12 Ferro-Fibrous
Armament: 42 tons of pod space available

Manufacturer: Bulldog Enterprises, Cosara Weaponries (under license)
Primary Factory: Proserpina, Northwind
Communications System: Sipher CommSys 1
Targeting and Tracking System: TargiTrack 717

Overview

Following the success of the improved Tokugawa heavy tank manufactured jointly by Bulldog Enterprises and Buda Imperial Vehicles, the DCMS High Command commissioned a new vehicle that would specialize in fire-support.

At the same time that the Combine High Command was looking for a new assault vehicle, Bulldog Enterprises was in negotiations with Cosara Weaponries of Northwind, which was expanding its production capabilities and looking to enter the vehicle market. The DCMS commission for a new vehicle proved to be a tailor-made opportunity for a joint design venture, and after several months of discussion, Bulldog and Cosara submitted the Schiltron for approval by the DCMS High Command.

The High Command showed immediate interest in the Schiltron, not least because they were aware of the Northwind Highlanders' intention to establish an exclusive relationship with Cosara Weaponries. The High Command also concluded that the Highlanders, with their long history of putting vehicles to good use, would be the perfect unit to field-test the Schiltron. Fortunately, the Combine was on good terms with the Highlanders following the successful conclusion of Stirling's Fusiliers' Deep Periphery contract with the Dragon in 3058. The invasion of the Smoke Jaguar Occupation Zone during Operation Bulldog gave the Highlanders an excellent opportunity to test the new design.

Capabilities

The Schiltron was the DCMS's first contract for a modular vehicle using Omni technology. With the successful construction—and even more successful battlefield debut—of eight OmniMechs, the High Command felt confident experimenting with modular vehicles. Wolf's Dragoons had proved the usefulness of such vehicles with the Bandit hovercraft and the Badger tracked transport. Unlike those two designs, however, which were made to transport infantry, the High Command wanted a modular vehicle that could act as a mobile fire-support platform. The Schiltron fit that bill perfectly.

The use of the C³ system in every configuration of the vehicle also pleased the High Command, because many Combine commanders had long wished to see this valuable piece of equipment used more fully on the battlefield. Their inclusion of the C³ proved to be the deciding factor in awarding the contract to Bulldog Enterprises and Cosara Weaponries.

With more than 40 tons of pod space, the Schiltron potentially can mount as many weapons as the heaviest Inner Sphere OmniMech. Even the Clans, with their vastly superior technology, have a hard time matching the Schiltron for the sheer volume of firepower it can deliver.

Critics of this unusual design (who also comment disparagingly on its being tested by a "mere" mercenary unit) have cited its relative lack of armor for a vehicle of its size, as well as its tremendous production costs, as reason to limit its development.

Deployment

Initially, several Schiltrons were assigned to the Second and Third battalions of Stirling's Fusiliers as well as MacLeod's Regiment. Following Stirling's Fusiliers report of outstanding successes with the Schiltron during Operation Bulldog, Cosara Weaponries and Bulldog Enterprises saw a significant increase in orders, leading many analysts to comment that the Schiltron is here to stay.

Type: **Schiltron**
Technology Base: Inner Sphere
Movement Type: Wheeled
Tonnage: 80
Battle Value: 776

Equipment		**Mass**
Internal Structure:		8
Engine:	220	7.5
Type:	XL Fusion	
Cruising MP:	3	
Flank MP:	5	

Heat Sinks:	10	0
Control Equipment:		4
Lift Equipment:		0
Power Amplifier:		0
Turret:		2
Armor Factor:	179	10
	Armor Value	
Front	46	
R/L Side	34/34	
Back	25	
Turret	40	

Fixed Equipment	**Location**	**Tonnage**
C^3 Master	Body	5
Guardian ECM Suite	Body	1.5

Weapons and Ammo	**Location**	**Tonnage**
Primary Configuration		
Arrow IV System	Front	15
Arrow IV System	Front	15
Ammo (Arrow) 40	Body	8
Med. Laser	Turret	1
Med. Laser	Turret	1
Small Laser	Turret	.5
Small Laser	Turret	.5
Small Laser	Turret	.5
Small Laser	Turret	.5
Battle Value: 1,088		
Alternate Configuration A		
MRM 40	Front	12
MRM 40	Front	12
Ammo (MRM) 36	Body	6
MRM 10	Turret	3
MRM 10	Turret	3
Ammo (MRM) 48	Body	2
Med. Laser	Turret	1
Med. Laser	Turret	1
Small Laser	Turret	.5
Small Laser	Turret	.5
Small Laser	Turret	.5
Small Laser	Turret	.5
Battle Value: 1,088		
Alternate Configuration B		
LRM 15	Turret	7
Artemis IV FCS	Turret	1
LRM 15	Turret	7
Artemis IV FCS	Turret	1
LRM 15	Front	7
Artemis IV FCS	Body	1
LRM 15	Front	7
Artemis IV FCS	Body	1
Ammo (Ammo) 64	Body	8
Med. Laser	Turret	1
Small Laser	Turret	.5
Small Laser	Turret	.5
Battle Value: 1,117		
Alternate Configuration C		
Large Laser	Turret	5
Large Laser	Turret	5
Large Laser	Turret	5
Large Laser	Turret	5
22 Heat Sinks	Body	22
Battle Value: 714		

BATTLEFORCE 2
Type: Schiltron

MP	**Damage PB/M/L**	**Overheat**	**Class**
3w	4/3/4	—	A
Armor/Structure	**Point Value**	**Specials**	
—/7	8	omni, c3m, ecm, artA	

Alternate Configuration A

MP	**Damage PB/M/L**	**Overheat**	**Class**
3w	8/4/—	—	A
Armor/Structure	**Point Value**	**Specials**	
—/7	10	omni, c3m, ecm	

Alternate Configuration B

MP	**Damage PB/M/L**	**Overheat**	**Class**
3w	4/5/5	—	A
Armor/Structure	**Point Value**	**Specials**	
—/7	11	omni, c3m, ecm, if	

Alternate Configuration C

MP	**Damage PB/M/L**	**Overheat**	**Class**
3w	3/3/—	—	A
Armor/Structure	**Point Value**	**Specials**	
—/7	7	omni, c3m, ecm	

DEMOLISHER II HEAVY TANK

Mass: 100 tons
Movement Type: Tracked
Power Plant: Vlar 300 Fusion
Cruising Speed: 32 kph
Flank Speed: 54 kph
Armor: Starslab/6 Ferro-Fibrous with CASE

Armament:
1 Defiance Disintegrator LB 20-X Autocannon
1 Defiance Thunder Ultra AC/20 Autocannon
2 Coventry Light Autoguns

Manufacturer: Defiance Industries of Hesperus II

Primary Factory: Hesperus II
Communications System: Niel 9000
Targeting and Tracking System: Angst Clear View 2A

Overview

When the Jade Falcons captured the original Demolisher factory on Sudeten during the Clan invasion, the Federated Commonwealth solicited bids for a new urban combat vehicle. The Typhoon urban assault vehicle began production in early 3057, with the majority shipping to Davion Guards units. Consequently, when Katrina Steiner issued her recall to all Lyran troops following the Marik-Liao invasion of the Sarna March, almost no Typhoon vehicles remained in Lyran Alliance hands. The Lyran Alliance Armed Forces asked Defiance Industries of Hesperus II to create a new assault vehicle whose capabilities would exceed the Typhoon's. The Demolisher II Heavy Tank is a direct result of that effort.

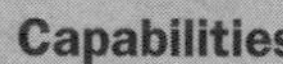

Capabilities

The showcase weapons of the Demolisher II Heavy Tank are the new Defiance Disintegrator LB 20-X autocannon and Defiance Thunder Ultra AC/20 autocannon. With their traditional love of large-bore weaponry, the LAAF devoted considerable time and resources into replicating the Clans' largest autocannons. Though the Disintegrator autocannon had been in production in the Lyran Alliance for years, Lyran scientists seemed unable to bridge the gap between the two weapon types. The final breakthrough came when Imperator Weaponries of Atreus in the Free Worlds League began production of its Ultra-10 autocannon, which it was willing to sell to anyone. Shortly afterward, the Lyran Alliance began field-testing its new large-bore autocannons.

The original Demolisher was created to concentrate the devastating firepower of twin Type-20 autocannons in one vehicle. However, the new LB-X and Ultra versions of those weapons increase the usefulness and fearsomeness of the Demolisher II. As with the original Demolisher, both these weapon systems are mounted in a turret. Almost as an afterthought, twin machine guns are fixed in the front firing arc as an anti-infantry deterrent.

Deployment

The Demolisher II began full production in late 3059, only months after Operation Bulldog concluded. Currently, under direct orders from the Lyran Alliance, Defiance Industries of Hesperus II has refused all orders for this new assault vehicle outside of the Lyran Alliance.

DEMOLISHER II HEAVY TANK

Type: **Demolisher II Heavy Tank**
Technology Base: Inner Sphere
Movement Type: Tracked
Tonnage: 100
Battle Value: 1,039

Equipment		**Mass**
Internal Structure:		10
Engine:	300	28.5
Type:	Fusion	
Cruising MP:	3	
Flank MP:	5	
Heat Sinks:	10	0
Control Equipment:		5
Lift Equipment:		0
Power Amplifier:		0
Turret:		3
Armor Factor:	260	14.5

	Armor Value
Front	60
R/L Side	50/50
Rear	40
Turret	60

Weapons and Ammo	**Location**	**Tonnage**
LB 20-X AC	Turret	14
Ammo (LB-X) 20	Body	4
Ultra AC/20	Turret	15
Ammo (Ultra) 20	Body	4
Machine Gun	Front	.5
Machine Gun	Front	.5
Ammo (MG) 100	Body	.5
CASE	Body	.5

BATTLEFORCE 2

MP	**Damage PB/M/L**	**Overheat**	**Class**
3t	5/5/—	—	A

Armor/Structure	**Point Value**	**Specials**
—/10	10	

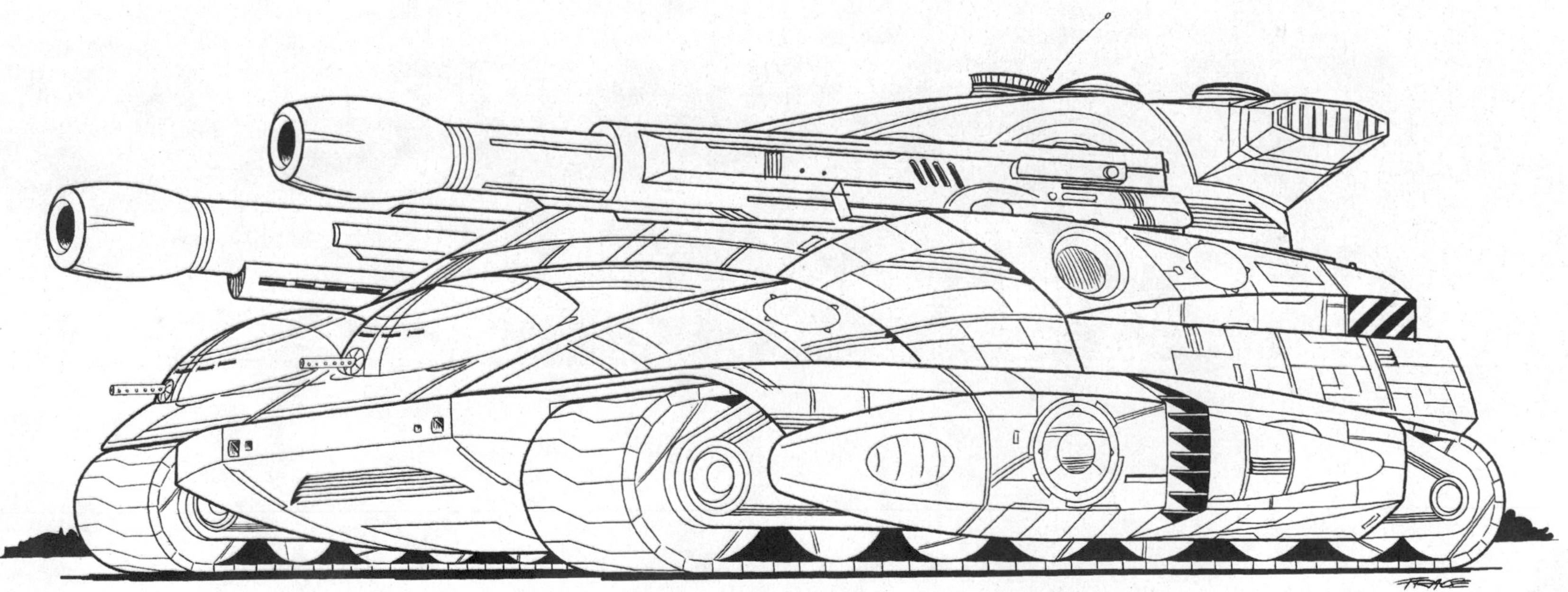

CLAN VEHICLES

Nicholas Kerensky's reform of the society created by his father Aleksandr placed BattleMechs and aerospace fighters at the forefront of the new social order he named the Clans. Combat vehicles and other arms of the military were relegated to supporting roles as security and paramilitary police, and most were denied a place in the liberation of the Pentagon. These non-'Mech units soon formed a second tier within the warrior caste. As Kerensky's honor-based traditions of one-on-one combat gained pre-eminence, vehicles, which relied on teamwork, fell further out of favor. By the 2830s, many had been abandoned or scavenged for spare parts.

The second ilKhan of the Clans, Jerome Winson, saw the folly of this way of thinking. As Clan society entered what is known as its Golden Century and began serious colonization efforts, it became clear that more troops would be needed to garrison these worlds. Because 'Mechs were viewed as the province of the elite, armored vehicles were the logical choice for garrison duty, but most were in poor condition. In 2842, ilKhan Winson commissioned new designs that would be inexpensive to produce and use the latest technology.

Named for war gods from many Terran cultures, the original designs were little better than those found in the Inner Sphere today. Unwilling to repeat the mistake of ignoring conventional vehicles, however, Clan leaders have demanded that vehicles selected for production continue to be refitted and upgraded. While each improvement incorporates current technological advances, efficiency and cost-effectiveness remain cornerstones of the designs. While most use fusion rather than extralight engines, Clan vehicles make use of the Clans' lighter and more efficient weaponry, as well as enhanced armor composites, to gain an advantage on the battlefield.

Though many Clan vehicles contain compatible components that simplify maintenance, most do not use modular weapon packs. The Clans view combat vehicles as unfit for front-line deployment, and see no benefit in incorporating Omni flexibility into vehicle design. The main exception to this mindset is Clan Hell's Horses, whose use of vehicles is well known. Their Epona design, which served as the basis for several Wolf's Dragoons vehicles (primarily the Badger and Bandit), is the only true OmniVehicle in the Clans.

It would be a grave mistake, however, to consider Clan vehicles weak. The largest, the Mars, is a match for any Inner Sphere tank and can defeat most light or medium 'Mechs. While Clan vehicles do not enjoy as great an advantage over Inner Sphere vehicles as do Clan OmniMechs over their Inner Sphere counterparts, they still represent a potent, if underused, fighting force.

—Jared Pascal, Adept XVI-Omega
Deep Periphery, 25 November 3060

SHAMASH RECONNAISSANCE VEHICLE

Mass: 11 tons
Movement Type: Hover
Power Plant: Fusion 60
Cruising Speed: 140 kph
Flank Speed: 216 kph
Armor: Compound JX2 Ferro-Fibrous

Armament:
4 Series 1 Extended Range Small Lasers
Manufacturer: York Vehicle Y2 Facility
Communications System:
Consolidated Type 2M
Targeting and Tracking System:
Consolidated Type V TTS

Overview

Weakened militarily by years of feuding with Clan Burrock and deprived of all significant planetary resources, in the latter part of the twenty-ninth century Clan Blood Spirit found itself in desperate need of raw materials. The loss of the Clan's holdings on Foster, a relatively recent acquisition through colonization, as a result of renewed raiding by the Burrocks exacerbated the situation. Clan Blood Spirit concluded that it needed a faster, cheaper vehicle that it could use in the reconnaissance role of the Asshur, one of the original vehicles commissioned by ilKhan Jerome Winson. Aware that Clan Hell's Horses had recently constructed and fielded a new vehicle design, Khan Boques decided the Blood Spirit scientist caste also should begin working on a new, faster, cheaper vehicle that the Spirits could deploy quickly to repel other Clans' incursions into their territory. The Shamash reconnaissance vehicle is the product of that decision.

Capabilities

The key to the success of the Shamash is its unrivaled speed. Able to travel at more than 200 kilometers per hour, the Shamash can outmaneuver almost any battlefield unit deployed by either the Clans or the Inner Sphere. In open terrain, it can even keep pace with most VTOL/VSTOL aircraft, most of which are specifically designed for speed.

Another factor in the phenomenal success of this vehicle was the unique combination of armor and firepower for a vehicle of its size. Mounting four Series 1 extended-range small lasers, the Shamash is able to deliver a withering fusillade of fire almost equal to the attack capabilities of the Asshur, a vehicle almost twice the size of the Shamash. These weapons mounted in the turret give the Shamash a full 360-degree arc of fire for maximum flexibility.

The final factor that contributed significantly to the Shamash's success was not immediately apparent: the decision to design the vehicle to be operated by a single crew member was made to lower the overall cost of the vehicle and allow rapid deployment. This decision had an unexpected long-term effect on its drivers, however, who, in repeated testing, demonstrated a sharp rise in their overall performance in standard field exercises as well as actual combat and Trials of Position. After months of evaluation, the Clan was forced to accept what was for them a deeply disturbing conclusion. Because Shamash drivers face the enemy alone, rather than with a team of crewmen, they quickly adopt the independent, highly motivated and loyal mindset of a MechWarrior. Like most Clans, Blood Spirit accepts vehicles as necessary to their Clan's survivability but maintains a prejudice against their crews as lesser warriors than 'Mech pilots. The dramatic performances of Shamash drivers, however, may force at least Clan Blood Spirit to reevaluate that attitude.

Deployment

From the time it first rolled off the assembly line at the York Vehicle Y2 facility, Clan Blood Spirit jealously guarded the Shamash against all Trials of Possession. Unfortunately, the disastrous Absorption War waged by Clan Blood Spirit against Clans Star Adder and Burrock left many of these vehicles in the hands of Clan Star Adder.

SHAMASH RECONNAISSANCE VEHICLE

Type: **Shamash Reconnaissance Vehicle**
Technology Base: Clan
Movement Type: Hover
Tonnage: 11
Battle Value: 406

Equipment		**Mass**
Internal Structure:		1.5
Engine:	60	2.5
Type:	Fusion	
Cruising MP:	13	
Flank MP:	20	
Heat Sinks:	10	0
Control Equipment:		1
Lift Equipment:		1.5
Power Amplifier:		0
Turret		.5

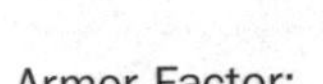

Armor Factor:	38	2
	Armor Value	
Front	9	
R/L Side	7/7	
Rear	7	
Turret	8	

Weapons and Ammo	**Location**	**Tonnage**
4 ER Small Lasers	Turret	2

BATTLEFORCE 2

MP	**Damage PB/M/L**	**Overheat**	**Class**
13h	2/2/—	—	L

Armor/Structure	**Point Value**	**Specials**
—/1	4	

ASSHUR ARTILLERY SPOTTER

Mass: 20 tons
Movement Type: Hover
Power Plant: Fusion 95
Cruising Speed: 97 kph
Flank Speed: 151 kph
Armor: Compound JX2 Ferro-Fibrous

Armament:
2 Series 2b Extended Range Medium Lasers
1 Pattern J6 Streak-6 SRM Launcher
1 ICD Type 4 Target Acquisition Gear
Manufacturer: Various

Communications System: Consolidated Type 2M
Targeting and Tracking System: Consolidated Type V TTS

Overview

The lightest of the original designs commissioned by Jerome Winson, the Asshur fast reconnaissance vehicle was named for an Assyro-Babylonian god of war. When the scientists of Clan Blood Spirit introduced the even lighter Shamash to serve the same purpose, the Asshur immediately became a candidate for decommissioning. Rather than abandoning the serviceable Asshur, however, Blood Spirit technicians replaced its hull-mounted machine guns with a TAG system, and the Asshur proved an ideal artillery spotter.

Capabilities

Only moderately armored, the Asshur's primary defense against opposing 'Mechs and armor is its speed. Capable of achieving speeds in excess of 150 kilometers per hour, it can outrun almost any ground vehicles currently fielded. In addition, a pair of turret-mounted extended-range medium lasers provide accurate fire out to 450 meters, allowing the Asshur to maintain a respectable distance from its target. These beam weapons are backed by a sophisticated short-range missile system, also mounted in the turret. Though the Asshur carries only enough ammunition for fifteen missile volleys, the use of Streak technology guarantees a hit by every round.

The vehicle's primary "weapon" is the TAG system. Initial attempts to mount the device in the turret caused problems with the traverse mechanism, hindering both the TAG system and the Asshur's ability to defend itself. As a result, the designator was mounted fixed-forward, which proved to be less of a problem than might be expected. Though the crew is required to maneuver their vehicle face-on to the target, the vehicle's speed and agility means they are rarely exposed to effective counter-fire.

Deployment

Though most Clans use Asshurs, only the Ghost Bears and Steel Vipers have deployed them in the Inner Sphere. They saw action in several engagements, the most notable being a raid by the mercenary company Armstrong's Archers in 3054. Under contract to the Federated Commonwealth, the Archers staged a raid against the Steel Vipers on Graus, encountering elements of the Thirty-eighth Phalanx 250 kilometers north of New Paris. A mixed Star of vehicles and 'Mechs faced off against the mercenary company, and the Inner Sphere commander expected a quick victory against the garrison unit.

Because the commander was unaware that one of the vehicles was an Asshur spotter vehicle, the mercenaries ignored the vehicles and launched a mass assault against the Star's two 'Mechs, perceiving them as the greater threat. The mercenaries' action freed the Vipers from the need to adhere to the strict rules of engagement, and the Asshur ran circles around the Inner Sphere 'Mechs, repeatedly designating the nearest for Arrow-IV artillery missiles inbound from a pair of tanks located several kilometers from the battlefield. No mercenaries survived the engagement.

ASSHUR ARTILLERY SPOTTER

Type: **Asshur Artillery Spotter**
Technology Base: Clan
Movement Type: Hover
Tonnage: 20
Battle Value: 809

Equipment		**Mass**
Internal Structure:		2
Engine:	95	4.5
Type:	Fusion	
Cruising MP:	9	
Flank MP:	14	
Heat Sinks:	10	0
Control Equipment:		1
Lift Equipment:		2
Power Amplifier:		0
Turret		.5
Armor Factor:	58	3

	Armor Value
Front	13
R/L Side	11/11
Rear	10
Turret	13

Weapons and Ammo	**Location**	**Tonnage**
2 ER Med. Lasers	Turret	2
Streak SRM 6	Turret	3
Ammo (Streak) 15	Body	1
TAG	Front	1

BATTLEFORCE 2

MP	**Damage PB/M/L**	**Overheat**	**Class**
9h	3/3/—	—	L

Armor/Structure	**Point Value**	**Specials**
—/2	8	tag

ODIN SCOUT TANK

Mass: 20 tons
Movement Type: Wheeled
Power Plant: Fusion 140
Cruising Speed: 86 kph
Flanking Speed: 130 kph
Armor: Compound 2110 Ferro-Fibrous

Armament:
2 Kolibri Omega Series Medium Pulse Lasers
1 Series 1 Extended Range Small Laser
1 Pattern J2 Streak-2 SRM Launcher
Manufacturer: Various

Communications System: Consolidated BMR 6
Targeting and Tracking System: TRTTS Mark II

Overview

Though slower than both the Asshur and the Shamash, the Odin remains a staple of second-line forces thanks to its sophisticated sensor suite. Fully integrated with the communication and targeting systems, this sensor suite uses magnetic resonance, IR and electromagnetic intercepts to develop a detailed picture of the area surrounding the tank to 150 meters, making the Odin an ideal vehicle for surveying cluttered terrain and identifying hidden enemy troops.

Capabilities

Like many scout tanks, the Odin sacrifices armor for speed and equipment. Its 1.5 tons of ferro-fibrous armor serve primarily to protect the crew and equipment from damage caused by collisions during off-road movement and from enemy small-arms fire, and do little to shield them from the heavier weapons of 'Mechs and other vehicles. Instead, the Odin relies on its speed to avoid damage. Powered by a lightweight fusion plant, the vehicle can attain speeds of up to 130 kph both on and off the road, but the need to avoid damage to the vehicle's suspension and the crew usually restricts off-road speeds to less than 90 kph.

Turret-mounted dual pulse lasers provide a limited defensive-fire capability, trading range and mass for volume of fire and so increasing the Odin crew's chance of hitting its intended target. Additional fire support is provided by a short-range missile pack. By using Streak technology, this unit offers a longer range than regular SRMs and eliminates the wasted ammunition common to unguided ballistic weapons. These weapons are under the command of the vehicle's gunner, who also commands the vehicle and operates the sensor suite. A nose-mounted small laser allows the driver to engage enemies in the front arc while the gunner discourages pursuit.

Deployment

Contrary to Clan tradition, the two-man crew of an Odin often train together and serve as a team throughout their military career, a strategy required by the high level of teamwork needed to maneuver and fight with the small but sophisticated vehicle. Poor teamwork among Odin crews, and the resulting poor quality of the intelligence they gathered, led to Clan Jade Falcon suffering disastrous results in several engagements against Clan Ghost Bear on the Bear world of Tokasha. Taking their cue from the Jade Falcons' miscalculation, other Clans modified their training and deployment procedures to ensure an appropriate level of performance. In keeping with their traditionally extreme reaction to every situation, however, the Jade Falcons immediately relegated all vehicles to a training or support role.

ODIN SCOUT TANK

Type: **Odin Scout Tank**
Technology Base: Clan
Movement Type: Wheeled
Tonnage: 20
Battle Value: 619

Equipment		**Mass**
Internal Structure:		2
Engine:	140	7.5
Type:	Fusion	
Cruising MP:	8	
Flank MP:	12	
Heat Sinks:	10	0
Control Equipment:		1
Lift Equipment:		0
Power Amplifier:		0
Turret:		0.5
Armor Factor:	29	1.5

	Armor Value
Front	7
R/L Side	6/6
Rear	4
Turret	6

Weapons and Ammo	**Location**	**Tonnage**
2 Med. Pulse Lasers	Turret	4
Streak SRM 2	Turret	1
ER Small Laser	Front	0.5
Ammo (Streak) 50	Body	1
Active Probe	Body	1

BATTLEFORCE 2

MP	**Damage PB/M/L**	**Overheat**	**Class**
8w	2/2/—	—	L

Armor/Structure	**Point Value**	**Specials**
—/1	6	prb

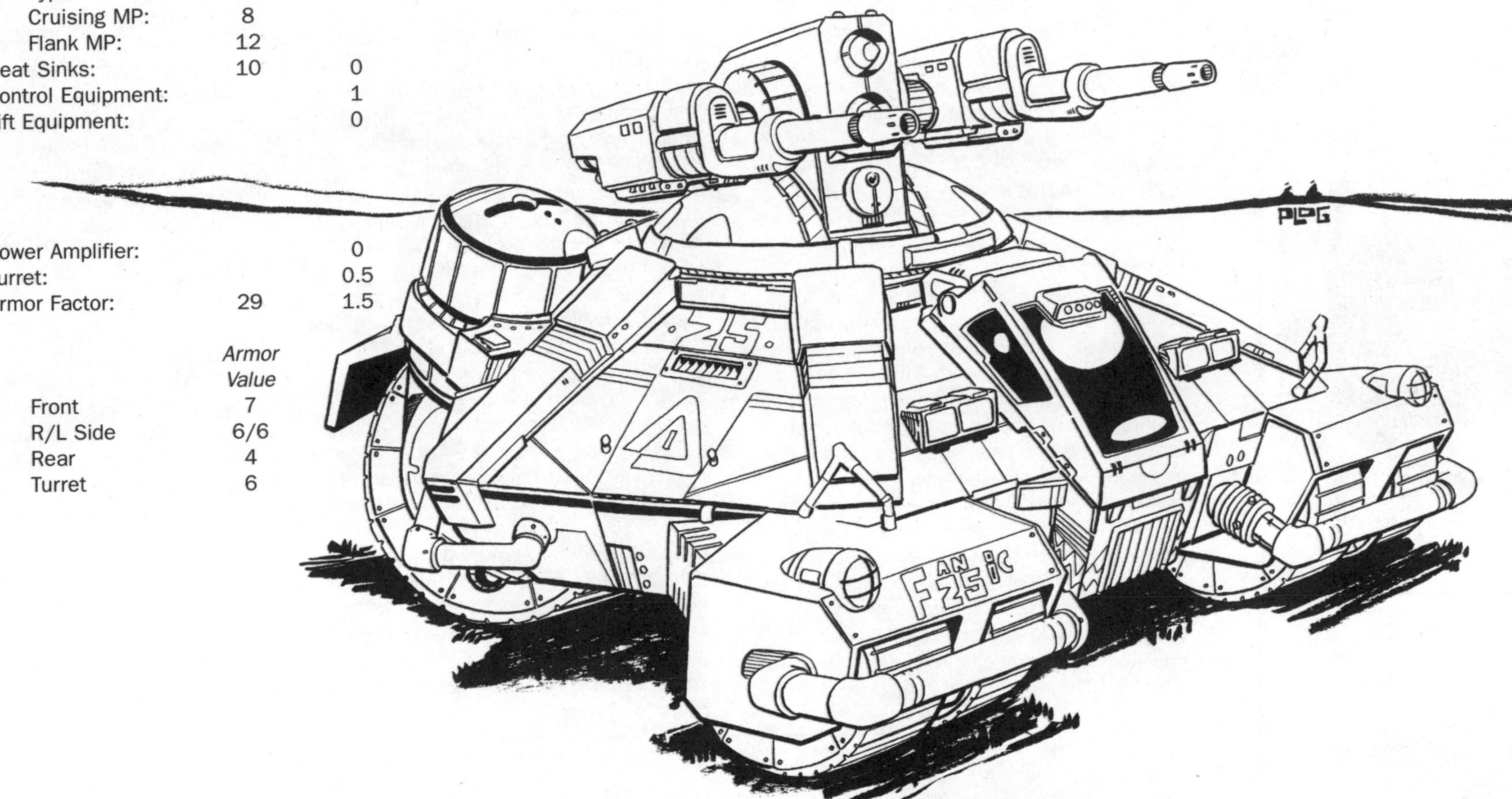

DONAR ASSAULT HELICOPTER

Mass: 21 tons
Movement Type: VTOL
Power Plant: Fusion 50
Cruising Speed: 97 kph
Flanking Speed: 151 kph
Armor: Compound A2F Ferro-Fibrous

Armament:
1 Series 7J Extended Range Large Laser
2 Pattern J2 Streak-2 SRM Launcher
Manufacturer: Various
Communications System: Unit 2J "Boxer"
Targeting and Tracking System: HT9 TTS

Overview

Similar in concept to the Inner Sphere Warrior attack helicopter, the Donar is fast and lethal. A more recent addition to the Clan arsenal, the design was commissioned to fill a need in the Clan Touman for a fast assault unit capable of providing long-range fire support.

Capabilities

The armored cockpit of the Donar contains positions for two crewmen seated in a tandem configuration, a pilot and copilot/gunner (CPG). Designed to be occupied by Clan aerospace warriors, these positions are cramped and uncomfortable for others. These crew positions offer many of the same readouts, allowing either warrior to fly the aircraft or use its weapon systems. This redundancy covers only the most basic operations, however, because the forward copilot/gunner position contains additional readouts for the weapon, targeting and navigation systems, while the rear pilot's position contains additional avionics displays.

Heavily armored for a VTOL, the Donar carries three tons of ferro-fibrous armor, but even the best efforts of Clan scientists to sufficiently protect the Donar's rotors leave that component relatively vulnerable. The rotors' armor protection does prevent accidental damage and keeps them operational even when struck by fire of up to 40mm caliber. Larger-caliber weapons frequently destroy a section of the rotor, forcing the Donar to crash-land, but structural reinforcement normally allows the crew to survive low-speed and low-altitude crashes.

The Donar's primary weapon is an underslung extended-range large laser capable of delivering accurate fire against targets up to 750 meters away. A pair of pylon-mounted Streak SRMs provides a second layer of firepower. Both systems are aimed using a "look-hit" smart system that tracks the firer's eye movements and correlates that movement with electronic sensor data to select and lock-on to the target. The system allows an experienced pilot to identify and destroy threats swiftly and efficiently, but is very difficult for novice pilots to master.

Deployment

Most Clans use the Donar, though the role varies considerably. Clan Hell's Horses use it as a cavalry helicopter for anti-armor and fire-support missions. Clan Steel Viper uses the craft in some second-line clusters as a mobile fire-support platform for infantry. Most Clans, however, particularly Goliath Scorpion and Ice Hellion, use the Donar as a scout. The SLDF gained several intact Donars when they overran Smoke Jaguar bases during Operation Bulldog.

Variants

One of only two variants of a conventional vehicle in standard use by the Clans, the reconnaissance variant of the Donar used by Clan Goliath Scorpion replaces the twin SRM launchers and missiles with an active probe, an ECM system and a TAG designator.

CLAN

DONAR ASSAULT HELICOPTER

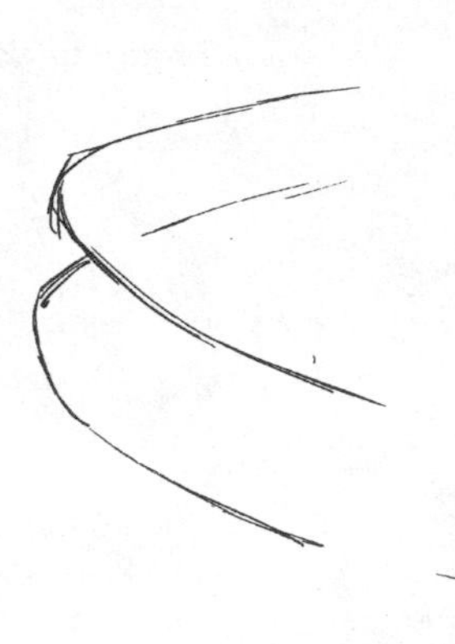

Type: **Donar Assault Helicopter**
Technology Base: Clan
Movement Type: VTOL
Tonnage: 21
Battle Value: 1,435

Equipment		**Mass**
Internal Structure:		2.5
Engine:	50	2.5
Type:	Fusion	
Cruising MP:	9	
Flank MP:	14	
Heat Sinks:	12	2
Control Equipment:		1.5
Lift Equipment:		2.5
Power Amplifier:		0
Armor Factor:	58	3

	Armor Value
Front	16
R/L Side	14/14
Rear	12
Rotor	2

Weapons and Ammo	**Location**	**Tonnage**
ER Large Laser	Front	4
2 Streak SRM 2	Front	2
Ammo (Streak) 50	Body	1

BATTLEFORCE 2

MP	**Damage PB/M/L**	**Overheat**	**Class**
9v	2/2/1	—	L

Armor/Structure	**Point Value**	**Specials**
—/2	14	

MITHRAS LIGHT TANK

Mass: 25 tons
Movement Type: Tracked
Power Plant: Fusion 150
Cruising Speed: 65 kph
Flanking Speed: 97 kph
Armor: Compound Alpha Ferro-Fibrous

Armament:
2 Series 2b Extended Range Medium Lasers
1 Type 25 Ultra Autocannon 2
Manufacturer: Various
Communications System:
Consolidated BMR 6c

Targeting and Tracking System:
TRTTS Mark II CWS

Overview

Originally designed as a scout vehicle that could also fill the role of a light tank, the Mithras eventually ceded the scout role to lighter and faster hover vehicles. The design's serviceable mix of speed, firepower and armor, however, make it ideal for supporting a wide variety of other operations. Able to traverse all but the most difficult terrain, the design enjoys many advantages over lighter and faster vehicles. The most common deployment is in support of conventional infantry, or to harry an enemy's flanks.

Capabilities

The Mithras carries a two-man crew. The driver is responsible for sensor operations and maneuvering the vehicle on the battlefield, while the gunner/commander operates the weapons and communication systems, as well as serving as navigator. An integrated fire control system known as the Combined Weapon System (CWS) allows the gunner, seated halfway up the turret, to both aim and fire. Though this allows for swift target identification and engagement, the lack of a secondary gun sight means that the turret weapons cannot be fired if the vehicle's sensors become inoperative.

The Mithras's turret-mounted Series 2b autocannon allows accurate, sustained fire against targets up to one thousand meters from the vehicle. The system's advanced autoloader allows the gunner to select a variable rate of fire, and at full speed the 50mm cannon can fire twelve rounds a minute. However, as with many fast-load systems, the recoil mechanism is prone to foul the autoloader track, effectively rendering the weapon useless. To give the Mithras limited defensive capabilities in this event, and to provide additional firepower within the cannon's dead zone, the Mithras mounts an extended-range medium laser coaxially with the main weapon. Both systems are controlled by the gunner/commander, while a second laser is mounted on the front of the tank. Though nominally under the control of the driver, this weapon can also be operated by the gunner using the CWS, allowing the driver to concentrate on maneuvering the vehicle.

The Mithras carries only three tons of armor, but the use of a ferro-fibrous compound gives protection equivalent to more than four tons of regular plating, allowing the vehicle to survive a single hit from all but the largest weapons. This tank's only weakness is its rear armor, which can sustain only a single hit from a light or medium weapon before being breached.

Deployment

All Clans field the Mithras, but the Fire Mandrill Kindraa Kline possesses a notable concentration of the design, captured from the Ice Hellions during that Clan's "Hellion's Fury" campaign of ill-advised assaults on its fellow Clans following the Ice Hellions' failure to win a place in the invasion force. The Mandrills' Twenty-first Vanguard Cluster finds the design ideally suited to their particular style of defensive operations; while the 'Mech and Elemental forces hold their position and grind down the enemy, the light tanks harass the enemy flanks and rear positions, forcing them to either withdraw troops to deal with the "gnat bite" attacks or risk being slowly worn down.

MITHRAS LIGHT TANK

Type: **Mithras Light Tank**
Technology Base: Clan
Movement Type: Tracked
Tonnage: 25
Battle Value: 506

Equipment		**Mass**
Internal Structure:		2.5
Engine:	150	8.5
Type:	Fusion	
Cruising MP:	6	
Flank MP:	9	
Heat Sinks:	10	0
Control Equipment:		1.5
Lift Equipment:		0
Power Amplifier:		0
Turret:		1
Armor Factor:	67	3.5

	Armor Value
Front	16
R/L Side	14/14
Rear	9
Turret	14

Weapons and Ammo	**Location**	**Tonnage**
ER Med. Laser	Turret	1
Ultra AC/2	Turret	5
Ammo (Ultra) 45	Body	1
ER Med. Laser	Front	1

BATTLEFORCE 2

MP	**Damage PB/M/L**	**Overheat**	**Class**
6t	2/2/—	—	L

Armor/Structure	**Point Value**	**Specials**
—/3	5	

ANHUR TRANSPORT

Mass: 30 tons
Movement Type: VTOL
Power Plant: Fusion 100
Cruising Speed: 86 kph
Flanking Speed: 130 kph
Armor: Airframe Pattern 2841 Ferro-Fibrous

Armament:
1 Series 2f Extended Range Medium Laser
2 Kolibri Delta Series Medium Pulse Lasers
Manufacturer: Various

Communications System: Khan-series (Type 2)
Targeting and Tracking System: Mark 11 IHADS

Overview

The Clans engage in short, goal-oriented military engagements whenever possible, but the need to maintain a flow of materiel and equipment to the battlefield has long been a concern, exacerbated during the Inner Sphere invasion. While DropShips serve to carry necessary equipment and supplies between worlds, their use is too expensive for on-world transport. As a practical alternative, the Clans use transport vehicles like the Anhur. One of the few designs to pre-date ilKhan Winson's vehicle design review, the Anhur is based on the classic Star League Cobra chassis.

Capabilities

Like the NETC/ComStar Karnov UR design, also based on the Cobra, the Anhur uses a tilt-rotor design, giving it V/STOL capabilities. Capable of taking off or landing without the benefit of a prepared runway, the vehicle is suitable for delivering supplies directly to units in the field. This role all but guarantees encounters with enemy troops, and so the Anhur carries a formidable array of weapons.

Nose-mounted extended-range and pulse lasers provide both range and volume of fire, allowing the Anhur to discourage threats on the ground and in the air. A pulse laser mounted to the rear of the airframe discourages pursuit and can provide covering fire when loading or unloading cargo.

The cavernous cargo bay is rated for loads of up to seven tons and can carry anything from light vehicles or cargo to conventional infantry platoons. Three tons of advanced armor composites provide the crew and cargo with considerable protection against enemy fire, but the Anhur relies primarily on speed and terrain masking to avoid being seen or engaged. The vehicle's crew, consisting of a pilot, copilot and loadmaster, specializes in ground-hugging flights. Accustomed to the violent pitching and rolling that accompanies such flights, they often appear to take a perverse pleasure in the discomfort this causes passengers.

Deployment

All Clans use the Anhur for logistical operations, but relatively few use them for combat operations. Only Clans Blood Spirit, Hell's Horses, and Star Adder permanently assign the vehicle to combat units as an infantry transport. Clans Fire Mandrill, Goliath Scorpion, Ice Hellion and Snow Raven use the design for combat duties on an ad-hoc basis.

ANHUR TRANSPORT

Type: **Anhur Transport**
Technology Base: Clan
Movement Type: VTOL
Tonnage: 30
Battle Value: 1,221

Equipment		**Mass**
Internal Structure:		3
Engine:	100	4.5
Type:	Fusion	
Cruising MP:	8	
Flank MP:	12	
Heat Sinks:	13	3
Control Equipment:		1.5
Lift Equipment:		3
Power Amplifier:		0
Turret:		0
Armor Factor:	58	3

	Armor Value
Front	15
R/L Side	14/14
Rear	13
Rotor	2

Weapons and Ammo	**Location**	**Tonnage**
ER Med. Laser	Front	1
Med. Pulse Laser	Front	2
Med. Pulse Laser	Rear	2
Cargo	Body	7

BATTLEFORCE 2

MP	**Damage PB/M/L**	**Overheat**	**Class**
8v	2/2/—	—	L

Armor/Structure	**Point Value**	**Specials**
—/2	12	tran7

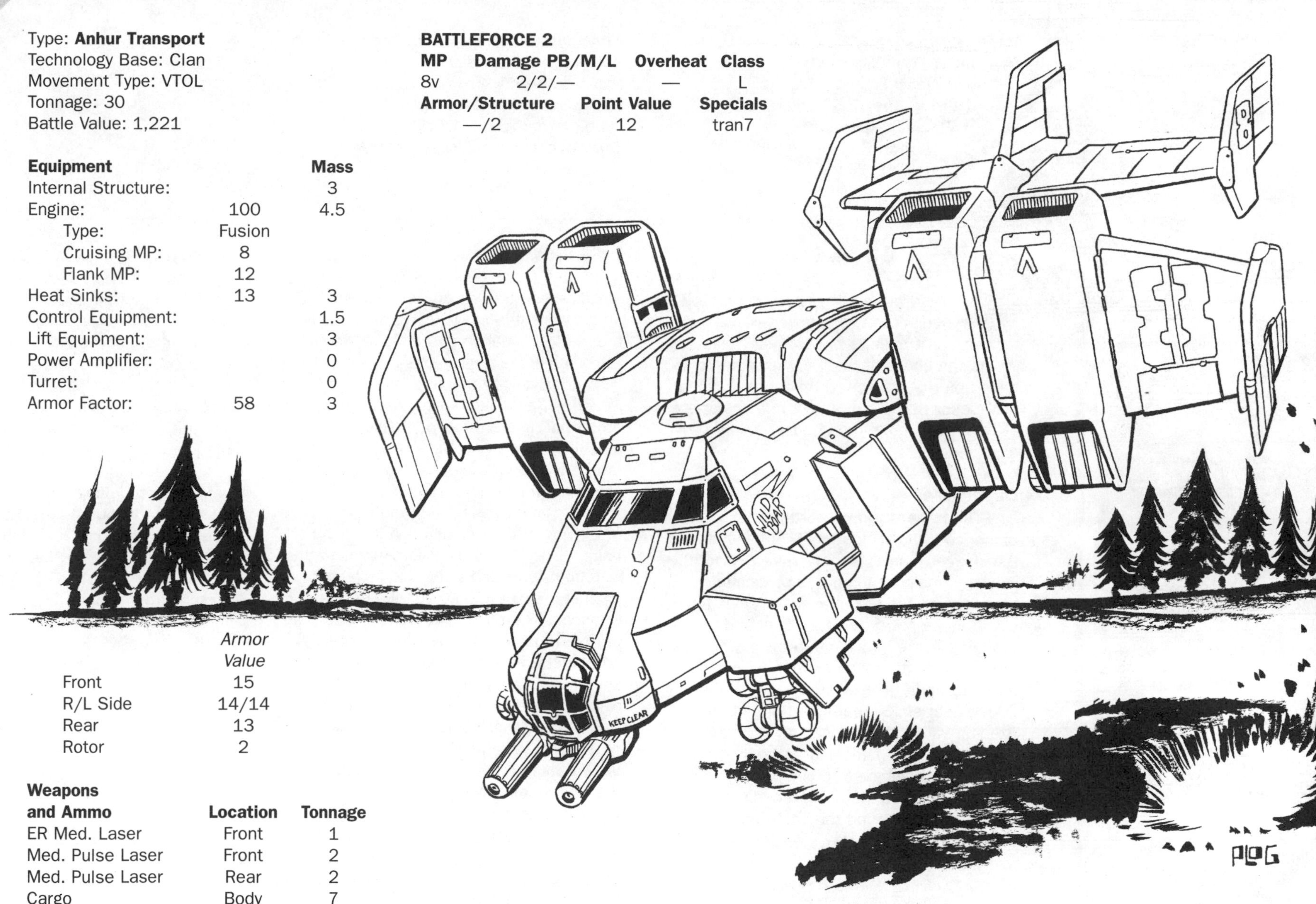

INDRA INFANTRY TRANSPORT

Mass: 35 tons
Movement Type: Wheeled
Power Plant: Fusion 155
Cruising Speed: 54 kph
Flanking Speed: 86 kph
Armor: Compound K4 Ferro-Fibrous

Armament: 4 Series IX Machine Guns
1 Type 22 Extended Range PPC
Manufacturer: Various
Communications System: Consolidated Type 2I
Targeting and Tracking System: Series VI KITT

Overview

The Indra is heavily armed and armored for its size and role. Though the two vehicles serve vastly different roles, a strong rivalry exists between crews of the Indra and the Zorya, based on the fact that the infantry transport is superior to the Zorya light tank in almost every area, though the opposite might be expected.

Capabilities

The Indra is named for the Brahmanic archer-god who wields a bolt of lightning, so the choice of an extended-range PPC for the vehicle's main armament is particularly appropriate. The PPC masses only six tons, but its huge power requirements and the resulting waste heat require the manufacturer to install almost as much mass again in heat sinks. Even with the added heat sinks, repeated firing of the fixed-forward main gun can make the infantry compartment unbearably hot. One modification designed to compensate for this flaw involved installing a dedicated cooling circuit around the cargo bay, but this change ultimately made little difference.

Anti-personnel defense comes from quadruple chain guns mounted in the micro-turret. These provide devastating anti-infantry fire through 360 degrees, allowing the swift elimination of unarmored infantry while "smart targeting" ensures minimal casualties among friendly troops. The turret weapons have also proven effective against armor and aircraft, fouling tracks, turret mechanisms and control surfaces to deadly effect and far in excess of their commonly accepted anti-armor abilities.

To give its passengers the best chance of arriving at their destination unhurt, the Indra carries five tons of ferro-fibrous armor, with both front and sides well-protected against a single hit by even the heaviest weapons. The turret and rear are less well-armored, but will hold against small arms and most anti-vehicle weapons. The weak link, as with all similar vehicles, is the drive train and the wheels, but the Indra's tires contain a light armor weave and make use of the same self-sealing gels (Harjel) used on WarShips and Elemental suits, allowing them to repair any breach and re-inflate as needed. This system is effective against up to 50mm caliber weapon attacks, as the entry and exit holes produced by larger rounds are too large for the Harjel to provide a sufficient seal.

Deployment

The most notorious Inner Sphere deployment of the Indra occurred on the world of Turtle Bay. When rioting broke out following the occupation, Clan Smoke Jaguar dispatched a number of vehicles to control the violence, using Indras to attempt to intimidate the population into submission. This ploy failed, and in the central marketplace of the city of Edo the crowd actually attempted to seize control of two vehicles, prompting the crew to open fire. In less than a minute the tanks killed nearly five hundred people, escalating the situation to the extent that the Jaguar commander declared the situation insoluble and razed the city from orbit.

INDRA INFANTRY TRANSPORT

Type: **Indra Infantry Transport**
Technology Base: Clan
Movement Type: Wheeled
Tonnage: 35
Battle Value: 689

Equipment		**Mass**
Internal Structure:		3.5
Engine:	155	8.5
Type:	Fusion	
Cruising MP:	5	
Flank MP:	8	
Heat Sinks:	15	5
Control Equipment:		2
Lift Equipment:		0
Power Amplifier:		0
Turret:		.5
Armor Factor:	96	5

	Armor Value
Front	25
R/L Side	20/20
Rear	14
Turret	17

Weapons and Ammo	**Location**	**Tonnage**
ER PPC	Front	6
4 Machine Guns	Turret	1
Ammo (MG) 100	Body	.5
Cargo	Body	3

BATTLEFORCE 2

MP	**Damage PB/M/L**	**Overheat**	**Class**
5w	2/2/2	—	L

Armor/Structure	**Point Value**	**Specials**
—/4	7	tran3

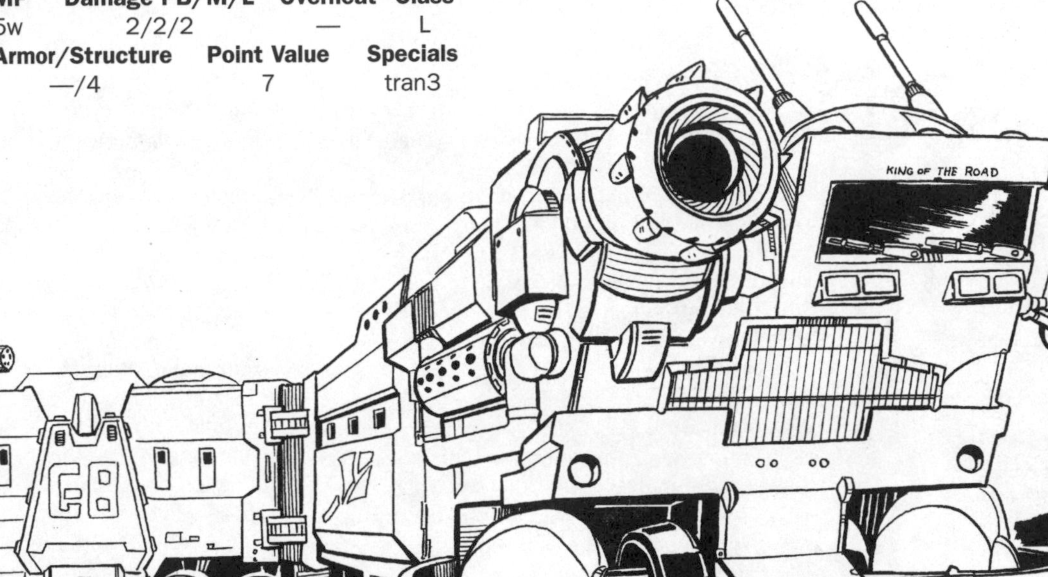

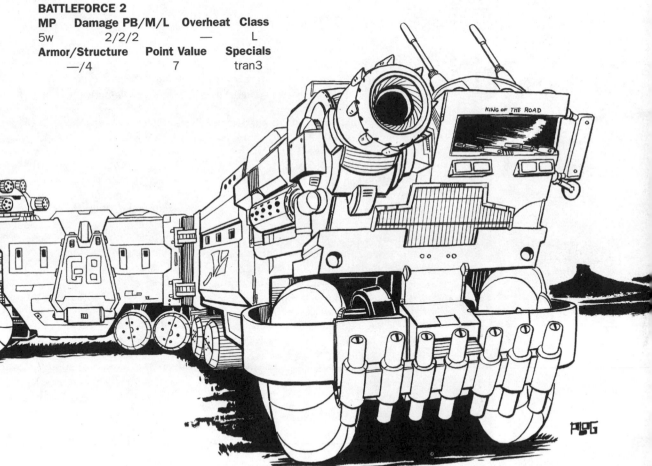

SVANTOVIT INFANTRY FIGHTING VEHICLE

Mass: 35 tons
Movement Type: Hover
Power Plant: Fusion 175
Cruising Speed: 108 kph
Flanking Speed: 162 kph
Armor: Compound Alpha Ferro-Fibrous

Armament: 2 Series IX Machine Guns
2 Type V "Longbow" LRM-5 Launchers
2 Pattern J2 Streak-2 SRM Launchers
Manufacturer: Various
Communications System: Consolidated Type 2I
Targeting and Tracking System: Series II GPS

Overview

In front-line units, the handholds on OmniMechs provide battle armor troops with a means of rapidly moving across a battlefield. Second-line 'Mechs lack these hand-holds, and Elementals assigned to such units, or to vehicle-only garrison units, are forced to move under their own power or to seek alternative transport. The Svantovit was developed to transport and support a Point of troops.

Capabilities

Formerly a conventional infantry transport, the Svantovit's original weaponry was downgraded to increase the size of the infantry compartment. This redesign still left the Svantovit with a formidable array of firepower. Twin long-range missile packs fixed to fire into the vehicle's forward arc comprise the Svantovit's primary weaponry; they are used primarily for fire support once the troops have disembarked and the vehicle can withdraw from the immediate conflict and bring the launchers to bear. Turret-mounted Streak SRM launchers provide a defense against close assault during the deployment of troops. The SRM launchers cannot fire on targets close to the sides of the vehicle, but side-mounted machine guns discourage enemy troops from approaching this dead zone. The massive exit hatch dominates the rear facing of the vehicle, prohibiting any weapons from being mounted there.

A number of Elemental Points have experimented with on-the-move deployment from the Svantovit, with no real success. Not only do the disembarking troops risk being injured, but the sudden weight reduction causes major handling problems for the vehicles' pilots. To reduce the number of crashes, standard operating procedure calls for the Svantovit to come to a full stop before opening the rear hatch. As might be expected, many vehicle crews quickly learned to crash-decelerate from near-flank speed to stationary in a few seconds; though rough on the crew and passengers, this maneuver minimizes the vehicle's vulnerability to enemy fire.

Deployment

Svantovits are manufactured and used by every Clan. Because they generally use the largest number of vehicles and infantry, Clans Blood Spirit and Hell's Horses field the greatest number of Svantovits, while Clans Star Adder and Jade Falcon deploy the fewest. Clan Jade Falcon uses the design solely for training purposes.

Variants

A few Clans continue to use the original configuration of the Svantovit. The cargo capacity of this variant is only three tons, barely sufficient for a platoon of foot infantry in cramped conditions, but the turret-mounted missile launchers carry the Streak-4 system.

SVANTOVIT INFANTRY FIGHTING VEHICLE

Type: **Svantovit Infantry Fighting Vehicle**
Technology Base: Clan
Movement Type: Hover
Tonnage: 35
Battle Value: 546

Equipment		**Mass**
Internal Structure:		3.5
Engine:	175	10.5
Type:	Fusion	
Cruising MP:	10	
Flank MP:	15	
Heat Sinks:	10	0
Control Equipment:		2
Lift Equipment:		3.5
Power Amplifier:		0
Turret:		.5
Armor Factor:	58	3

	Armor Value
Front	14
R/L Side	11/11
Rear	10
Turret	12

Weapons and Ammo	**Location**	**Tonnage**
Machine Gun	Left	.25
Machine Gun	Right	.25
Ammo (MG) 100	Body	.5
2 LRM 5	Front	2
Ammo (LRM) 24	Body	1
2 Streak SRM 2	Turret	2
Ammo (Streak) 50	Body	1
Cargo	Body	5

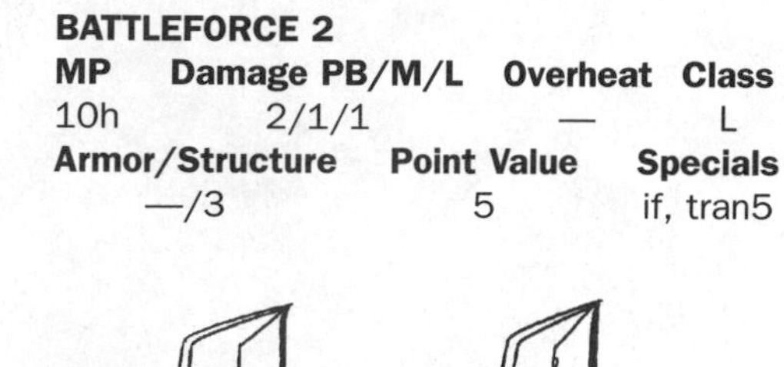

BATTLEFORCE 2

MP	**Damage PB/M/L**	**Overheat**	**Class**
10h	2/1/1	—	L

Armor/Structure	**Point Value**	**Specials**
—/3	5	if, tran5

ZORYA LIGHT TANK

Mass: 35 tons
Movement Type: Tracked
Power Plant: ICE 140
Cruising Speed: 43 kph
Flanking Speed: 65 kph
Armor: Forging OTR17b

Armament: 1 Type OVR-X LB 5-X Autocannon
1 Type X "Short Bow" LRM-10 Launchers with Artemis IV FCS
Manufacturer: Various
Communications System: Consolidated BMR 6c
Targeting and Tracking System: TRTTS Mark II with Artemis IV FCS

Overview

Named for a Slavic warrior goddess, the Zorya is the most common armored vehicle used by the Clans. Comprised of readily available parts, it is inexpensive to manufacture, and its simple control systems make it easy for crews to learn to operate the vehicle.

Capabilities

One of the few Clan fighting vehicles to use an ICE engine, the Zorya is slower than many of its peers, with a top speed of only 65 kph. Because this vehicle is intended to be used in static positions, as indicated by its armor configuration, its speed is rarely an issue. The front hull and turret carry almost double the armor of the side and rear facings, but this armor is conventional forged rather than ferro-fibrous, making it 20 percent less effective than it could be. A sophisticated ECM suite, however, adequately supplements the armor by degrading the performance of enemy fire-control and sensor systems.

Compared to other Clan vehicles of its tonnage, the Zorya mounts a large crew, requiring a driver, gunner and commander. The division of labor between the crew members, however, allows soldiers to operate most systems in the vehicle with minimal training. Save for the lock-in harness and narrow vision slit, the driver position is little different than that in a standard ground car. The gunner position, located behind the driver, controls the turret and the vehicle's weapon systems. Equipped with a 360-degree vision strip, the gunner simply aligns the cross hairs of each weapon system on the target and depresses the firing stud. The commander, who also serves as sensor, communications and electronic warfare officer, can also designate a target on his console for the gunner, which is then highlighted on the gunnery screen.

The Zorya's primary weapon is a 40mm LB-X series autocannon. Capable of firing both solid and cluster rounds, the weapon is devastatingly effective against armor and infantry units. The Zorya carries 40 rounds of ammunition for the main gun, divided between two ammunition bins. Most Zoryas carry an equal mix of solid and cluster rounds. A 10-tube long-range missile pack provides additional firepower, but small ammunition bins limit the launcher's endurance and versatility. An Artemis fire-control system slaved to the LRM launcher has improved the number of missiles that strike the intended target, but some Clans have removed this device in favor of an extra ton of ammunition.

Deployment

All Clans use the Zorya. Clans Blood Spirit and Cloud Cobra initially deployed the largest number, though many of the Blood Spirit Zoryas were destroyed when the Clan intervened in the Star Adder-Burrock Trial of Absorption and have yet to be replaced. Clan Wolf recently has begun to make extensive use of the Zorya, because of its easy-to-learn controls, to repopulate its garrison ranks. Forced to acknowledge the weakened condition of his military following the invasion of the Inner Sphere and the Refusal War, Khan Vlad Ward took the desperate step of recruiting members of the non-warrior castes, through Trials of Position, to crew Zoryas and other vehicles.

ZORYA LIGHT TANK

Type: **Zorya Light Tank**
Technology Base: Clan
Movement Type: Tracked
Tonnage: 35
Battle Value: 415

Equipment		**Mass**
Internal Structure:		3.5
Engine:	140	10
Type:	ICE	
Cruising MP:	4	
Flank MP:	6	
Heat Sinks:	0	0
Control Equipment:		2
Lift Equipment:		0
Power Amplifier:		0
Turret:		1.5
Armor Factor:	56	3.5

	Armor Value
Front	15
R/L Side	9/9
Rear	9
Turret	14

Weapons and Ammo	**Location**	**Tonnage**
LB 5-X AC	Turret	7
Ammo (LB-X) 40	Body	2
LRM 10	Turret	2.5
Artemis IV FCS	Turret	1
Ammo (LRM) 12	Body	1
ECM Suite	Body	1

BATTLEFORCE 2

MP	**Damage PB/M/L**	**Overheat**	**Class**
4t	1/1/1	—	L

Armor/Structure	**Point Value**	**Specials**
—/3	4	if, ecm

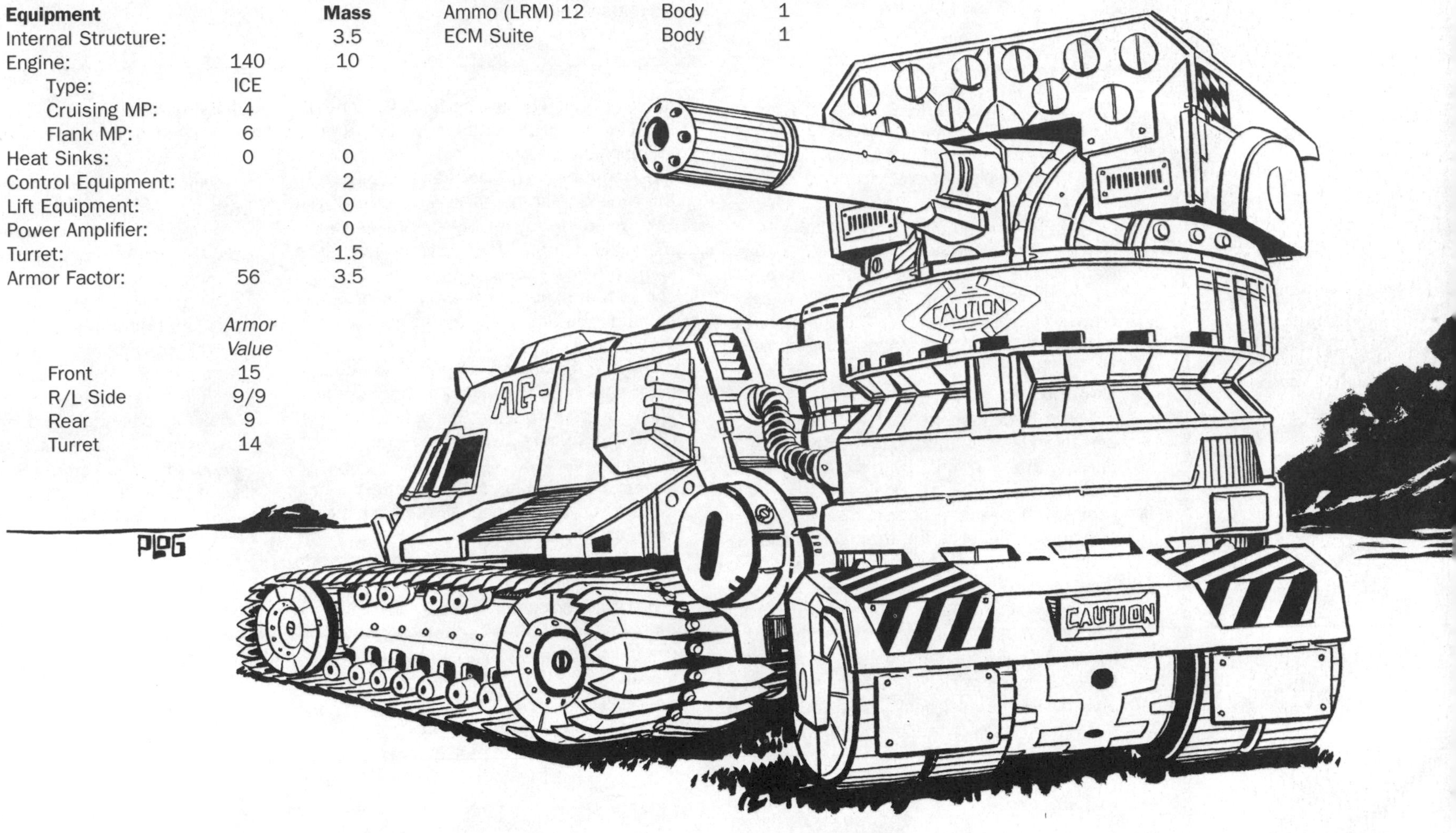

PLOG

ARES MEDIUM TANK

Mass: 40 tons
Movement Type: Tracked
Power Plant: Fusion 200
Cruising Speed: 54 kph
Flanking Speed: 86 kph
Armor: Compound G5 Ferro-Fibrous

Armament:
1 Series 7Ja Extended Range Large Laser
1 Type X "Short Bow" LRM-10 launchers with Artemis IV FCS
1 Type XV "Crossbow" LRM-15 launchers with Artemis IV FCS

Manufacturer: Various

Communications System: 2SH C3
Targeting and Tracking System: Build 4 JVJ TTS with Artemis IV FCS

Overview

Designed to provide direct and indirect fire support, the Ares tank operates well in a wide range of roles. Specifically, the vehicle's top speed of 86 kph makes it an ideal escort for armored personnel carriers (APCs) and transports. Though the Ares is not classified as an infantry fighting vehicle, most Ares crews are trained to work in conjunction with both battle armor and standard infantry.

Capabilities

The three-man crew of the Ares is protected by four and a half tons of ferro-fibrous armor, which provides consistent protection on all sides. Unlike most vehicles, the Ares' rear armor is only marginally inferior to the front glacis and sides, and that only because the rear location carries CASE blowout panels. Designed to channel the blast away from the vehicle's most delicate components in the event of an internal ammunition explosion, the CASE system allows the crew to survive an otherwise catastrophic explosion, though the vehicle itself is rendered inoperable. Most vehicles equipped with CASE can be repaired and returned to active duty after an ammunition explosion; at the very least, most of the systems are salvageable. With the exception of the driver's bulletproof view port, none of the crew have a direct view of the exterior of the tank. Instead, they rely on camera feeds or periscope sights, a design choice that minimizes the number of weak points in the armor and increases crew survivability.

A turret-mounted, extended-range large laser serves as the tank's primary weapon, allowing accurate direct-fire against targets up to 750 meters away. Prone to slight warping when fired repeatedly, the barrel of the weapon is monitored by the fire-control system, which automatically compensates for heat-induced distortion.

Hull-mounted missile launchers provide secondary direct-fire capability. The ten- and fifteen-tube box-launchers can also use targeting data from other vehicles to loft indirect fire against targets masked by terrain features. Because ammunition for the missile tubes is strictly limited by the vehicle's carrying capacity, most commanders favor the turret laser.

Deployment

Most commonly found in Clans Wolf and Coyote, the Ares has played an increasingly significant role in the Wolves' homeworld garrison forces since the Refusal War. Troop shortages in the invasion force prompted the transfer of many warriors to the Inner Sphere and, in a dramatic and desperate strategy, these warriors have been replaced by recruits from the lower castes. Because vehicle training is less intense than that required for 'Mech operations, most soldiers recruited through these "garrison-level" Trials of Position have been assigned to the crews of newly manufactured tanks and APCs. After the Zorya, the Ares crews have seen the largest influx of recruits.

ARES MEDIUM TANK

Type: **Ares Medium Tank**
Technology Base: Clan
Movement Type: Tracked
Tonnage: 40
Battle Value: 938

Equipment		**Mass**
Internal Structure:		4
Engine:	200	13
Type:	Fusion	
Cruising MP:	5	
Flank MP:	8	
Heat Sinks:	12	2
Control Equipment:		2
Lift Equipment:		0
Power Amplifier:		0
Turret:		.5
Armor Factor:	86	4.5

	Armor Value
Front	19
R/L Side	17/17
Rear	16
Turret	17

Weapons and Ammo	**Location**	**Tonnage**
ER Large Laser	Turret	4
LRM 10	Front	2.5
Artemis IV FCS	Front	1
Ammo (LRM) 12	Body	1
LRM 15	Front	3.5
Artemis IV FCS	Front	1
Ammo (LRM) 8	Body	1

BATTLEFORCE 2

MP	**Damage PB/M/L**	**Overheat**	**Class**
5t	3/3/3	—	M

Armor/Structure	**Point Value**	**Specials**
—/4	9	if

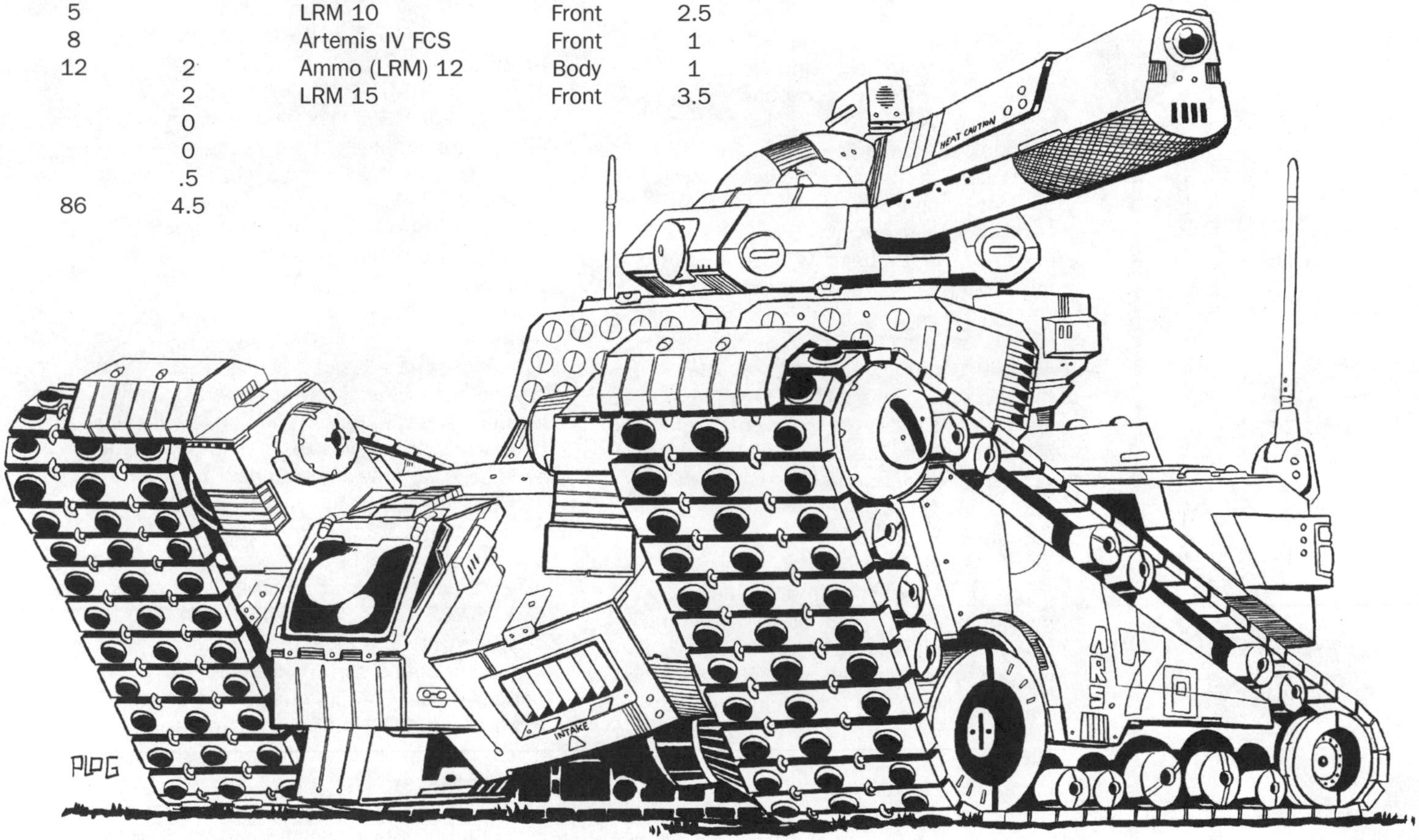

EPONA PURSUIT TANK

Mass: 50 tons
Movement Type: Hover
Power Plant: Fusion 215
Cruising Speed: 97 kph
Flanking Speed: 150 kph
Armor: Compound VM20 Ferro-Fibrous

Armament: 17 tons pod space (maximum of 10 tons in turret)
Manufacturer: Niles Industriplex Alpha
Communications System: Build 1700/5 Tacticom
Targeting and Tracking System: Series XL FWS

Overview

Clan Hell's Horses maintains a high regard for the usefulness of conventional forces, and as such are the only Clan to manufacture and deploy the Epona. Other Clans consider the pod technology wasted on conventional vehicles, but the Horses, who regularly use vehicles in front-line roles, have enjoyed the benefits of the flexibility of this design for more than seventy years. Though the success of the Epona might have been expected to prompt the design and production of more OmniVehicles, the Clanwide bias toward BattleMech supremacy even among the Horses prevents expansion of this concept. The Epona remains the only vehicle of its kind in use among the Clans.

Capabilities

Based on the heaviest hovertank chassis possible in order to achieve maximum speed potential and structural integrity, the Epona is purpose-built as a recon and pursuit craft, very similar in design to the Dragoons' Bandit hovercraft (likely an offshoot of the Epona). The major difference between the two is that the Epona mounts roughly half the armor of the Bandit, but carries more than double the pod space.

The primary configuration of the Epona reflects the favored attack mode of Clan Hell's Horses by employing an effective mix of pulse lasers and SRMs. The next most common Epona configuration features twin turret-mounted LRM-20s, supported by a pair of forward-fixed extended-range medium lasers. Apparently meant as a heavy artillery-support unit, this version also features target acquisition gear to spot for even heavier artillery units after first softening up the target with its own weapons.

The Epona's B and C configurations favor engagements in relatively open terrain, featuring a single, massive weapon backed up by short-range missiles. The C configuration adds an ECM array and features TAG.

The modular technology that makes these variations possible does create one minor problem for Epona crews. The roles of driver, gunner and commander, usually specialized in other vehicles, become less distinct in the Epona, as each crew member's duties can change with the weapons load. For this reason, the controls at each station in this vehicle are easily programmable for all possible tasks to make transitions between roles easier. Still, new crews must drill for weeks in the proper use of an Epona before taking it into the field.

Deployment

Hell's Horses is the only Clan to use the Epona, despite its relatively long career in service. As with OmniMechs, Eponas are considered front-line units, meant for the most elite of warriors, and are concentrated in the Clan's primary Galaxies.

Type: **Epona Pursuit Tank**
Technology Base: Clan OmniVehicle
Movement Type: Hover
Tonnage: 50
Battle Value: 1,242

Equipment		**Mass**
Internal Structure:		5
Engine:	215	14.5
Type:	Fusion	
Cruising MP:	9	
Flank MP:	14	
Heat Sinks:	10	0
Control Equipment:		2.5
Lift Equipment:		5
Power Amplifier:		0
Turret:		1
Armor Factor:	96	5

	Armor Value
Front	21
R/L Side	20/20
Rear	18
Turret	17

TRACKED

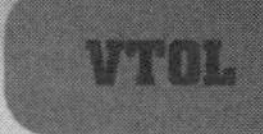

OMNI

CLAN

EPONA PURSUIT TANK

Weapons and Ammo	Location	Tonnage
Primary Configuration		
4 Med. Pulse Lasers	Turret	8
Streak SRM 4	Turret	2
Ammo (Streak) 25	Body	1
6 Heat Sinks	Body	6
Configuration A		
LRM 20	Turret	5
Ammo (LRM) 12	Body	2
LRM 20	Turret	5
Ammo (LRM) 12	Body	2
2 ER Med. Lasers	Front	2
TAG	Front	1
Battle Value: 1,741		
Configuration B		
Ultra AC/10	Turret	10
Ammo (Ultra) 20	Body	2
2 Streak SRM 4	Front	4
Ammo (Streak) 25	Body	1
Battle Value: 1,022		
Configuration C		
ER PPC	Turret	6
Streak SRM 6	Turret	3
Ammo (Streak) 15	Body	1
5 Heat Sinks	Body	5
ECM Suite	Body	1
TAG	Front	1
Battle Value: 1,322		

BATTLEFORCE 2

Type: **Epona Pursuit Tank**

MP	**Damage PB/M/L**	**Overheat**	**Class**
9h	4/4/—	—	M

Armor/Structure	**Point Value**	**Specials**
—/4	12	omni

Configuration A

MP	**Damage PB/M/L**	**Overheat**	**Class**
9h	4/4/2	—	M

Armor/Structure	**Point Value**	**Specials**
—/4	17	omni, if, tag

Configuration B

MP	**Damage PB/M/L**	**Overheat**	**Class**
9h	3/3/2	—	M

Armor/Structure	**Point Value**	**Specials**
—/4	10	omni

Configuration C

MP	**Damage PB/M/L**	**Overheat**	**Class**
9h	3/3/2	—	M

Armor/Structure	**Point Value**	**Specials**
—/4	13	omni, ecm, tag

HACHIMAN FI[illegible]E SUPPORT TAN[illegible]

Mass: 50 tons
Movement Type: Tracked
Power Plant: Fusion 200
Cruising Speed: 43 kph
Flanking Speed: 65 kph
Armor: Compound G5 Ferro-Fibrous

Armament:
- 2 Series 2d Extended Range Medium Lasers
- 2 Type XX "Great Bow" LRM-20 Launchers with Artemis IV FCS
- 1 Pattern J6 Streak-4 SRM Launcher

Manufacturer: Various

Communications System: JNE Integrated
Targeting and Tracking System: Build 2 JRD TTS with Artemis IV FCS

Overview

Designed as a fire-support platform, the Hachiman receives little respect from warriors, but its effectiveness ensures that most Clans field several in their toumans. Moderately armed and armored, this vehicle is equally at home in a stand-off or close support role, but lacks the ammunition for prolonged engagements.

Capabilities

The armor and structure of the Hachiman use advanced composites and construction techniques to provide the vehicle and its crew with maximum protection. Each of the crew members operates from within his own armored compartment, and core systems such as the power plant and ammo bins are similarly protected. Though a lucky hit may still disable a vital system, most armor facings are proof against multiple hits. Even the weak rear armor can sustain an attack by the largest caliber autocannons and leave the vehicle operable. Intended to minimize the effects of a penetrating hit, this compartmentalized system has met with mixed success.

An advanced tactical coordination system (TCS) aids communication between the crew compartments, yet all but the best-trained crews suffer a noticeable reduction in inter-crew communication, which in turn reduces fighting effectiveness. Crews and commanders scorn the Hachiman's interior configuration, but scientist-caste studies indicate that it gives the Hachiman the highest crew survival rate of any Clan armored vehicle, as well as the highest incidence of salvageable equipment.

In most circumstances, the Hachiman does not allow an enemy to approach close enough to cause potentially fatal damage. Its primary armament is a pair of LRM-20 launchers, which provides a devastating stand-off punch. Unhindered by the arming delay used by Inner Sphere systems, these launchers can also engage a target at pointblank range. In either case, the mating of a sophisticated fire-control system with the launcher ensures a tight grouping of missiles and improves the volley's damage potential. Because the Hachiman carries only enough ammunition for two minutes of continual LRM attacks, the turret also includes a pair of extended-range medium lasers to provide defense when the ammunition is exhausted. A fixed-forward Streak SRM rack rounds out the Hachiman's armament.

Deployment

Though predominantly found in garrison Clusters, the Hachiman is regarded as an offensive rather than defensive platform. As such, several of the pro-vehicle Clans, including the Blood Spirits, Hell's Horses and Star Adders, employ them in front-line roles. Indeed, both the Alpha and Omega Keshiks of Clan Hell's Horses incorporate this design.

HACHIMAN FIRE SUPPORT TANK

Type: **Hachiman Fire Support Tank**
Technology Base: Clan
Movement Type: Tracked
Tonnage: 50
Battle Value: 1,245

BATTLEFORCE 2

MP	Damage PB/M/L	Overheat	Class
4t	5/5/3	—	M

Armor/Structure	Point Value	Specials
—/5	12	if

Equipment		Mass
Internal Structure:		5
Engine:	200	13
Type:	Fusion	
Cruising MP:	4	
Flank MP:	6	
Heat Sinks:	10	0
Control Equipment:		2.5
Lift Equipment:		0
Power Amplifier:		0
Turret:		1.5
Armor Factor:	134	7

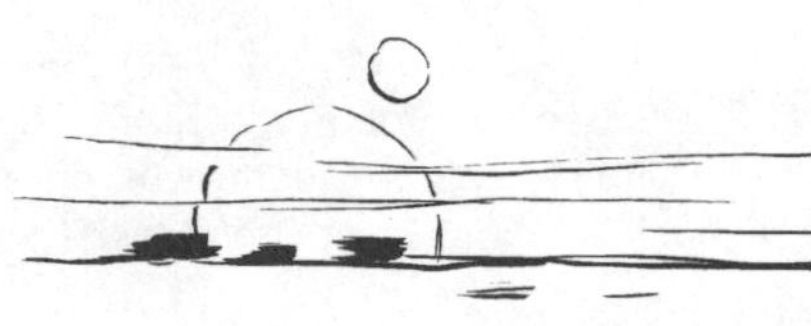

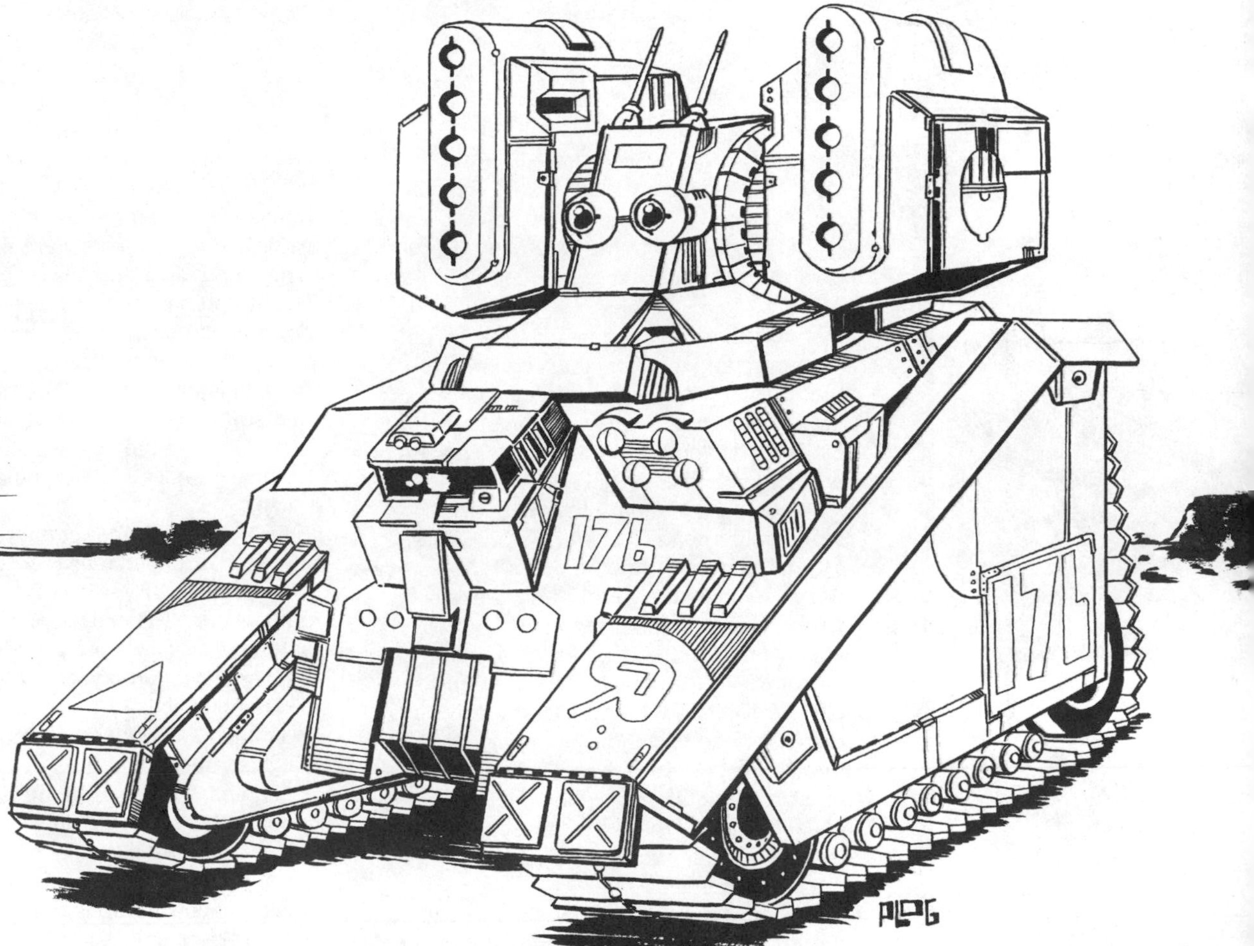

	Armor Value
Front	30
R/L Side	29/29
Rear	19
Turret	27

Weapons and Ammo	Location	Tonnage
2 ER Med. Lasers	Turret	2
2 LRM 20	Turret	10
2 Artemis IV FCS	Turret	2
Ammo (LRM) 24	Body	4
Streak SRM 4	Front	2
Ammo (Streak) 25	Body	1

KU WHEELED ASSAULT TANK

Mass: 50 tons
Movement Type: Wheeled
Power Plant: Fusion 180
Cruising Speed: 43 kph
Flanking Speed: 65 kph
Armor: "Magnum" Ferro-Fibrous Composite

Armament:
1 Series 7J Extended Range Large Laser
1 Series 1 Extended Range Small Laser
1 Type 9 Ultra Autocannon 10
1 Pattern JX Streak-4 SRM Launcher
Manufacturer: Various
Communications System:
Build 1685 Tacticom

Targeting and Tracking System:
Series VI Integrated TTS

Overview

Based on the SLDF Turhan chassis, the Ku assault tank was designed with a single goal in mind: closing with the enemy and inflicting the maximum amount of damage.

Capabilities

Powered by a class-180 fusion plant, the Ku is capable of speeds up to 65 kph. Its wheeled drive system, however, while making excellent use of the power plant's output, limits the terrain across which the tank can pass without sustaining damage to the undercarriage to open or urban sites.

Seven tons of the Magnum ferro-fibrous armor compound give the tank crew and systems considerable protection from enemy fire. Further, the armor is only marginally biased toward the front and sides, reflecting the fact that the vehicle is regularly used to penetrate enemy formations and so requires even its rear to be able to withstand multiple hits. As is usual for tanks, the turret possesses the least protection, but its design limits exposure to enemy fire.

Though small, the crew compartment of the Ku provides all the facilities the driver, gunner and commander need to conduct an extended campaign in enemy territory. The cabin is fully pressurized, allowing the vehicle to operate in a vacuum or tainted atmosphere, and the commander's exit hatch serves as a compact but functional airlock. A built-in heating element allows the crew to prepare field rations, and a fold-down bunk above the gunner's position even allows the crew to sleep in shifts. Unfortunately, sanitary facilities are limited and so Ku crews have developed special procedures to prevent the atmosphere becoming unpleasant during extended campaigns.

Offensive firepower is provided by a Series 7 extended-range large laser mounted coaxially with a Type 9 75mm autocannon. The clip-reload system for the autocannon allows the gunner to select a one- or two-round burst, giving the tank a devastating volley-fire capability. A cupola-mounted extended-range small laser provides secondary fire capabilities, as does a quad-pack short-range missile launcher mounted above the driver's position. The gunner controls all weapon systems, but secondary fire controls at the commander's position allow the tank to continue fighting even if the gunner is disabled.

Deployment

The best-known use of the Ku occurred on Arcadia in 3002, when Clans Ghost Bear and Steel Viper clashed over control of a manufacturing complex. The Vipers considered defense of the facility a low priority and so assigned the site only a vehicle Trinary from the Ninety-third Viper Assault Cluster (The Immortals). The Viper commander chose to defend his position despite the apparent inequality of forces, and though the Vipers eventually lost control of the factory, a Star of Ku assault tanks crippled or destroyed an equal number of Ghost Bear OmniMechs.

CLAN

KU WHEELED ASSAULT TANK

Type: **Ku Wheeled Assault Tank**
Technology Base: Clan
Movement Type: Wheeled
Tonnage: 50
Battle Value: 831

Equipment		**Mass**
Internal Structure:		5
Engine:	180	10.5
Type:	Fusion	
Cruising MP:	4	
Flank MP:	6	
Heat Sinks:	14	4
Control Equipment:		2.5
Lift Equipment:		0
Power Amplifier:		0
Turret:		1.5
Armor Factor:	134	7

	Armor Value
Front	30
R/L Side	29/29
Rear	26
Turret	20

Weapons and Ammo	**Location**	**Tonnage**
ER Large Laser	Turret	4
ER Small Laser	Turret	.5
Ultra AC/10	Turret	10
Ammo (Ultra) 20	Body	2
Streak SRM 4	Front	2
Ammo (Streak) 25	Body	1

BATTLEFORCE 2

MP	**Damage PB/M/L**	**Overheat**	**Class**
4w	4/3/3	—	M

Armor/Structure	**Point Value**	**Specials**
—/5	8	

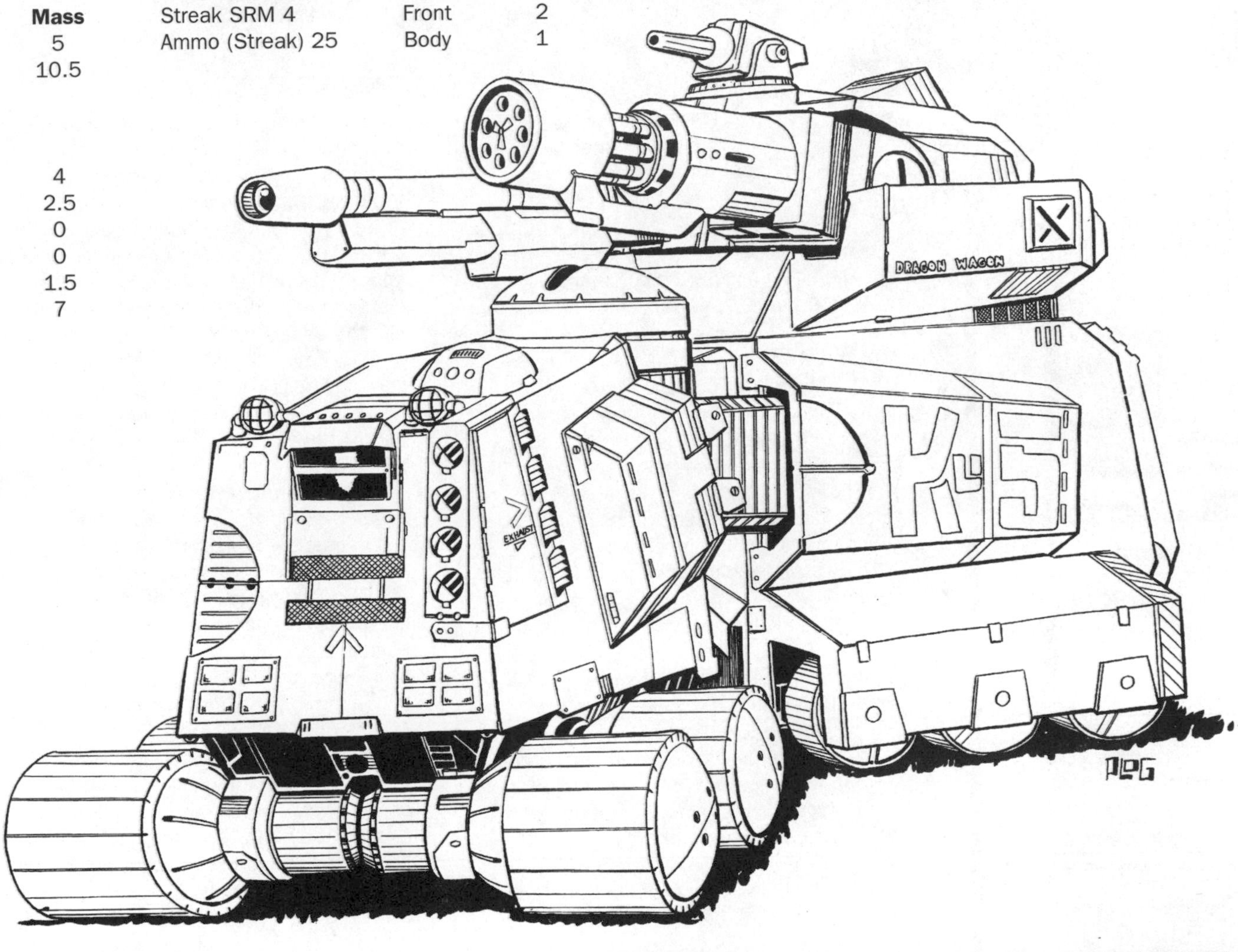

ORO HEAVY TANK

Mass: 60 tons
Movement Type: Tracked
Power Plant: Fusion 240
Cruising Speed: 43 kph
Flanking Speed: 65 kph
Armor: Compound 3092/3 Ferro-Fibrous

Armament:
1 Series 2d Extended Range Medium Laser
1 Kolibri Delta Series Large Pulse Laser
1 Type J LB-20X Autocannon
Manufacturer: Various
Communications System: Q2 Block 7

Targeting and Tracking System:
Build 2 JRD TTS

Overview

Designed specifically to oppose vehicles and aircraft, the Oro is a feared sight on the battlefield. Its presence can provide a decisive edge over enemy troops, making it a tank sought after by commanders as well as a prime target for enemy fire.

Capabilities

Built around the rugged G6 fusion power plant, the Oro can attain speeds up to 65 kph despite carrying more than twenty-five tons of weapons and armor. The Compound 3092/3 ferro-fibrous armor allows the tank to sustain considerable punishment, though Inner Sphere commanders would consider it inadequately armored when compared to Inner Sphere tanks of similar size such as the Manticore and Po. The Clans consider the armor load a simple statement of the value, or lack thereof, attached to vehicle crews.

While the turret-mounted Kolibri Delta large pulse laser provides long-range high-volume fire, the Oro's most feared weapon is the Type J autocannon. Designed to fire both standard rounds and cluster ammunition, it is equally effective against 'Mechs, vehicles and aircraft. The standard rounds can shred even the thickest armor, but the cluster-shot is more insidious, sanding off armor and any exposed systems. The movement and control systems of tanks and aircraft are particularly vulnerable to this form of attack, and one or two hits are usually sufficient to disable them. The limited ammunition storage capacity of the Oro, only five rounds of each type, forces tank commanders to carefully husband their shots. A nose-mounted medium laser provides a means of defense even in the event of major damage to the turret.

The Oro uses the same targeting system as the Hachiman, though it lacks the necessary hookups for the Artemis missile control system. The Oro is also equipped with a comparable tactical coordination system, but lacks the compartmentalization of the smaller vehicle. In the Oro, the TCS allows the gunner and commander to assume the other's role in the event that one or the other is incapacitated by combat damage. However, the likelihood of any crew surviving the shrapnel that would result from such a penetrating hit is slim, and both designers and crew have questioned the value of installing the sophisticated system.

Deployment

Originally designed to carry a conventional AC-20, Clan Steel Viper developed the current version of the Oro as a counter to the air power of Clan Snow Raven. Devastatingly effective against aerospace fighters, the new version quickly earned acceptance throughout the Clans and was found to be equally useful in other roles. Ironically, Clan Snow Raven fields many Oros, mostly at the Ravenshead training facility where they are used to expose aerospace pilots to tactics for avoiding anti-air fire.

ORO HEAVY TANK

Type: **Oro Heavy Tank**
Technology Base: Clan
Movement Type: Tracked
Tonnage: 60
Battle Value: 873

Equipment		**Mass**
Internal Structure:		6
Engine:	240	17.5
Type:	Fusion	
Cruising MP:	4	
Flank MP:	6	
Heat Sinks:	15	5
Control Equipment:		3
Lift Equipment:		0
Power Amplifier:		0
Turret:		2
Armor Factor:	106	5.5

	Armor Value
Front	24
R/L Side	21/21
Rear	18
Turret	22

Weapons and Ammo	**Location**	**Tonnage**
ER Med. Laser	Front	1
Large Pulse Laser	Turret	6
LB 20-X AC	Turret	12
Ammo (LB-X) 10	Body	2

BATTLEFORCE 2

MP	**Damage PB/M/L**	**Overheat**	**Class**
4t	4/4/1	—	H

Armor/Structure	**Point Value**	**Specials**
—/5	9	

ISHTAR HEAVY FIRE SUPPORT TANK

Mass: 65 tons
Movement Type: Wheeled
Power Plant: Fusion 110
Cruising Speed: 32 kph
Flanking Speed: 54 kph
Armor: Compound E91 Ferro-Fibrous

Armament:
1 "Goalkeeper" Anti-Missile System
1 Type KOV LB-10X Autocannon
1 Type 9 Ultra Autocannon 10
1 Type XV "Crossbow" LRM-15 Launcher with Artemis IV FCS
2 Series 2b Extended Range Medium Lasers

Manufacturer: Various
Communications System: Build 1685/3 Tacticom
Targeting and Tracking System: Series XXVI IWS with Artemis IV FCS

Overview

Because vehicle crews consider it too cumbersome, the Ishtar has never attained the popularity of the lighter, similar-use Hachiman. Personal preference aside, the Ishtar's deadly weapons array makes it a vital part of heavy armor units.

Capabilities

The original version of the Ishtar was capable of speeds up to 65 kph, but over the centuries since ilKhan Winson commissioned the design, the size of the power plant has been reduced in favor of a larger weapons load. The current version has a flank speed of only 54 kph, and its crews colorfully describe its handling characteristics as similar to those of a beached whale. Rather than maneuverability, it relies on armor and defensive systems to survive on the battlefield. The tank's first line of defense is the hull-mounted Goalkeeper anti-missile system, which can track and engage missiles inbound against the tank. Unfortunately, the system is positioned on the forward glacis of the tank, creating a dead zone for this important defense to the sides and rear of the vehicle.

Controlled by the sophisticated Series XXVI Integrated Weapons System (IWS), the primary armament of the Ishtar is a pair of turret-mounted 75mm autocannons. Though both are capable of firing standard 75mm rounds, their loading mechanisms and barrels have widely differing capabilities. The loader of the smoothbore KOV-series cannon can switch between standard rounds and cluster ammunition, which the gunner may select up to the moment of firing. The Type 9 cannot switch ammunition types, but makes use of a clip-reload system that provides gunner-selected volley-style fire. Both systems use 20-round ammunition bins, but the differing barrel types prevent cross-loading of ammunition.

A hull-mounted "Crossbow" missile launcher provides secondary firepower and can supply indirect fire in conjunction with a spotter. When used for direct fire, the low-power infrared designating laser of an Artemis fire-control system provides the missiles with course-correction data, increasing the number that hit the target. Standard practice places these missiles under the control of the tank's commander, but the IWS allows the gunner to aim and fire them as needed. The IWS also allows the gunner or commander to fire the twin lasers slaved to the driver's position, though the driver's IWS console does not allow him or her to control other weapon systems.

Deployment

Clans Hell's Horses and Star Adder primarily manufacture and use the Ishtar, though every Clan fields a few and has the capability to build more. Current data indicates that the Nova Cats have established a very limited trade agreement with the Draconis Combine to exchange military hardware for Inner Sphere goods, and Clan vehicles have begun to appear in very limited numbers among DCMS forces, chiefly the Ishtar. There is no indication that the Nova Cats plan to trade Clan BattleMechs in this fashion.

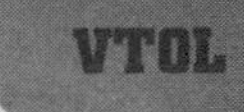

ISHTAR HEAVY FIRE SUPPORT TANK

Type: **Ishtar Heavy Fire Support Tank**
Technology Base: Clan
Movement Type: Wheeled
Tonnage: 65
Battle Value: 1,128

Equipment		**Mass**
Internal Structure:		6.5
Engine:	110	10.5
Type:	Fusion	
Cruising MP:	3	
Flank MP:	5	
Heat Sinks:	10	0
Control Equipment:		3.5
Lift Equipment:		0
Power Amplifier:		0
Turret:		2
Armor Factor:	144	7.5

	Armor Value
Front	32
R/L Side	30/30
Rear	24
Turret	28

Weapons and Ammo	**Location**	**Tonnage**
2 ER Med. Lasers	Front	2
Anti-Missile System	Front	.5
Ammo (AMS) 48	Body	2
LB 10-X AC	Turret	10
Ammo (LB-X) 20	Body	2
Ultra AC/10	Turret	10
Ammo (Ultra) 20	Body	2
LRM 15	Front	3.5
Artemis IV FCS	Front	1
Ammo (LRM) 16	Body	2

BATTLEFORCE 2

MP	**Damage PB/M/L**	**Overheat**	**Class**
3w	5/5/4	—	H

Armor/Structure	**Point Value**	**Specials**
—/6	11	

ATHENA COMBAT VEHICLE

Mass: 75 tons
Movement Type: Tracked
Power Plant: Fusion 225
Cruising Speed: 32 kph
Flanking Speed: 54 kph
Armor: Compound VH30 Ferro-Fibrous

Armament:
2 Series 2h Extended Range Medium Lasers
2 Type AA4 Gauss Rifles
2 Type AP40 Machine Guns
1 Type Xa LRM-10 Launcher
Manufacturer: Niles Industriplex Alpha

Communications System: Build 1690/2 Tacticom
Targeting and Tracking System: Consolidated Type VII TTC with Mark-5 Series Targeting Enhancement Computer

Overview

Another example of Clan Hell's Horses' unClanlike infatuation with conventional forces is the unconventional Athena combat vehicle. Like the Epona, which uses modular technology to obtain its battlefield edge, the Athena also claims a distinction the Clans normally reserve for their BattleMechs: the advanced targeting computer system. Able to deliver massive destructive potential at long range with uncommon accuracy, the Athena can threaten even the heaviest BattleMechs.

Capabilities

The Athena is a "sniper" tank, capable of delivering serious damage to hostile units while lying beyond the range of most return fire. It carries twin Gauss rifles, fixed in the forward compartment for stability and backed up by a 10-rack LRM launcher. With this firepower, the Athena possesses the potential to cripple a light or medium 'Mech with a single, well-placed volley. In an effort to make such a shot possible, the Horses took the extraordinary step of equipping the Athena with a sophisticated targeting computer system. This system is exactly like those carried by some of the most deadly Clan 'Mechs. The targeting computer aids in bringing the Athena's main guns to bear on enemy units, and even allows more experienced crews to place their slugs where the damage can be most effective.

While this emphasis on offensive capabilities suits the Athena for joining heavy forces in assault operations, its defenses are achingly limited. It possesses only enough speed and maneuverability to keep pace with the heaviest and slowest elements in today's armies, and its armor protection is significantly weaker than that carried by Inner Sphere vehicles of the same mass. In what appears to be a half-hearted attempt to mitigate these flaws without sacrificing the primary weapons array and targeting computer requirements, the Athena's designers added smaller, shorter-ranged weaponry in a semi-independent turret assembly. A secondary, "defensive" gunner mans this turret, which carries two medium lasers with computer-enhanced targeting and a pair of machine guns for defense in close-quarters combat. Despite the importance of this system, the defensive gunner usually is the lowest-ranked warrior in his crew, as the Athena's primary role tends to keep his contributions to a minimum.

Despite the defensive drawbacks of the Athena, Clan Hell's Horses have made successful use of this design for more than fifty years. In the last battle for Niles Industriplex Alpha against Clan Ghost Bear, a Trinary of Athenas, freshly manufactured and attached to Alpha Galaxy, helped to turn the Bears' advance by crippling nearly two full BattleMech Binaries.

Deployment

Athenas appear in the heavy and assault vehicle Stars of almost every front-line Cluster and Galaxy in Clan Hell's Horses. Deemed too valuable by the Horses' command to risk their loss, these potent vehicles are rarely deployed without some form of BattleMech or Elemental support.

ATHENA COMBAT VEHICLE

Type: **Athena Combat Vehicle**
Technology Base: Clan
Movement Type: Tracked
Tonnage: 75
Battle Value: 1,461

Equipment		**Mass**
Internal Structure:		7.5
Engine:	225	15
Type:	Fusion	
Cruising MP:	3	
Flank MP:	5	
Heat Sinks:	10	0
Control Equipment:		4
Lift Equipment:		0
Power Amplifier:		0
Turret:		.5
Armor Factor:	144	7.5

	Armor Value
Front	38
R/L Side	26/26
Rear	24
Turret	30

Weapons and Ammo	**Location**	**Tonnage**
2 ER Med. Lasers	Turret	2
2 Machine Guns	Turret	.5
Ammo (MG) 100	Body	.5
2 Gauss Rifles	Front	24
Ammo (Gauss) 32	Body	4
LRM 10	Front	2.5
Ammo (LRM) 12	Body	1
Targeting Computer	Body	6

BATTLEFORCE 2

MP	**Damage PB/M/L**	**Overheat**	**Class**
3t	6/5/4	—	H

Armor/Structure	**Point Value**	**Specials**
—/6	15	

HUITZILOPOCHTLI ASSAULT TANK

Mass: 85 tons
Movement Type: Tracked
Power Plant: ICE 170
Cruising Speed: 22 kph
Flanking Speed: 32 kph
Armor: Forging ZK11

Armament:
- 2 Kolibri Omega Series Medium Pulse Lasers
- 1 Series 1 Extended Range Small Laser
- 1 Type 31 Ultra Autocannon 5
- 2 Series IX Machine Guns
- 2 Arrow IV Launchers

Manufacturer: Various
Communications System: TJ6 "Bell" Integrated
Targeting and Tracking System: Series VI TTS

Overview

Designed to meet the Clans' need for mobile artillery, the Huitzilopochtli (better known as the "Huey") is a descendent of the Padilla artillery tank. The Star League Defense Forces who joined Kerensky in the Exodus included few artillery pieces in their armament, and most of those were destroyed in the Civil War, leaving the Clans woefully lacking in support weapons. Equipping 'Mechs with Arrow IV launchers proved moderately effective but was considered a misuse of 'Mechs, and assignment to such hybrid machines was not highly regarded. As a result, Nicholas Kerensky was forced to concede the need for a new tank-based artillery platform, and thus was born the Huitzilopochtli.

Capabilities

The Huitzilopochtli carries an internal combustion engine rather than the extra-light fusion engine used in the Star League Padilla, making it considerably slower than the Padilla. The Clans accept this disadvantage, however, because they are loath to waste such technology on a vehicle. At a flanking speed of 32 kph, the Huitzilopochtli is considered too slow to cross long distances under its own power, and so Hueys are usually transported by DropShip to their general area of operations.

Twin Arrow IV box-launchers dominate the forward section of the tank, each capable of hitting a target more than three kilometers away. The Huey carries 10 rounds for each launcher, usually evenly divided between TAG-homing missiles (with a focused warhead that allows precision strikes) and area-effect impact fused rounds. A third type of warhead developed by the Clans allows the Arrow system to cover an area with field artillery scatterable mine (FASCAM) submunitions.

While the Arrow IV provides the Huey with a devastating weapon system, it is unsuited to defense, and so the tank carries several layers of secondary weapons. Mounted in the compact turret are a pair of Kolibri medium pulse lasers, designed to saturate an area with fire and so increase the probability of a successful attack. Their primary role is anti-infantry defense, and they have proved effective against both armored and unarmored troops. The turret also contains an ER small laser that provides additional firepower against targets within 180 meters. A nose-mounted fast-load 40mm autocannon can be used against both armored infantry and vehicles, but is of minimal use against regular infantry. Rounding out the Huey's armaments are side-mounted machine guns that can deliver a devastating barrage of fire against unarmored troops.

The tank's defensive systems center on a sophisticated broad-band ECM unit that jams enemy sensor and targeting systems. Though it fails to completely hide the vehicle, it successfully degrades the performance of enemy systems, making it harder to engage the Huey. Its armor is considerably lower-tech; because the tank is regarded as a rear-echelon unit, it carries standard forged armor rather than ferro-fibrous compounds.

Deployment

One of the few vehicles used by Clan Jade Falcon in a non-training role (the Falcons classify them as support units rather than combatants), several Huitzilopochtli were deployed to Coventry in the campaign of 3058. As Clan Jade Falcon sought to prove its honor and prowess against the combined might of the Great Houses, they also proved the effectiveness of the Huitzilopochtli.

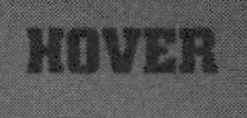

TRACKED

VTOL

CLAN

HUITZILOPOCHTLI ASSAULT TANK

Type: **Huitzilopochtli Assault Tank**
Technology Base: Clan
Movement Type: Tracked
Tonnage: 85
Battle Value: 769

Equipment		**Mass**
Internal Structure:		8.5
Engine:	170	12
Type:	ICE	
Cruising MP:	2	
Flank MP:	3	
Heat Sinks:	10	10
Control Equipment:		4.5
Lift Equipment:		0
Power Amplifier:		.5
Turret:		.5
Armor Factor:	88	5.5

	Armor Value
Front	20
R/L Side	18/18
Rear	16
Turret	16

Weapons and Ammo	**Location**	**Tonnage**
2 Med. Pulse Lasers	Turret	4
ER Small Laser	Turret	.5
Ultra AC/5	Front	7
Ammo (Ultra) 40	Body	2
Machine Gun	Left	.25
Machine Gun	Right	.25
Ammo (MG) 100	Body	.5
2 Arrow IV Systems	Front	24
Ammo (Arrow) 20	Body	4
ECM Suite	Body	1

BATTLEFORCE 2

MP	**Damage PB/M/L**	**Overheat**	**Class**
2t	5/5/5	—	A

Armor/Structure	**Point Value**	**Specials**
—/4	8	artA, ecm

MARS ASSAULT VEHICLE

Mass: 100 tons
Movement Type: Tracked
Power Plant: Fusion 200
Cruising Speed: 22 kph
Flanking Speed: 32 kph
Armor: Compound Zeta Ferro-Fibrous

Armament:
1 Series 7N Extended Range Large Laser
1 CRG Gauss Rifle
2 Series IX Machine Guns
1 Type KOV LB-10X Autocannon
3 Type XV "Crossbow" LRM-15 Launchers with Artemis IV FCS
2 Pattern J6c Streak-6 SRM Launchers

Manufacturer: Various
Communications System: Q2 Block 9
Targeting and Tracking System: Series XXXII Multitrack IWS with Artemis IV FCS

Overview

One of the most formidable vehicles ever built, the Mars dedicates more than half its weight to weapons, ammunition and associated systems. Popular legend attributes the design of the tank to ilKhan Winson himself, but even if this were the case, little remains in the current version of the original configuration created more than two centuries ago.

Capabilities

Carrying more than eleven tons of advanced-composite armor, the Mars can sustain multiple hits with minimal risk of penetration. A general-purpose ECM unit degrades the abilities of many of the sophisticated fire-control systems an enemy force is likely to use, further reducing the chances of a successful hit. This armor protection and vast weapons array, however, has the unfortunate result of making the Mars ponderously slow and incapable of withdrawing from a fight.

A CRG Gauss rifle serves as the vehicle's main gun, while a coaxial large laser allows the Mars to snipe out to ranges at which Gauss slugs would likely be wasted. A hull-mounted 150mm LB-X autocannon provides devastating anti-vehicle firepower, but the gun can be raised only 10 degrees above horizontal and is of minimal use against aerial targets. Three Artemis-slaved long-range missile packs give the Mars the ability to deliver devastating barrages, but only one ton of ammunition per launcher dictates that the LRMs be held in reserve until a critical juncture in the fight.

The Mars also carries a number of systems designed to defend the vehicle. Turret-mounted machine guns provide an effective anti-infantry weapon, while side-mounted SRM Streak launchers discourage opponents from exploiting the tank's weaker side and rear armor.

The crew operates from two self-contained compartments linked by a tactical coordination system. The driver sits in an armored cockpit in the nose of the vehicle and, in addition to looking though the armored view slit, wears a sophisticated helmet that presents navigation information on the Heads Up Display (HUD). The gunner and commander sit in a second compartment beneath the turret.

Deployment

Occupying the same battlefield niche as heavy- and assault-class BattleMechs, the Mars is a common sight among active garrison Clusters. While most Clans replace vehicles only as needed, Clan Hell's Horses maintains an almost constant production of the Mars.

Variants

Clan Hell's Horses are currently conducting limited experiments with a modified version of the Mars. Once again going against standard Clan practice, they have rebuilt the engine compartments of two vehicles and replaced their power plants with 300-rated XL fusion engines. They have also removed the machine guns and their ammunition and have downgraded the armor by a half-ton. These modifications increase the vehicles' flank speed to a respectable 54 kph. The Horses expect to begin field-testing this variant in the next few months.

Type: **Mars Assault Vehicle**
Technology Base: Clan
Movement Type: Tracked
Tonnage: 100
Battle Value: 1,620

Equipment		**Mass**
Internal Structure:		10
Engine:	200	13
Type:	Fusion	
Cruising MP:	2	
Flank MP:	3	
Heat Sinks:	12	2
Control Equipment:		5
Lift Equipment:		0
Power Amplifier:		0
Turret:		2
Armor Factor:	220	11.5

	Armor Value
Front	50
R/L Side	43/43
Rear	37
Turret	47

Weapons and Ammo	**Location**	**Tonnage**
ER Large Laser	Turret	4
Gauss Rifle	Turret	12
Ammo (Gauss) 16	Body	2
2 Machine Guns	Turret	.5
Ammo (MG) 100	Turret	.5
LB 10-X AC	Front	10
Ammo (LB-X) 20	Body	2
3 LRM 15	Front	10.5
3 Artemis IV FCS	Front	3
Ammo (LRM) 24	Body	3
Streak SRM 6	Left	3
Streak SRM 6	Right	3
Ammo (Streak) 30	Body	2
ECM Suite	Body	1

BATTLEFORCE 2

MP	**Damage PB/M/L**	**Overheat**	**Class**
2t	9/9/6	—	A
Armor/Structure	**Point Value**	**Specials**	
—/9	16	ecm	

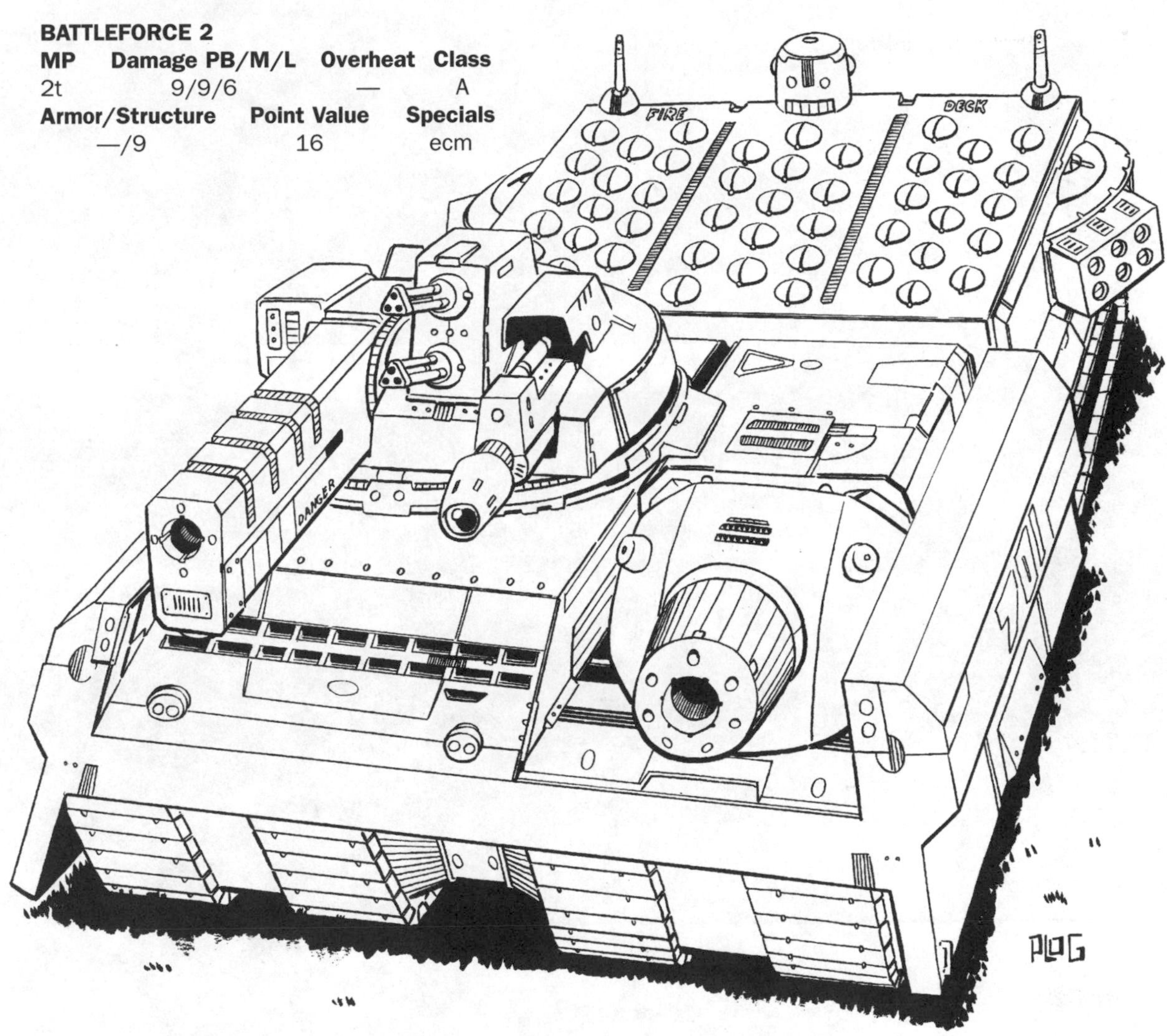

INNER SPHERE BATTLEMECHS

As the Inner Sphere prepared to launch Operation Bulldog against the Smoke Jaguar Occupation Zone, cooperation among the Great Houses of the Inner Sphere increased. This cooperation has spurred innovative BattleMech and OmniMech developments, producing impressive, powerful designs throughout the Inner Sphere. Whether this cooperation will continue now that the Clan threat has diminished remains to be seen.

The Inner Sphere has rapidly closed the technological gap with the Clans in both weapon technologies and equipment. Additionally, Inner Sphere manufacturers have explored new avenues in BattleMech construction, producing 'Mechs with unusual tonnages, specialized weapon configurations and varying speed. Even the four-legged BattleMech chassis, much maligned over the centuries, flourishes as several new QuadMechs have recently seen action in the Inner Sphere.

This technical briefing, compiled from ComStar's latest intelligence, is an attempt to stay abreast of these rapid developments.

—Frances Pryce
Adept XII-Omega
ComStar Archives, Terra
20 October 3060

C-SK1 COSSACK

Mass: 20 tons
Chassis: Taijian Series X Endo
Power Plant: Hermes 120 Extralight
Cruising Speed: 65 kph
Maximum Speed: 97 kph
Jump Jets: Pitban LFT-65
Jump Capacity: 360 meters
Armor: ArcShield VII Mk. 6

Armament:
1 MilDouglas "Duke" SRM-6 Launcher
1 Kajuka Type 2 "Bright Blossom" Medium Laser
2 Jackson Model 12 Small Lasers
Manufacturer: Ceres Metals Industries
Primary Factory: Warlock

Communications System:
Endicott Type 22 Maser
Targeting and Tracking System:
Wentland Cyber-Track

Overview

After the success of their latest 'Mech designs, the leaders of the St. Ives Military were eager to bring newer and lighter designs into their noticeably heavy arsenal. In an effort to create a 'Mech that would be popular with pilots, Caroline Seng, Commander of the St. Ives Military, brought together her regimental commanders and an engineering team to agree on basic specs for the new machine. Initially, the design team called for the fastest recon 'Mech that Ceres Metals could design and build. After some deliberation, however, they settled for a moderately fast recon unit with significant firepower. The involvement of more offices and departments in the St. Ives Military led to four more design revisions, and Ceres engineers received requests for several more changes even after the prototype began combat trials. Seng tried to end the influx of conflicting requirements by officially contracting with Ceres for a 'Mech based on the first redesign, the well-armed recon unit. Even as the first 'Mechs began to enter service, however, whole new sets of requirements continued to flood Ceres' new offices on Warlock.

Capabilities

The *Cossack* is a relatively inexpensive design intended to fill a number of roles in the expanding roster of the St. Ives Military. Even with the expense of its extralight power plant, the design is still extremely affordable. As a scout, the *Cossack* performs only adequately. Its jump jets allow it to quickly pass over rough terrain, but a top speed of just under 100 kph leaves it too slow to escape some of the leading elements it may face. Likewise, its armor is not sufficient to protect it while making a fighting retreat.

In line regiments, however, the *Cossack* should make an excellent harasser. Teamed with similarly armed 'Mechs and/or vehicles, it will probe an enemy's flank for weakness, or be dispatched to finish off battlefield stragglers. Its relatively heavy weapons load gives it the firepower to effectively undertake such missions. If the *Cossack* encounters heavier resistance than expected, its moderate speed and jumping power should enable it to evade and re-engage at will.

The *Cossack*'s true destiny may lie in the Home Guard units scattered across the St. Ives Compact. It costs little more than most other light 'Mechs, making it an ideal choice for the limited budgets of militia units. While the *Cossack* cannot hope to stand alone against most of the 'Mechs it might face in combat, a full lance of *Cossacks* can produce a rain of fire that few MechWarriors would wish to weather. Against any other enemy, vehicle or infantry, the *Cossack* will reign supreme.

Deployment

Named for Khorsakov's Cossacks in honor of that mercenary unit's faithful service, the first *Cossacks* will be a gift to their namesake unit. Others are tentatively assigned to the St. Ives Academy Training Cadre. With relations between the Compact and the Capellan Confederation rapidly deteriorating, however, a number of these new 'Mechs will undoubtedly replace other light 'Mechs lost in battle. The *Cossack* is likelier to receive its trial by fire far sooner than its creators anticipated.

C-SK1 COSSACK

Type: **Cossack**
Technology Base: Inner Sphere
Tonnage: 20
Battle Value: 374

Equipment		**Mass**
Internal Structure:	Endo Steel	1
Engine:	120 XL	2
Walking MP:	6	
Running MP:	9	
Jumping MP:	6	
Heat Sinks:	10	0
Gyro:		2
Cockpit:		3
Armor Factor:	48	3

	Internal Structure	*Armor Value*
Head	3	7
Center Torso	6	7
Center Torso (rear)		2
R/L Torso	5	6
R/L Torso (rear)		1
R/L Arm	3	4
R/L Leg	4	5

Weapons and Ammo	**Location**	**Critical**	**Tonnage**
SRM 6	CT	2	3
Ammo (SRM) 15	RT	1	1
Small Laser	RT	1	.5
Small Laser	LT	1	.5
Med. Laser	LA	1	1
Jump Jet	RT	1	.5
Jump Jet	LT	1	.5
Jump Jets	RL	2	1
Jump Jets	LL	2	1

BATTLEFORCE 2

MP	**Damage PB/M/L**	**Overheat**	**Class**
6J	2/1/—	—	L

Armor/Structure	**Point Value**	**Specials**
1/1	4	

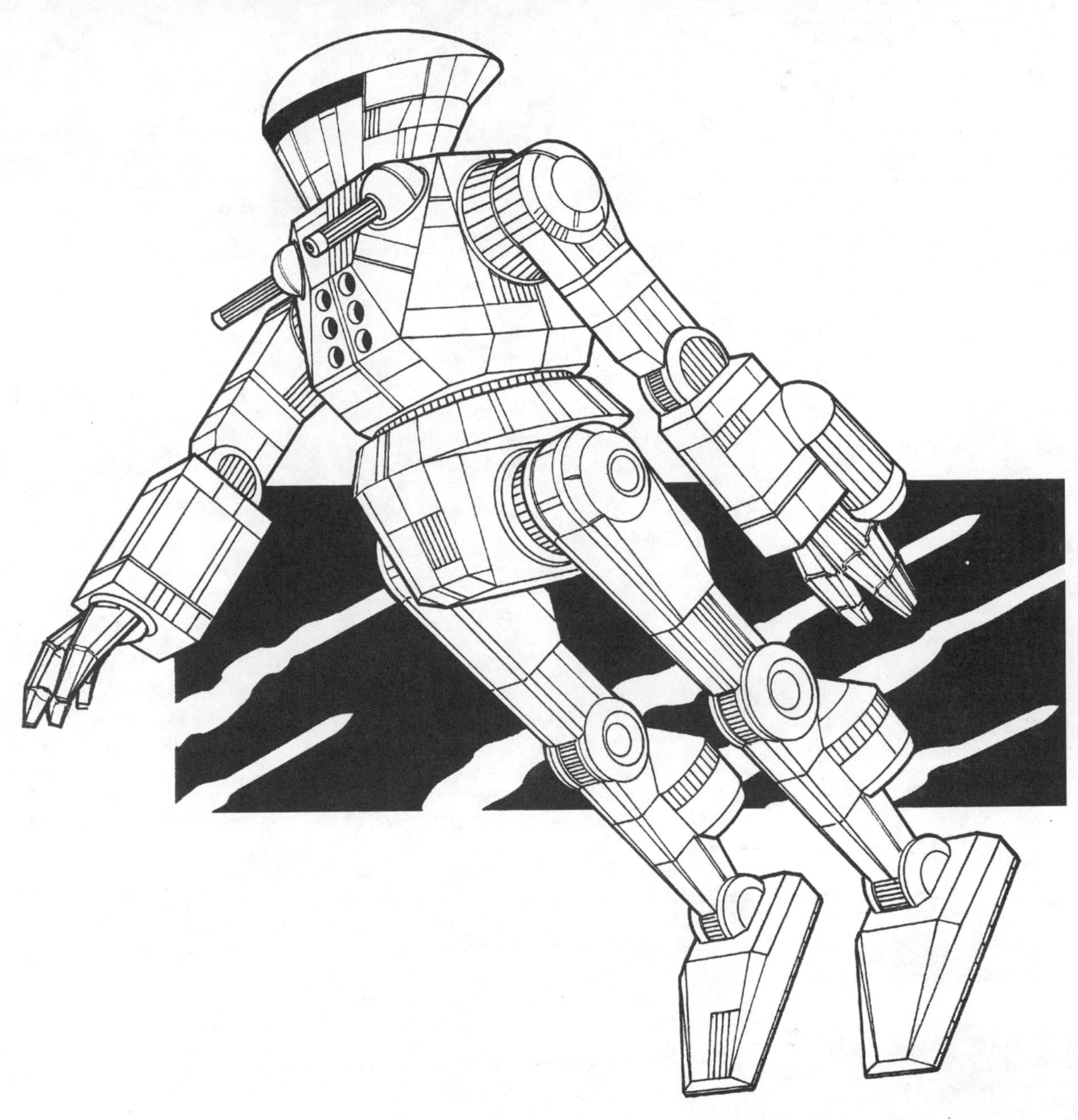

KBO-7A KABUTO

Mass: 20 tons
Chassis: Chariot Type 1a
Power Plant: Leenex 140 XL
Cruising Speed: 76 kph
Maximum Speed: 119 kph
Jump Jets: None
Jump Capacity: None
Armor: Starshield A
Armament: 2 Guided Technologies 2nd Gen Streak-4 SRM Launchers
Manufacturer: Diplan 'Mechyards
Primary Factory: Ozawa
Communications System: Sipher CommCon SCU-4
Targeting and Tracking System: Cat's Eyes 5

Overview

For many decades, the Draconis Combine Mustered Soldiery lacked 'Mechs in the 20- to 35-ton category. During this time, Bushido ("the Way of the Warrior") and single 'Mech-on-'Mech combat were considered the only honorable ways of fighting. Because most light 'Mechs cannot stand toe-to-toe against larger 'Mechs, light 'Mechs had no place in the DCMS.

The arrival of the Clans changed all that. Also believers in single combat, the Clans had superior training and technology, with which they defeated the DCMS at almost every turn. Combine warriors could defeat Clan opponents only by putting the honor of the Draconis Combine before each individual warrior's honor and using all available military assets in combination. The Combine made use of light 'Mechs for fast recon, lighting raids and other attacks. New Combine light 'Mech designs, perfectly suited for these rediscovered tactics, quickly made their way onto the battlefield. The most recent addition is the *Kabuto*, named for the elaborate "helmet" of armor that encases the 'Mech's head assembly.

Capabilities

The *Kabuto* is patterned after the highly successful *Hitman* BattleMech design. The *Hitman* quickly became a mainstay of the DCMS, being exceptionally fast, armed with impressive firepower for a 'Mech of its class, and loaded with specialized electronics. Even the *Hitman*'s hefty price tag could not detract from its success on the battlefield. Eager to repeat that success, the design teams at Diplan 'Mechyards were ready to begin field-testing the *Kabuto* by late 3059. The thorough testing of the *Hitman* by the student MechWarriors of the Sun Zhang Academy on New Samarkand had so impressed Diplan 'Mechyards that they arranged to test the *Kabuto* in the same fashion.

In creating the *Kabuto*, Diplan 'Mechyards fulfilled their goal of developing a light 'Mech with exceptional speed, armor and firepower at a low price. With more firepower and armor than any other 'Mech of its weight class and a top speed of well over 110 kph, the *Kabuto* is a prime example of superior DCMS design and manufacturing. Even the price tag—just under 2.5 million C-bills—is a bargain considering this 'Mech's battlefield performance.

Deployment

The *Kabuto* has finished its testing, though it has yet to see combat. The DCMS has begun to issue the 'Mech to units that lost light 'Mechs during Operation Bulldog.

KBO-7A KABUTO

Type: **Kabuto**
Technology Base: Inner Sphere
Tonnage: 20
Battle Value: 448

Equipment		**Mass**
Internal Structure:	Endo Steel	1
Engine:	140 XL	2.5
Walking MP:	7	
Running MP:	11	
Jumping MP:	0	
Heat Sinks:	10	0
Gyro:		2
Cockpit:		3
Armor Factor:	69	4.5
	Internal Structure	*Armor Value*
Head	3	9
Center Torso	6	9
Center Torso (rear)		3
R/L Torso	5	8
R/L Torso (rear)		2
R/L Arm	3	6
R/L Leg	4	8

Weapons and Ammo	**Location**	**Critical**	**Tonnage**
Streak SRM 4	LT	1	3
Streak SRM 4	RT	1	3
Ammo (Streak) 25	RT	1	1

BATTLEFORCE 2

MP	**Damage PB/M/L**	**Overheat**	**Class**
7	2/2/—	—	L

Armor/Structure	**Point Value**	**Specials**
2/1	4	

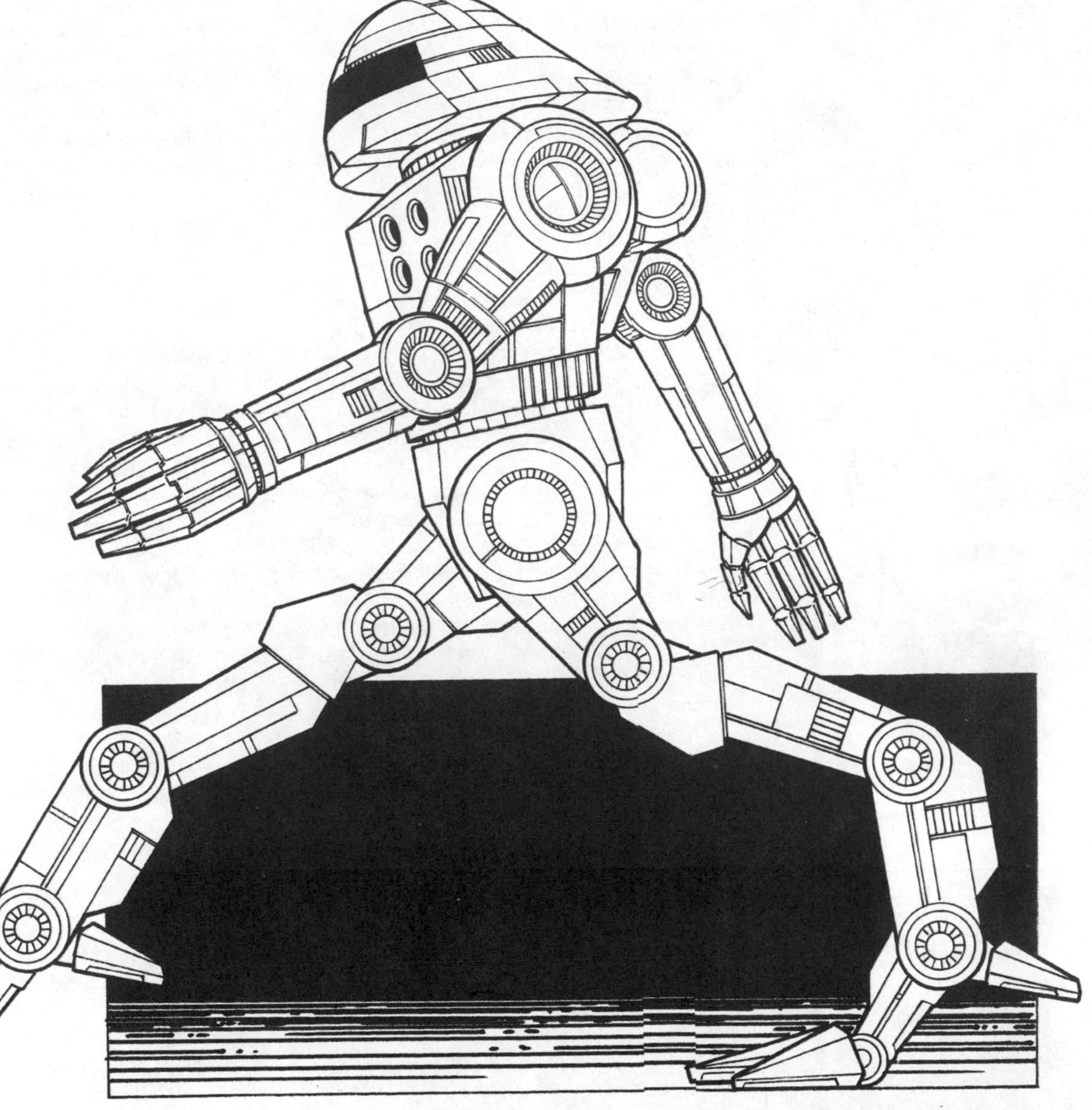

D9-G9 DUAN GUNG

Mass: 25 tons
Chassis: Chariot Type II Endo Steel
Power Plant: 175 Omni XL
Cruising Speed: 76 kph
Maximum Speed: 119 kph
Jump Jets: Chilton 360
Jump Capacity: 180 meters
Armor: Valiant Defco
Armament: 1 Zeus LRM-10 Launcher
2 Martell Medium Lasers
Manufacturer: Shengli Arms
Primary Factory: Victoria
Communications System:
Dian-bao Comms, Standard
Targeting and Tracking System:
Dynatec 990 T&T

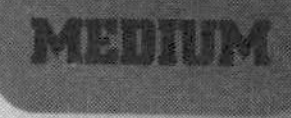

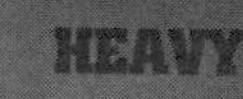

Overview

With only a handful of production facilities left in the Capellan Confederation, and a technological renaissance sweeping the Inner Sphere, Chancellor Sun-Tzu Liao turned his attention to the old Star League factory on the world of Victoria. Despite difficulties refurbishing the production plant, a fully functioning prototype of the *Duan Gung* design finally walked off the assembly line in late 3057, and the BattleMech was put into limited production in 3058. This 'Mech is one of four designs that the Star League facility was set up to manufacture; everything but its jump jets and targeting system is currently produced on-site.

Basing the new 'Mech on a design named the *Sling* by the Star League Defense Force, CCAF Strategic Director Talon Zahn renamed it the *Duan Gung*, meaning *Short Bow*. The design shows many similarities to the Clan OmniMech known as the *Koshi*. The few prototype *Slings* that existed in 2780 likely traveled with the Exodus Fleet to the Clan homeworlds, where the design later proved adaptable to Clan OmniMech technology. The Capellan technicians reworked part of the design as well, replacing the *Sling*'s cramped, box-like cockpit with the slightly more roomy turret-style cockpit seen on the *JagerMech*.

Capabilities

At speeds approaching 120 kilometers per hour, the *Duan Gung* can move across a battlefield quickly, presenting a minimal target. In rough terrain, its impressive jumping ability gives it a mobility that rivals or exceeds other BattleMechs of a similar weight class. The *Duan Gung* is designed to shower its target with long-range missiles as it nears, switching to its medium lasers for close-range punch.

In trial runs by the Red Lancers and Warrior House Daidachi, the 'Mech's only weakness was its thin armor. This 'Mech can easily lose an arm to a particle projector cannon or even a large laser, and its valuable XL engine is very exposed. However, when used as part of a recon force or as a missile support 'Mech for a light or medium lance, the *Duan Gung* performed admirably. House Daidachi was especially pleased with the way it complemented the *Raven*, the Confederation's primary scout 'Mech.

In single-combat tests, the *Duan Gung* can stand toe-to-toe with any Inner Sphere 'Mech of similar weight. The surprise came in a series of trials held in the Da-jiao-tang Mountains on Grand Base. In severe terrain, such as bluffs or thick forests, the *Duan Gung* took down non-jumping 'Mechs two or even three times its own weight. Pilots accomplished this by maneuvering within jumping range and then performing a series of strikes in which they jumped into a target's rear quarter, fired, and then jumped away before enemy weapons could be brought to bear against them. This maneuver is terrain-specific, and is not always effective, as a single hit from a large weapon tends to finish off the *Duan Gung*. A MechWarrior in this situation can expect no room for error.

Deployment

After its test deployment in the Red Lancers and House Daidachi, the *Duan Gung* began to spread in small numbers throughout the Confederation Armed Forces. In 3059 Chancellor Liao also offered it for sale to current Star League units, or any unit with ties to the original Star League Defense Force. Upgrades to the Victoria facility came just in time to meet an increased demand. The yearly production numbers on the *Duan Gung* have doubled, and this light 'Mech should spread throughout the Star League.

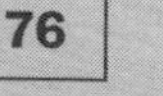

D9-G9 DUAN GUNG

Type: **Duan Gung**
Technology Base: Inner Sphere
Tonnage: 25
Battle Value: 729

Equipment		**Mass**
Internal Structure:	Endo Steel	1.5
Engine:	175 XL	3.5
Walking MP:	7	
Running MP:	11	
Jumping MP:	6	
Heat Sinks:	10 [20]	0
Gyro:		2
Cockpit:		3
Armor Factor:	64	4

	Internal Structure	*Armor Value*
Head	3	9
Center Torso	8	10
Center Torso (rear)		3
R/L Torso	6	8
R/L Torso (rear)		2
R/L Arm	4	5
R/L Leg	6	6

Weapons and Ammo	**Location**	**Critical**	**Tonnage**
LRM 10	CT	2	5
Ammo (LRM) 12	RT	1	1
Med. Laser	RA	1	1
Med. Laser	LA	1	1
Jump Jets	RT	3	1.5
Jump Jets	LT	3	1.5

BATTLEFORCE 2

MP	**Damage PB/M/L**	**Overheat**	**Class**
7	2/2/1	—	L

Armor/Structure	**Point Value**	**Specials**
2/1	7	if

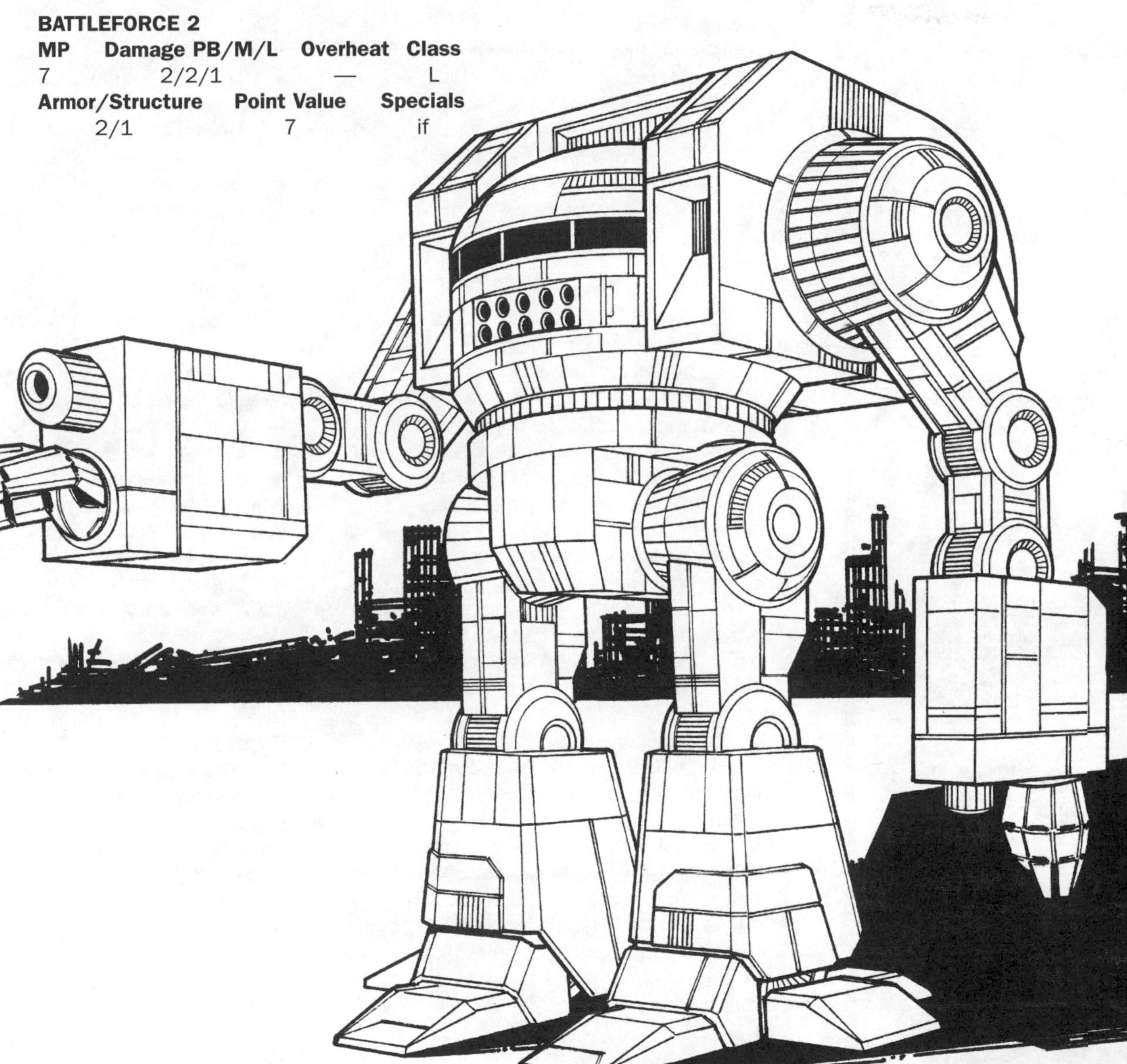

EGL-2M EAGLE

Mass: 25 tons
Chassis: Curtiss Eagle
Power Plant: Vlar 125
Cruising Speed: 54 kph
Maximum Speed: 86 kph
Jump Jets: CurtissJet 55
Jump Capacity: 150 meters

Armor: Kallon FWL
Armament:
1 Diverse Optics Sunbeam Extended Range Large Laser
1 Diverse Optics Extended Range Medium Laser
Manufacturer: Curtiss Militech
Primary Factory: Paradise

Communications System: CurtissComm Mark II
Targeting and Tracking System: Dynatech 12B with TAG

Overview

The *Eagle* is Curtiss Militech's foray into the light BattleMech class, a follow-up to their highly successful and extremely popular *Wraith* medium 'Mech. The Curtiss designers chose to keep the *Wraith*'s mobility, though they made the *Eagle* somewhat slower to make room for weaponry. They also equipped the *Eagle* with a standard engine, hoping to keep down production costs and increase the 'Mech's survivability. The *Eagle*'s standard chassis design makes battlefield repair easier; the shipments of replacement parts that the *Wraith* required cut deeply into profits.

The original *Eagle* design, the EGL-1M, lacked the TAG system. When the LCCC introduced the new semi-guided LRMs, Curtiss designers added the TAG, expecting great demand for a speedy light 'Mech that could target for such missiles. So far, they seem to have been right; the Free Worlds League and Capellan militaries have both placed orders, many from units that already use the *Wraith* and feel they can depend on a Curtiss-built 'Mech.

Capabilities

Though not as fast as many 'Mechs in its weight class, the *Eagle* packs quite a punch at long ranges and runs fairly cool despite the high heat generated by its weaponry. Though intended to supplement the ER large and medium lasers, the TAG gear is also capable of targeting units for either Arrow IV systems or the deadly new semi-guided missiles. Should neither be available as support for the *Eagle*'s unit, the *Eagle* can deal a significant amount of damage for its size with its lasers. This 'Mech's multiple uses make it valuable to commanders, and its initial sales reflect that fact.

Deployment

*Eagle*s have been shipped to units all over the Free Worlds League, and small numbers have shipped to the Capellan Confederation. Various Marik Militia units received the majority, followed by Fusiliers of Oriente units.

Variants

Curtiss has produced a few of the original EGL-1M design, though they are scarce. Most were slated for the Capellan military, the rest scattered across the Free Worlds League. The 1M lacks the TAG system and extended-range medium laser; instead, it carries an anti-missile system with one ton of ammunition and an ER small laser.

EGL-2M EAGLE

Type: **Eagle**
Technology Base: Inner Sphere
Tonnage: 25
Battle Value: 745

Equipment		**Mass**
Internal Structure:	Endo Steel	1.5
Engine:	125	4
Walking MP:	5	
Running MP:	8	
Jumping MP:	5	
Heat Sinks:	10 [20]	0
Gyro:		2
Cockpit:		3
Armor Factor:	80	5

	Internal Structure	*Armor Value*
Head	3	9
Center Torso	8	12
Center Torso (rear)		3
R/L Torso	6	10
R/L Torso (rear)		2
R/L Arm	4	7
R/L Leg	6	9

Weapons and Ammo	**Location**	**Critical**	**Tonnage**
ER Large Laser	RA	2	5
ER Med. Laser	LA	1	1
TAG	LT	1	1
Jump Jet	CT	1	.5
Jump Jets	RT	2	1
Jump Jets	LT	2	1

BATTLEFORCE 2

MP	**Damage PB/M/L**	**Overheat**	**Class**
5J	2/1/1	—	L

Armor/Structure	**Point Value**	**Specials**
2/2	7	tag

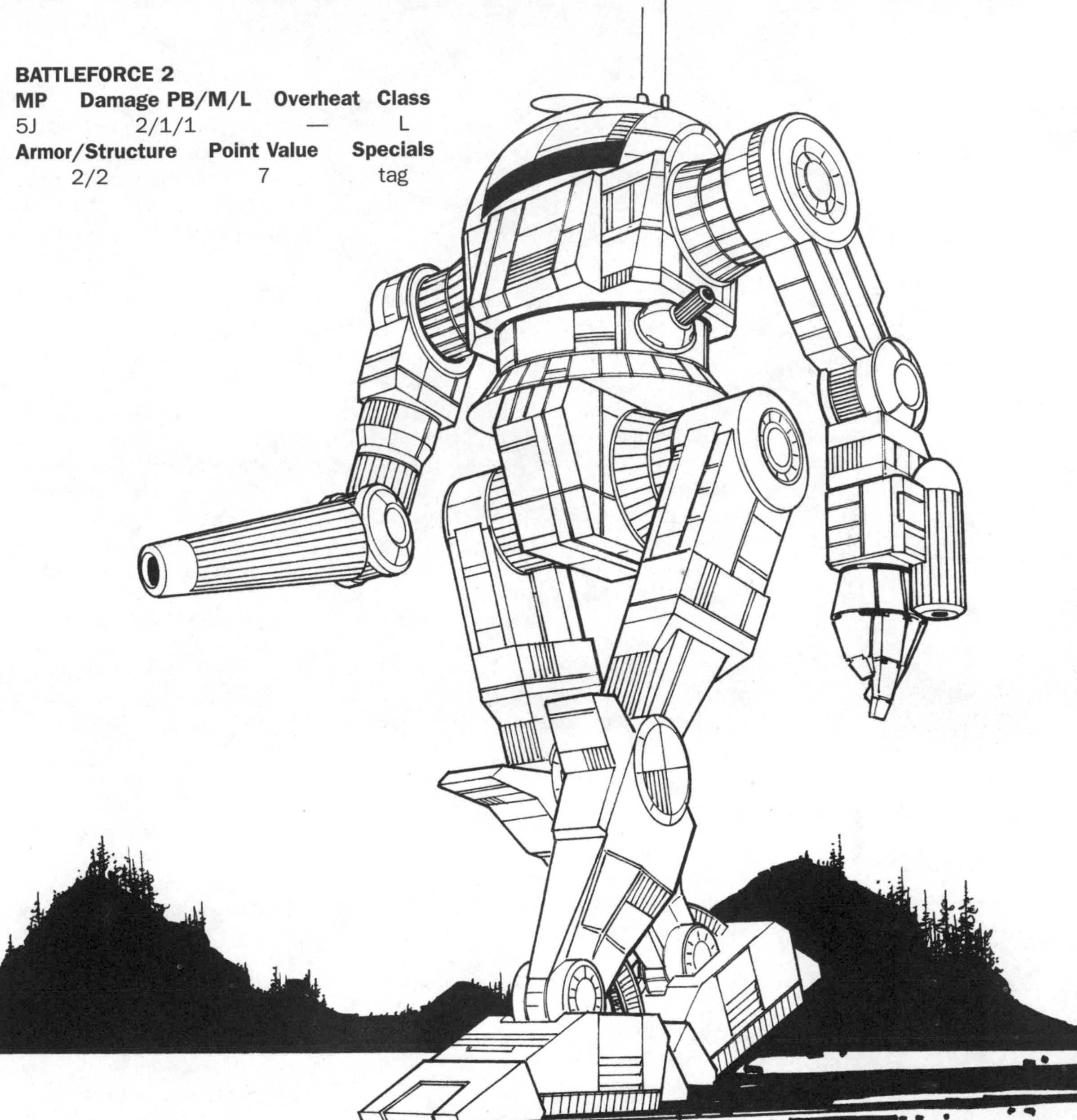

AF1 ARCTIC FOX

Mass: 30 tons
Chassis: AR-3 Endo Steel
Power Plant: 180 GM XL
Cruising Speed: 65 kph
Maximum Speed: 97 kph
Jump Jets: None
Jump Capacity: None
Armor: Royal-7 Standard

Armament:
14 tons of pod space available
Manufacturer: Arc-RoyalMechWorks
Primary Factory: Arc-Royal
Communications System:
K9 Communications System
Targeting and Tracking System:
Type IV Bloodhound T&T System

Overview

The Kell Hounds' first OmniMech came with their salvage from Luthien. Recognizing the value of a reconfigurable 'Mech Morgan Kell had the Arc-Royal facilities attempt a clone of the machine. However, nly after Phelan Kell and his Wolves-in-Exile arrived were the final bugs worked out.

In return for the Kell Hounds' material support for Phelan's Wolves, Clan technical advisors helped the Kells finish reverse-engineering a Clan *Uller* (known to the Clans as a *Kit Fox*). Though the Kells have access to Clan materials, the *Arctic Fox* is built with only Inner Sphere technology, for logistical as well as strategic reasons. The Kell Hounds use most of the Clan material they get for the upkeep of their captured Clan 'Mechs. Also, with their support of "training farm" units and ARDC defense regiments, the Kells wished to offer this versatile design to those who could afford it, but had no Clan technology.

The Kell Hounds do not use the designation of AF1. In Clan fashion, they refer to the basic machine as the *Arctic Fox* Prime. The name evokes the 'Mech's progenitor, the Clan *Kit Fox*, as well as the new Wolf-in-Exile Clan 'Mech, the *Arctic Wolf*. Variants are designated A, B, C and D.

Capabilities

Well armored for a light 'Mech, the *Arctic Fox* can stand up to most Inner Sphere designs of similar weight. Upon reaching an efficient range for its weapons load, the OmniMech is best used holding that range and taking advantage of natural cover. For warriors with a penchant for up-close-and-personal combat, however, the *Arctic Fox* does not disappoint.

The *Arctic Fox's* snarling visage is backed by fourteen tons of pod space for weapons. Its primary variant relies on an extended-range PPC, backed by an array of medium-range weapons. The A variant borrows from the Clan *Black Hawk*, mounting a blistering array of medium and short-range lasers. The B and D variations are both support machines, the former packing an LB-10X shotgun-style autocannon, while the latter is a straight missile-support 'Mech. The C variant is a dueling machine. Its combination of an extended-range PPC and a large pulse laser give it impressive power, made for single combat rather than lance or company actions.

Deployment

In addition to its position in the Kell Hound regiments, *Arctic Foxes* have been noted in the mercenary Blue Star Irregulars and Dioscuri outfits. The *Arctic Fox* has also been adopted by a few garrison force warriors of Phelan's Wolves, who suffer the Inner Sphere weapons in return for the ability to reconfigure their 'Mechs.

Type: **Arctic Fox**
Technology Base: Inner Sphere OmniMech
Tonnage: 30
Battle Value: 766

Equipment		**Mass**
Internal Structure:	Endo Steel	1.5
Engine:	180 XL	3.5
Walking MP:	6	
Running MP:	9	
Jumping MP:	0	
Heat Sinks:	10 [20]	0
Gyro:		2
Cockpit:		3
Armor Factor:	96	6
	Internal Structure	*Armor Value*
Head	3	9
Center Torso	10	15
Center Torso (rear)		4
R/L Torso	7	11
R/L Torso (rear)		3
R/L Arm	5	10
R/L Leg	7	10

Weight and Space Allocation

Location	*Fixed*	*Spaces Remaining*
Head		1
Center Torso	2 Endo Steel	0
Right Torso	3 XL Engine 2 Double Heat Sinks	3
Left Torso	3 XL Engine Double Heat Sink	6
Right Arm	4 Endo Steel	4
Left Arm	4 Endo Steel	4
Right Leg	2 Endo Steel	0
Left Leg	2 Endo Steel	0

AF1 ARCTIC FOX

Weapons and Ammo	Location	Critical	Tonnage
Primary Weapons Configuration			
Med. Laser	LA	1	1
SRM 4	LT	1	2
Ammo (SRM) 25	LT	1	1
ER PPC	LT	3	7
SRM 4	RT	1	2
Med. Laser	RA	1	1
Alternate Configuration A			
Small Pulse Laser	H	1	1
2 Med. Pulse Lasers	LA	2	4
2 Small Pulse Lasers	LT	2	2
Jump Jets	LT	3	1.5
Jump Jets	RT	3	1.5
2 Med. Pulse Lasers	RA	2	4
Battle Value: 736			
Alternate Configuration B			
LB 10-X AC	LA	6	11
Ammo (LB-X) 20	LT	2	2
Med. Laser	RT	1	1
Battle Value: 634			
Alternate Configuration C			
ER PPC	LA	3	7
Large Pulse Laser	RA	2	7
Battle Value: 747			
Alternate Configuration D			
LRM 10	LA	2	5
Artemis IV FCS	LA	1	1
Ammo (LRM) 12	LA	1	1
LRM 10	RA	2	5
Artemis IV FCS	RA	1	1
Ammo (LRM) 12	RA	1	1
Battle Value: 643			

BATTLEFORCE 2

Type: **Arctic Fox**

MP	Damage PB/M/L	Overheat	Class
6	3/2/1	1	L
Armor/Structure	**Point Value**	**Specials**	
2/1	8	omni	

Alternate Configuration A

MP	Damage PB/M/L	Overheat	Class
6J	3/2/—	1	L
Armor/Structure	**Point Value**	**Specials**	
2/1	7	omni	

Alternate Configuration B

MP	Damage PB/M/L	Overheat	Class
6	2/2/1	—	L
Armor/Structure	**Point Value**	**Specials**	
2/1	6	omni	

Alternate Configuration C

MP	Damage PB/M/L	Overheat	Class
6	2/1/1	1	L
Armor/Structure	**Point Value**	**Specials**	
2/1	7	omni	

Alternate Configuration D

MP	Damage PB/M/L	Overheat	Class
6	1/2/2	—	L
Armor/Structure	**Point Value**	**Specials**	
2/1	6	omni, if	

GRM-01A GAR

Mass: 35 tons
Chassis: Johnston Biped L-25-a2
Power Plant: 175 Omni
Cruising Speed: 57 kph
Maximum Speed: 89 kph
Jump Jets: Rawlings 80-Beta
Jump Capacity: 150 meters

Armor:
Johnston Duraweave 6000 Ferro-Fibrous
Armament: 1 Mydron Excel 5SG Autocannon
1 Federated LRM -10 Launcher
Manufacturer: Johnston Industries
Primary Factory: New Syrtis
Communications System: Lynx-shur 4.5

Targeting and Tracking System:
Sync Tracker (55-42071)

Overview

Named for the mythological hound that guarded the entrance to the Norse realm of the dead, the *Garm* was designed as a light support 'Mech for Federated Commonwealth fire lances. The *Garm* entered a field dominated for centuries by the famed *Valkyrie*, which has been a signature 'Mech of the AFFC. The two 'Mechs share similar capabilities. Despite its heavy firepower, however, the *Garm* met with limited success, selling mostly to mercenary units and some Periphery states. Johnston Industries was prepared to kill the model when news reports from the Periphery showed several lances of the *Garm* handily fending off pirate raids on the Taurian Concordat world of Mithron. These reports earned the notice of AFFC military officials, who ordered the *Garm* for several of their own units.

Capabilities

Slightly less well-armored than other 'Mechs of its weight class, the *Garm* carries greater long-range striking ability with its newly developed Mydron Excel 5SG Class autocannon. Pairing the autocannon with the Federated 10-Shot long-range missile launcher, the 'Mech can quickly shave away armor on light opponents. The *Garm* is also maneuverable, with enough ground speed to match most heavier scouts. The *Garm* also comes equipped with jump jets, adding a necessary edge.

The *Garm* also has two fully functional hands. Though they were not part of the original design, engineers at Johnston saw a need for them, particularly with the growing presence of armored infantry on the modern battlefield. The hands also complement the jump jets when navigating tricky mountainous terrain.

Deployment

In its first years of production, the *Garm* made few inroads into the AFFC military, but did find some takers in mercenary units serving in the Chaos March. The biggest break for the *Garm* came when the Defense Forces of the Taurian Concordat, a nearby Periphery state, picked up several production runs. After that, the AFFC began to take serious notice of the design and ordered several hundred of the 'Mechs to fill its frontline units.

Variants

The one variant of the *Garm* is nearly as popular as the standard model. The 01B design replaces the autocannon with an extended-range large laser, an additional ton of armor and two extra heat sinks. The remaining ton is used to mount an Artemis IV fire-control system for the LRM-10 launcher. This design retains the 'Mech's long-distance punch, but forces the pilot to engage in careful heat management, despite the extra heat sinks.

GRM-01A GARM

Type: **Garm**
Technology Base: Inner Sphere
Tonnage: 35
Battle Value: 662

Equipment		**Mass**
Internal Structure:	Endo Steel	2
Engine:	175	7
Walking MP:	5	
Running MP:	8	
Jumping MP:	5	
Heat Sinks:	10	0
Gyro:		2
Cockpit:		3
Armor Factor:	63	3.5

	Internal Structure	*Armor Value*
Head	3	7
Center Torso	11	10
Center Torso (rear)		2
R/L Torso	8	9
R/L Torso (rear)		1
R/L Arm	6	6
R/L Leg	8	6

Weapons and Ammo	**Location**	**Critical**	**Tonnage**
LB 5-X AC	RT	5	8
Ammo (LB-X) 20	RT	1	1
LRM 10	LT	2	5
Ammo (LRM) 12	LT	1	1
Jump Jets	RL	2	1
Jump Jets	LL	2	1
Jump Jet	CT	1	.5

BATTLEFORCE 2

MP	**Damage PB/M/L**	**Overheat**	**Class**
5J	2/1/1	—	L

Armor/Structure	**Point Value**	**Specials**
2/3	7	if

INI-02 INITIATE

Mass: 40 tons
Chassis: Geometric 1000 Endo Steel
Power Plant: LTV 160
Cruising Speed: 43 kph
Maximum Speed: 65 kph
Jump Jets: None
Jump Capacity: None
Armor: Strasbourg Armaments Type 3
Armament:
3 Diverse Optics Extended Range Small Lasers
2 Irian Weapons Works Super 6 Medium Lasers
1 Irian Weapons Works V7 LRM-15 Launcher
1 Irian Weapons Works 60mm SRM-6 Launcher
1 McArthur Anti-Missile System
Manufacturer: Martinson Armaments
Primary Factory: Australia, Terra
Communications System: Blow 55 Net
Targeting and Tracking System: Scope 2000

Overview

Immediately after Word of Blake conquered Terra, technicians began reopening and repairing mothballed factories. The *Initiate*, the first 'Mech to walk out of one of these refurbished factories, comes from the Martinson Armaments production center that once produced the *Spartan*. Though the Martinson factory was destroyed when Stefan Amaris took Terra some three centuries ago, it was repaired in a surprisingly short time, and now produces *Initiate*s as well as *Spartan*s.

The *Initiate* design was based in part on the *Albatross*, sharing many of that assault 'Mech's weapons systems and imitating its eclectic weapons mix.

Capabilities

Loaded with weapons and armor, the *Initiate*'s only drawback is a decided lack of speed and maneuverability. At long range, the LRM provides quite a bit of punch for a 'Mech this size, and the *Initiate*'s firepower is stronger as it closes in. The combined punch of the ER small lasers, the medium lasers and the SRM can disable smaller 'Mechs quickly and efficiently, and the anti-missile system defends the 'Mech from incoming missile barrages.

Deployment

Production of the *Initiate* continues at record speed, and each one quickly gets a pilot. *Initiate*s are being spread equally among all Word of Blake divisions.

INI-02 INITIATE

Type: **Initiate**
Technology Base: Inner Sphere
Tonnage: 40
Battle Value: 913

Equipment		**Mass**
Internal Structure:	Endo Steel	2
Engine:	160	6
Walking MP:	4	
Running MP:	6	
Jumping MP:	0	
Heat Sinks:	11 [22]	1
Gyro:		2
Cockpit:		3
Armor Factor:	136	8.5

	Internal Structure	*Armor Value*
Head	3	9
Center Torso	12	17
Center Torso (rear)		6
R/L Torso	10	15
R/L Torso (rear)		5
R/L Arm	6	12
R/L Leg	10	20

Weapons and Ammo	**Location**	**Critical**	**Tonnage**
2 Med. Lasers	LA	2	2
3 ER Small Lasers	RA	3	1.5
LRM 15	LT	3	7
Ammo (LRM) 8	LT	1	1
Anti-Missile System	LT	1	.5
Ammo (AMS) 12	LT	1	1
CASE	LT	1	.5
SRM 6	RT	2	3
Ammo (SRM) 15	RT	1	1

BATTLEFORCE 2

MP	**Damage PB/M/L**	**Overheat**	**Class**
4	4/3/1	—	M

Armor/Structure	**Point Value**	**Specials**
3/3	9	if

SNT-04 SENTRY

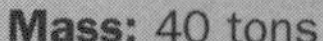

Mass: 40 tons
Chassis: Dorwinion Hyperactive 3 Endo Steel
Power Plant: Nissan 200
Cruising Speed: 55 kph
Maximum Speed: 87 kph
Jump Jets: HildCo Model 12
Jump Capacity: 150 meters
Armor: Starshield A
Armament: 1 Parti-Kill Heavy Cannon
2 Magna 200P Small Pulse Lasers
1 Zippo Flamer
4 SperryBrowning Machine Guns
Manufacturer: Robinson Standard BattleWorks
Primary Factory: Robinson
Communications System: Archernar Electronics HICS-15
Targeting and Tracking System: Federated Hunter Type 3

Overview

Fearing the possibility of another invasion, the leaders of the various Federated Commonwealth Marches demanded a new 'Mech with more advanced technology than the *Watchman*, which had been designed in Prince Hanse Davion's day for their defense. In response, Prince Victor Steiner-Davion had a new wing added to the *Watchman* factory on Robinson for production of the *Sentry*.

Prince Victor made sure that all of the new 'Mech's parts would be interchangeable, as with the *Watchman*, to ease the introduction of the *Sentry* into the various planetary militia units. Like the *Watchman*, the *Sentry* uses as many surplus parts from other units as possible, such as extra Zippo flamers from the *Berserker* and SperryBrowning machine guns from older *Vulcan* models. The Parti-Kill heavy cannon came from a stockpile formed when the Manticore heavy tank was upgraded, and the Magna 200P small pulse lasers are leftovers from an overstock for the *Dart*.

Capabilities

The *Sentry* is just as tough as its counterpart, with the same heavy armor protection and mobility that marked the earlier *Watchman* design. The *Sentry* also includes the CASE system, to protect the machine gun ammunition. The *Sentry*'s weapons are geared toward anti-personnel combat, with an impressive arsenal of four machine guns and a flamer. MechWarriors who underestimate this design do so at their peril; the PPC packs quite a punch, and the deadly-accurate fire of the small pulse lasers can destroy 'Mechs as easily as the ballistic weapons take down infantry.

Deployment

The first production run of the *Sentry* was divided evenly among the various Marches, much to the annoyance of Duke Sandoval of the Draconis March. Though Prince Hanse Davion had allowed Duke Sandoval first crack at the *Watchman*, Prince Victor declined to do the same with the *Sentry*, refusing to give favored status to bitter enemies of the Draconis Combine.

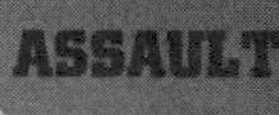

SNT-04 SENTRY

Type: **Sentry**
Technology Base: Inner Sphere
Tonnage: 40
Battle Value: 961

Equipment		**Mass**
Internal Structure:	Endo Steel	2
Engine:	200	8.5
Walking MP:	5	
Running MP:	8	
Jumping MP:	5	
Heat Sinks:	10 [20]	0
Gyro:		2
Cockpit:		3
Armor Factor:	136	8.5
	Internal Structure	*Armor Value*
Head	3	9
Center Torso	12	17
Center Torso (rear)		6
R/L Torso	10	15
R/L Torso (rear)		5
R/L Arm	6	12
R/L Leg	10	20

Weapons and Ammo	**Location**	**Critical**	**Tonnage**
2 Small Pulse Lasers	RA	2	2
4 Machine Guns	LA	4	2
PPC	LA	3	7
Ammo (MG) 200	LT	1	1
CASE	LT	1	.5
Flamer	H	1	1
Jump Jet	CT	1	.5
Jump Jets	LL	2	1
Jump Jets	RL	2	1

BATTLEFORCE 2

MP	**Damage PB/M/L**	**Overheat**	**Class**
5J	3/1/1	—	M

Armor/Structure	**Point Value**	**Specials**
3/3	10	

BEO-12 BEOWULF

Mass: 45 tons
Chassis: Beowulf 3
Power Plant: GM 270 XL
Cruising Speed: 65 kph
Maximum Speed: 97 kph, w/MASC 130 kph
Jump Jets: Odin Type II
Jump Capacity: 180 meters
Armor: Wall Type 6 Ferro-Fibrous
Armament:
1 Blankenburg Large Pulse Laser
2 Diverse Optics Extended Range Medium Lasers
Manufacturer: Odin Manufacturing
Primary Factory: Orestes
Communications System: Dash-2 Standard
Targeting and Tracking System: Blade 12 with Beagle Active Probe and TAG

Overview

After the Clan defeat on Tukayyid, ComStar immediately began upgrading several small production facilities in the Free Rasalhague Republic into 'Mech factories. The largest, Odin Manufacturing's facility on Orestes, was the first to produce a new 'Mech design, the *Beowulf*.

In 3058, when ComStar was driven from Terra, all of its *Mongoose* scout 'Mechs were destroyed. Rather than order more, the Precentor Martial decided to build a new 'Mech that would serve as a scout without the *Mongoose*'s lack of firepower and mobility. The new 'Mech, the *Beowulf*, is nearly twice as heavy as the *Mongoose* and has jump capability.

Capabilities

The *Beowulf* is extremely mobile, combining an XL engine with MASC for extra speed and with a 180-meter jump radius. Combined with that mobility is the firepower provided by a large pulse laser and two of the newly developed ER medium lasers, purchased from the Free Worlds League. As a scout 'Mech, the *Beowulf* is also equipped with a Beagle active probe and a TAG system to direct incoming artillery.

Deployment

Half of the *Beowulf*s produced go to the Com Guards, the other half to the Rasalhague Küngsarmé. To date, only the 321st Division of the Com Guards and the Fourth Kavalleri of the Küngsarmé have received *Beowulf*s.

BEO-12 BEOWULF

Type: **Beowulf**
Technology Base: Inner Sphere
Tonnage: 45
Battle Value: 1,147

Equipment		**Mass**
Internal Structure:		4.5
Engine:	270 XL	7.5
Walking MP:	6	
Running MP:	9 (12)	
Jumping MP:	6	
Heat Sinks:	12 [24]	2
Gyro:		3
Cockpit:		3
Armor Factor:	152	8.5

	Internal Structure	*Armor Value*
Head	3	9
Center Torso	14	20
Center Torso (rear)		7
R/L Torso	11	16
R/L Torso (rear)		6
R/L Arm	7	14
R/L Leg	11	22

Weapons and Ammo	**Location**	**Critical**	**Tonnage**
Large Pulse Laser	RA	2	7
2 ER Med. Lasers	LA	2	2
Beagle Active Probe	CT	2	1.5
TAG	H	1	1
MASC	RT	2	2
Jump Jets	LT	2	1
Jump Jet	LL	1	.5
Jump Jets	RT	2	1
Jump Jet	RL	1	.5

BATTLEFORCE 2

MP	**Damage PB/M/L**	**Overheat**	**Class**
6J	3/2/—	—	M

Armor/Structure	**Point Value**	**Specials**
4/2	11	prb, tag

BSN-3K BISHAMON

Mass: 45 tons
Chassis: Fortune VII Endo Steel (quad)
Power Plant: 315 GM XL
Cruising Speed: 76 kph
Maximum Speed: 119 kph
Jump Jets: None
Jump Capacity: None
Armor: Nimakachi Type 3

Armament: 1 Shigunga MRM-20 Launcher
2 Diverse Optics Extended Range Medium Lasers
2 Tronel XII Medium Pulse Lasers
Manufacturer:
Nimakachi Fusion Products Ltd.
Primary Factory: Tematagi

Communications System: Omicron 5000
Targeting and Tracking System:
Eagle Eye B-18

Overview

Impressed by the success of the *Venom* design, Draconis Combine officials approached Nimakachi Fusion Products about producing a slightly larger scout 'Mech that used some of the newer technology available. Intrigued by the challenge, Nimakachi designers began work on what would become the *Bishamon*.

In their first and most important decision, the designers chose to use a four-legged chassis. Seeking a more stable platform for scouting, Nimakachi found the unorthodox quad configuration to be the best choice. The designers also felt that a heavily armed scout could go more places on the battlefield than lighter-armed and armored 'Mechs could, and so made full use of several new weapons. Unfortunately, this left no room for jump jets, but Nimakachi's designers felt that the combination of heavier weapons and armor, speed and the stable quad chassis would make up for the lack of jump capability. After reviewing the design, the DCMS agreed.

Capabilities

The *Bishamon* was built using all of the latest materials; sparing no expense, Nimakachi included a 315 XL engine and an endo steel chassis. The innate space limitations of a quad design precluded the use of ferro-fibrous armor, but the designers added 10.5 tons of standard armor, more than any bipedal 'Mech of the *Bishamon*'s size can carry.

For weapons, Nimakachi first chose the newly available medium-range missiles, adding a rack of twenty and enough ammunition to keep the *Bishamon* supplied during the scouting missions for which it was intended. Supplementing the missiles are two Tronel XII medium pulse lasers, weapons with a proven track record on the *Venom*. The designers also purchased Diverse Optics ER medium lasers from the Free Worlds League, whose weapons manufacturers are selling much of their advanced technology across the Inner Sphere.

Deployment

The *Bishamon* has so far been distributed only to the First Sword of Light regiment, which is fitting. The First Sword are known as the "Ivory Dragon," representing religious devotion, and the *Bishamon* is named for a Japanese god—one of the Seven Fortunes. This symbolism is likely deliberate.

Variants

Only one variant of the basic design has been produced, at a ratio of one variant model to every four standard models. The variant replaces the MRM-20 with an MRM-10 and both ER medium lasers with ER small lasers, and adds a C^3 master computer. This variant is meant to lead lances of light and medium Combine OmniMechs.

BSN-3K BISHAMON

Type: **Bishamon**
Technology Base: Inner Sphere
Tonnage: 45
Battle Value: 1,089

Equipment		**Mass**
Internal Structure:	Endo Steel	2.5
Engine:	315 XL	11
Walking MP:	7	
Running MP:	11	
Jumping MP:	0	
Heat Sinks:	10 [20]	0
Gyro:		4
Cockpit:		3
Armor Factor:	168	10.5
	Internal Structure	*Armor Value*
Head	3	9
Center Torso	14	21
Center Torso (rear)		6
R/L Torso	11	17
R/L Torso (rear)		5
R/L Front Leg	11	22
R/L Rear Leg	11	22

Weapons and Ammo	**Location**	**Critical**	**Tonnage**
ER Med. Laser	LT	1	1
ER Med. Laser	RT	1	1
Med. Pulse Laser	LT	1	2
Med. Pulse Laser	RT	1	2
MRM 20	RT	3	7
Ammo (MRM) 12	RT	1	1

BATTLEFORCE 2

MP	**Damage PB/M/L**	**Overheat**	**Class**
7	4/3/—	—	M

Armor/Structure	**Point Value**	**Specials**
4/2	11	

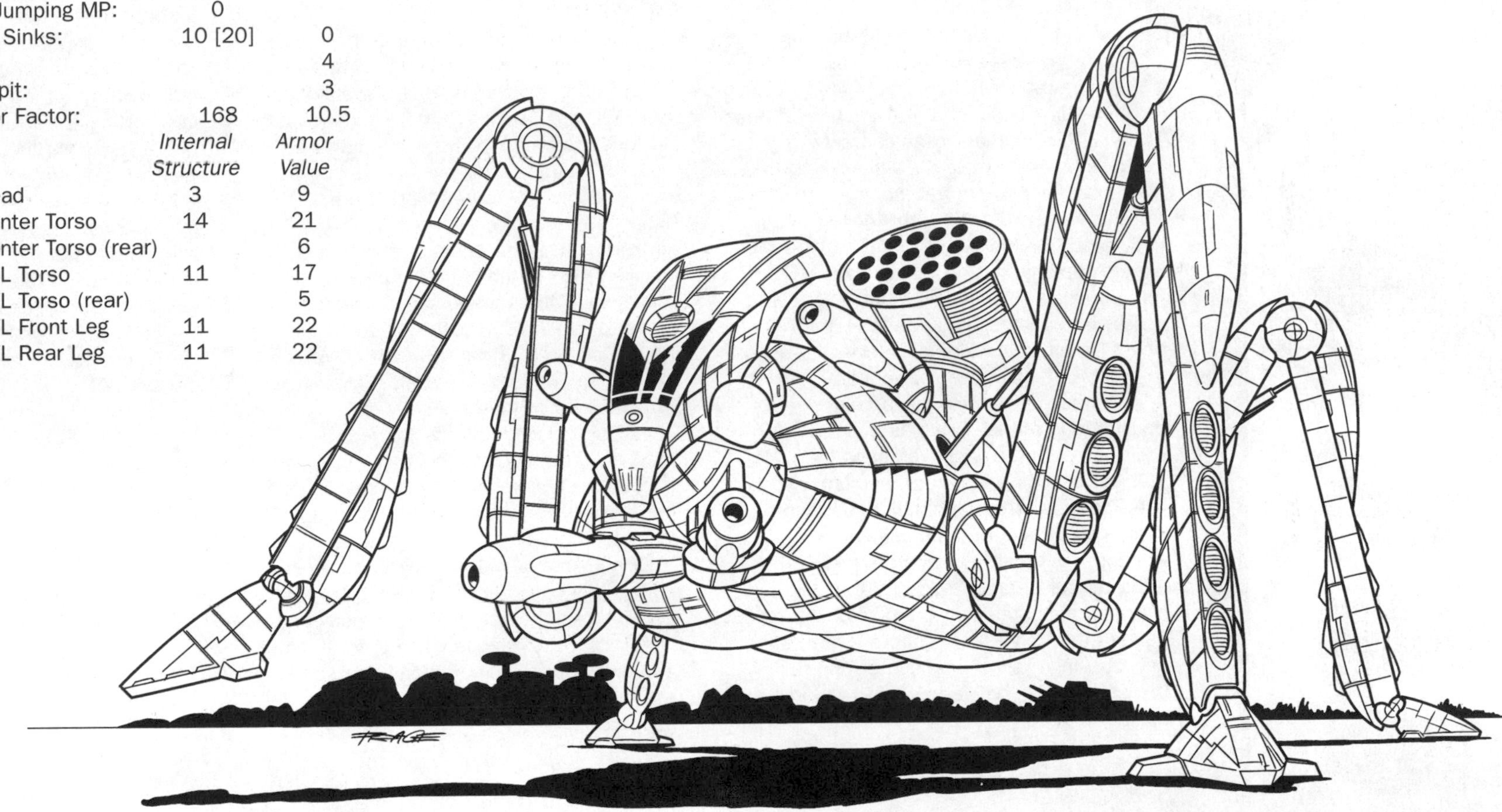

CBR-02 COBRA

Mass: 45 tons
Chassis: Defiance 450 Endo Steel
Power Plant: VOX 225
Cruising Speed: 54 kph
Maximum Speed: 87 kph
Jump Jets: None
Jump Capacity: None

Armor: Lexington Ltd. High Grade Ferro-Fibrous
Armament:
2 Coventry Star Fire LRM-15 Launchers
2 Defiance B3M Medium Lasers
Manufacturer: Defiance Industries
Primary Factory: Hesperus II

Communications System:
TharHes Calliope 270
Targeting and Tracking System:
TharHes Ares LM

Overview

During the Marik/Liao invasions of 3057, Lyran Alliance commanders were impressed by the fire-support actions of the enemy's new *Apollo* 'Mech. The Lyrans contacted Earthwerks, makers of the *Apollo*, only to learn that Earthwerks had been instructed to refuse any orders for the *Apollo* from the Federated Commonwealth, and that they were extending that refusal to the newly formed Lyran Alliance. Undaunted, LAAF officials contacted Defiance Industries about developing a similar 'Mech, a request to which Defiance gladly responded.

Defiance engineers used field descriptions of the *Apollo* as the basis for their new 'Mech design, retaining the LRM-15s but choosing standard medium lasers over the less effective small pulse lasers. They also changed the placement of the weapons, putting them all in the 'Mech's arms to give a larger field of fire. LAAF officials requested that the new design—dubbed the *Cobra* for its hood-like targeting and tracking system—be lighter and faster than the *Apollo*, but retain the standard engine to keep costs down.

Capabilities

The *Cobra* is intended as a fire-support 'Mech, and it serves admirably in that role. Though it lacks Artemis IV FCS systems for its LRMs, the *Cobra*'s mobility enables it to get to a good firing position and gives it a range of motion that provides the missiles with a nearly 360-degree field of fire. Defiance chose to copy the missile arrangement of the *Zeus*, arranging the missile tubes around and set back from a solid core. This arrangement allows the *Cobra* to punch without fear of damaging the missile rack. Backing up the LRMs is a pair of medium lasers, classic short-range protection for a fire-support 'Mech.

Using a standard engine keep costs down and also adds to the survivability of the *Cobra*. Despite all the miracles Defiance managed to work, however, the design contains some flaws. It leaves no space for CASE equipment, a drawback that makes some pilots consider the *Cobra* a deathtrap. Also, despite the use of ferro-fibrous alloys, the Cobra lacks adequate armor for a 'Mech of its size, sacrificing protection for speed. Only time will tell if that trade-off was a wise one.

Deployment

The *Cobra* has so far gone only to the Third Donegal Guards, undergoing a testing period with them. It is fairly certain that LAAF officials approve of the design, however, as production has begun in earnest despite the fact that testing has not yet been completed. Other realms barred from purchasing *Apollo*s havc also expressed interest. The LAAF is expected to authorize sales to the Free Rasalhague Republic, but it seems unlikely that either the Federated Commonwealth or the St. Ives Compact will be allowed to purchase the design.

CBR-02 COBRA

Type: **Cobra**
Technology Base: Inner Sphere
Tonnage: 45
Battle Value: 994

Equipment		**Mass**
Internal Structure:	Endo Steel	2.5
Engine:	225	10
Walking MP:	5	
Running MP:	8	
Jumping MP:	0	
Heat Sinks:	10 [20]	0
Gyro:		3
Cockpit:		3
Armor Factor:	116	6.5
	Internal Structure	*Armor Value*
Head	3	9
Center Torso	14	16
Center Torso (rear)		5
R/L Torso	11	15
R/L Torso (rear)		4
R/L Arm	7	11
R/L Leg	11	13

Weapons and Ammo	**Location**	**Critical**	**Tonnage**
LRM 15	LA	3	7
Med. Laser	LA	1	1
Ammo (LRM) 32	LT	4	4
LRM 15	RA	3	7
Med. Laser	RA	1	1

BATTLEFORCE 2

MP	**Damage PB/M/L**	**Overheat**	**Class**
5	3/3/2	—	M

Armor/Structure	**Point Value**	**Specials**
3/4	10	if

BTZ-3F BLITZKRIEG

Mass: 50 tons
Chassis: Coventry BTZ-VII
Power Plant: 350 Magna XL
Cruising Speed: 76 kph
Maximum Speed: 119 kph
Jump Jets: None
Jump Capacity: None

Armor: Lexington Ltd. High Grade Ferro-Fibrous
Armament:
1 Defiance Thunder Ultra AC/20 Autocannon
Manufacturer: Coventry Metal Works
Primary Factory: Coventry

Communications System: TharHes Muse 54-58K
Targeting and Tracking System: Cyclops 9b

Overview

After five years of relative peace, Clan forces forged deep into the Lyran Alliance in 3058, ending their bloody campaign on Coventry. The Coventry Metal Works facility was a prime target, and though the bulk of the fighting took place more than a kilometer away from the plant, the factory suffered significant collateral damage. Combined with the loss of nearly all of its defending 'Mech force, the damage meant that CMW faced a long period of rebuilding.

One of CMW's primary products had been the *Hollander*, a 'Mech disliked by many members of the Lyran Alliance Armed Forces. Critics cited its lack of secondary weapons, poor speed, light armor, and inherent instability as weaknesses that, though minor when considered individually, combined to make the *Hollander* ineffective when facing Clan forces head-on. The critics were vindicated by the weak performance of the *Hollanders* defending the plant against Clan Jade Falcon attackers during the Battle of Coventry.

Salvage claimed from that battle provided the spark for a new design based on the *Hollander.* Among the salvage pulled from wrecked Clan 'Mechs were a number of intact Clan autocannons, including an Ultra-20 class weapon in perfect condition. This rare item, combined with recent technological exchanges with the Free Worlds League, allowed scientists at Defiance Industries to develop a working Ultra/20 autocannon for full-scale production. First used on the upgraded Demolisher heavy tank, the weapon would soon see use in a radical new BattleMech, the *Blitzkrieg.*

Capabilities

The BTZ-3F *Blitzkrieg* addresses almost every pilot complaint about the *Hollander.* First and foremost, a massive 350 XL engine drives the 'Mech's 50-ton frame at speeds of more than 100 kph, allowing the 'Mech to outflank all but the fastest opponents. This speed is vital, because the Defiance Thunder Ultra-20 Autocannon—the *Blitzkrieg's* only weapon—has only half the effective range of the *Hollander*'s Gauss rifle. However, with a potential damage curve more than twice that of the Gauss rifle, the autocannon can slice target 'Mechs in half in a matter of seconds, especially if the *Blitzkrieg* circles behind its target to hit the rear armor.

The *Blitzkrieg* is also tougher than its predecessor, with a stronger chassis and almost twice the armor protection. Combined with its high speed, this makes the newer 'Mech much more likely to survive contact with the enemy. Designers were also careful about the placement of the huge cannon on the 'Mech's frame. By placing counterweights and ammo feeds to the right of the weapon, designers ensured proper balance on uneven terrain.

Despite these improvements, the *Blitzkrieg* has only a single weapon system, and when it runs out of ammunition (which it tends to do very quickly), it must retreat behind friendly lines for resupply. Given its other design advances, however, the need to resupply is a minor weakness in an otherwise devastating fast-strike 'Mech.

Deployment

Because of cost overruns and other delays, the *Blitzkrieg* is still not in full-scale production. A lance of the new 'Mechs has been shipped to the Twenty-fourth Arcturan Guards on Barcelona for field testing. Full-scale production is due to begin in 3061. The Free Worlds League will have the option of purchasing up to 25 percent of all *Blitzkriegs* manufactured on Coventry.

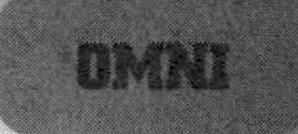

BTZ-3F BLITZKRIEG

Type: **Blitzkrieg**
Technology Base: Inner Sphere
Tonnage: 50
Battle Value: 1,092

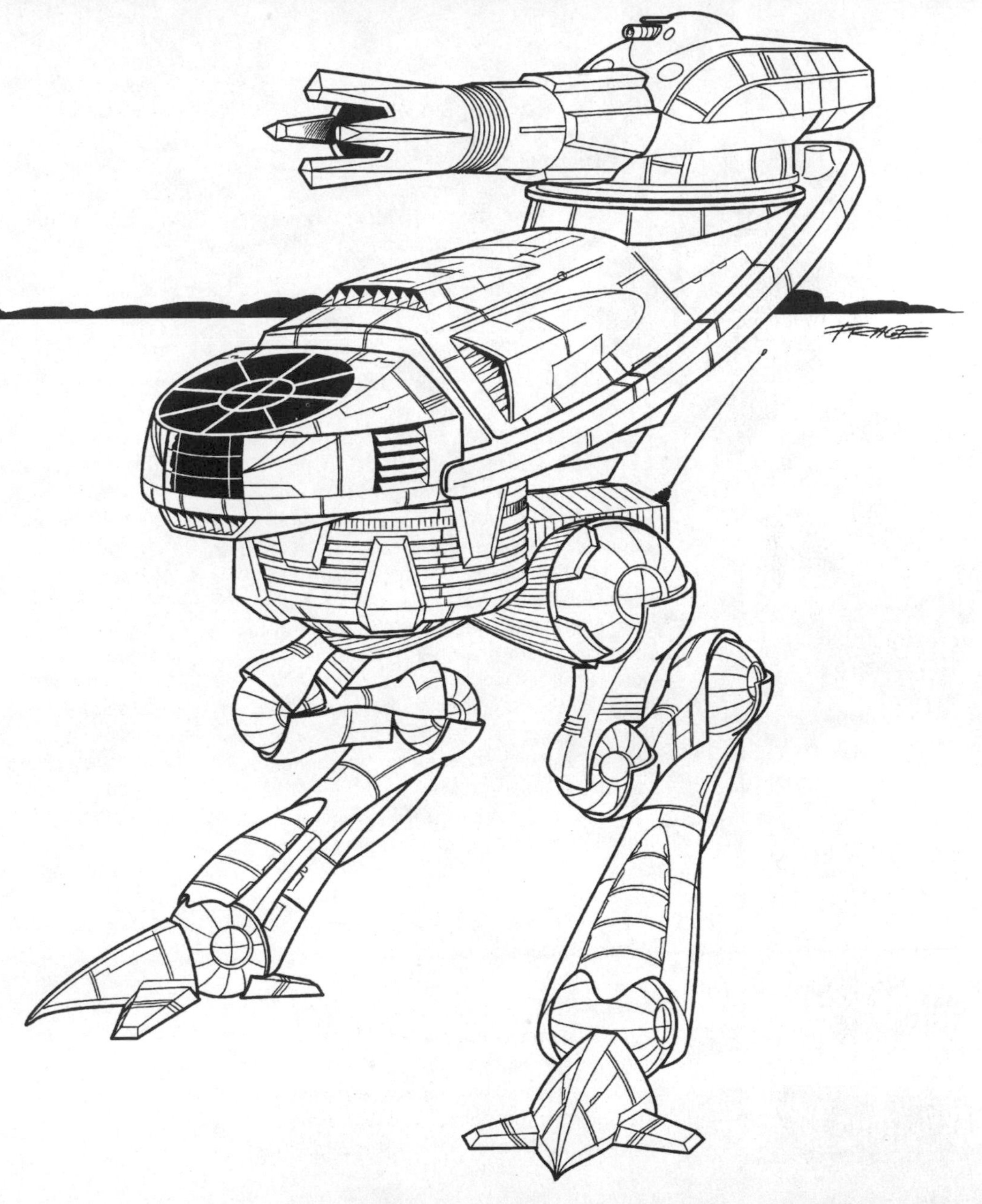

Equipment		**Mass**
Internal Structure:	Endo Steel	2.5
Engine:	350 XL	15
Walking MP:	7	
Running MP:	11	
Jumping MP:	0	
Heat Sinks:	10 [20]	0
Gyro:		4
Cockpit:		3
Armor Factor:	116	6.5

	Internal Structure	*Armor Value*
Head	3	8
Center Torso	16	17
Center Torso (rear)		5
R/L Torso	12	13
R/L Torso (rear)		4
R/L Arm	8	10
R/L Leg	12	16

Weapons and Ammo	**Location**	**Critical**	**Tonnage**
Ultra AC/20	LT/CT	10	15
Ammo (Ultra) 20	RT	4	4

BATTLEFORCE 2

MP	**Damage PB/M/L**	**Overheat**	**Class**
7	4/3/—	—	M

Armor/Structure	**Point Value**	**Specials**
3/2	11	

ENF-6M ENFORCER III

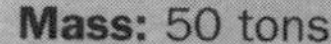

Mass: 50 tons
Chassis: Dorwinion Standard-Alpha
Power Plant: Magna 250 XL
Cruising Speed: 55 kph
Maximum Speed: 87 kph
Jump Jets: McCloud Specials
Jump Capacity: 150 meters

Armor: StarGuard CIV Standard
Armament:
1 BlazeFire Sweetshot Extended Range Large Laser
1 Mydron Excel Ultra Type 10 Autocannon
1 ChisComp 2000 Extended Range Small Laser

Manufacturer: Achernar BattleMechs, Kallon Weapon Industries
Primary Factory: New Avalon (Achernar), Talon (Kallon)
Communications System: Achernar Electronic HICS-12
Targeting and Tracking System: Federated Hunter

Overview

The *Enforcer* has long been the workhorse medium-weight 'Mech for the Federated Suns and, later, the Federated Commonwealth. Considered a Davion design, the *Enforcer* is one of the most recognized 'Mechs in the AFFC.

Its history as a Davion 'Mech made it an obvious choice for experiments with technology newly developed by Federated Commonwealth engineers. Archon Prince Victor Steiner-Davion hoped to rebuild his image by taking a military icon and improving upon it. The *Enforcer* III, using the latest in military technology, has become one of the flagship 'Mechs of the AFFC.

This new design, while heralded as an improvement, has sparked some controversy over the changes—controversy the young Prince does not need in the wake of the split with the Lyran portion of the Federated Commonwealth.

Capabilities

When Independence Weaponries technicians reverse-engineered an Inner Sphere version of the deadly Clan Ultra-10 autocannon, the public relations division of the AFFC saw a perfect opportunity to aid Prince Victor in rebuilding his image by including the Ultra autocannon on the newly revamped *Enforcer*. Putting a foreign weapon on the 'Mech that would become the new flagship design of the AFFC was a risk, but they believed it would show that Prince Victor was attempting to form alliances, and could help his people forget the Free Worlds Leaguc's invasion of the Federated Commonwealth. Convinced of the plan's validity, Prince Victor gave his okay for the design.

Replacing the Mydron Excel LB-X autocannon with the newly developed Ultra version significantly improved the 'Mech's damage spread. The new weapon gave the *Enforcer* a more concentrated punch, as well as enhancing its ability to cripple 'Mechs of its own weight class or lighter. The change sparked controversy among many *Enforcer* MechWarriors, however. These pilots had grown accustomed to fighting with the LB-X autocannon, which causes less damage but whose cluster rounds give it a wider spread. The damage pattern of the Ultra autocannon, by contrast, usually resulted in longer engagements, forcing many MechWarriors to change their battle tactics and strategies.

Despite their concerns, the changes went through. Initial field tests seemed to bear out the pilots' arguments. However, when the redesigned 'Mech was fielded by green warriors, the change of weapon did not appear to affect their or the 'Mech's performance.

Deployment

Because design changes from the earlier *Enforcer* were minimal, the new *Enforcer* III design is rapidly finding placement in numerous units along Federated Commonwealth borders. Publicity has been heavy for the new design and its counterpart, the *JagerMech* III. Posters bearing the image of the new *Enforcer*, along with the phrase "Upgraded for more enforcement" have become commonplace throughout the Commonwealth. Surprisingly, there has been no backlash regarding the use of a foreign-made Ultra autocannon.

ENF-6M ENFORCER III

Type: **Enforcer III**
Technology Base: Inner Sphere
Tonnage: 50
Battle Value: 1,427

Equipment		**Mass**
Internal Structure:	Endo Steel	2.5
Engine:	250 XL	6.5
Walking MP:	5	
Running MP:	8	
Jumping MP:	5	
Heat Sinks:	12 [24]	2
Gyro:		3
Cockpit:		3
Armor Factor:	160	10

	Internal Structure	*Armor Value*
Head	3	9
Center Torso	16	24
Center Torso (rear)		7
R/L Torso	12	19
R/L Torso (rear)		5
R/L Arm	8	16
R/L Leg	12	20

Weapons and Ammo	**Location**	**Critical**	**Tonnage**
ER Large Laser	LA	2	5
ER Small Laser	LT	1	.5
Ultra AC/10	RA	7	13
Ammo (Ultra) 20	RT	2	2
Jump Jet	CT	1	.5
Jump Jets	LL	2	1
Jump Jets	RL	2	1

BATTLEFORCE 2

MP	**Damage PB/M/L**	**Overheat**	**Class**
5J	3/2/2	1	M

Armor/Structure	**Point Value**	**Specials**
4/2	14	

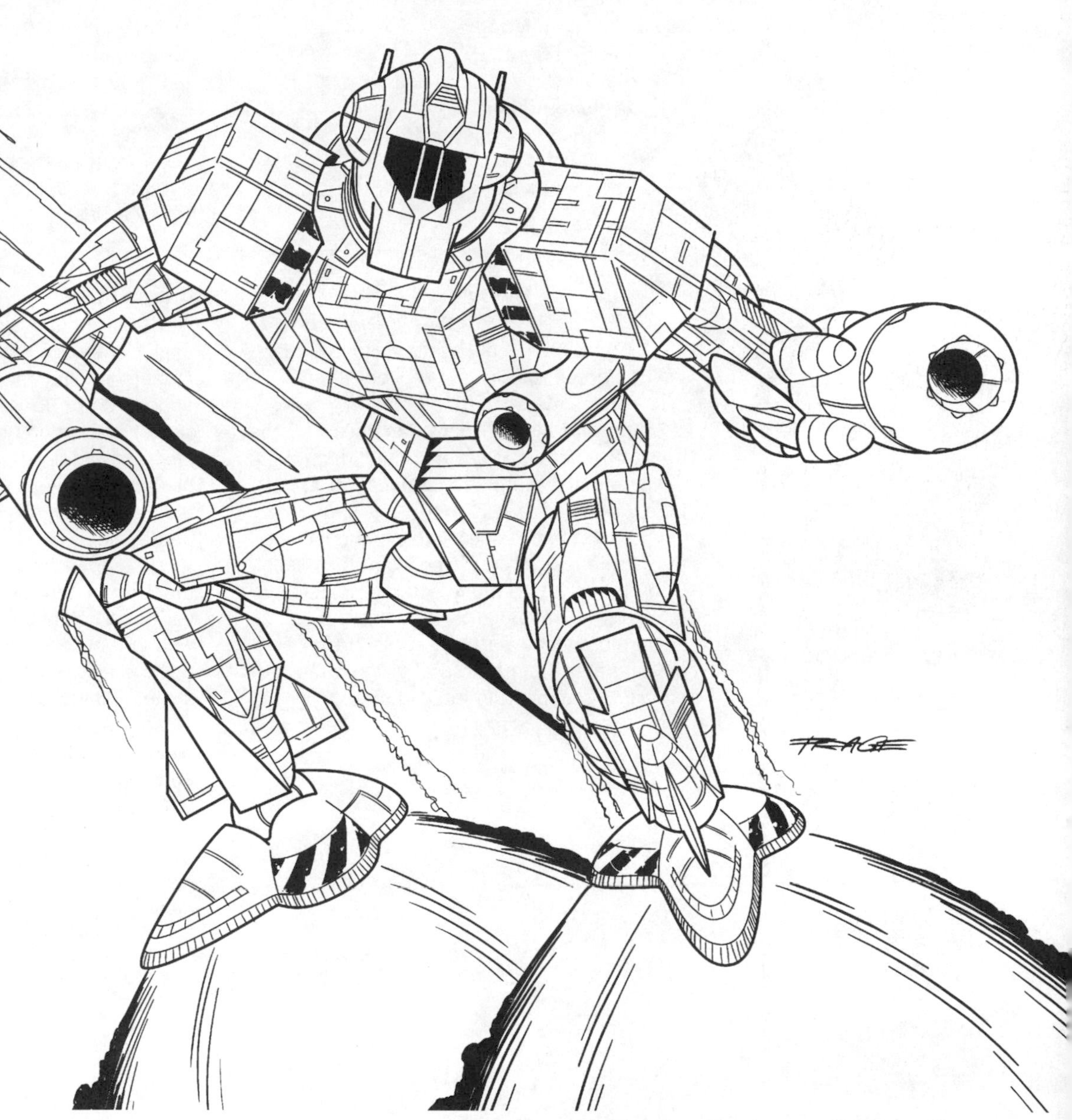

BCN-3 BUCCANEER

Mass: 55 tons
Chassis: Standard
Power Plant: Vox 330 XL
Cruising Speed: 65 kph
Maximum Speed: 97 kph
Jump Jets: None
Jump Capacity: None

Armor: Kallon FWL Special Ferro-Fibrous
Armament:
1 Irian Weapon Works 60mm SRM-6 Launcher with Artemis FCS
1 Diverse Optics Sunbeam Extended Range Large Laser
4 Diverse Optics Type 18 Medium Lasers
1 Starflash Medium Pulse Laser

Manufacturer: Gibson Federated BattleMechs
Primary Factory: Gibson
Communications System: Easy Talk 2
Targeting and Tracking System: RCA Instatrac Mark XIII with Artemis IV system

Overview

After their arrival on Gibson, the Word of Blake armed forces had far more pilots than 'Mechs. To solve this problem, Precentor Martial Trent Arian called for the mass production of several new 'Mech designs using materials produced in the Free Worlds League.

One design rushed into production was the *Buccaneer*, a prototype ComStar 'Mech that had yet to be manufactured on Terra. After a swift redesign to accommodate League-produced parts, the 'Mech went through an accelerated trial program and entered production in late 3055.

Capabilities

Built around a compact Vox 330 XL engine, the *Buccaneer* has above-average maneuverability for its size and is capable of speeds up to 95 kph. When forced by weight restrictions to choose between jump jets and additional weapons and armor, the designers chose the latter; consequently, the *Buccaneer* is a sturdy opponent on the battlefield.

Intended for close combat in cities and other restricted terrain, the *Buccaneer* carries a hatchet in its left hand. This weapon, built around an ultra-dense core of depleted uranium, allows the *Buccaneer* to severely damage opponents within arm's reach. A battery of lasers and an Irian Weapon Works 60mm SRM launcher provide additional close-in support. The *Buccaneer*'s major long-range weapon, a Diverse Optics Sunbeam extended-range large laser, makes overheating a problem, but compensates for this with its ability to do damage at long distances.

Deployment

The Word of Blake has given several *Buccaneer*s to the Free Worlds League as part of an ongoing technology exchange, but the majority of these 'Mechs remain in service with the Word of Blake Militia. The first units saw action in the Nestor campaign, in which the Blake Militia defeated the 21st Centauri Lancers.

The 'Mech's first real test came during the Terra campaign, with several deployed in task forces Steel, Silver and Brass. The most notable was piloted by Adept Will Clark in the Sandhurst campaign; Adept Clark accounted for three Com Guard BattleMechs in the twenty-two hours of near-continuous fighting that raged across the southern British Isles.

BCN-3R BUCCANEER

Type: **Buccaneer**
Technology Base: Inner Sphere
Tonnage: 55
Battle Value: 1,092

Equipment		**Mass**
Internal Structure:		5.5
Engine:	330 XL	12.5
Walking MP:	6	
Running MP:	9	
Jumping MP:	0	
Heat Sinks:	10 [20]	0
Gyro:		4
Cockpit:		3
Armor Factor:	179	10
	Internal Structure	*Armor Value*
Head	3	9
Center Torso	18	27
Center Torso (rear)		9
R/L Torso	13	19
R/L Torso (rear)		6
R/L Arm	9	17
R/L Leg	13	25

Weapons and Ammo	**Location**	**Critical**	**Tonnage**
Hatchet	LA	4	4
SRM 6	LT	2	3
Artemis IV FCS	LT	1	1
Ammo (SRM) 15	LT	1	1
ER Large Laser	RA	2	5
Med. Laser	H	1	1
2 Med. Lasers	CT	2	2
Med. Laser	RT	1	1
Med. Pulse Laser	LT	1	2

BATTLEFORCE 2

MP	**Damage PB/M/L**	**Overheat**	**Class**
6	4/3/1	1	M

Armor/Structure	**Point Value**	**Specials**
4/2	11	

MHL-X1 MARSHAL

Mass: 55 tons
Chassis: Earthwerk GRF
Power Plant: Magna 220
Cruising Speed: 43 kph
Maximum Speed: 65 kph
Jump Jets: Rawlings 55
Jump Capacity: 120 meters

Armor: Durallex Medium Ferro-Fibrous
Armament: 1 Sunglow Type 2 Large Laser
1 Diverse Optics Type 27 Medium Pulse Laser
1 Diverse Optics Type 18 Medium Laser
1 Hotshot Flamer
1 Delta Dart LRM-5 Launcher
2 SperryBrowning Machine Guns

Manufacturer: Taurus Territorial Industries
Primary Factory: Taurus
Communications System: Neil 9000-A
Targeting and Tracking System: Octagon Tartrac System C

Overview

The Treaty of Taurus, recently signed with the Magistracy of Canopus, requires the Taurian Concordat to provide members of its Colonial Marshals force with BattleMechs and technical support. The Concordat's initial practice of issuing each marshal the 'Mech most conveniently available at the time of his posting, however, meant that many marshals received substandard machines. To remedy this problem, Concordat leader Jeffrey Calderon commissioned Taurus Technical Industries to develop a 'Mech specially suited to the Colonial Marshals' needs. The MHL-1X *Marshal* promises to be an exceptional boon to the marshals and the Taurian military.

Capabilities

The *Marshal* is a versatile medium-weight 'Mech with exceptional armor, endurance and firepower. It is somewhat slow for a 'Mech of its class, though its leg-mounted jump jets enable it to traverse difficult terrain with ease. Ten tons of ferro-fibrous armor give the 'Mech excellent protection, though some critics complain that the difficulty of repairing ferro-fibrous armor in the field makes the armor a poor choice.

In recognition of the scarcity of ammunition on the worlds patrolled by the Colonial Marshals, the new 'Mech's arsenal features a broad spectrum of energy weapons favored for their reliability. Large and medium lasers and medium pulse lasers comprise the core of the *Marshal*'s armament, which also features a torso-mounted flamer that is ideal for non-combat uses as well.

Both arms of the *Marshal* are equipped with fully articulated hand actuators, which make the 'Mech a helpful construction vehicle in peacetime. For anti-personnel and riot duty, the 'Mech is equipped with a pair of lethal SperryBrowning machine guns. A single LRM-5 rack provides the *Marshal* with long-range firepower.

Deployment

Production of the *Marshal* began in 3059. Barring any major delays, all Colonial Marshal units are expected to be fully equipped with the new BattleMechs by the end of 3060. After that, newly produced *Marshals* will be issued to the Taurian Defense Force. All of the *Marshal*'s components are manufactured in or near the Concordat, virtually ensuring that spare parts for *Marshals* will be readily available.

MHL-X1 MARSHAL

Type: **Marshal**
Technology Base: Inner Sphere
Tonnage: 55
Battle Value: 995

Equipment		**Mass**
Internal Structure:		5.5
Engine:	220	10
Walking MP:	4	
Running MP:	6	
Jumping MP:	4	
Heat Sinks:	18	8
Gyro:		3
Cockpit:		3
Armor Factor:	179	10

	Internal Structure	*Armor Value*
Head	3	9
Center Torso	18	26
Center Torso (rear)		8
R/L Torso	13	20
R/L Torso (rear)		6
R/L Arm	9	18
R/L Leg	13	24

Weapons and Ammo	**Location**	**Critical**	**Tonnage**
Large Laser	RA	2	5
Med. Pulse Laser	RT	1	2
Med. Laser	LA	1	1
2 Machine Guns	LT	2	1
Ammo (MG) 100	LT	1	.5
Flamer	CT	1	1
LRM 5	RT	1	2
Ammo (LRM) 24	RT	1	1
Jump Jets	RL	2	1
Jump Jets	LL	2	1

BATTLEFORCE 2

MP	**Damage PB/M/L**	**Overheat**	**Class**
4J	4/2/—	—	M

Armor/Structure	**Point Value**	**Specials**
4/5	10	

MS1-O MEN SHEN

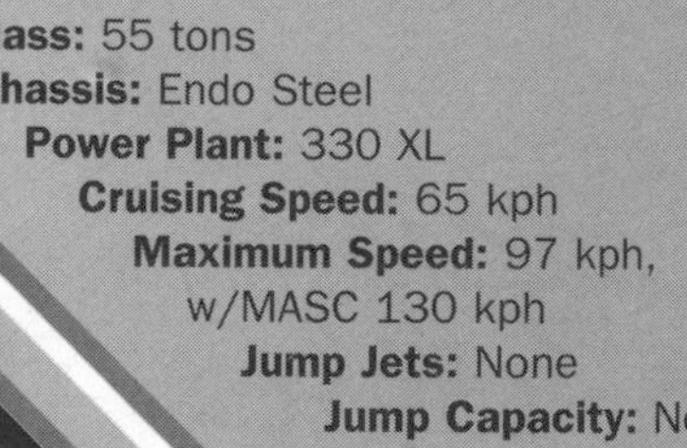

Mass: 55 tons
Chassis: Endo Steel
Power Plant: 330 XL
Cruising Speed: 65 kph
Maximum Speed: 97 kph, w/MASC 130 kph
Jump Jets: None
Jump Capacity: None

Armor: Standard
Armament:
17 tons of pod space available
Manufacturer: Hellespont Industries
Primary Factory: Sian
Communications System: Unknown
Targeting and Tracking System:
Beagle Active Probe

Overview

The first Capellan-produced OmniMech, the *Men Shen* is based on the successful *Raven* design. Hellespont Industries, which also produces the *Raven,* acquired the necessary technology through trade agreements with Kali Yama Weapons Industries of the Free Worlds League. The *Men Shen* also relies heavily on advanced sensor and ECM technologies.

The 'Mech was named by Chancellor Sun-Tzu Liao in a speech at the 'Mech's unveiling, when he said that "this new OmniMech will act as a *men shen* for the Confederation, protecting us from all enemies." *Men shen* are door gods from ancient China who are said to protect houses from evil.

Capabilities

With its fast speed and Beagle active probe, the *Men Shen* makes a perfect scout, though its considerable firepower and solid armor protection also allow it to hold its own in a stand-up fight. Four medium pulse lasers and an LRM-15, augmented by the Artemis IV fire-control system, make the primary configuration of the *Men Shen* a dangerous opponent at all ranges. The 'Mech's other configurations are equally dangerous regardless of range, except for the C variant, which is designed for close-in assaults and carries a Guardian ECM suite to help it close in on enemy 'Mechs unnoticed.

In addition to several Free Worlds League weapon systems that appear on various configurations of the *Men Shen*, the 'Mech also features the new Capellan-made LB-X Type 2 autocannon, giving this weapon system a powerful debut.

Deployment

A lance of *Men Shen*s has been delivered to each of the Capellan Warrior Houses, and the Death Commandos may have received some as well. The next shipment is expected to go to units stationed on Capellan Confederation borders.

Type: **Men Shen**
Technology Base: Inner Sphere OmniMech
Tonnage: 55
Battle Value: 1,199

Equipment		Mass
Internal Structure:	Endo Steel	3
Engine:	330 XL	12.5
Walking MP:	6	
Running MP:	9 (12)	
Jumping MP:	0	
Heat Sinks:	10 [20]	0
Gyro:		4
Cockpit:		3
Armor Factor:	176	11

	Internal Structure	*Armor Value*
Head	3	9
Center Torso	18	26
Center Torso (rear)		7
R/L Torso	13	20
R/L Torso (rear)		6
R/L Arm	9	17
R/L Leg	13	24

Weight and Space Allocation

Location	*Fixed*	*Spaces Remaining*
Head	None	1
Center Torso	Beagle Active Probe	0
Right Torso	3 Engine	9
Left Torso	3 Engine 3 MASC	6
Right Arm	5 Endo Steel	3
Left Arm	5 Endo Steel	3
Right Leg	2 Endo Steel	0
Left Leg	2 Endo Steel	0

Weapons and Ammo	Location	Critical	Tonnage
Primary Weapons Configuration			
2 Med. Pulse Lasers	LA	2	4
2 Med. Pulse Lasers	RA	2	4
LRM 15	RT	3	7
Artemis IV FCS	RT	1	1
Ammo (LRM) 8	RT	1	1

LIGHT
MEDIUM
HEAVY
ASSAULT
OMNI

INNER SPHERE

Alternate Configuration A

TAG	H	1	1
3 ER Med. Lasers	LA	3	3
LB 10-X AC	RT	6	11
Ammo (LB-X) 20	RT	2	2

Battle Value: 1,232

Alternate Configuration B

LB 2-X AC	LA	4	6
LB 2-X AC	RA	4	6
Ammo (LB-X) 45	LT	1	1
2 ER Med. Lasers	LT	2	2
2 ER Med. Lasers	RT	2	2

Battle Value: 1,128

Alternate Configuration C

ER Small Laser	H	1	.5
Large Pulse Laser	LA	2	7
Large Pulse Laser	RA	2	7
Guardian ECM Suite	RT	2	1.5
Double Heat Sink	RT	3	1

Battle Value: 1,151

Alternate Configuration D

SRM 4	LA	1	2
SRM 4	RA	1	2
Ammo (SRM) 25	LT	1	1
2 Med. Pulse Lasers	LT	2	4
ER PPC	RT	3	7
Double Heat Sink	RT	3	1

Battle Value: 1,157

BATTLEFORCE 2

Type: Men Shen

MP	**Damage PB/M/L**	**Overheat**	**Class**
6	4/3/1	—	M
Armor/Structure	**Point Value**	**Specials**	
4/2	12	omni, prb, if	

Alternate Configuration A

MP	**Damage PB/M/L**	**Overheat**	**Class**
6	4/3/1	—	M
Armor/Structure	**Point Value**	**Specials**	
4/2	12	omni, prb, tag	

Alternate Configuration B

MP	**Damage PB/M/L**	**Overheat**	**Class**
6	4/2/—	—	M
Armor/Structure	**Point Value**	**Specials**	
4/2	11	omni, prb	

Alternate Configuration C

MP	**Damage PB/M/L**	**Overheat**	**Class**
6	3/2/—	—	M
Armor/Structure	**Point Value**	**Specials**	
4/2	12	omni, prb, ecm	

Alternate Configuration D

MP	**Damage PB/M/L**	**Overheat**	**Class**
6	4/3/1	—	M
Armor/Structure	**Point Value**	**Specials**	
4/2	12	omni, prb	

HEL-3D HELIOS

Mass: 60 tons
Chassis: Overlord Mk. 3 Endo Steel
Power Plant: 240 Pitban
Cruising Speed: 43 kph
Maximum Speed: 65 kph
Jump Jets: Swingline X-1200
Jump Capacity: 120 meters
Armor: Taijian StarShield II

Armament:
1 MilDouglas "Emperor Bones" series Gauss Rifle
2 BlazeFire Longshot Extended Range Medium Lasers
2 MilDouglas "Duke" SRM-6 Launchers
Manufacturer: Ceres Metals Industries
Primary Factory: Warlock

Communications System: Ceres SuperComm 3
Targeting and Tracking System: Wentland Giga-Track

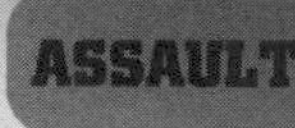

Overview

Ever since Duchess Candace Liao broke the St. Ives Compact away from the Capellan Confederation in 3029, her military commanders have pressured her to expand the military industries within her realm. Until the Clan invasion, she was content to supplement the Compact's limited BattleMech production runs with units bought from the Federated Commonwealth. With the coming of the Clans, however, that changed.

While HildCo and StarCorps each moved to quickly reintroduce proven Star League-era designs, engineering teams from Ceres Metals worked closely with St. Ives Military officers to design a new heavy BattleMech. The *Helios* design languished for a few years until Ceres could complete its new facility on Warlock, which was already turning out *Blackjack* OmniMechs. Another addition to that plant, quietly financed by ComStar, increased the number of *Helios* production lines to four.

Capabilities

With such designs as the *Victor*, the *Emperor* and the *Pillager* in service, the St. Ives Military is noticeably heavy. While those designs mount considerable firepower, they also rank among the most costly BattleMechs currently in production. The *Helios* was conceived as a low-cost "bodyguard" for such valuable units. As such, it has no need to be extremely maneuverable; its top speed is only 20 kph higher than HildCo's *Pillager*. Likewise, its mission profile suggested only sporadic close-in combat, prompting its designers to mount minimal armor protection. That left almost half of the 'Mech's mass available for weapons and ammunition.

Constructed almost entirely with Compact-built equipment, the *Helios* is designed to complement the 'Mechs it defends. The *Helios'* main hitting power comes from its Gauss rifle, giving it the capability to engage enemy units at the same range as its charges. Paired short-range missile launchers and medium lasers provide the additional firepower needed to take down any enemies that stray too close.

The basic configuration of the *Helios* changed slightly when Ceres expanded its Warlock factory. ComStar financing of the Ceres addition provided the funding necessary to purchase the new extended-range medium lasers from the Free Worlds League, which replaced the two standard medium lasers. *Helios* 'Mechs already in service will be scheduled for a retrofit of the new weapons as soon as sufficient stock is available.

Deployment

The first two runs of this 'Mech put the *Helios* in service in every St. Ives BattleMech regiment. Half of the third run is slated for ComStar, which will undoubtedly use it to make up for losses suffered in action against Clan Smoke Jaguar.

Variants

In light of recent deals signed with the Draconis Combine, two variants have been rushed into production. Candace Liao hopes these variants will boost her own military by providing new weapons to St. Ives troops, and also prove a monetary boon to the St. Ives economy when Ceres begins selling them to the Draconis Combine. The first variant removes one of the lasers to make room for a C^3 computer link. That version has only been seen twice, operating as a part of a trial C^3 unit. The second variant, the 4A, adds two tons of much-needed armor and completely revises the weapons load. An extended-range PPC, an MRM-20 launcher and three standard medium lasers turn this 'Mech into an effective close-range brawler.

HEL-3D HELIOS

Type: **Helios**
Technology Base: Inner Sphere
Tonnage: 60
Battle Value: 1,559

Equipment		Mass
Internal Structure:	Endo Steel	3
Engine:	240	11.5
Walking MP:	4	
Running MP:	6	
Jumping MP:	4	
Heat Sinks:	10 [20]	
Gyro:		3
Cockpit:		3
Armor Factor:	144	9

	Internal Structure	*Armor Value*
Head	3	9
Center Torso	20	22
Center Torso (rear)		7
R/L Torso	14	18
R/L Torso (rear)		5
R/L Arm	10	15
R/L Leg	14	15

Weapons and Ammo	Location	Critical	Tonnage
Gauss Rifle	RA	7	15
Ammo (Gauss) 16	RT	2	2
SRM 6	RT	2	3
Ammo (SRM) 15	RT	1	1
CASE	RT	1	.5
SRM 6	LT	2	3
2 ER Med. Lasers	LA	2	2
Jump Jets	RL	2	2
Jump Jets	LL	2	2

BATTLEFORCE 2

MP	Damage PB/M/L	Overheat	Class
4J	4/3/1	1	H

Armor/Structure	Point Value	Specials
4/5	16	

TSG-9H TI TS'ANG

Mass: 60 tons
Chassis: SL Special
Power Plant: 360 Hermes XL
Cruising Speed: 65 kph,
76 kph w/Triple-Strength Myomer
Maximum Speed: 97 kph,
119 kph w/Triple-Strength Myomer

Jump Jets: Chevron I
Jump Capacity: 180 meters
Armor: Durallex Heavy
Armament:
5 Diverse Optics Extended Range Medium Lasers
4 Diverse Optics Extended Range Small Lasers

Manufacturer: Ceres Metals Industries
Primary Factory: Capella
Communications System:
CeresCom Model 21-Rs
Targeting and Tracking System:
C-Apple Churchill

Overview

At the end of the Fourth Succession War, the Capellan Confederation had lost half its worlds to aggressors. Of the more than 150 Capellan regular and mercenary battalions at the beginning of the war, 65 had been utterly destroyed and an additional 46 had been captured or had defected. In capturing such a large swath of Capellan territory, the Armed Forces of the Federated Suns juggernaut had destroyed that nation's pride in itself.

When Sun Tzu Liao assumed the Celestial Throne in 3052, he immediately began several programs to restore the Confederation's reputation as a powerful nation, not only in the eyes of the other Great Houses, but also in the hearts of its own citizens. The latest and most important of these programs is the *Xin Sheng* movement, meaning new birth. Capitalizing on his position as First Lord of the new Star League, Sun-Tzu Liao has begun to preach "manifest destiny" among his people.

To aid in this endeavor, Sun-Tzu recently commissioned a series of new BattleMechs intended to epitomize the essence of House Liao. The first of these designs has overt tones of Chinese design worked into the armor of the 'Mech, similar to Draconis Combine 'Mechs that clearly display Japanese workmanship. Chancellor Liao named the new design *Ti Ts'ang*—King of the Earth's Womb and the lord of *Yen-Lo-Wang*.

Capabilities

The *Ti Ts'ang* is the Capellan Confederation's first attempt at a 'Mech equipped with a weapon designed for hand-to-hand combat: an ax. With the success of such new designs as the *Scarabus*, *Nightsky* and *Berserker* as well as the older *Hatchetman* and *Axman* BattleMechs, Chancellor Liao wished to create a 'Mech along the same lines for his own military.

Relying heavily on weapons purchased from the Free Worlds League, the *Ti Ts'ang* mounts a plethora of extended-range medium and small lasers that give it a blistering fusillade of firepower at short ranges. The Confederation may have problems purchasing these weapons, however, as relations between it and the Free Worlds League deteriorate.

The most stunning feature of the new 'Mech is the inclusion of triple-strength myomer, a technology pioneered by the Federated Suns. In his speech announcing the debut of this 'Mech, Sun-Tzu said, "It is time we overcame our fear of symbols from the past. That we were tricked into using defective myomer during the Fourth War is common knowledge. That it aided in our most ignominious defeat is recorded in every Great House's history books. With this BattleMech, we conquer the demon of failure and show our enemies that we have the will to use any tool available to fulfill our destiny."

Deployment

The first *Ti Ts'ang*s were delivered to Capellan units stationed on the border of the St. Ives Compact. One was also presented to the Fourth Tau Ceti Rangers, a mercenary unit that recently became a Capellan Confederation House unit.

Variants

The only variant currently in use stems from the *Ti Ts'ang* 's lack of long-range weapons. The 9J variant removes an extended-range medium laser from each torso, two ER small lasers from the left arm, the TAG and one double heat sink to free up tonnage for an ER large laser mounted in the center torso.

TSG-9H TI TS'ANG

Type: **Ti Ts'ang**
Technology Base: Inner Sphere
Tonnage: 60
Battle Value: 1,462

Equipment		**Mass**
Internal Structure:	Endo Steel	3
Engine:	360 XL	16.5
Walking MP:	6 (7)	
Running MP:	9 (11)	
Jumping MP:	6	
Heat Sinks:	13 [26]	3
Gyro:		4
Cockpit:		3
Armor Factor:	200	12.5

	Internal Structure	*Armor Value*
Head	3	9
Center Torso	20	30
Center Torso (rear)		9
R/L Torso	14	22
R/L Torso (rear)		6
R/L Arm	10	20
R/L Leg	14	28

Weapons and Ammo	**Location**	**Critical**	**Tonnage**
Hatchet	RA	4	4
2 ER Med. Lasers	RT	2	2
2 ER Med. Lasers	LT	2	2
ER Med. Laser	LA	1	1
4 ER Small Lasers	LA	4	2
TAG	CT	1	1
Triple-Strength Myomer	LT/RT	6	0
Jump Jets	LL	2	2
Jump Jet	LT	1	1
Jump Jet	RT	1	1
Jump Jets	RL	2	2

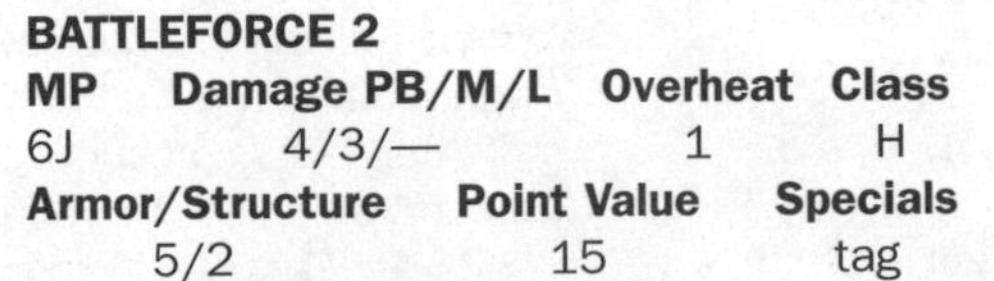

BATTLEFORCE 2

MP	**Damage PB/M/L**	**Overheat**	**Class**
6J	4/3/—	1	H

Armor/Structure	**Point Value**	**Specials**
5/2	15	tag

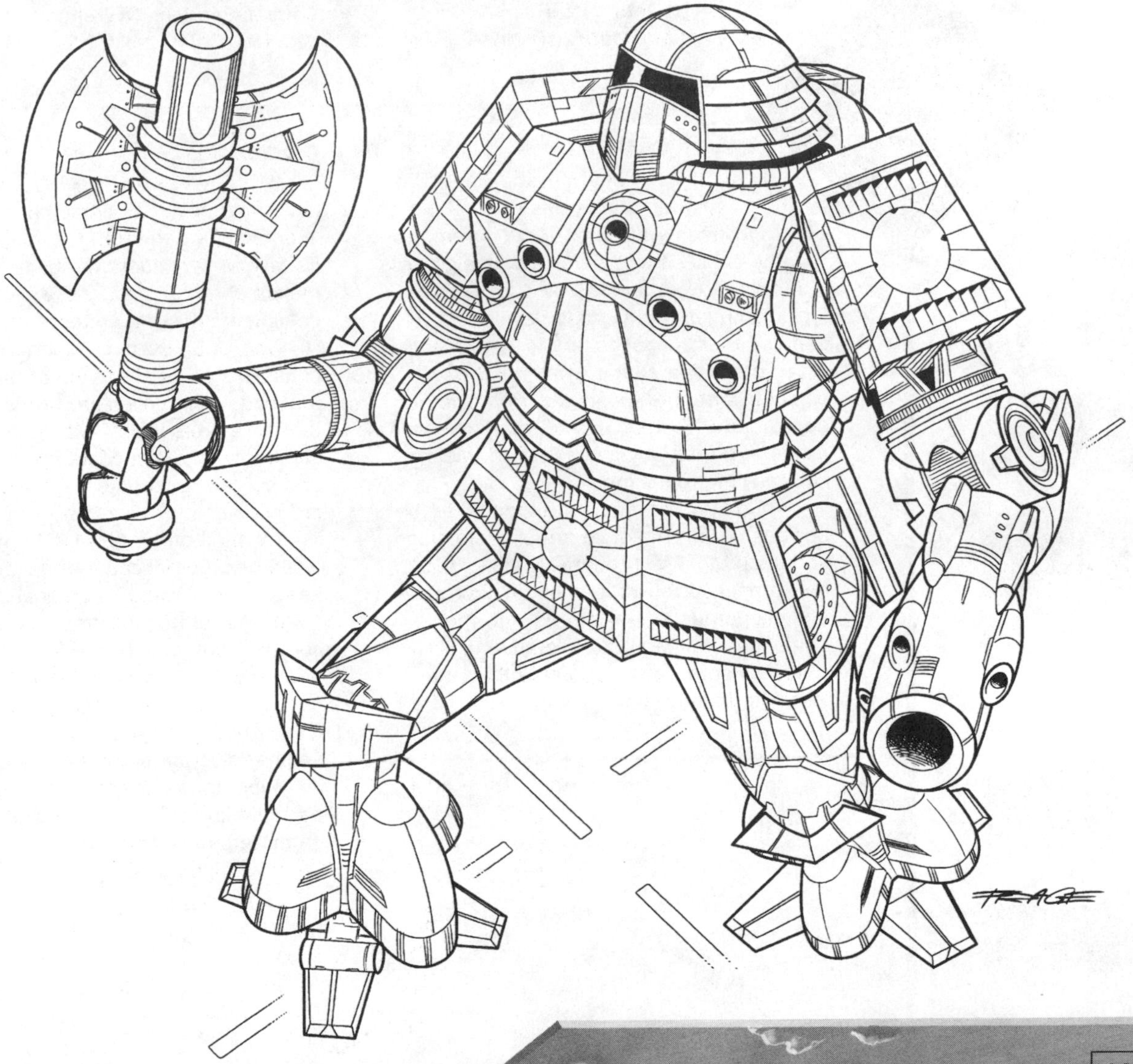

YMN-6Y YEOMAN

Mass: 60 tons
Chassis: Curtiss Yeoman
Power Plant: Pitban 240
Cruising Speed: 43 kph
Maximum Speed: 65 kph
Jump Jets: None
Jump Capacity: None

Armor: Kallon FWL Special Ferro-Fibrous
Armament: 2 Zeus LRM-15 Launchers
2 Zeus LRM-10 Launchers
Manufacturer: Curtiss Militech
Primary Factory: Paradise
Communications System:
CurtissComm Mark IV

Targeting and Tracking System:
Dynatec MissileTrac X

Overview

Along with the *Eagle*, the *Yeoman* represents Curtiss Militech's attempt to capitalize on the success of their *Wraith* design. In a departure from the *Wraith*, the *Yeoman* lacks jump jets, as Curtiss developers deemed them unnecessary for the 'Mech's main role of fire support. Intended to compete with the *Apollo* and *Trebuchet* designs, the *Yeoman* carries more missiles for its size than any Inner Sphere 'Mech currently in production.

To load on so many missile racks, the designers had to reduce armor protection and keep the 'Mech relatively slow, though they managed to avoid using an expensive and dangerous XL engine. As with the *Eagle*, the *Yeoman* uses a standard chassis, more easily reparable than the *Wraith*'s, to keep down costs.

Capabilities

With two LRM-15 racks, two LRM 10 racks and plenty of ammunition, the *Yeoman* is a dedicated fire-support 'Mech. Its lack of secondary weapons, however, makes potential pilots nervous. Curtiss designers chose to protect both side torsos with the CASE system, which will likely see considerable use because of the 'Mech's reduced armor coverage. Curtiss believed that as a fire-support 'Mech, the *Yeoman* should avoid direct contact with the enemy, and so gave priority to weapons over armor protection.

With all of the new LRM ammunition types being produced in the Free Worlds League, the *Yeoman*'s arsenal will likely see quite a bit of use. Curtiss has tried to convince potential buyers that the *Yeoman* is a natural companion to the *Eagle* because the latter's TAG system can target for the new semi-guided LRMs; the LCCC seems reluctant to believe such hype, however, apparently remembering the failed partnership of the *Hammer* and *Anvil* promoted so strongly by Free Worlds Defense Industries.

Deployment

Though the first shipment of *Yeoman*s turned up throughout the FWLM, the vast majority were distributed to the various Free Worlds Legionnaires units. Surprisingly, the Capellan Confederation has shown little interest in the new design, apparently preferring its own older *Catapult* designs for fire support.

YMN-6Y YEOMAN

Type: **Yeoman**
Technology Base: Inner Sphere
Tonnage: 60
Battle Value: 1,222

Equipment		**Mass**
Internal Structure:	Endo Steel	3
Engine:	240	11.5
Walking MP:	4	
Running MP:	6	
Jumping MP:	0	
Heat Sinks:	10 [20]	0
Gyro:		3
Cockpit:		3
Armor Factor:	152	8.5

	Internal Structure	*Armor Value*
Head	3	9
Center Torso	20	23
Center Torso (rear)		6
R/L Torso	14	21
R/L Torso (rear)		6
R/L Arm	10	15
R/L Leg	14	15

Weapons and Ammo	**Location**	**Critical**	**Tonnage**
LRM 15	RT	3	7
LRM 10	RT	2	5
Ammo (LRM) 16	RT	2	2
Ammo (LRM) 12	RT	1	1
CASE	RT	1	.5
LRM 15	LT	3	7
LRM 10	LT	2	5
Ammo (LRM) 16	LT	2	2
Ammo (LRM) 12	LT	1	1
CASE	LT	1	.5

BATTLEFORCE 2

MP	**Damage PB/M/L**	**Overheat**	**Class**
4	3/3/3	—	H

Armor/Structure	**Point Value**	**Specials**
4/5	12	if

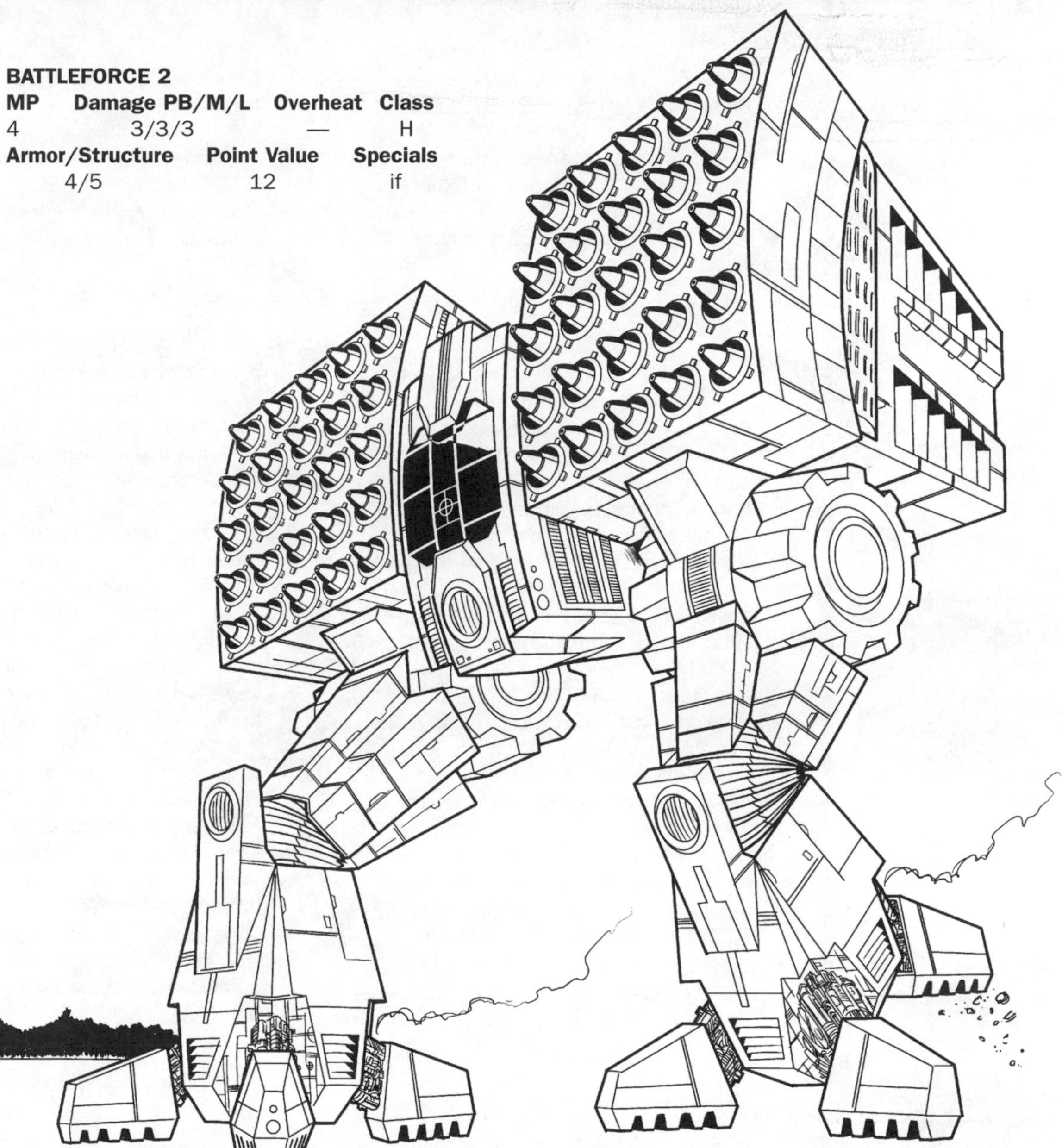

JM6-D3 JAGERMECH III

Mass: 65 tons
Chassis: Kallon Type XIV Endo Steel
Power Plant: 325 VOX XL
Cruising Speed: 57 kph
Maximum Speed: 89 kph
Jump Jets: None
Jump Capacity: None

Armor: Kallon Unity Weave Ferro-Fibrous
Armament:
2 Mydron Model D-rf Light Autocannons
2 Johnston Parti-Cannon PPCs
2 Intek Medium Lasers
Manufacturer: Kallon Industries, Independence Weaponry

Primary Factory: Talon (Kallon), Quentin (Independence)
Communications System: Garret T12-S
Targeting and Tracking System: Garret T11fc

Overview

As part of dealing with the domestic nightmare of the Federated Commonwealth's breakup, Archon Prince Victor Steiner-Davion has been forced to work overtime to repair his tarnished image as leader among his people and his troops. Returning to his warrior roots, Victor decided to boost the spirits of his subjects by commissioning updated designs of longtime mainstays of the old Federated Suns military and the AFFC. One of these updates is the *JagerMech* III. Long a favorite 'Mech of the Prince's father, the formidable Hanse Davion, the *JagerMech* was Prince Victor's first choice for a refit. Kallon Industries, manufacturer of the original design, quickly went to work.

Capabilities

The *JagerMech* was customarily relegated to support and fire roles, lacking a reputation for strength in stand-up slugfests. On Prince Victor's orders, the designers of the *JagerMech* III hoped to move the new 'Mech to high-visibility frontline roles.

To that end, the *JagerMech* III is far more robust than its predecessor. In place of the dual Ultra autocannons, the new version sports twin particle projector cannons and enough heat sinks to compensate for the heat they generate. In place of the older Type 2 autocannons, designers installed a pair of new Mydron Ultra Type 2 autocannons. Kallon technicians also upgraded the fusion reactor to give the 'Mech enough speed to keep up with Inner Sphere and Clan 'Mechs of the same weight class. The final design improvement was upgraded armor protection. The *JagerMech* III can do immense damage at long ranges; its only major drawback is a lack of significant close-range firepower.

Early field tests of the new design proved its worth. Pilots commented that the 'Mech's slightly lower center of gravity aided in maneuverability at high speeds. The *JagerMech* III also appears to blend well with FedCom heavy lances in mock simulations against Clan and Inner Sphere opponents.

Deployment

With two production runs completed, the *JagerMech* III began to appear in AFFC units. Commanders have stated that the new design will see widespread use; the initial models were placed in units bordering the Chaos March.

Even more critical than the appearance of the design is the publicity surrounding it. Both the *JagerMech* III and the *Enforcer* III are seen as important elements in rehabilitating Archon Prince Victor's image and revitalizing the morale of his nation. Using the latest technology to improve a respected design is seen as a solid move in that direction.

JM6-D3 JAGERMECH III

Type: **JagerMech III**
Technology Base: Inner Sphere
Tonnage: 65
Battle Value: 1,225

Equipment		**Mass**
Internal Structure:	Endo Steel	3.5
Engine:	325 XL	12
Walking MP:	5	
Running MP:	8	
Jumping MP:	0	
Heat Sinks:	12 [24]	2
Gyro:		4
Cockpit:		3
Armor Factor:	170	9.5

	Internal Structure	*Armor Value*
Head	3	9
Center Torso	21	26
Center Torso (rear)		7
R/L Torso	15	22
R/L Torso (rear)		6
R/L Arm	10	16
R/L Leg	15	20

Weapons and Ammo	**Location**	**Critical**	**Tonnage**
PPC	RA	3	7
PPC	LA	3	7
Ultra AC/2	RA	3	7
Ultra AC/2	LA	3	7
Ammo (Ultra) 45	RT	1	1
Med. Laser	LT	1	1
Med. Laser	RT	1	1

BATTLEFORCE 2

MP	**Damage PB/M/L**	**Overheat**	**Class**
5	3/3/2	1	H

Armor/Structure	**Point Value**	**Specials**
4/3	12	

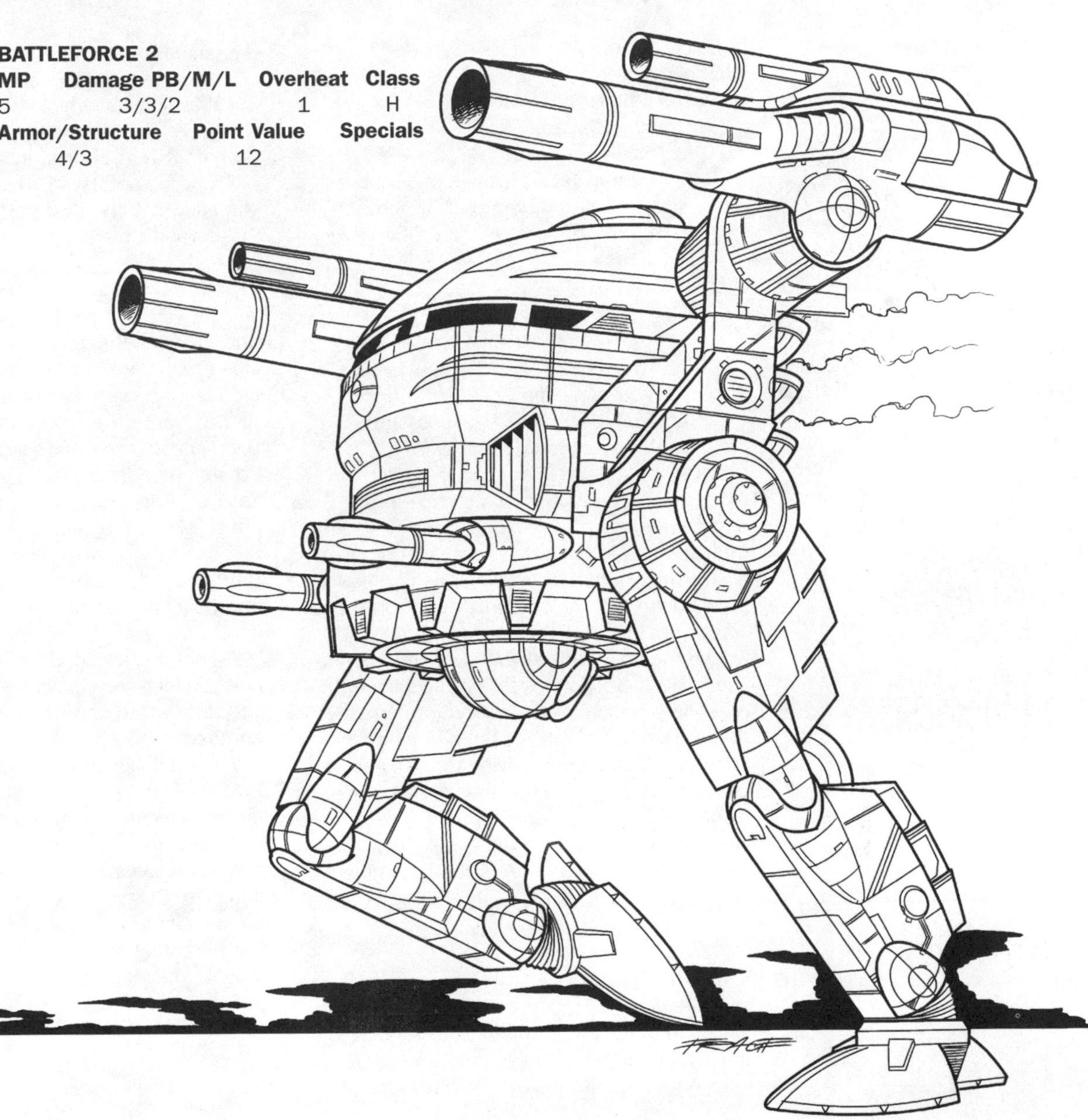

JN-G8A JINGGAU

Mass: 65 tons
Chassis: Chariot Type II Endo Steel
Power Plant: 325 VOX XL
Cruising Speed: 54 kph
Maximum Speed: 86 kph
Jump Jets: Hellespont Leapers
Jump Capacity: 150 meters
Armor: Valiant DefCo
Armament: 1 Zhi-tong-yao Gauss Rifle
4 Diverse Optics Extended Range Medium Lasers
1 Raker-IV Medium Pulse Laser
Manufacturer: Shengli Arms
Primary Factory: Victoria
Communications System: Dian-bao Comms, heavily insulated
Targeting and Tracking System: Dynatec Special T&T

Overview

Toward the end of 3058, Word of Blake's Toyama faction began providing Capellan Chancellor Sun-Tzu Liao with technicians and material resources to help finish overhauling the old Star League production facility on Victoria. This assistance, apparently part of a personal debt owed to Chancellor Liao, increased production of the *Duan Gung* BattleMech design and helped the Capellans to quickly finish work on the *Jinggau* assembly line. The first *Jinggau* (which means siren) reportedly came off the line in early 3059, though for undisclosed reasons production was halted for more than a year, and then resumed in limited numbers. Engineers studying the *Jinggau* are curious about its extended-range medium lasers, which are produced in the Free Worlds League. As with the *Duan Gung*, all parts for the *Jinggau* except for its jumpjets and targeting system are intended to be built on Victoria.

Capabilities

The *Jinggau* is designed to wade into the middle of combat rather than skulking around the edges or hoping for a few lucky long-range hits. Its top-end mobility for its weight, with a running speed of over 85 kph and 150-meter jump capability, allow it to close fairly rapidly in almost any terrain. For crossing open areas or engaging in stand-up battles, more than eleven tons of armor give the *Jinggau* excellent odds of survival. Presenting a lance of *Jinggau* to the Fourth Tau Ceti Rangers, Sun-Tzu Liao said, "This is not a 'Mech relegated to support roles, or reconnaissance or garrison duty. This is a BattleMech for seeking out your opponent and doing him harm. This is a 'Mech with which to make your enemy miserable."

That misery comes primarily from the new *Zhi-tong-yao* ("painkiller") Gauss rifle. The rifle, which can worry the pilot of even an assault 'Mech, delivers hard blows until the *Jinggau* closes to the range of its Diverse Optics lasers. At that point, the lasers seek weakened spots to eviscerate an enemy machine, while the Gauss rifle continues to deliver its knock-down power punches. Carrying sixteen rounds of ammunition, in the hands of an experienced MechWarrior the *Jinggau* can expect to match up against three other BattleMechs before requiring a reload.

Deployment

Chancellor Liao presented the Fourth Tau Ceti Rangers with one of the first *Jinggau* lances, on the day they accepted his offer to become a regular House Liao regiment. Other *Jinggau* have been seen in the Daidachi and Kamata Warrior Houses, and the Chancellor's Death Commandos will likely field them as well.

Even as the *Jinggau* made its debut, however, rumors regarding the Shengli Arms facility continued to spread, especially with regard to this design. Stories circulate of off-limits areas, and portions of the *Jinggau* assembly line that are shut down and under guard. Post-production analysis of the BattleMech bears out some of the rumors, in that both arm sections have obviously been redesigned. This could account for the delays in reaching full production, but begs the question of why the CCAF apparently fielded a variant ahead of the primary design.

JN-G8A JINGGAU

Type: **Jinggau**
Technology Base: Inner Sphere
Tonnage: 65
Battle Value: 1,915

Equipment		**Mass**
Internal Structure:	Endo Steel	3.5
Engine:	325 XL	12
Walking MP:	5	
Running MP:	8	
Jumping MP:	5	
Heat Sinks:	13 [26]	3
Gyro:		4
Cockpit:		3
Armor Factor:	184	11.5
	Internal Structure	*Armor Value*
Head	3	9
Center Torso	21	28
Center Torso (rear)		9
R/L Torso	15	24
R/L Torso (rear)		6
R/L Arm	10	17
R/L Leg	15	22

Weapons and Ammo	**Location**	**Critical**	**Tonnage**
Gauss Rifle	RA	7	15
Ammo (Gauss) 16	RT	2	2
Med. Pulse Laser	RA	1	2
4 ER Med. Lasers	LA	4	4
Jump Jets	RL	2	2
Jump Jet	CT	1	1
Jump Jets	LL	2	2

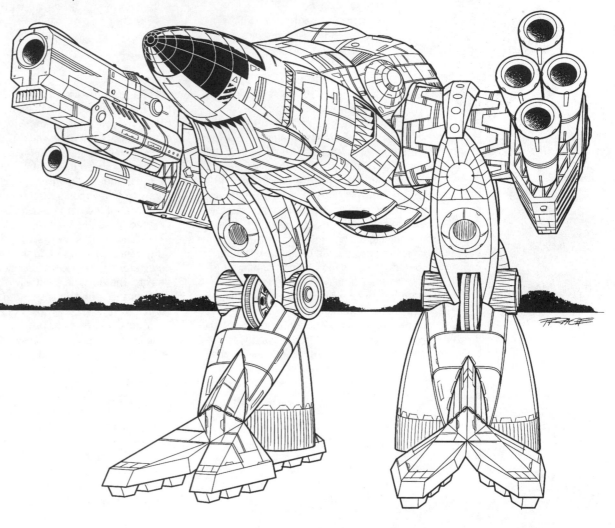

BATTLEFORCE 2

MP	**Damage PB/M/L**	**Overheat**	**Class**
5J	4/4/1	—	H

Armor/Structure	**Point Value**	**Specials**
5/3	19	

BGS-1T BARGHEST

Mass: 70 tons
Chassis: Earthwerk GRF Quad
Power Plant: 350 Magna XL
Cruising Speed: 54 kph
Maximum Speed: 86 kph
Jump Jets: None
Jump Capacity: None
Armor: Durallex Heavy

Armament:
2 BlazeFire Sweetshot Extended Range Large Lasers
1 Defiance Disintegrator LB 20-X Autocannon
Manufacturer: TharHes Industries
Primary Factory: Tharkad

Communications System:
TharHes Euterpe HM-14
Targeting and Tracking System:
TharHes Ares-8a

Overview

This new and unusual design was the brainchild of Katrina Steiner, Archon of the Lyran Alliance. The Archon informed TharHes Industries of Tharkad that she wished to create a new design with a terrifying visage, like that of the *Atlas* or the *Banshee*. She also wanted to make it a four-legged design. TharHes executives attempted to dissuade her from the quad design, which has been much maligned for centuries, but failed. Only during the final testing of the new 'Mech, when new four-legged designs appeared in the Draconis Combine and Free Worlds League militaries, did TharHes Industries appreciate the political and military implications of a new quad design in the Lyran Alliance Armed Forces. Upon viewing the finished 'Mech's animalistic grace and power, the Archon named it *Barghest*, after the savage, wolf-like creatures of mythology.

Capabilities

Early in the design process, several designers noticed the similarities between preliminary designs for the *Barghest* and the highly successful *Bushwacker*, with its exceptionally long, low chassis. The engineers moved the *Bushwacker*'s legs forward, enabling them to install the rear legs and to overcome many of the complicated interior layout problems that so plagued the early *Bushwacker*.

Many months were spent on simulators and live-fire ranges to find the weapons configuration that would best suit this new design. The designers initially rejected the weapon that proved the most effective complement to a four-legged design, the large-bore autocannon. Unwilling to mount such an antiquated weapon on their new 'Mech, they spent considerable time looking for another solution. The entire project was on the verge of shutdown when Defiance Industries of Hesperus II made the breakthrough into large-bore LB-X and Ultra autocannons. An LB-X Type 20 autocannon was shipped to Tharkad, where designers mounted it on the *Barghest* alongside twin extended-range large lasers. This weapon configuration was extremely successful, and the new 'Mech soon began full production.

Deployment

The first *Barghests* went to five newly christened units of the Alliance Jaegers: the Bolan, Skye, Donegal, Coventry and Alarion Jaegers. Each unit began as a battalion, charged by the Archon to form an elite regiment from one of the five new Lyran Alliance provinces. With each unit drawing recruits from only one province, the Archon hopes to inspire feelings of Lyran national pride.

Variants

The only variant currently available switches the LB-X for an Ultra/20 autocannon and exchanges the twin extended-range large lasers for a single extended-range PPC. The additional tonnage freed up by the weapons change made room for one more double heat sink to increase heat dissipation, along with one more ton of armor.

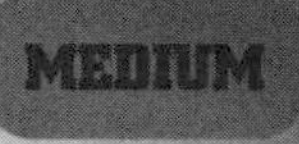

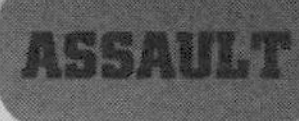

BGS-1T BARGHEST

Type: **Barghest**
Technology Base: Inner Sphere
Tonnage: 70
Battle Value: 1,205

Equipment		**Mass**
Internal Structure:		7
Engine:	350 XL	15
Walking MP:	5	
Running MP:	8	
Jumping MP:	0	
Heat Sinks:	10 [20]	0
Gyro:		4
Cockpit:		3
Armor Factor:	208	13

	Internal Structure	*Armor Value*
Head	3	9
Center Torso	22	30
Center Torso (rear)		9
R/L Torso	15	21
R/L Torso (rear)		6
R/L Front Legs	15	27
R/L Rear Legs	15	26

Weapons and Ammo	**Location**	**Critical**	**Tonnage**
2 ER Large Lasers	LT	4	10
LB 20-X AC	RT/CT	11	14
Ammo (LB-X) 10	LRL	2	2
Ammo (LB-X) 10	RRL	2	2

BATTLEFORCE 2

MP	**Damage PB/M/L**	**Overheat**	**Class**
5	3/2/1	2	H

Armor/Structure	**Point Value**	**Specials**
5/3	12	

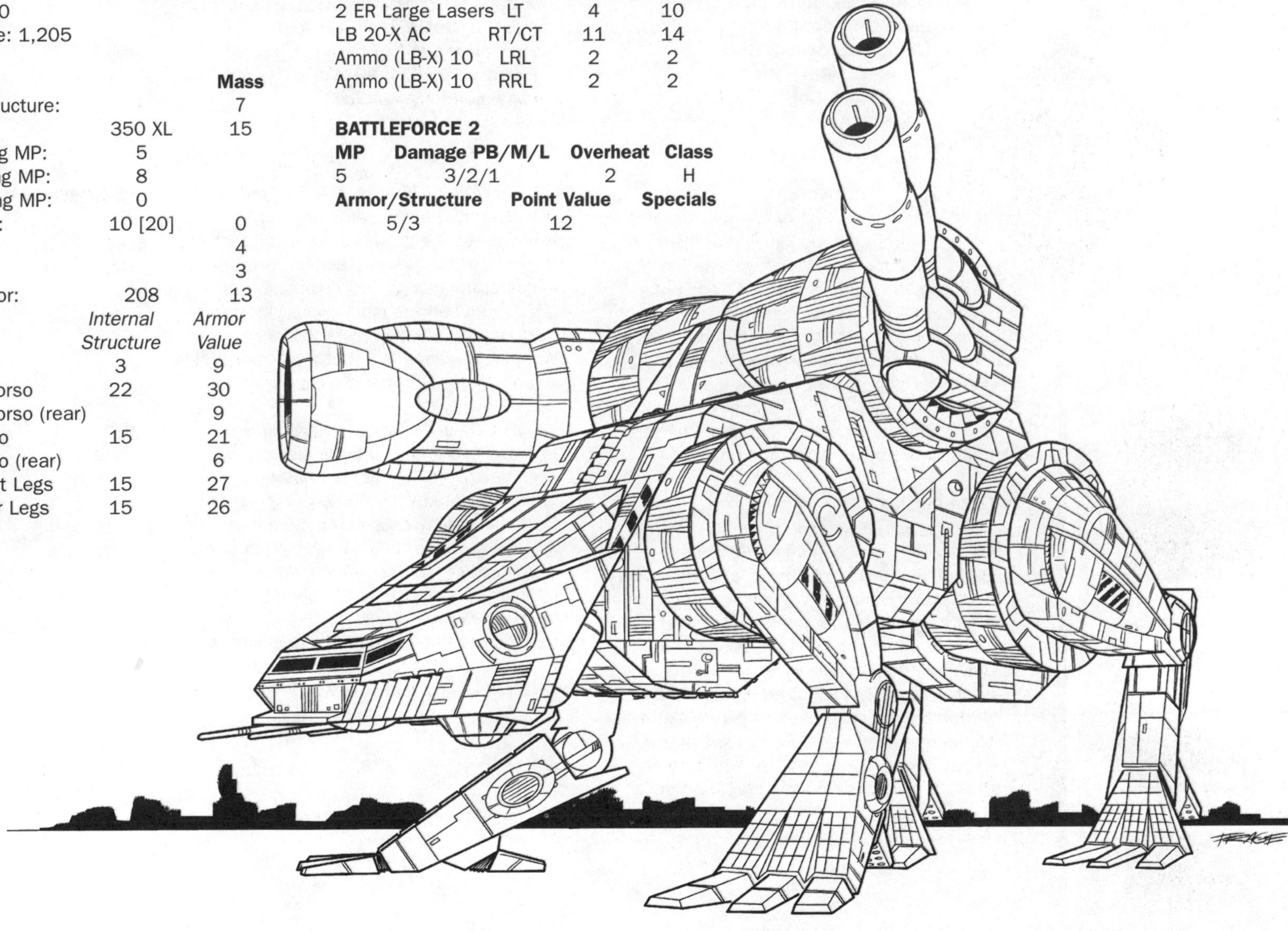

SJA-7D SHUGENJA

Mass: 75 tons
Chassis: Alshain Type Heavy Chi
Power Plant: 300 Vlar XL
Cruising Speed: 54 kph
Maximum Speed: 86 kph
Jump Jets: None
Jump Capacity: None
Armor: Ferro-Fibrous

Armament:
1 Lord's Light Extended Range PPC
2 Diverse Optics Type 30 Large Lasers
1 Shigunga MRM-30 Launcher
Manufacturer: Independence Weaponry
Primary Factory: Quentin
Communications System:
Garret T-19F with C^3 Computer

Targeting and Tracking System:
Cat's Eyes 5

Overview

One of two new designs from Independence Weaponry on Quentin, the *Shugenja*, like the *Tai-sho*, is equipped with a C^3 computer system. This new design follows in the footsteps of the *Naginata*, also produced by Independence Weaponry. As the C^3 computer has finally begun to lose its stigma among Combine warriors, Independence expects sales of all three units to skyrocket within the next year.

Capabilities

Impressed with the maneuverability and survivability of the unusual *Komodo* BattleMech design, Independence Weaponry contacted Luthien Armor Works to purchase the design specs for its base Alshain-type chassis. After acquiring the chassis, designers began altering it to support an additional thirty tons of equipment and armor. The finished chassis bears a striking similarity to the *Komodo*, causing several executives at Luthien Armor Works to call the new design "*Komodo*'s big brother."

As with the *Tai-sho*, the *Shugenja* is built around a C^3 master computer. However, unlike the *Tai-sho* and *Naginata* designs, which mount standard low-cost engines, the design specifications of this 'Mech required the more expensive extra-light engine. However, Independence Weaponry is confident that the power of this new design morc than offsets the higher price tag.

The 'Mech's weapons complement includes two standard large lasers, an extended-range PPC and an MRM-30 launcher armed with the new Shigunga medium-range missiles. The seemingly mystical ability of this new design to bring that firepower to bear on almost any opponent regardless of the speeds or terrain involved—thanks to the superior targeting of the C^3 system in conjunction with the 'Mech's lance mates—gave the*Shugenja* its name, which means "magic user."

Deployment

As with the *Tai-sho*, the first *Shugenja*s have been shipped to the Genyosha regiments.

SJA-7D SHUGENJA

Type: **Shugenja**
Technology Base: Inner Sphere
Tonnage: 75
Battle Value: 1,274

Equipment		**Mass**
Internal Structure:		7.5
Engine:	300 XL	9.5
Walking MP:	4	
Running MP:	6	
Jumping MP:	0	
Heat Sinks:	15 [30]	5
Gyro:		3
Cockpit:		3
Armor Factor:	231	13

	Internal Structure	*Armor Value*
Head	3	9
Center Torso	23	35
Center Torso (rear)		11
R/L Torso	16	24
R/L Torso (rear)		8
R/L Arm	12	24
R/L Leg	16	32

Weapons and Ammo	**Location**	**Critical**	**Tonnage**
ER PPC	LA	3	7
MRM 30	LT	5	10
Ammo (MRM) 16	LT	2	2
2 Large Lasers	RA	4	10
C^3 Computer	RT	5	5

BATTLEFORCE 2

MP	**Damage PB/M/L**	**Overheat**	**Class**
4	4/2/1	1	H

Armor/Structure	**Point Value**	**Specials**
6/3	15	c3m

TYM-1A TOYAMA

Mass: 75 tons
Chassis: Endo Steel
Power Plant: 300 VLAR XL
Cruising Speed: 43 kph
Maximum Speed: 65 kph
Jump Jets: None
Jump Capacity: None
Armor: Durallex Heavy

Armament:
2 Diverse Optics Sunbeam Extended Range Large Lasers
1 Doombud LRM-20 Launcher
3 Magna Mark II Medium Lasers
1 Imperator Code Red LB 10-X Autocannon

Manufacturer:
Gibson Federated BattleMechs
Primary Factory: Gibson
Communications System: Basix 200
Targeting and Tracking System: Garret a99

Overview

The *Toyama*, like the *Buccaneer* and the *Grand Crusader*, was designed and built for the Word of Blake following their exodus to Gibson. Unlike many other new Word of Blake 'Mechs, the *Toyama* was designed by an outsider—Dr. Thaddeus Anable, a military technology consultant with the Free Worlds League's Heliopolis design labs. As part of an arrangement with Captain-General Thomas Marik, Anable passed the design to the Word of Blake, who put it into production in early 3057.

Capabilities

Designed as a multi-purpose 'Mech, the *Toyama* can engage in extended operations without resupply. Its main weapons are a pair of Diverse Optics Sunbeam extended-range large lasers mounted in the right arm. A Doombud LRM-20 in the torso and an Imperator Code Red autocannon in the left arm provide additional firepower in short engagements. With storage capacity for two full tons of autocannon ammunition, the *Toyama* can carry a mix of rounds, allowing the pilot to tailor the 'Mech's loadout to his own preference or mission requirements. A cluster of lasers in the 'Mech's torso provides additional firepower, though their effective range is less than 300 meters and their tracking capabilities are limited.

The *Toyama* also carries a state-of-the-art defense measure in the right torso: the Guardian ECM system, which limits the effectiveness of advanced targeting and tracking systems used in close proximity to the 'Mech. The original design called for an anti-missile system to be installed alongside the ECM system, but space considerations ultimately caused the designers to omit the anti-missile system in favor of a larger LRM launcher.

Deployment

To date, the *Toyama* has been deployed only with the Word of Blake Militia. Plans to ship several to the Atrean Dragoons were postponed when the Word of Blake launched Operation Odysseus, in which Blake Militia troops masquerading as the mercenary 21st Centauri Lancers infiltrated and sabotaged ComStar's defenses on Terra. During that operation, the Blakist forces used at least four *Toyama*s.

TYM-1A TOYAMA

Type: **Toyama**
Technology Base: Inner Sphere
Tonnage: 75
Battle Value: 1,352

Equipment		**Mass**
Internal Structure:	Endo Steel	4
Engine:	300 XL	9.5
Walking MP:	4	
Running MP:	6	
Jumping MP:	0	
Heat Sinks:	14 [28]	4
Gyro:		3
Cockpit:		3
Armor Factor:	192	12

	Internal Structure	*Armor Value*
Head	3	9
Center Torso	23	30
Center Torso (rear)		9
R/L Torso	16	20
R/L Torso (rear)		7
R/L Arm	12	20
R/L Leg	16	25

Weapons and Ammo	**Location**	**Critical**	**Tonnage**
2 ER Large Lasers	RA	4	10
LRM 20	RT	5	10
Ammo (LRM) 12	RT	2	2
3 Med. Lasers	LT	3	3
Guardian ECM Suite	RT	2	1.5
LB 10-X AC	LA	6	11
Ammo (LB-X) 20	LA	2	2

BATTLEFORCE 2

MP	**Damage PB/M/L**	**Overheat**	**Class**
4	4/4/3	1	H

Armor/Structure	**Point Value**	**Specials**
5/3	14	ecm

BKW-7 BLACK WATCH

Mass: 85 tons
Chassis: Norse Heavy XT2-1A
Power Plant: Strand 255
Cruising Speed: 32 kph
Maximum Speed: 54 kph
Jump Jets: Rawlings 54
Jump Capacity: 90 meters

Armor: Valiant Lamellor with CASE
Armament:
1 Imperator Light Gauss Rifle
1 Imperator Automatic Ultra-10 Autocannon
1 Shigunga MRM-40 Launcher
Manufacturer: Cosara Weaponries
Primary Factory: Northwind

Communications System:
O/P AIR500 with C^3 Slave Unit
Targeting and Tracking System:
DLK Type Phased Array Sensor System

Overview

The prototype *Black Watch* currently undergoing testing is the fulfillment of several dreams. The first dream was that of Cosara Weaponries, producers of the *Crab* 'Mech, who wanted to expand their operations. The second dream was dear to the Northwind Highlanders, who have long craved the independence that Wolf's Dragoons and the Kell Hounds enjoy in having their own private suppliers of military hardware. Finally, Captain Neil Campbell of the Royal Black Watch Company dreamed of creating a 'Mech that would symbolize the new spirit of unity in the Inner Sphere by incorporating technologies from various Successor States. The *Black Watch* is the result of all these dreams coming together.

Capabilities

The *Black Watch* is built around the same chassis as the SLDF's training 'Mech, the *Crockett*. Cosara Weaponries chose that design for its ruggedness and its jump jets—the latter an unusual feature on an assault 'Mech.

Early in the planning stages, the engineers wanted to install an extralight engine. However, that soon changed because of the extent to which an XL engine makes a 'Mech vulnerable in battle. Though XL engines weigh less than standard engines, allowing a 'Mech to carry considerably more weaponry and equipment, they are also bulky, taking up vast areas of the 'Mech's torso. Attacks that damage the torso are therefore much more likely to inflict critical damage to an XL engine than to a standard model.

When the designers were selecting weaponry for the *Black Watch*, the debate centered around the new 'Mech's mission. Captain Campbell pushed the idea that, while this 'Mech must be combat-ready, its primary goal is to act as a reminder that the Inner Sphere can and must face the Clans united. He therefore petitioned to incorporate Draconis Combine and Free Worlds League weaponry into the design. After many months of negotiation, the new Shigunga medium-range missile system and C^3 slave equipment from the Draconis Combine, as well as Imperator Automatic Weaponry's new light Gauss rifle and Ultra-10 autocannon from the Free Worlds League, were shipped to Northwind to be installed on the new 'Mech.

Many critics of the new design believe that its haphazard creation will be its downfall. As proof, they point out that additional shipments of weapons and equipment from the Free Worlds League and the Draconis Combine hinge upon the results of the 'Mech's initial testing.

Deployment

The *Black Watch* is currently in the prototype stage, undergoing testing that will decide its future. However, the Clan Elders on Northwind have already stated that the first machines off the production line will go to the Royal Black Watch Company, after which they will begin to fill requests from other Highlander units.

LIGHT

MEDIUM

BKW-7R BLACK WATCH

Type: **Black Watch**
Technology Base: Inner Sphere
Tonnage: 85
Battle Value: 1,855

Equipment		**Mass**
Internal Structure:	Endo Steel	4.5
Engine:	255	13
Walking MP:	3	
Running MP:	5	
Jumping MP:	3	
Heat Sinks:	10 [20]	0
Gyro:		3
Cockpit:		3
Armor Factor:	240	15
	Internal Structure	*Armor Value*
Head	3	9
Center Torso	27	37
Center Torso (rear)		12
R/L Torso	18	26
R/L Torso (rear)		10
R/L Arm	14	24
R/L Leg	18	31

Weapons and Ammo	**Location**	**Critical**	**Tonnage**
Light Gauss Rifle	LA	5	12
Ammo (Light Gauss) 16	LT	1	1
Ultra AC/10	RA	7	13
Ammo (Ultra) 20	RT	2	2
MRM 40	LT	7	12
Ammo (MRM) 12	RT	2	2
CASE	RT	1	.5
C³ Slave	H	1	1
Jump Jet	RT	1	1
Jump Jet	CT	1	1
Jump Jet	LT	1	1

BATTLEFORCE 2

MP	**Damage PB/M/L**	**Overheat**	**Class**
3J	4/3/2	—	A

Armor/Structure	**Point Value**	**Specials**
6/7	16	c3s

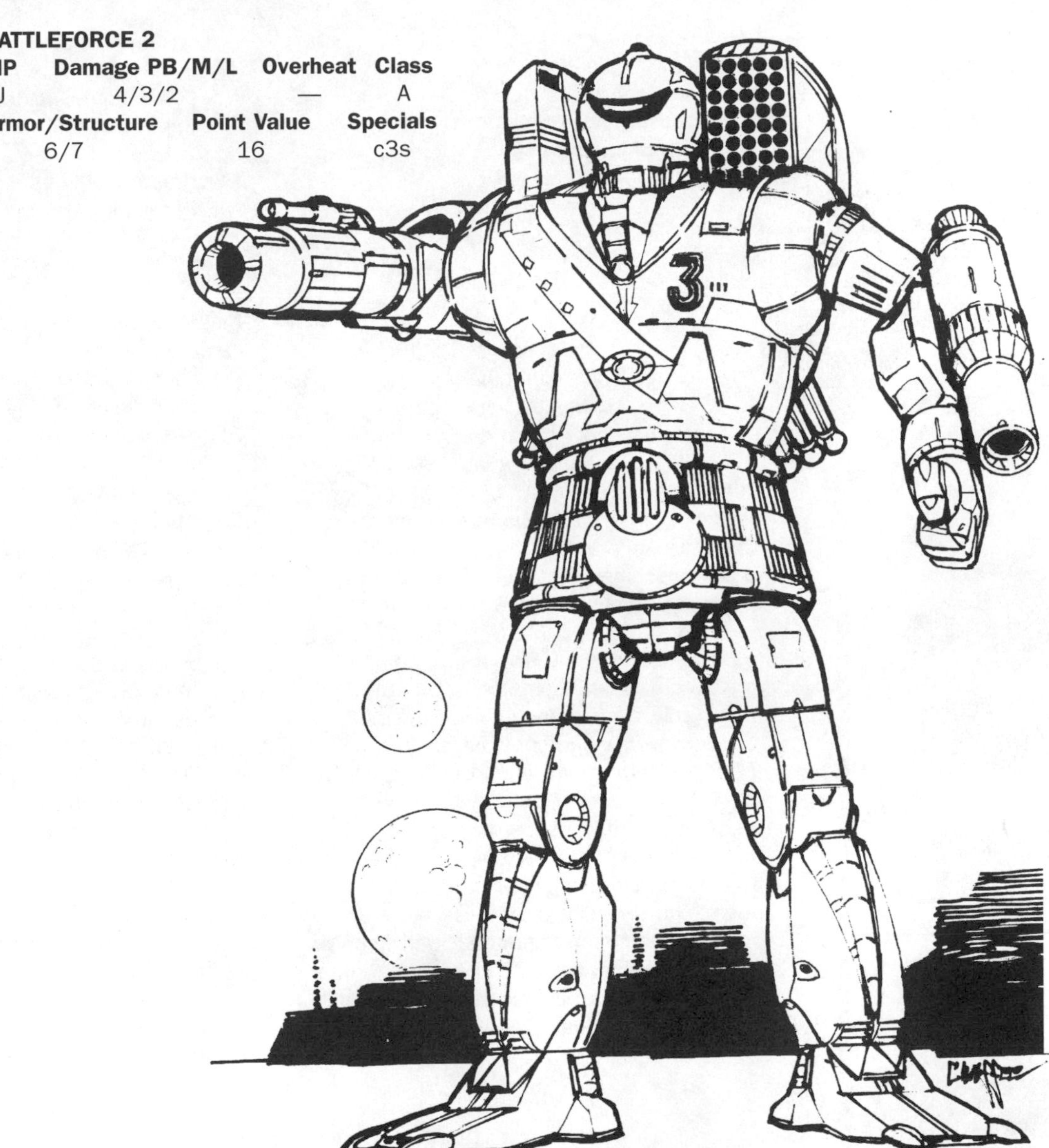

TSH-7S TAI-SHO

Mass: 85 tons
Chassis: Star League XT
Power Plant: 255 Strand
Cruising Speed: 32 kph
Maximum Speed: 54 kph
Jump Jets: None
Jump Capacity: None

Armor: Durallex with Ferro-Fibrous
Armament:
2 Lord's Light 2 Extended Range PPCs
1 Imperator Automatic Ultra-10 Autocannon
Manufacturer: Independence Weaponry
Primary Factory: Quentin

Communications System:
Garret T-19G with dual C^3 Computer
Targeting and Tracking System:
Cat's Eyes 5

Overview

For ten years, the Draconis Combine has possessed the C^3 computer system, a technological marvel designed to coordinate lance and company actions. Despite the best efforts of the DCMS, however, the system has rarely been used. The Draconis Combine has historically lacked machines that incorporate the C^3, and most Combine MechWarriors are resistant to change. Many are particularly loath to abandon the samurai tradition of single combat and combine to fire on a single unit, a tactic the C^3 encourages.

However, the spectacular success of the C^3 system in Operation Bulldog against the Smoke Jaguars finally overcame the reservations of Combine warriors regarding this equipment. The deciding event seems to have occurred when *Tai-sa* Hohiro Kurita, heir to the Combine throne, led a C^3-equipped company of the elite Genyosha regiment against the 362nd Assault Cluster on Kiamba. There, in Hecate's Swamp, Hohiro's forces destroyed the Assault Cluster's Command Trinary. These events meant considerable profits for Independence Weaponry, as that manufacturer's two newest designs, the *Tai-sho* and the *Shugenja*, both incorporate C^3 master systems.

Capabilities

The *Tai-sho* was intended as the centerpiece of a C^3-equipped company of twelve units. By designing the *Tai-sho* to carry two C^3 masters, Independence Weaponry produced a 'Mech that carries maximum armor protection for its size, as well as mounting impressive firepower despite the tonnage lost to the C^3 systems.

Twin extended-range particle projector cannons, plus an Ultra type 10 autocannon purchased from the Free Worlds League, give the *Tai-sho* its devastating punch. Using a standard engine rather than an extra-light model prolongs the 'Mech's life on the battlefield and also cuts production costs considerably.

Deployment

The first *Tai-sho*s produced were slated for assignment to the First Genyosha, the regiment with the most C^3-equipped units in the DCMS, once they returned from their efforts to finish off the Smoke Jaguars in the Deep Periphery. Units produced subsequently will be assigned to other DCMS regiments.

To express their gratitude and to honor the heir to the Dragon, Independence Weaponry planned to give Hohiro Kurita the first *Tai-sho* off the assembly lines. Whether he will trade his Clan-manufactured *Daishi* for the new 'Mech remains to be seen.

TSH-7S TAI-SHO

Type: **Tai-sho**
Technology Base: Inner Sphere
Tonnage: 85
BattleValue: 1,518

Equipment		**Mass**
Internal Structure:		8.5
Engine:	255	13
Walking MP:	3	
Running MP:	5	
Jumping MP:	0	
Heat Sinks:	13 [26]	3
Gyro:		3
Cockpit:		3
Armor Factor:	269	15

	Internal Structure	*Armor Value*
Head	3	9
Center Torso	27	41
Center Torso (rear)		13
R/L Torso	18	27
R/L Torso (rear)		9
R/L Arm	14	28
R/L Leg	18	36

Weapons and Ammo	**Location**	**Critical**	**Tonnage**
ER PPC	RA	3	7
ER PPC	LA	3	7
Ultra AC/10	RT	7	13
Ammo (Ultra) 20	RT	2	2
CASE	RT	1	.5
2 C3 Computers	LT	10	10

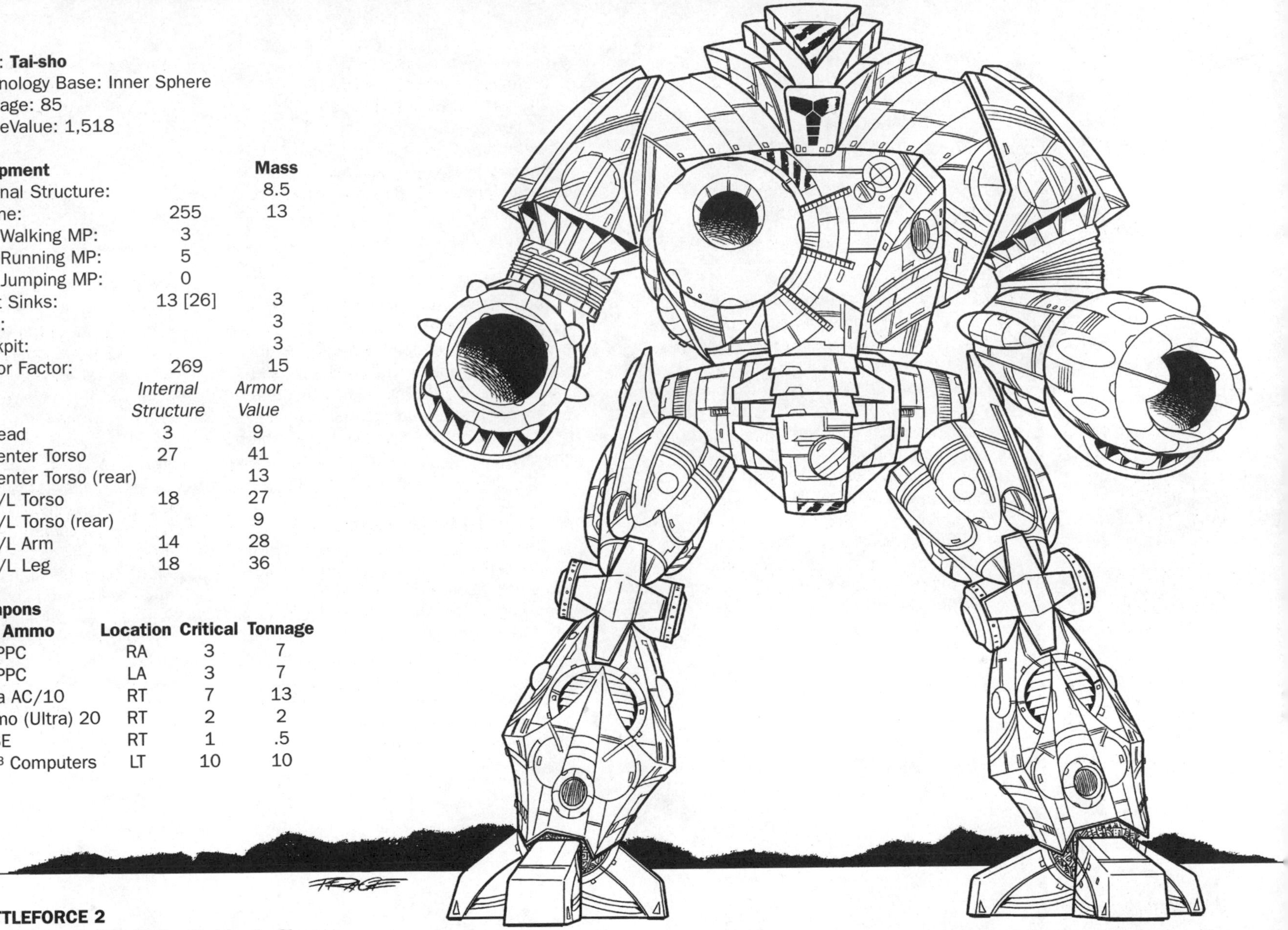

BATTLEFORCE 2

MP	**Damage PB/M/L**	**Overheat**	**Class**
3	3/2/2	2	A

Armor/Structure	**Point Value**	**Specials**
7/7	15	c3m, c3m

VKG-2F VIKING

Mass: 90 tons
Chassis: GC Type 1 Endo Steel
Power Plant: GM 270
Cruising Speed: 32 kph
Maximum Speed: 54 kph
Jump Jets: None
Jump Capacity: None
Armor: GC Slab

Armament: 2 Shigunga LRM-20 Launchers
2 Shigunga LRM-15 Launchers
2 ChisComp 32 Small Lasers
4 SperryBrowning Machine Guns
Manufacturer: Grumium Creations
Primary Factory: Grumium
Communications System: GC Wave 12B

Targeting and Tracking System:
GC MultiTrac System Type 6

Overview

The *Viking* is the second 'Mech co-produced by ComStar and the Free Rasalhague Republic, following quickly on the heels of the *Beowulf*. ComStar chose to upgrade the Grumium Creations factory, taking a small company that provided various parts and systems and turning it into a production powerhouse. Second only to Odin Manufacturing in the Free Rasalhague Republic, Grumium Creations looks to turn a profit from now on, having obtained contracts to produce several other units for ComStar and the Free Rasalhague Republic in the future.

Capabilities

When ComStar officials requested a new fire-support BattleMech that could take over for the aging *Bombardier*, Grumium was happy to oblige. The company used connections in the Draconis Combine to obtain permits to purchase large numbers of Shigunga missile launchers, and built the chassis and internal workings of the *Viking* around the launchers. Grumium designers gave each launcher plenty of ammunition, and equipped the launchers with the Artemis IV fire-control system to improve their accuracy. Backup weaponry consists of two small lasers and four machine guns, a somewhat paltry short-range assortment.

The *Viking* lacks an XL engine because its mahufacturer could not afford them, so its speed is poor compared to the *Bombardier*. However, Grumium designers hope that the *Viking*'s heavy armor and dual CASE systems will make it attractive to pilots all the same.

Deployment

As with the *Beowulf*, half the *Viking*s produced go to the Com Guards, the other half to the Rasalhague Kungsärmé. *Viking*s have so far appeared only in the Third Hussars of the Kungsärmé and the 403rd Division of the Com Guards.

Variants

Grumium has produced one variant of the *Viking*, popular with the Third Hussars. An unusual variant, practically a new design, it replaces all of the standard weaponry with a large pulse laser in the right arm and three medium pulse lasers in the left. A Gauss rifle rests in the right torso and an LB 10-X autocannon sits in the left, each with two tons of ammunition. The variant, dubbed the 2G, retains the CASE systems and adds two tons of armor, a Guardian ECM suite and two double heat sinks.

VKG-2F VIKING

Type: **Viking**
Technology Base: Inner Sphere
Tonnage: 90
Battle Value: 1,749

Equipment		**Mass**
Internal Structure:	Endo Steel	4.5
Engine:	270	14.5
Walking MP:	3	
Running MP:	5	
Jumping MP:	0	
Heat Sinks:	10 [20]	0
Gyro:		3
Cockpit:		3
Armor Factor:	248	15.5
	Internal Structure	*Armor Value*
Head	3	9
Center Torso	29	33
Center Torso (rear)		10
R/L Torso	19	31
R/L Torso (rear)		7
R/L Arm	15	30
R/L Leg	19	30

Weapons and Ammo	**Location**	**Critical**	**Tonnage**
LRM 20	RA	5	10
Artemis IV FCS	RA	1	1
LRM 20	LA	5	10
Artemis IV FCS	LA	1	1
LRM 15	RT	3	7
Artemis IV FCS	RT	1	1
Small Laser	RT	1	.5
Ammo (LRM) 12	RT	2	2
Ammo (LRM) 16	RT	2	2
CASE	RT	1	.5
LRM 15	LT	3	7
Artemis IV FCS	LT	1	1
Small Laser	LT	1	.5
Ammo (LRM) 12	LT	2	2
Ammo (LRM) 8	LT	1	1
Ammo (MG) 100	LT	1	.5
CASE	LT	1	.5
2 Machine Guns	RL	2	1
2 Machine Guns	LL	2	1

BATTLEFORCE 2

MP	**Damage PB/M/L**	**Overheat**	**Class**
3	6/6/6	—	A

Armor/Structure	**Point Value**	**Specials**
6/7	18	if

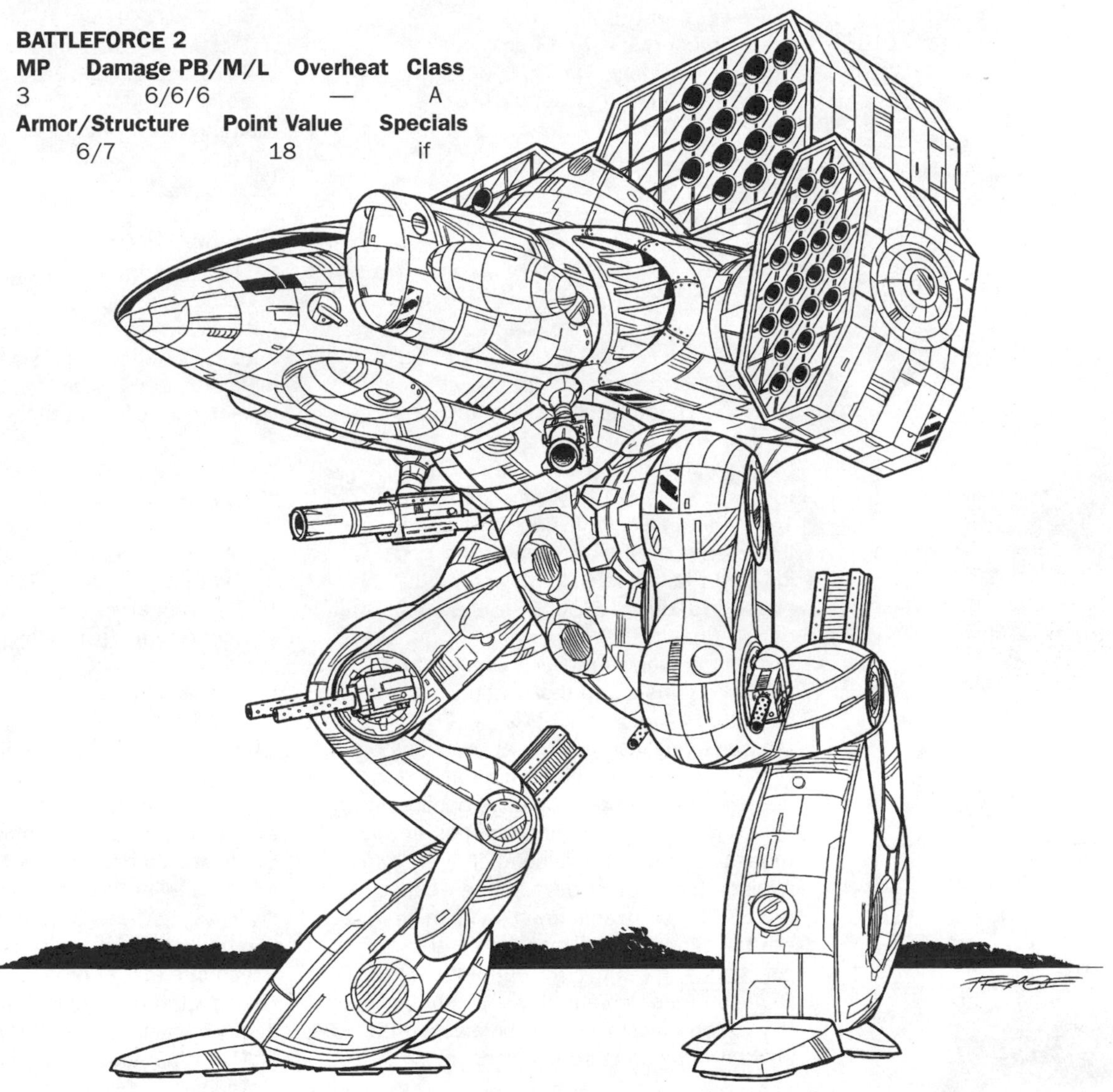

Y-H9G YU HUANG

Mass: 90 tons
Chassis: Chariot Type II Endo Steel
Power Plant: 360 Hermes XL
Cruising Speed: 43 kph
Maximum Speed: 65 kph
Jump Jets: Rodan-90s
Jump Capacity: 120 meters
Armor: Star Shell Standard

Armament:
1 LB-20X Autocannon
1 Extended Range PPC
1 Zeus LRM-10 Launcher
2 Martell Medium Lasers
1 Raker-IV Medium Pulse Laser
Manufacturer: Shengli Arms
Primary Factory: Victoria

Communications System:
Dian-bao Comms, Standard
Targeting and Tracking System:
O/P 911 Targeting and Tracking System

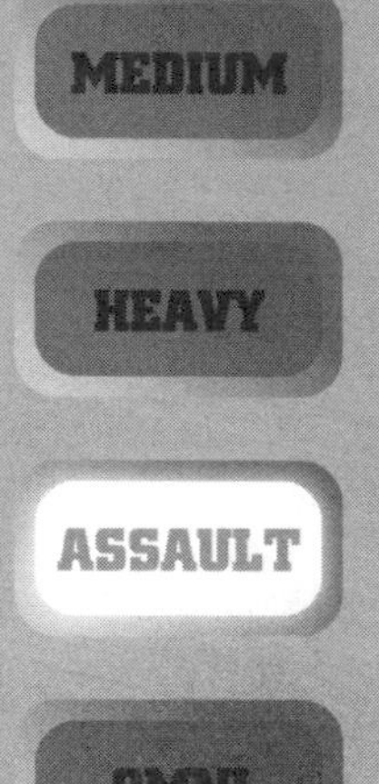

Overview

The *Yu Huang* is the third design from Shengli Arms, a Confederation-sponsored enterprise that refurbished an old Star League production facility on Victoria with help from the Word of Blake. Chancellor Sun-Tzu Liao ordered cosmetic changes in the 'Mech to suggest a greater Chinese influence, reinforcing his call for "Capellan renewal." The first *Yu Huang*, named for the Jade Emperor who rules the heavenly court, entered trials in late 3059, and production began in January of 3060. At the 'Mech's debut, Chancellor Liao promised that, "it shall sit in judgment over a battlefield, meting out justice to those who would transgress against us." Like the *Ti Ts'ang*, the *Yu Huang* incorporates suggestions of Chinese design and bears the name of a deity from the ancient Chinese pantheon.

Though early detractors of this design thought that it would depend on the Lyran Alliance for its most devastating weapon, the LB-20X autocannon, no such shipments are taking place. The most obvious conclusion, given the current state of Capellan research and development, is that the Victoria facility already possessed the ability to manufacture the weapon.

Capabilities

As with any well-designed assault 'Mech, the *Yu Huang* aims to dominate the battlefield. In addition to its war-god appearance, this machine boasts one of the highest speeds of any assault-class BattleMech. Often overlooked are its Rodan jump jets, which lend it extra mobility atypical of a ninety-ton machine. Its endo steel frame and an extralight engine allow the *Yu Huang* to carry maximum armor as well as an impressive array of weaponry.

With its PPC and LRM launcher, the *Yu Huang* can deliver a long-range sting, but is still considered lacking by many MechWarriors when compared to other assault 'Mechs. Such negative comments fade, however, after trial battles. *Yu Huang* pilots quickly assume an air of invulnerability, shunning covering terrain and relying on speed and armor to protect them as they rapidly close to bring the BattleMech's massive LB 20-X autocannon into play. With three tons of ammunition, switching between slug and cluster rounds can bring down even the sturdiest assault 'Mech in a matter of seconds. The *Yu Huang*'s trio of medium lasers offers a sturdy back-up barrage for times when the LRMs or the autocannon would be inefficient.

Deployment

Except for a full lance of *Yu Huangs* sent immediately to Warrior House Imarra, this 'Mech is slowly being deployed in every regiment of the CCAF in singles and pairs. Chancellor Liao has even made a few of the assault machines available to mercenary units of longstanding service, at an impressive discount. Clearly, *Yu Huang* BattleMechs will become common on any battlefield with Capellan troops, joining the ranks of other "Capellan flagship" designs such as the *Vindicator* and *Raven*.

Variants

In an effort to bolster the CCAF with this latest assault 'Mech, the Y-H10G was quickly brought into production. This variant changes the payload of the 'Mech, relying heavily on extended-range medium lasers imported from the Free Worlds League. Six extended-range medium lasers, three in each torso, combined with an extended-range large laser and a Gauss rifle, as well as a Guardian ECM Suite and a Beagle active probe for defense, give this variant massive punch.

Y-H9G YU HUANG

Type: **Yu Huang**
Technology Base: Inner Sphere
Tonnage: 90
Battle Value: 1,781

Equipment		**Mass**
Internal Structure:	Endo Steel	4.5
Engine:	360 XL	16.5
Walking MP:	4	
Running MP:	6	
Jumping MP:	4	
Heat Sinks:	13 [26]	3
Gyro:		4
Cockpit:		3
Armor Factor:	272	17
	Internal Structure	*Armor Value*
Head	3	9
Center Torso	29	43
Center Torso (rear)		14
R/L Torso	19	28
R/L Torso (rear)		9
R/L Arm	15	29
R/L Leg	19	37

Weapons and Ammo	**Location**	**Critical**	**Tonnage**
LB 20-X AC	RA/RT	11	14
Ammo (LB-X) 15	RT	3	3
LRM 10	CT	2	5
Ammo (LRM) 12	RT	1	1
ER PPC	LA	3	7
2 Medium Lasers	LA	2	2
Medium Pulse Laser	LA	1	2
Jump Jets	LL	2	4
Jump Jets	RL	2	4

BATTLEFORCE 2

MP	**Damage PB/M/L**	**Overheat**	**Class**
4J	5/4/1	1	A

Armor/Structure	**Point Value**	**Specials**
7/3	18	

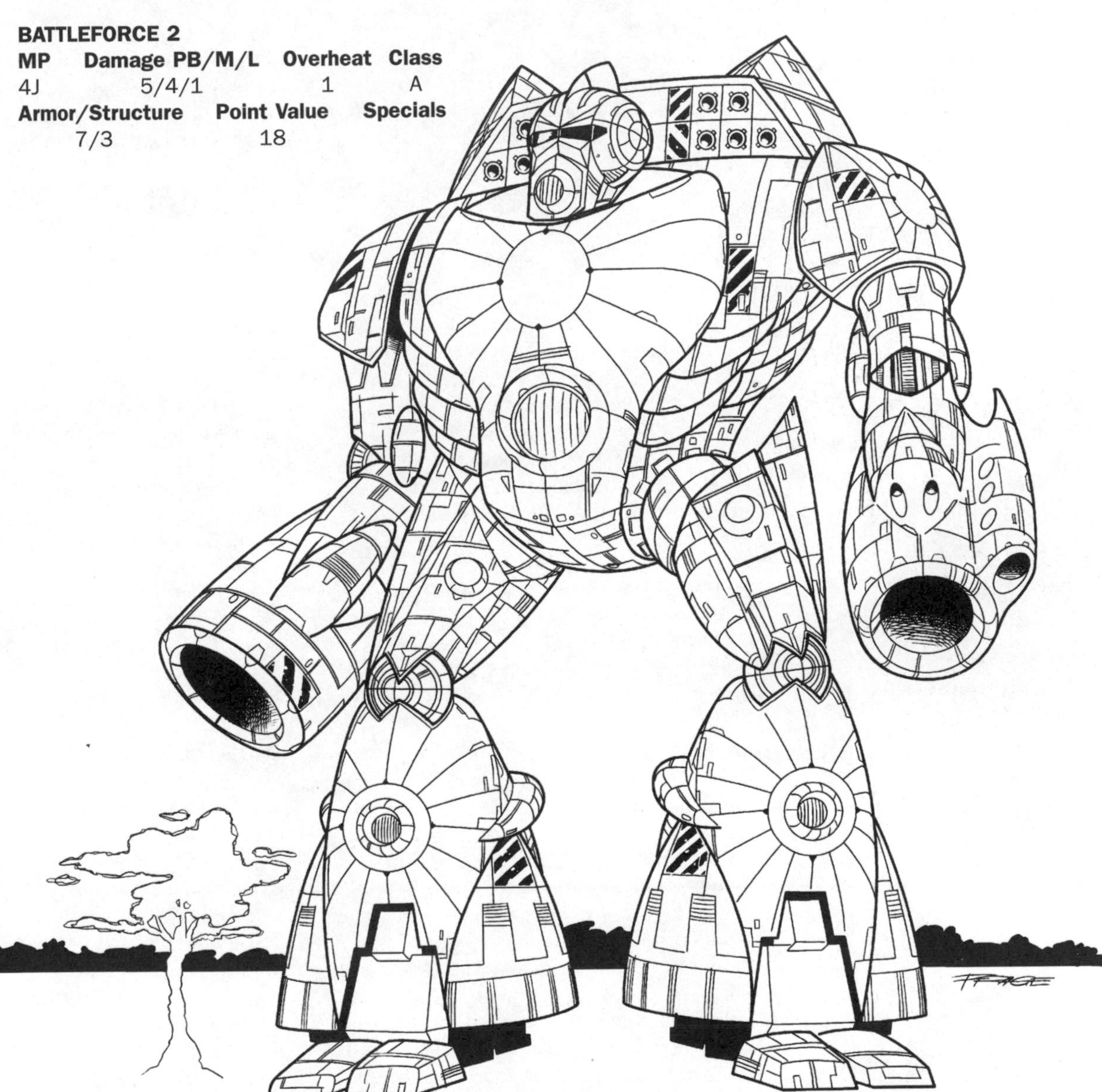

HA1-O HAUPTMANN

LIGHT
MEDIUM
HEAVY
ASSAULT
OMNI

Mass: 95 tons
Chassis: Standard
Power Plant: 285 Standard
Cruising Speed: 32 kph
Maximum Speed: 54 kph
Jump Jets: None
Jump Capacity: None
Armor: Standard
Armament: 43 tons of pod space available
Manufacturer: Coventry Metal Works
Primary Factory: Coventry
Communications System: Unknown
Targeting and Tracking System: Unknown

Overview

The *Hauptmann*, the Lyran Alliance's first OmniMech design, is based on captured Clan *Daishi*s. Coventry Metal Works, producer of the Draconis-designed *Firestarter* OmniMech, took what they learned from producing the *Firestarter* and applied it to a much larger chassis. Oddly, the *Hauptmann* lacks an XL engine. There is certainly room in the chassis, and Coventry Metal Works can afford the cost. Rumor has it that Coventry designers cannot make OmniMechs with XL engines; however, it is more likely that they simply wanted to save money.

Capabilities

The *Hauptmann*'s primary configuration is deadly at all ranges, combining paired ER large lasers with medium pulse lasers and the newly developed LB 20-X autocannon. Extremely well-armored, the Prime configuration also carries enough heat sinks to make efficient use of its weapons, as well as the added protection of a Guardian ECM suite. The A configuration is designed for close combat, utilizing hand actuators for punching and jump jets for maneuverability. It carries four ER medium lasers, bought from the Free Worlds League, and two SRM-6 launchers, each augmented with the Artemis IV fire-control system. For long-range weaponry, the A variant carries a Gauss rifle that is more than enough to discourage smaller opponents.

The B configuration returns to the all-around approach of the Prime, carrying two ER PPCs for long-range attacks and three medium pulse lasers for closer opponents. It also mounts the frightening new Ultra AC/20, carrying enough ammunition to keep it supplied for some time. Unfortunately, it lacks the heat sinks to support all of its weaponry.

Deployment

In a unique move, Archon Katrina Steiner named the new Lyran Alliance OmniMech *Hauptmann*, to honor all the hauptmanns who command in the Lyran Alliance Armed Forces. The highest officers who consistently see battle, the hauptmanns of the LAAF have long held the greatest respect among enlisted and non-com officers. The first models of the new OmniMech were assigned to hauptmanns in the new Bolan, Skye, Donegal, Coventry and Alarion Jaegers units. The remaining *Hauptmann*s produced so far have been sent to Skye Rangers units. Several *Hauptmann*s have been assigned to garrison units on Coventry, with Coventry Metal Works retaining some to protect its main factories.

Type: **Hauptmann**
Technology Base: Inner Sphere OmniMech
Tonnage: 95
Battle Value: 1,819

Equipment		**Mass**
Internal Structure:		9.5
Engine:	285	16.5
Walking MP:	3	
Running MP:	5	
Jumping MP:	0	
Heat Sinks:	11 [22]	1
Gyro:		3
Cockpit:		3
Armor Factor:	293	18.5

	Internal Structure	*Armor Value*
Head	3	9
Center Torso	30	45
Center Torso (rear)		15
R/L Torso	20	30
R/L Torso (rear)		10
R/L Arm	16	32
R/L Leg	20	40

Weight and Space Allocation

Location	*Fixed*	*Spaces Remaining*
Head	None	1
Center Torso	None	2
Right Torso	CASE	11
Left Torso	None	12
Right Arm	None	8
Left Arm	None	8
Right Leg	None	2
Left Leg	None	2

HA1-O HAUPTMANN

Weapons and Ammo	Location	Critical	Tonnage
Primary Weapons Configuration			
ER Small Laser	H	1	.5
ER Large Laser	LA	2	5
Med. Pulse Laser	LA	1	2
2 Double Heat Sinks	LA	6	2
LB 20-X AC	LT	11	14
Guardian ECM Suite	CT	2	1.5
Streak SRM 2	LT	1	1.5
Streak SRM 2	RT	1	1.5
Ammo (LB-X) 15	RT	3	3
Ammo (Streak) 50	RT	1	1
2 Double Heat Sinks	RT	6	2
ER Large Laser	RA	2	5
Med. Pulse Laser	RA	1	2
2 Double Heat Sinks	RA	6	2
Alternate Configuration A			
2 ER Med. Lasers	LA	2	2
SRM 6	LA	2	3
Artemis IV FCS	LA	1	1
Double Heat Sink	LA	3	1
4 Double Heat Sinks	LT	12	4
Gauss Rifle	RT	7	15
Ammo (Gauss) 16	RT	2	2
Ammo (SRM) 30	RT	2	2
Jump Jet	CT	1	2
Jump Jet	LL	1	2
Jump Jet	RL	1	2
2 ER Med. Lasers	RA	2	2
SRM 6	RA	2	3
Artemis IV FCS	RA	1	1
Double Heat Sink	RA	3	1
Battle Value: 2,172			
Alternate Configuration B			
Med. Pulse Laser	H	1	2
ER PPC	LA	3	7
Med. Pulse Laser	LA	1	2
Double Heat Sink	LA	3	1
3 Double Heat Sinks	LT	9	3
Ultra AC/20	RT/CT	10	15
Ammo (Ultra) 15	RT	3	3
ER PPC	RA	3	7
Med. Pulse Laser	RA	1	2
Double Heat Sink	RA	3	1
Battle Value: 1,662			

BATTLEFORCE 2

Type: **Hauptmann**

MP	Damage PB/M/L	Overheat	Class
3	7/5/2	1	A
Armor/Structure	**Point Value**	**Specials**	
7/7	18	omni, ecm	

Alternate Configuration A

MP	Damage PB/M/L	Overheat	Class
3J	7/6/2	—	A
Armor/Structure	**Point Value**	**Specials**	
7/7	22	omni	

Alternate Configuration B

MP	Damage PB/M/L	Overheat	Class
3	5/4/2	3	A
Armor/Structure	**Point Value**	**Specials**	
7/7	17	omni	

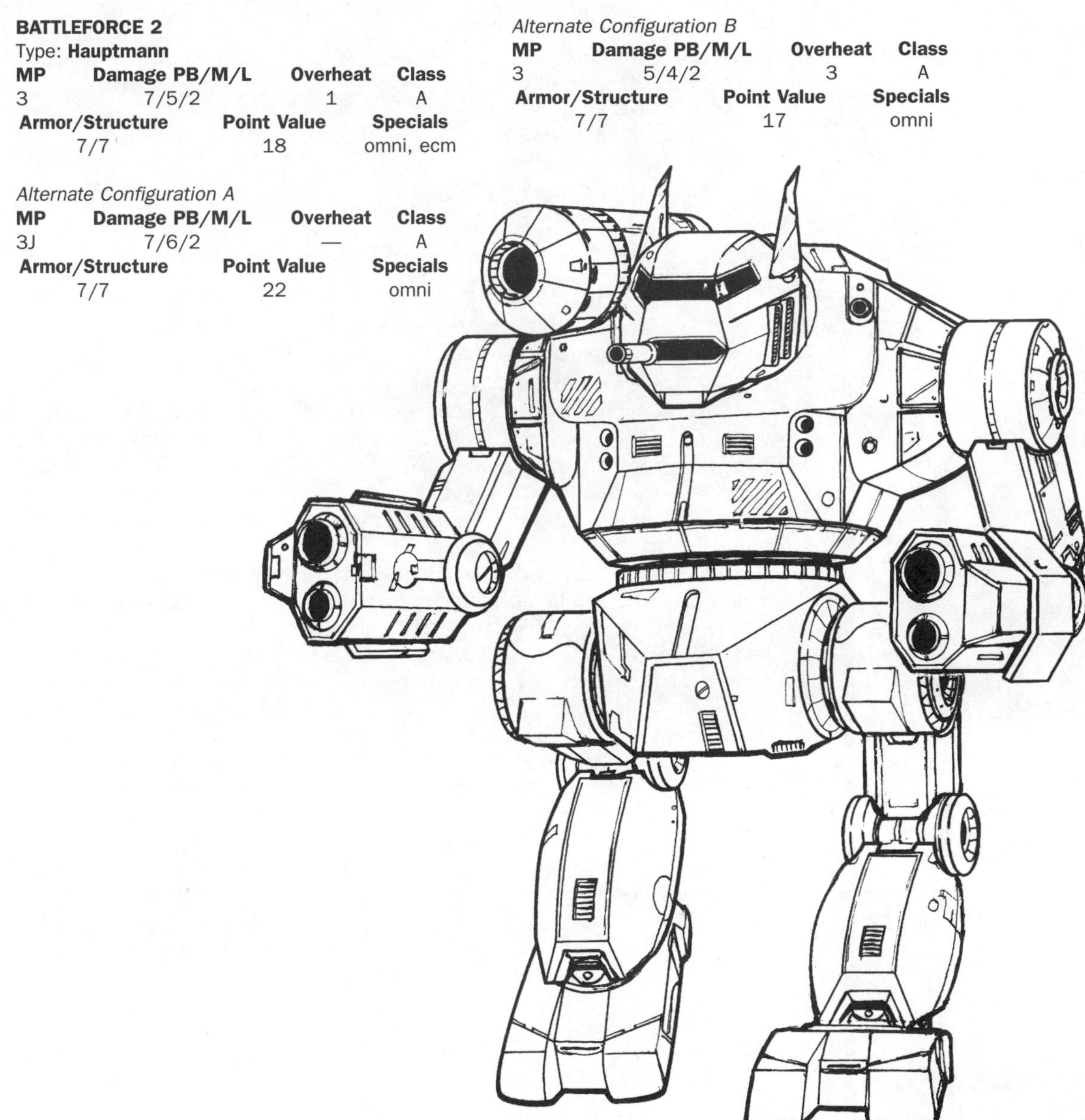

SRC-3C SIROCCO

Mass: 95 tons
Chassis: Corean IX (quad)
Power Plant: 285 Pitban
Cruising Speed: 32 kph
Maximum Speed: 54 kph
Jump Jets: None
Jump Capacity: None
Armor: Starshield

Armament:
2 Imperator Automatic Ultra-10 Autocannons
6 Diverse Optics Extended Range Medium Lasers
1 Diverse Optics Medium Pulse Laser
2 Ma Mien Anti-Personnel Pods

Manufacturer: Corean Enterprises MacAdams-Suharno
Primary Factory: Stewart
Communications System: Corean TransBand-J9 with Guardian ECM Suite
Targeting and Tracking System: Corean B-Tech

Overview

In the late 3040s, Corean Enterprises MacAdams-Suharno of the Free Worlds League decided to take a another look at the four-legged 'Mech chassis. They upgraded their aging *Goliath* design, and in the early 3050s the company introduced the *Tarantula*, a four-legged light scout 'Mech. To overcome the prevailing negative stereotype of quad 'Mechs, Corean launched an ambitious ad campaign using actual battle footage and MechWarrior testimonials. The company also took the unprecedented step of giving a number of *Tarantula*s to several premier units around the Inner Sphere. By 3057, this impressive effort paid off, and sales of the *Tarantula* skyrocketed. This response persuaded Corean that a new quad assault 'Mech should replace the aging *Goliath*. By early 3059, the *Sirocco* was undergoing field testing.

Capabilities

The *Sirocco*'s main firepower centers around twin Ultra-10 autocannons produced by Imperator Weaponries. Large ammo bins mounted in each of the 'Mech's rear legs feed the autocannon. To provide additional firepower at close range, the *Sirocco* adds six extended-range medium lasers. Because four-legged 'Mech designs do not have arm-mounted weapons, the design also incorporates two rear-facing lasers.

For defensive purposes, an electronic countermeasures suite reduces the effectiveness of enemy long-range scanning and surveillance equipment. Additionally, because of the unique nature of four-legged designs, Corean Enterprises was able to mount more armor protection than ever previously incorporated into any 'Mech design.

Finally, the *Sirocco* incorporates Capellan-produced anti-personnel pods that mimic their Clan counterparts. Captain-General Thomas Marik agreed to purchase the anti-infantry weapons in an effort to appease Capellan Chancellor Sun-Tzu Liao, who is becoming increasingly irate over Marik's refusal to set a wedding date between Sun-Tzu and Marik's daughter Isis.

Deployment

Executives at Corean Enterprises realized early on that the survival of the company's new design depended on making sure it reached the right MechWarriors as quickly as possible. They therefore devised a contract that allowed the Free Worlds League Military to buy the first production run at a much-reduced cost, provided that these first*Sirocco*s were assigned to a premier unit. The first *Sirocco*s off the production line have been shipped to the Second Knights of the Inner Sphere.

Variants

The only variant currently in production provides more diverse firepower as well as longer-range weapons. Field tested at the same time as the 3C version, the 5C variant exchanges the paired Ultra AC/10s for a pair of light Gauss rifles. It drops two of the ER medium lasers in favor of two SRM-4 launchers with CASE in either torso, and mounts two additional anti-personnel pods.

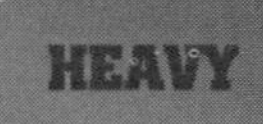

ASSAULT

SRC-3C SIROCCO

Type: **Sirocco**
Technology Base: Inner Sphere
Tonnage: 95
Battle Value: 1,807

Equipment		**Mass**
Internal Structure:		9.5
Engine:	285	16.5
Walking MP:	3	
Running MP:	5	
Jumping MP:	0	
Heat Sinks:	13 [26]	3
Gyro:		3
Cockpit:		3
Armor Factor:	309	19.5

	Internal Structure	*Armor Value*
Head	3	9
Center Torso	30	40
Center Torso (rear)		20
R/L Torso	20	25
R/L Torso (rear)		15
R/L Front Leg	20	40
R/L Rear Leg	20	40

Weapons and Ammo	**Location**	**Critical**	**Tonnage**
ER Med. Laser	LFL	1	1
A-Pod	LFL	1	.5
ER Med. Laser	RFL	1	1
A-Pod	RFL	1	.5
ER Med. Laser	RT	1	1
ER Med. Laser	RT (R)	1	1
Ultra AC/10	RT	7	13
Ammo (Ultra) 20	RRL	2	2
ER Med. Laser	LT	1	1
ER Med. Laser	LT (R)	1	1
Ultra AC/10	LT	7	13
Ammo (Ultra) 20	LRL	2	2
Med. Pulse Laser	H	1	2
Guardian ECM Suite	CT	2	1.5

BATTLEFORCE 2

MP	**Damage PB/M/L**	**Overheat**	**Class**
3	5/4/2	2	A

Armor/Structure	**Point Value**	**Specials**
8/7	18	ecm

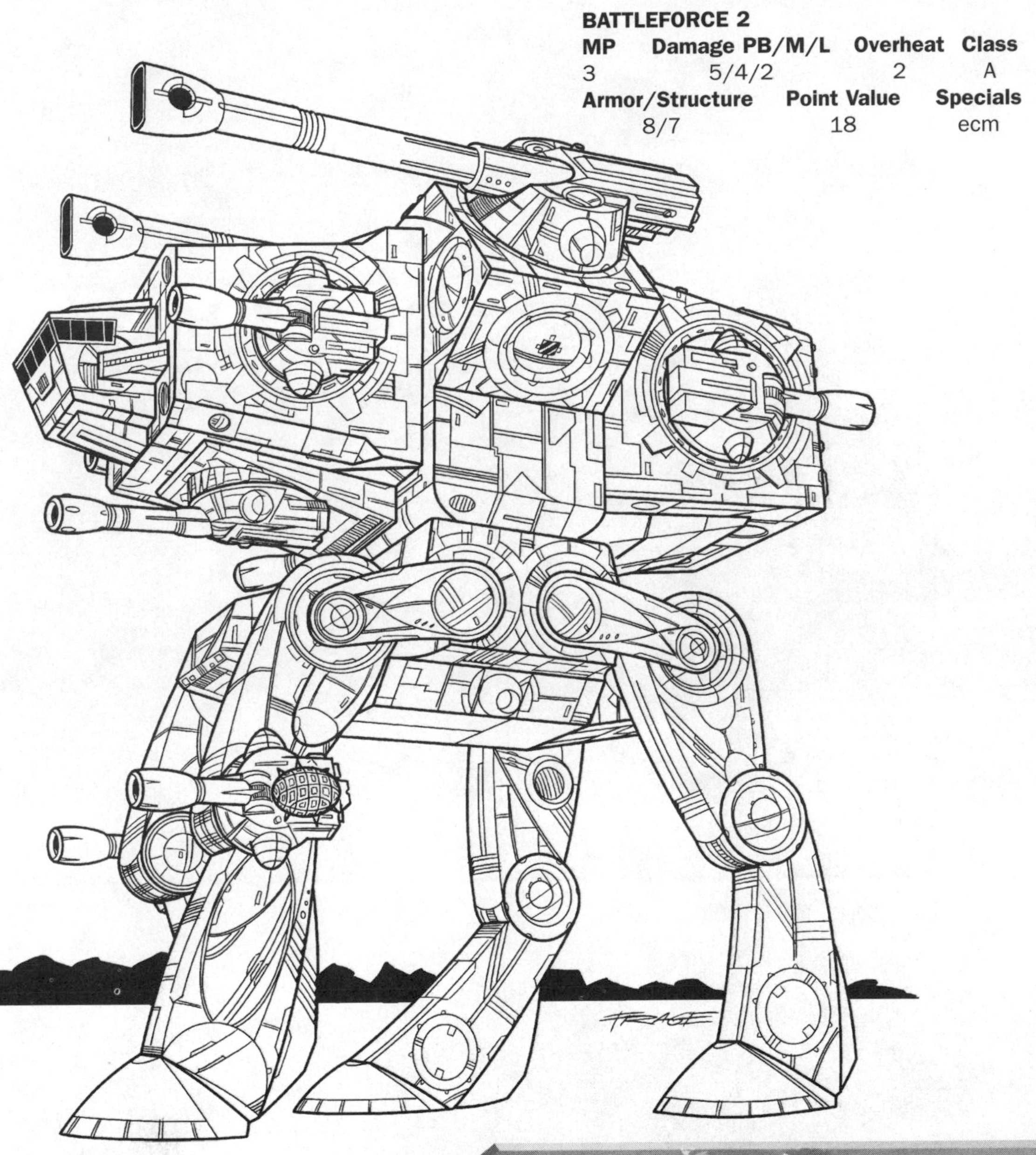

CLAN BATTLEMECHS

ComStar's intelligence-gathering efforts since the Truce of Tukayyid have uncovered the nature of most of the Clans' current military deployment in the Inner Sphere, and the Inner Sphere's strike against the Clan Smoke Jaguar homeworld of Huntress in 3060 captured Jaguar military files that revealed many never-before-seen BattleMech designs. Though the majority of these units are second-line 'Mechs, my report does not exaggerate the continuing viability of these designs and the level of threat they represent. It is of further interest that the Clans field four-legged 'Mechs, contrary to popular opinion among Inner Sphere military leaders. In fact, according to decrypted Clan reports, one of the four-legged 'Mech designs recently seen fighting for the Clans is a direct response to the success of the *Tarantula* BattleMech.

A much more disturbing trend in Clan armament is the new heavy laser weapon system now being identified on 'Mechs of all types and among all the Clans. Though the Clans still hold a significant technological lead on the Inner Sphere, we have been slowly closing that gap. My own research indicates that the Clans have not introduced new technology to their BattleMech designs in more than one hundred years; I fear that our desire to match their technological achievements has finally moved the Clan's scientist castes from their lassitude. We must redouble our efforts to close the technological gap between the Inner Sphere and the Clans before the Clans make another leap forward—and hope that the scientist castes have become too complacent over the past century to develop new and effective weapons quickly.

—Jared Pascal
Precentor I-Omega
Deep Periphery
17 November 3060

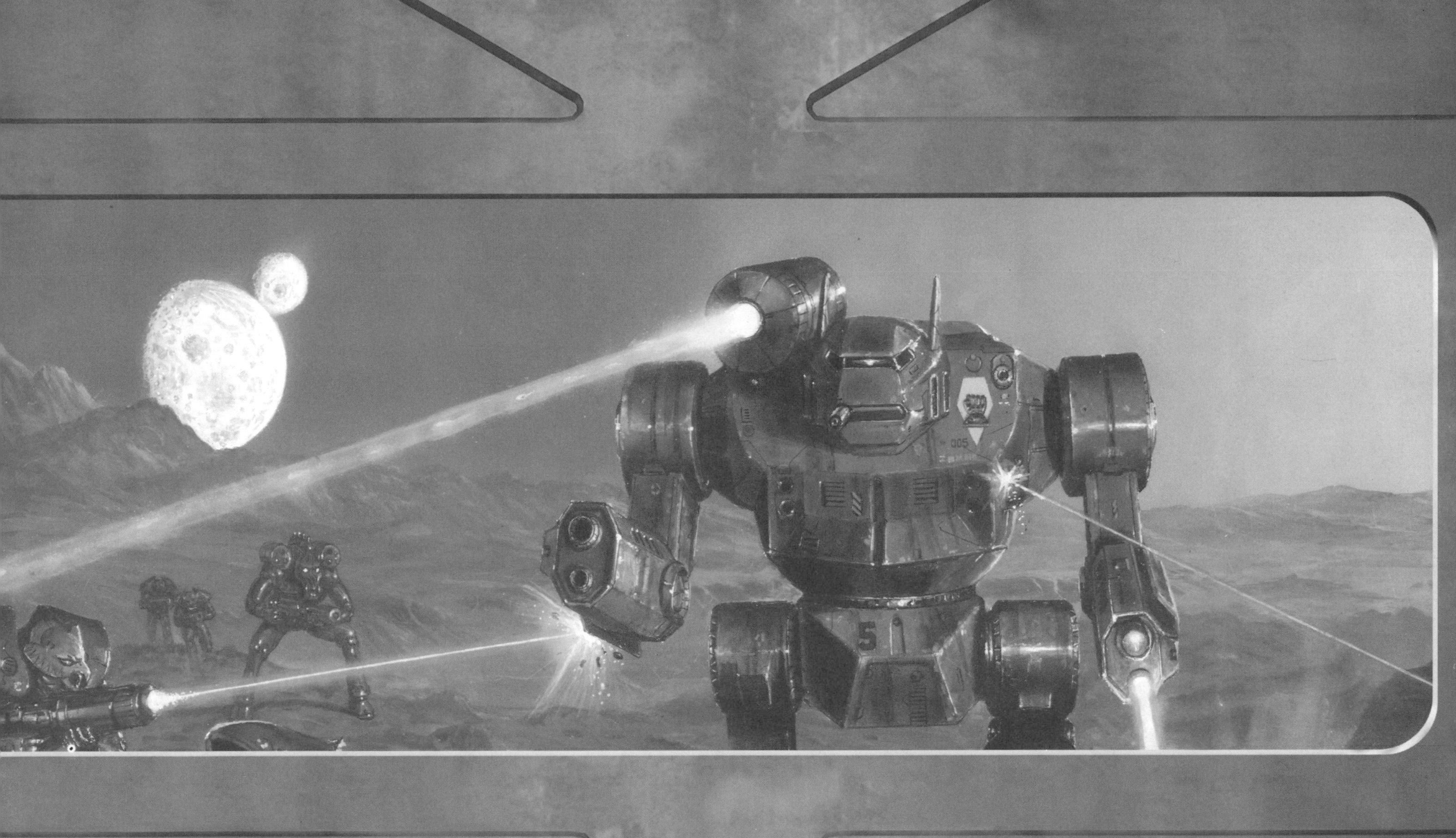

SNOW FOX

Mass: 20 tons
Chassis: Hellion Slopeback V1 (Quad)
Power Plant: 160 Standard
Cruising Speed: 85 kph
Maximum Speed: 127 kph, 172 kph w/MASC
Jump Jets: None
Jump Capacity: None

Armor: Compound Alpha Ferro-Fibrous
Armament:
1 Series 2f Extended Range Medium Laser
2 Series 1-s Extended Range Small Lasers
Manufacturer:
Hector MechWorks Facility Beta

Communications System: HCFA 3035 2.0
Targeting and Tracking System:
HCFA 3047 1.5

Overview

The *Snow Fox* is Clan Ice Hellion's attempt to create a fast, multi-role 'Mech that is both aesthetically pleasing and functional. Designed around the lightest version of the Slopeback Quad chassis, the *Snow Fox* possesses an intentional and well-executed resemblance to a predator common to the icy plains of the Ice Hellion world of Hector.

The designers deliberately attempted to create a 'Mech that would instill fear in attackers. This concept worked to a limited degree—the *Snow Fox*'s speed does create an unfamiliar and therefore unsettling trotting sound that matches its unique gait.

The *Snow Fox* is an integrated design, not a modular OmniMech, as it was designed primarily to fill what the Clans describe as a cavalry role: swift, swooping attacks and immediate disengagements. Because the *Snow Fox* is one of only a few new designs developed in the past fifty years, its rarity makes it noticeable—and its effectiveness makes the 'Mech popular.

Proponents of the design have tried to use it as astep toward creating a quad-style OmniMech, but have made little progress. Too many warriors consider two-legged 'Mechs to be more intimidating than quads. They also enjoy the option of having working hands, and are more comfortable piloting the familiar two-legged, upright shape.

Capabilities

The *Snow Fox* is an extremely fast and surprisingly agile 'Mech. MechWarriors find it takes more training to become accustomed to the 'Mech's loping gait, and warriors unfamiliar with how the 'Mech handles frequently tip it over. The movement of the *Snow Fox* gives it an extra edge, often making it difficult for enemy 'Mechs to obtain a target lock. This defense is enhanced when the *Snow Fox*'s MASC equipment is engaged, creating an extra burst of speed.

Lightly armed with a single medium and two small lasers, the *Snow Fox* is not designed to engage in stand-up fights. As with most Hellion-designed 'Mechs, its primary weapon is its speed, which can be used to deadly effect. This was proved when other Clans attempted to win back holdings lost to the Ice Hellions during the Hellions Fury campaign. One engagement on the world of Marshall, jointly held by several Clans, saw the Seventh Hector Cavaliers pinned by the Second Falcon Velites in a wide canyon in the Firth mountain range.

An Ice Hellion Binary made up primarily of *Snow Foxes* arrived at the engagement and raced around the Falcon lines, harassing targets up and down the rear flank. This rapid activity created the illusion of a large force at the Falcons' rear. The ensuing confusion allowed the Hellion warriors an avenue of escape and gave them an opportunity to in turn flank the Falcons, eventually driving them off.

The *Snow Fox* has recently come into use as a deterrent to Elemental "headhunter" Stars. Its speed, paired with its laser weaponry, makes it ideal for swiftly crushing surprise attacks.

Deployment

As a second-line 'Mech, the *Snow Fox* appears only in garrison and cavalry-style units. The warriors of the Hellions' Zeta Galaxy, who prefer a mobile defense of their holdings, field a significant force of *Snow Foxes*. While other Clans do field this design, they generally rely on two-legged units as being more functional and appropriate to their fighting strategies.

Variants

The single known variant of the *Snow Fox* replaces the lasers with a single LRM 10-pack and one ton of ammunition to create a mobile fire platform. This variant has seen only limited use.

SNOW FOX

Type: **Snow Fox**
Technology Base: Clan
Tonnage: 20
Battle Value: 627

Equipment		**Mass**
Internal Structure:		2
Engine:	160	6
Walking MP:	8	
Running MP:	12 (16)	
Jumping MP:	0	
Heat Sinks:	10	0
Gyro:		2
Cockpit:		3
Armor Factor:	77	4

	Internal Structure	*Armor Value*
Head	3	9
Center Torso	6	9
Center Torso (rear)		3
R/L Torso	5	8
R/L Torso (rear)		2
R/L Front Leg	4	8
R/L Rear Leg	4	8

Weapons and Ammo	**Location**	**Critical**	**Tonnage**
ER Med. Laser	H	1	1
ER Small Laser	RT	1	.5
ER Small Laser	LT	1	.5
MASC	CT	1	1

BATTLEFORCE 2

MP	**Damage PB/M/L**	**Overheat**	**Class**
8	2/2/—	—	L

Armor/Structure	**Point Value**	**Specials**
2/2	6	

COMMANDO IIC

Mass: 25 tons
Chassis: Model ML-225 Endo Steel
Power Plant: Fusion 150 Standard
Cruising Speed: 65 kph
Maximum Speed: 97 kph
Jump Jets: None
Jump Capacity: None

Armor: Forging OTR17b with CASE
Armament:
2 Series 2d Extended Range Medium Lasers
1 Pattern J7 SRM-6 Launcher
3 SEP Class SRM-4 Launchers
Manufacturer:
Marshall Light Assembly Station

Communications System:
Build 1685/3 Tacticom
Targeting and Tracking System:
Mark 11 IHADS

Overview

Long the exclusive property of the Lyran Commonwealth, the *Commando* was once the premier scout 'Mech of House Steiner forces. For decades, the Lyrans fended off attempts by the Star League military to acquire the design. During the Amaris coup, however, several of the highly prized 'Mechs entered League service in the hands of volunteers disaffected by their House's neutral stance in the war. Organized into so-called Loyalist units, these and other Lyran citizens fought with distinction in the liberation of Terra alongside the SLDF.

Though history does not record the exact chain of events, a number of *Commando*s are known to have survived the second Exodus to become part of the Clan army organized by Nicholas Kerensky. Admired for their ability to easily destroy most light 'Mech opposition while maintaining their scouting role, these *Commando*s were produced in large numbers by Clans Smoke Jaguar and Goliath Scorpion. When radically lighter and less bulky construction materials were introduced, Clan Goliath Scorpion upgraded their aging line of *Commando*s to provide even more firepower for the deadly scout.

The resulting design, dubbed the *Commando* IIC, performed well in the tight, rocky confines of the Scorpions' early holdings on Dagda and Roche. Using the 'Mech in a lightning raid on Clan Hell's Horses' weakly defended Tokasha enclave in 2872, the Scorpions outflanked and destroyed the more numerous defenders and won access to two genetic legacies of the Horses. Eventually overshadowed by the rise of the more powerful OmniMechs, the *Commando* IIC was relegated to reserve status by most Clans in the late 2800s.

Capabilities

Information taken from Clan Wolf battle records of the invasion provides an interesting perspective on the strengths and weaknesses of the *Commando* IIC. The IIC mounts more than twice the weaponry and one-and-a-half times the armor of its Inner Sphere counterpart. This disparity translates into significantly improved survivability and a much higher kill potential for the Clan design.

Inner Sphere engineers, however, concentrated on improving the early *Commando*'s ammunition efficiency, which is a decided weakness of the *Commando* IIC. The Clan 'Mech does not mount the advanced Streak and Artemis technologies of the FedCom version, and when operating far from supply, its three SRM-4 launchers rapidly deplete its ammunition stock. This shortcoming does not diminish the *Commando* IIC's capability for destroying most light 'Mechs and even challenging heavier Clan designs like the *Ice Ferret*.

Deployment

Rare even among the Scorpions, the *Commando* IIC is often piloted by freeborn soldiers assigned to hunting bandits on the fringes of Clan space. Though criticized by most Scorpion warriors for its plethora of "inelegant" missile weapons, it is admired by those who have handled its responsive controls. Several *Commando* IICs were recently sighted among the Scorpion's Thirty-third Grenadiers; the pilots of Sharman's Boxers have nicknamed it the "Sucker Punch."

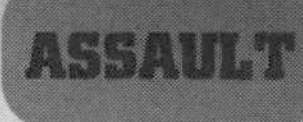

Type: **Commando IIC**
Technology Base: Clan
Tonnage: 25
Battle Value: 816

Equipment		**Mass**
Internal Structure:	Endo Steel	1.5
Engine:	150	5.5
Walking MP:	6	
Running MP:	9	
Jumping MP:	0	
Heat Sinks:	10 [20]	0
Gyro:		2
Cockpit:		3
Armor Factor:	72	4.5
	Internal Structure	*Armor Value*
Head	3	9
Center Torso	8	10
Center Torso (rear)		3
R/L Torso	6	8
R/L Torso (rear)		2
R/L Arm	4	6
R/L Leg	6	9

Weapons and Ammo	**Location**	**Critical**	**Tonnage**
2 ER Med. Lasers	LA	2	2
SRM 6	CT	1	1.5
Ammo (SRM) 15	RT	1	1
SRM 4	RA	1	1
SRM 4	LT	1	1
SRM 4	RT	1	1
Ammo (SRM) 25	RT	1	1

BATTLEFORCE 2

MP	**Damage PB/M/L**	**Overheat**	**Class**
6	4/3/—	1	L

Armor/Structure	**Point Value**	**Specials**
2/2	8	

ICESTORM

Mass: 25 tons
Chassis: Hellion Light V3
Power Plant: 300 XL
Cruising Speed: 126 kph
Maximum Speed: 190 kph
Jump Jets: None
Jump Capacity: None

Armor: Compound Alpha Standard
Armament:
1 Series 2f Extended Range Medium Laser
1 Pattern Alpha SRM-2 Launcher
1 Hellion Class Homing TAG
Manufacturer:
Hector MechWorks Facility Beta

Communications System:
Build 1685 Tacticom
Targeting and Tracking System:
Series VI Integrated TTS

Overview

Before the development of the *Fire Moth* OmniMech and other light recon designs, the *Icestorm* was the 'Mech of choice for scout Stars. Its fast speed and sophisticated communications and targeting gear suit the *Icestorm* to this role.

Based on a late-model Star League design known as the *Cameroon*, all prototypes and early models of what would become the *Icestorm* joined the Exodus fleet.

When Clan Ice Hellion was formed, Kerensky assigned that Clan the lion's share of the remaining *Cameroon*s. Recognizing it as a viable design, Khan Stephan Cage re-christened the 'Mech the *Icestorm*, ordered a build-up of the design and put it to good use in the following decades. The 'Mech remained popular among recon and support Stars even after the development of the OmniMech, and the *Icestorm* was one of the last Hellion 'Mechs to be replaced by the modular units.

Because it still serves a unique role, the *Icestorm* continues to have a working life nearly two centuries after its creation. Its exemplary track record makes it one of the few second-line 'Mechs that front-line units tolerate having in their ranks.

Capabilities

The *Icestorm* is an exceptionally fast 'Mech. With a top speed approaching 200 kph, it can outdistance most front-line light Omnis with ease. But what this 'Mech offers in speed, it lacks in protection. Outfitted with only a small amount of standard armor, the *Icestorm* cannot survive hits from any but the lightest Clan weaponry. *Icestorm* pilots frequently complain about the lack of sufficient protection in the 'Mech's head, but the Clan has so far failed to reallocate existing armor or upgrade it to ferro-fibrous.

This 'Mech's offensive armament also weighs in rather light for a 'Mech of this tonnage, though its extended-range medium laser and short-range missile launcher adequately support its role as a scout and spotter.

The *Icestorm* carries advanced target acquisition gear which, combined with the 'Mech's speed, makes the *Icestorm* a deadly artillery spotter. During the Pentagon Campaign in the early days of the Clans, Ice Hellion recon units used the *Icestorm* to deadly effect in crushing resistance on Babylon. Field use of the *Icestorm* increased during the Hellions' Fury campaign waged just prior to the Inner Sphere invasion, where its spotting ability helped soften up numerous enemy targets. Hellion commanders made a point of informing their vanquished foes that their defeat was due partly to the successful performance of the ancient design.

Deployment

Alpha Galaxy is the only Ice Hellion unit to contain no *Icestorms*. All other Galaxies, both front and second-line, count at least one *Icestorm* among their ranks, though most belong to second-line garrison forces. Theta Galaxy also fields few 'Mechs of this design, as the *Icestorm*'s mission profile clashes with their unit role as merchant escorts.

Of the other Clans, only Clan Wolf includes a respectable number of *Icestorm*s among its garrison forces.

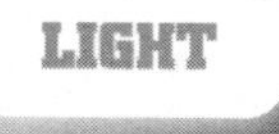

ICESTORM

Type: **Icestorm**
Technology Base: Clan
Tonnage: 25
Battle Value: 619

Equipment		**Mass**
Internal Structure:		2.5
Engine:	300 XL	9.5
Walking MP:	12	
Running MP:	18	
Jumping MP:	0	
Heat Sinks:	10	0
Gyro:		3
Cockpit:		3
Armor Factor:	56	3.5

	Internal Structure	*Armor Value*
Head	3	6
Center Torso	8	8
Center Torso (rear)		2
R/L Torso	6	6
R/L Torso (rear)		1
R/L Arm	4	6
R/L Leg	6	7

Weapons and Ammo	**Location**	**Critical**	**Tonnage**
ER Med. Laser	RA	1	1
SRM 2	H	1	0.5
Ammo (SRM) 50	RT	1	1
TAG	CT	1	1

BATTLEFORCE 2

MP	**Damage PB/M/L**	**Overheat**	**Class**
12	2/1/—	—	L

Armor/Structure	**Point Value**	**Specials**
1/2	6	tag

MANDRILL

Mass: 30
Chassis: Process 12 Endo Steel
Power Plant: Firebox 120 XL
Cruising Speed: 43 kph
Maximum Speed: 65 kph
Jump Jets: Type C Medium Lifters
Jump Capacity: 120 meters
Armor: Compound FM3 Ferro-Fibrous
Armament:
2 Type 20 "Great Bow" LRM-20 Launchers
1 Series 1 Extended Range Small Laser
Manufacturer:
Kindraa Sainze Primary Production Facility
Communications System:
JNE Integrated Communications
Targeting and Tracking System: Mark 4 TTS

LIGHT

MEDIUM

HEAVY

ASSAULT

OMNI

Overview

The *Mandrill* was the first of the so-called totem 'Mechs designed to resemble a Clan's totem animal. The design and production of the *Mandrill* BattleMech was one of the last truly unified efforts of Clan Fire Mandrill before it shattered into the various Kindraa. Designed by Kindraa Payne, the *Mandrill* is notably simian in appearance, with bulky shoulders, long arms and a cockpit resembling a mandrill's face. It also has the unique ability to walk on two legs or to use its exaggerated arms to scoot along with a gait similar to that of a quad 'Mech.

Some commanders consider *Mandrill*s to be an asset on the battlefield. The pride of piloting the Clan's totem makes their MechWarriors perform at their peak, as well as spurring their comrades to top performance. Others consider the *Mandrill* a second-rate fighting machine, its special gait a hindrance. Detractors also point out that totem 'Mechs create prime targets for enemy fire.

Though still in use by all Kindraas' second-line units, the *Mandrill* has not been produced in more than a century. OmniMechs use the same XL engine, endo steel and other components that made the *Mandrill* a successful design, and those resources quickly were allocated to production of the more standard combat machines. The Jade Falcons, however, impressed with the idea of a light, mobile, missile-firing 'Mech, borrowed the *Mandrill* design and scaled it down to become the *Baboon* design seen in many of their own second-line forces.

Capabilities

Those *Mandrill*s still operating continue to prove their worth in combat when required. With its devastating missile saturation assaults, a *Mandrill* can hold its own against any light 'Mech and many medium-weight designs. Its armor is sufficient to keep it in battle, especially in the one-on-one duels that the Clans favor. The head-mounted small laser may seem extraneous, but in a Fire Mandrill assault against the failing Smoke Jaguar positions on the Clan world of Atreus during the Inner Sphere attack, the *Mandrill*'s small lasers allowed the 'Mech to fight on once the missile bays ran empty.

Deployment

Every Kindraa keeps at least a Star's worth of this totem 'Mech in their second-line forces. Repairing and maintaining these machines is considered the tech caste's most important duty. In 3058, Khan Amanda Carrol formally requested that Kindraa Sainze retool their primary facility on the planet Shadow to produce a limited number of *Mandrill*s every year. Also at the Khan's request, Kindraa Sainze has begun trading these 'Mechs to other Kindraa at a reasonable rate of exchange to ensure that the 'Mech remains visible in all Fire Mandrill forces. Optimists among the Fire Mandrills see this as a sign of the dawn of a new age of cooperation among the Kindraa, kindling hopes that their Clan can once again emerge as a powerful, united force.

CLAN

Type: **Mandrill**
Technology Base: Clan
Tonnage: 30
Battle Value: 1,279

Equipment		**Mass**
Internal Structure:	Endo Steel	1.5
Engine:	120 XL	2
Walking MP:	4	
Running MP:	6	
Jumping MP:	4	
Heat Sinks:	10 [20]	0
Gyro:		2
Cockpit:		3
Armor Factor:	96	5

	Internal Structure	*Armor Value*
Head	3	8
Center Torso	10	14
Center Torso (rear)		6
R/L Torso	7	10
R/L Torso (rear)		4
R/L Arm	5	10
R/L Leg	7	10

Weapons and Ammo	**Location**	**Critical**	**Tonnage**
LRM 20	LT	4	5
Ammo (LRM) 12	LT	2	2
LRM 20	RT	4	5
Ammo (LRM) 12	RT	2	2
ER Small Laser	H	1	.5
Jump Jets	RT	2	1
Jump Jets	LT	2	1

BATTLEFORCE 2

MP	**Damage PB/M/L**	**Overheat**	**Class**
4J	4/3/3	—	L

Armor/Structure	**Point Value**	**Specials**
2/2	13	if

PACK HUNTER

Mass: 30 tons
Chassis: Type AR1 Endo Steel
Power Plant: Light Force (Standard) 210
Cruising Speed: 76 kph
Maximum Speed: 119 kph
Jump Jets: Leaper Model, L5
Jump Capacity: 210 meters
Armor: Royal-7 Standard

Armament:
1 Ripper Series A1 Extended Range PPC
Manufacturer: WC Site 3
Communications System:
K9 Communications System
Targeting and Tracking System:
Hunter (3) Dedicated TTS

Overview

The *Pack Hunter* represents a compromise design approved by the Clan Wolf-in-Exile as the initial 'Mech to be produced by the manufacturing arm of the Clan on their new home of Arc-Royal. Many warriors advocated producing a heavy OmniMech, wanting a flagship design that would command attention from the other Clans. Noting the well-maintained array of Omnis already in service with his Clan, however, Khan Phelan Kell instead focused the Clan's effort on producing a second-line machine of durable nature and immediate usefulness. This decision also allowed the manufacturing facilities to identify and fix problems in the new production line without the risk of producing a flawed OmniMech.

The endo-steel chassis is a product of the space-based production facility the Wolves-in-Exile brought to Arc-Royal. The 'Mech also carries standard composite armor, purchased from the Kell Hounds' production facilities as part of a trade agreement for access to the Clan-produced endo steel. As evidenced by the *Arctic Fox*, the Wolves and Hounds have chosen similar designations for apparently related designs, leading to speculation that they plan on further joint production efforts. The *Pack Hunter* also mounts a communications system of Kell Hound manufacture, though the Wolves-in-Exile will most likely replace it with one of their own as soon as they establish the appropriate production facilities.

Capabilities

Showing his preference for lighter, faster designs, Khan Phelan Kell directed his scientists to create a 'Mech offering "impressive speed but with a bite. A real pack hunter." The 30-ton *Pack Hunter* accomplishes this goal through a combination of high mobility and a hard-hitting primary weapon.

With a top-end speed of more than a hundred kilometers per hour and an impressive jumping range, the *Pack Hunter* is an excellent flanking or vanguard BattleMech. Though lacking the high-powered sensor unit that would make it an excellent scout, its ability to handle itself in nearly any situation makes up for that perceived deficiency. This 'Mech ranges all over the battlefield regardless of the underlying terrain and provides valuable tactical fire support.

The *Pack Hunter*'s only weapon is a Ripper series extended-range particle projection cannon. As with other designs that rely on a single large weapon, such as the *Panther* or *Wolfhound*, the ER PPC gives the *Pack Hunter* enough take-down power to give pause to even a medium or heavy BattleMech. In reported field tests, two *Pack Hunter*s repeatedly stood up to a *Dire Wolf*, relying on their greater mobility to remain at long range where the *Dire Wolf* could rarely get off a shot with any chance of success.

If the *Pack Hunter* may be said to have a weakness, it is the minimal allocation of armor that allows it to carry such a large weapon. Its standard engine with internal heat sinks only makes the 'Mech itself more durable, and any pilot making full use of the *Pack Hunter*'s mobility will offer a difficult target.

Deployment

The *Pack Hunter* saw limited action in 3059 against Clan Smoke Jaguar. Two garrison Stars appended to the First Wolf Strike Grenadiers, with two *Pack Hunter*s each, came under fire in a holding action on the world of Albiero. One *Pack Hunter* was lost to the destruction of its gyro, but the other three survived the battle and counted two heavy OmniMech kills between them.

Clan Wolf-in-Exile is deploying the *Pack Hunter* into second-line and garrison units as fast as they can be produced. A few *Pack Hunter*s have also been sighted in Kell Hound regiments, either for testing and training purposes or as further indication of future cooperation between Wolves-in-Exile and Kell Hounds.

PACK HUNTER

Type: **Pack Hunter**
Technology Base: Clan
Tonnage: 30
Battle Value: 1,384

Equipment		**Mass**
Internal Structure:	Endo Steel	1.5
Engine:	210	9
Walking MP:	7	
Running MP:	11	
Jumping MP:	7	
Heat Sinks:	10 [20]	0
Gyro:		3
Cockpit:		3
Armor Factor:	64	4
	Internal Structure	*Armor Value*
Head	3	7
Center Torso	10	10
Center Torso (rear)		3
R/L Torso	7	6
R/L Torso (rear)		2
R/L Arm	5	6
R/L Leg	7	8

Weapons and Ammo	**Location**	**Critical**	**Tonnage**
ER PPC	RT	2	6
Jump Jet	CT	1	.5
Jump Jets	LT	3	1.5
Jump Jets	RT	3	1.5

BATTLEFORCE 2

MP	**Damage PB/M/L**	**Overheat**	**Class**
7J	2/1/1	1	L

Armor/Structure	**Point Value**	**Specials**
2/3	14	

URBANMECH IIC

Mass: 30 tons
Chassis: Mk. VI Standard Light Chassis
Power Plant: Clan Model XT4 Standard
Cruising Speed: 32 kph
Maximum Speed: 54 kph
Jump Jets: Clan Light Series Mk. II
Jump Capacity: 90 meters

Armor: Forging ZK11 Standard
Armament:
1 Type 9 Ultra-10 Autocannon
1 Series 1 Extended Range Small Laser
Manufacturer: Beta Plant 2W
Communications System:
Build 1685 Tacticom
Targeting and Tracking System: HT9 TTS

Overview

The *UrbanMech* was never very popular with 'MechWarriors in the Inner Sphere, but the *UrbanMech* IIC has found a home in several Clans' second-line and freebirth units. The *UrbanMech* IIC is most popular with Clan Coyote, who have the only manufacturing plant in Clan space producing this 'Mech.

Capabilities

While Clan Coyote scientists were designing the OmniMech, the Coyote technician caste was looking at ways to upgrade the Coyotes' existing 'Mechs. The *UrbanMech* was the engineers' first such project. They began by reviewing battlevids from the Amaris Civil War to get a complete picture of the 'Mech's limitations.

They first changed the *UrbanMech* by replacing the old Leenex 60 series engine with a more powerful Model XT4 90 series engine, increasing the *UrbanMech*'s speed by more than 50 percent. Next, the techs replaced the jump jets with the newer Light Mk. II series, increasing the jump range from sixty to ninety meters. Next, they reviewed the weapons, replacing the old Imperator autocannon with an Ultra 10 autocannon, and the Harmon light laser with an extended-range small laser. Finally, the designers added CASE to the right torso of the 'Mech to protect the pilot in case of an ammunition explosion. To make up for the increased weight, the *UrbanMech* IIC is equipped with ten standard heat sinks, rather than the double heat sinks customary in Clan machines.

The newly christened *UrbanMech* IIC made an impact the first time it entered combat. Clan Burrock attempted to acquire Coyote genetic material by raiding the Coyotes' repository on Valin. Though caught off guard by the raid, the Eighteenth Assault Cluster from Lambda Galaxy won the right to fight the Burrock warriors. Fighting in the close confines of Mecca City, the warriors of the Eighteenth proved the *UrbanMech* IIC's worth by repeatedly rounding the corners of buildings, firing on the Burrock 'Mechs and jumping away. After a drawn-out fight, the Burrock warriors withdrew from the field without ever reaching the Coyotes' repository.

Deployment

Both Omicron and Nu Galaxies of Clan Coyote have several units equipped with the *UrbanMech* IIC. Clans Snow Raven, Ice Hellion and Hells Horses also field small numbers of the *UrbanMech* IIC.

Type: **UrbanMech IIC**
Technology Base: Clan
Tonnage: 30
Battle Value: 737

Equipment		**Mass**
Internal Structure:		3
Engine:	90	3
Walking MP:	3	
Running MP:	5	
Jumping MP:	3	
Heat Sinks:	10	0
Gyro:		1
Cockpit:		3
Armor Factor:	96	6

	Internal Structure	*Armor Value*
Head	3	9
Center Torso	10	11
Center Torso (rear)		8
R/L Torso	7	8
R/L Torso (rear)		4
R/L Arm	5	10
R/L Leg	7	12

Weapons and Ammo	**Location**	**Critical**	**Tonnage**
Ultra AC/10	RA	4	10
Ammo (Ultra) 20	RT	2	2
ER Small Laser	LA	1	.5
Jump Jet	LT	1	.5
Jump Jet	CT	1	.5
Jump Jet	RT	1	.5

BATTLEFORCE 2

MP	**Damage PB/M/L**	**Overheat**	**Class**
3J	2/2/1	—	L

Armor/Structure	**Point Value**	**Specials**
2/3	7	

COUGAR

Mass: 35 tons
Chassis: JF 3 Light Endo Steel
Power Plant: 175 JF Extralight
Cruising Speed: 55 kph
Maximum Speed: 86 kph
Jump Jets: None
Jump Capacity: None

Armor: Compound JF Ferro-Fibrous
Armament: 19 tons of pod space available
Manufacturer: Ironhold Alpha Complex
Communications System: JF Integrated
Targeting and Tracking System: Series JFVIII KITT

Overview

Following her Clan's Trial of Refusal against Clan Wolf in 3057, Khan Marthe Pryde of Clan Jade Falcon wanted to bring new and deadly OmniMechs to the field of battle. Knowing she had already taxed her Clan to the limit in the conflict with Clan Wolf, she took an unprecedented step. Rather than building a new OmniMech from the ground up, she assigned the Jade Falcon scientist caste the job of modifying a proven design into an even deadlier war machine. Beginning with a stock chassis from a Clan *Adder* (designated *Puma* by Inner Sphere forces), Clan Jade Falcon scientists managed to field a virtually new design, code-named the *Cougar*, in roughly half the time normally required to construct and test a new OmniMech.

Capabilities

Jade Falcon technicians gave the *Cougar* more pod space to allow for a greater variety of larger weapons. To accomplish this, they replaced the 210 XL engine with a 175 XL model. The overall consensus was that the increased firepower more than made up for the new 'Mech's slower movement rate.

The designers closely followed the *Puma*'s most common configurations. The increased tonnage for weapons enabled them to upgrade most of the OmniMech's systems while retaining the *Puma*'s tactic of ranged combat. The *Cougar*'s most common configuration uses the Clans' deadly pulse lasers to give this OmniMech an advantage against even the swiftest opponents. Two LRM-10 racks complement the lasers.

The *Cougar* A has immense potential as a rapid-deployment, indirect fire platform. The *Cougar* B is every bit as lethal as the *Puma* primary, but with greater heat-dissipation capacity.

The C configuration shows that the Jade Falcons have learned their lesson about dependence on ammunition. Its bristling array of lasers makes the accompanying Gauss rifle seem like an afterthought.

The *Cougar*'s final configuration, with its devastating combination of an Ultra autocannon and extended-range large laser, appears to be an upgrade of the *Puma* D.

Deployment

Though the *Cougar* first appeared among Jade Falcon forces during the battle of Coventry, it has since been seen in other Clan forces, most notably Clan Smoke Jaguar, where it was first spotted on Port Arthur during Operation Bulldog. Because it was built on the original *Puma* chassis and looks very similar to that 'Mech, many Inner Sphere units mistakenly believed they knew the *Cougar*'s capabilities. Not many lived to learn from their mistake.

Type: **Cougar**
Technology Base: Clan OmniMech
Tonnage: 35
Battle Value: 1,227

Equipment		**Mass**
Internal Structure:	Endo Steel	2
Engine:	175 XL	3.5
Walking MP:	5	
Running MP:	8	
Jumping MP:	0	
Heat Sinks:	10 [20]	0
Gyro:		2
Cockpit:		3
Armor Factor:	106	5.5

	Internal Structure	*Armor Value*
Head	3	8
Center Torso	11	14
Center Torso (rear)		6
R/L Torso	8	12
R/L Torso (rear)		4
R/L Arm	6	11
R/L Leg	8	12

Weight and Space Allocation

Location	*Fixed*	*Spaces Remaining*
Head		1
Center Torso	2 Endo Steel	0
Right Torso	2 XL Engine Double Heat Sink 3 Ferro-Fibrous	5
Left Torso	2 XL Engine 5 Endo Steel	5
Right Arm	Double Heat Sink	6
Left Arm	Double Heat Sink	6
Right Leg	2 Ferro-Fibrous	0
Left Leg	2 Ferro-Fibrous	0

Weapons and Ammo	Location	Critical	Tonnage
Primary Weapons Configuration			
Large Pulse Laser	LA	2	6
LRM 10	LT	1	2.5
Ammo (LRM) 12	LT	1	1
Large Pulse Laser	RA	2	6
LRM 10	RT	1	2.5
Ammo (LRM) 12	RT	1	1

Alternate Configuration A			
Small Pulse Laser	H	1	1
ER Med. Laser	LA	1	1
Ammo (LRM) 12	LA	2	2
LRM 20	LT	4	5
Artemis IV FCS	LT	1	1
ER Med. Laser	RA	1	1
Ammo (LRM) 12	RA	2	2
LRM 20	RT	4	5
Artemis IV FCS	RT	1	1
Battle Value: 1,429			

Alternate Configuration B			
ER Med. Laser	H	1	1
ER PPC	LA	2	6
Double Heat Sink	LA	2	1
2 Double Heat Sinks	LT	4	2
ER PPC	RA	2	6
Double Heat Sink	RA	2	1
2 Double Heat Sinks	RT	4	2
Battle Value: 1,564			

Alternate Configuration C			
ER Med. Laser	H	1	1
Gauss Rifle	LA	6	12
Ammo (Gauss) 16	LT	2	2
ER Med. Laser	RA	1	1
ER Med. Laser	RA	1	1
ER Med. Laser	RA	1	1
ER Med. Laser	RA	1	1
Battle Value: 1,442			

Alternate Configuration D			
ER Large Laser	LA	1	4
SRM 4	LT	1	1
Ultra AC/10	RA	4	10
Ammo (Ultra) 20	RT	2	2
SRM 4	RT	1	1
Ammo (SRM) 25	RT	1	1
Battle Value: 1,088			

BATTLEFORCE 2

Type: Cougar

MP	Damage PB/M/L	Overheat	Class
5	3/3/3	—	L
Armor/Structure	**Point Value**	**Specials**	
3/2	12	omni	

Alternate Configuration A

MP	Damage PB/M/L	Overheat	Class
5	5/4/3	—	L
Armor/Structure	**Point Value**	**Specials**	
3/2	14	omni, if	

Alternate Configuration B

MP	Damage PB/M/L	Overheat	Class
5	4/4/3	—	L
Armor/Structure	**Point Value**	**Specials**	
3/2	16	omni	

Alternate Configuration C

MP	Damage PB/M/L	Overheat	Class
5	4/4/1	1	L
Armor/Structure	**Point Value**	**Specials**	
3/2	14	omni	

Alternate Configuration D

MP	Damage PB/M/L	Overheat	Class
5	4/3/2	1	L
Armor/Structure	**Point Value**	**Specials**	
3/2	11	omni	

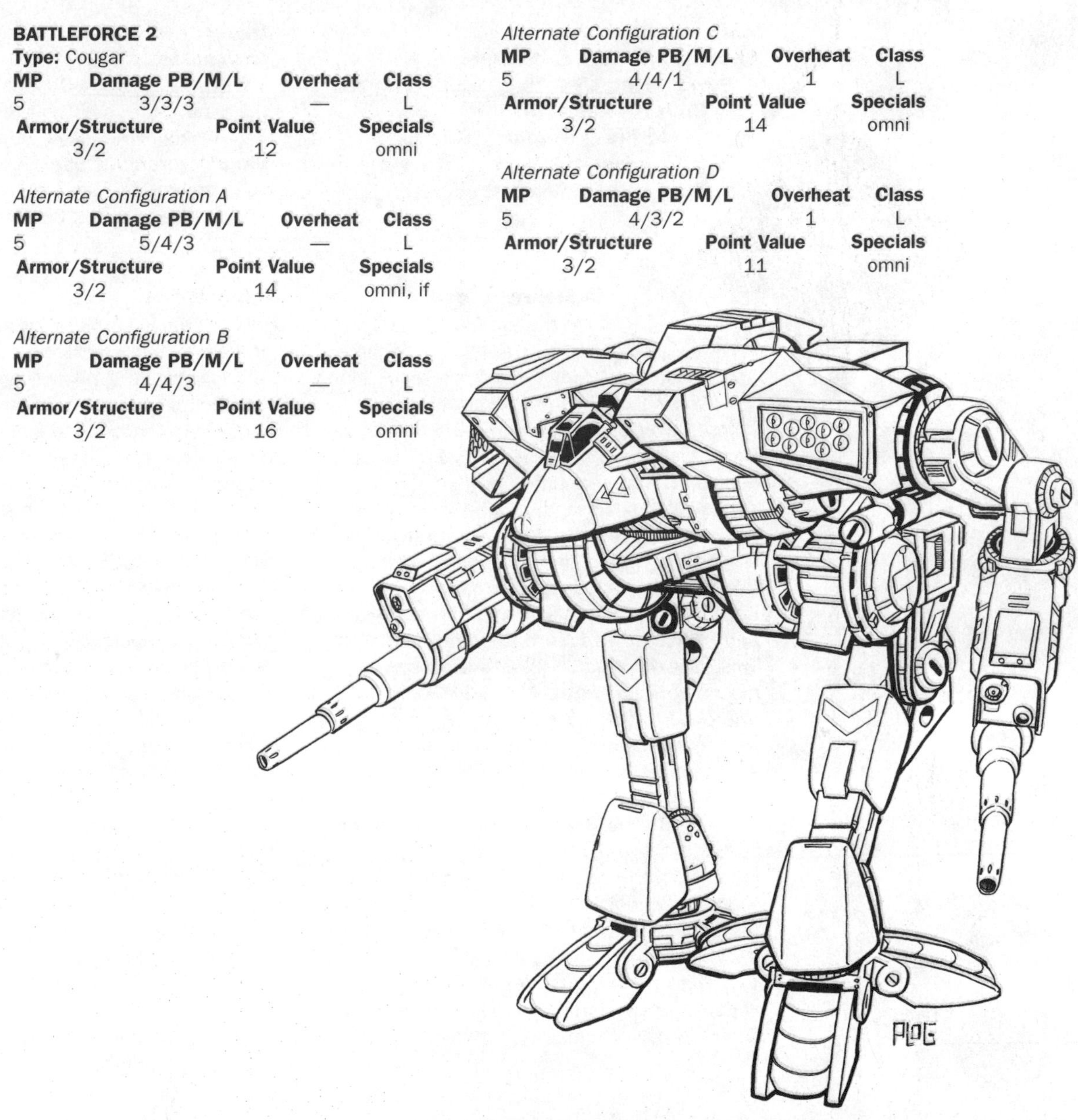

ARCTIC WOLF

Mass: 40
Chassis: Type AR1 Endo Steel
Power Plant: Light Force (ExtraLight) 280
Cruising Speed: 76 kph
Maximum Speed: 119 kph
Jump Jets: None
Jump Capacity: None

Armor: Royal-7 Standard
Armament:
6 Type 1 SRM Six-Shooters
2 Type 1 Cross-Pattern SRM 4 Launchers
1 Tracker Series Narc Beacon
Manufacturer: WC Site 1, Arc-Royal
Communications System:
HWLR Designation ComSys

Targeting and Tracking System:
Hunter (7) Dedicated TTS

Overview

In the process of gearing up their production lines on the southern continent of Arc-Royal, Clan Wolf-in-Exile has begun producing the *Arctic Wolf* BattleMech as a dry run for an OmniMech to be based on the same general design. In the meantime, its XL engine, double heat sinks and endo steel chassis promise to make the *Arctic Wolf* a favorite among the second-line units who will field this 'Mech. Loaded with SRMs, this BattleMech can rapidly close with an enemy and shower it with more than forty missiles. This capability has led Wolf warriors to nickname *Arctic Fox* pilots "MirvWarriors," a reference to the old strategic Multiple Independent Reentry Vehicles that separated into several missiles for saturation attacks.

As with the *Pack Hunter*, the armor and communications system for this 'Mech come from the Kell Hounds. The design team chose not to incorporate the Artemis fire control systems for the missile packages on this unit, because the SRM packages will be upgraded to Streak variants when the design is reworked as an OmniMech.

Capabilities

At nearly 120 kilometers per hour, the *Arctic Wolf* can quickly cross a battlefield while maintaining a low target-aspect ratio. Opponents of the design have noted the usual Clan tendency to ignore the machine's heat curve, as well as a reliance on weaponry that requires ammunition. However, firing a full salvo of missiles while running will barely hamper fire control and reduces mobility by less than 30 percent. This leaves the 'Mech sufficient mobility to evade hostile fire and maintain some offensive capability while waiting to cool down. Further, the *Arctic Wolf* cannot empty its bays in less than three minutes of continuous fire, for all practical purposes an eternity if engaged in a head-on slugging match. The *Arctic Wolf* should be able to stop nearly any opposing 'Mech design with two to four carefully placed missile flights (including Narc support in at least one flight), trusting to the efficiency of what Phelan Kell dubbed the "tandem-fire" effect of dozens of missiles independently seeking out weakened target locations. If the missile flights are accurately calculated, this gives the *Arctic Wolf* the potential to destroy up to four other machines before needing reloads, an impressive claim.

Deployment

The *Arctic Wolf* saw combat during Operation Bulldog as part of a second-line support Star appended to the First Wolf Legion for the assault on Bangor and again on Jeronimo. Problems with heat build-up were noted, but only for those warriors who violated the *Arctic Wolf*'s basic tactical doctrine of an engage-and-evade routine.

Variants

A single variant of the *Arctic Wolf* has been seen that drops the SRM-4s and their ammo and the two left-torso-mounted SRM Six-Shooters and replaces them with an Alpha Series large pulse laser in the left torso. This variant decreases ammo dependency and allows for some long-range attack capability, though it does not address heat dissipation problems. The rarity of this variant suggests that it is either very new or is only a test run for a proposed OmniMech configuration.

ARCTIC WOLF

Type: **Arctic Wolf**
Technology Base: Clan
Tonnage: 40
Battle Value: 1,044

Equipment		**Mass**
Internal Structure:	Endo Steel	2
Engine:	280 XL	8
Walking MP:	7	
Running MP:	11	
Jumping MP:	0	
Heat Sinks:	10 [20]	0
Gyro:		3
Cockpit:		3
Armor Factor:	96	6

	Internal Structure	*Armor Value*
Head	3	9
Center Torso	12	13
Center Torso (rear)		4
R/L Torso	10	14
R/L Torso (rear)		3
R/L Arm	6	8
R/L Leg	10	10

Weapons and Ammo	**Location**	**Critical**	**Tonnage**
2 SRM 6	RT	2	3
2 SRM 6	LT	2	3
SRM 6	RA	1	1.5
SRM 6	LA	1	1.5
Ammo (SRM) 45	LT	3	3
SRM 4	RA	1	1
SRM 4	LA	1	1
Ammo (SRM) 25	RT	1	1
Narc Missile Beacon	CT	1	2
Ammo (Narc) 6	RT	1	1

BATTLEFORCE 2

MP	**Damage PB/M/L**	**Overheat**	**Class**
7	4/4/—	2	M

Armor/Structure	**Point Value**	**Specials**
2/3	10	

CLINT IIC

Mass: 40
Chassis: SR 2830/b
Power Plant: Type 81 Fusion 240 XL
Cruising Speed: 65 kph
Maximum Speed: 97 kph
Jump Jets: Andoran Model JJII
Jump Capacity: 180 meters

Armor: Forging C629/j
Armament:
1 Type KOV LB-10X Autocannon
2 Series 2d Extended Range Medium Laser
Manufacturer:
Clan Snow Raven Industrial Complex Chi
Communications System: Raldon R1

Targeting and Tracking System:
Sloane 220 Lockover System

Overview

When the SLDF left the Inner Sphere in 2784, they took with them several prototype *Clint*s, each in the original configuration that carried the Armstrong Buster autocannon rather than the lighter cannon used in the mass-produced models. These prototypes went to storage in a Brian Cache on Circe and there they languished throughout the Exodus Civil War.

When Clan Snow Raven needed to rebuild after the Not-Named Clan's nuclear attack on their capital of Dehra Dun, they claimed the prototypes and pressed them into service. Snow Raven scientists worked to correct the stress problems on the 'Mech's frame caused by carrying the heavier autocannon, and by 2830 had transformed the poorly regarded prototype into a well-armed recon 'Mech.

Capabilities

The Ravens' key modification was replacing the large Pitban 240 fusion plant with a locally produced Type 81. While it offered the same output as the Pitban, the Type 81 was much lighter, allowing technicians to reinforce the arm and shoulder skeleton that repeatedly failed on the prototypes. Additional spare mass was used to increase the armor to seven tons and ammunition capacity to four tons.

During the Golden Century the design was further modified, replacing the Armstrong-Buster cannon with a KOV LB-10X that allowed selectable ammunition loads, and upgrading the lasers to extended-range variants. All other systems remained as in the original Andoran Industries model, and many retained their SLDF designations. Ironically in this age of modern technology, the *Clint* IIC still uses the original Sloane 220 Lockover TTS system.

Deployment

Clan Snow Raven used the *Clint* IIC in many clashes with other Clans during the Golden Century. The most notable was the defense of the Hellgate agrodomes in 2897. Though the speed and maneuverability of the *Clint* IIC provided the Ravens with a major advantage, the Ravens' battlefield inexperience cost them the fight, prompt the Clan to abandon the mining colony to the Steel Vipers only two years later.

With the Ravens' acquisition of OmniMech technology, many of their second-line 'Mechs were relegated to rear-echelon duty, including the *Clint* IIC. The Ravens chose to follow a policy of quality rather than quantity, and by the late thirtieth century they were faced with the choice of either decommissioning or mothballing the venerable design. The Blood Spirits' offer in 2977 to trade several of their WarShips for the Snow Raven 'Mech surplus came at a particularly good time. Along with many other older designs, most of the *Clint* IICs were transferred to the Spirits and became part of their Omicron Galaxy. Following the destruction of several Blood Spirit Galaxies in their battles with the Star Adders and Burrocks, however, few *Clint*s remained in Blood Spirit service.

In 3052, the Snow Ravens built the first new *Clint* IIC since production ceased in 2917, seeking to exploit the invading Clans' need for new equipment to replace their war losses. Clans Wolf and Ghost Bear acquired the largest numbers of the design, trading resources from the Inner Sphere for manufacturing output. The Ravens have refused to trade the design to either the Steel Vipers or the Jade Falcons because of ongoing feuds with those Clans.

Type: **Clint IIC**
Technology Base: Clan
Tonnage: 40
Battle Value: 1,176

Equipment		**Mass**
Internal Structure:	Endo Steel	2
Engine:	240 XL	6
Walking MP:	6	
Running MP:	9	
Jumping MP:	6	
Heat Sinks:	10	0
Gyro:		3
Cockpit:		3
Armor Factor:	112	7

	Internal Structure	*Armor Value*
Head	3	9
Center Torso	12	15
Center Torso (rear)		4
R/L Torso	10	13
R/L Torso (rear)		4
R/L Arm	6	9
R/L Leg	10	16

Weapons and Ammo	**Location**	**Critical**	**Tonnage**
LB 10-X AC	RA	5	10
Ammo (LB-X) 40	RT	4	4
ER Med. Laser	CT	1	1
ER Med. Laser	LT	1	1
Jump Jets	RL	2	1
Jump Jets	LL	2	1
Jump Jet	RT	1	.5
Jump Jet	LT	1	.5

BATTLEFORCE 2

MP	**Damage PB/M/L**	**Overheat**	**Class**
6J	2/1/1	1	M

Armor/Structure	**Point Value**	**Specials**
3/3	12	

CORVIS

Mass: 40 tons
Chassis: Model MH-24 Endo-Steel
Power Plant: Fusion 160 Standard
Cruising Speed: 43 kph
Maximum Speed: 65 kph
Jump Jets: 4 Model KT Boosters
Jump Capacity: 120 meters

Armor:
Compound H17 Ferro-Fibrous with CASE
Armament:
1 Type DL Ultra-10 Autocannon
2 Series 14a Medium Pulse Lasers
Manufacturer: Niles Industriplex Alpha

Communications System:
CH2 Series Integrated
Targeting and Tracking System:
Version Gamma-V TTS

Overview

By all accounts, the *Corvis* is a relic of Clan history. Apparently intended as a simple, inexpensive and easy-to-maintain 'Mech with great battle endurance, these very qualities ultimately limited its use in the field. Its lack of maneuverability relative to other 'Mechs in its weight class relegated the *Corvis* to defensive duty in built-up terrain, or as support for infantry and armor forces. Overshadowed within a decade of its unveiling by the development of the OmniMech, the *Corvis* fell quickly into disuse among virtually every Clan. Its demise would have been complete had Clan engineers not recognized some merit in the basic design, which included the same semi-modular techniques used in the lighter *Mercury*. Exploiting this flexibility to make improvements on the chassis, engine and weapons load by incorporating new Omni-technology, engineers ultimately transformed the tough but mediocre *Corvis* into the cutting-edge OmniMech known today as the *Stormcrow*. These changes created a far more flexible 'Mech and all but rang the death knell for the original model. Today, only Clan Hell's Horses continues to produce the original *Corvis*, which is usually employed in its traditional role of infantry and armor support.

Capabilities

The *Corvis* uses lightweight materials to conserve tonnage for its weapons array while maintaining nearly the maximum armor protection its mass allows. Unfortunately, the use of a standard 160-rated engine wastes the potential of this design by limiting its speed to that of 'Mechs twice its size. In an effort to offset this drawback, Clan engineers incorporated jump jets, allowing the *Corvis* to negotiate difficult terrain or move into better cover in a pinch. This makes the 'Mech most suitable for operations in overgrown or built-up areas such as jungles or urban environments.

The weapons of the *Corvis* are concentrated exclusively in the 'Mech's arms, allowing for the widest possible arc of fire. The Ultra-series autocannon in its right arm carries enough ammunition for more than three minutes of sustained fire at its maximum rate, and gives this 'Mech excellent endurance and punch at medium range. Paired medium pulse lasers ensure that even if the *Corvis* does run out of ammo, or (more likely) suffers a jam in its primary weapon, it can still strike the enemy from a suitable range. Another benefit of this weapons mix is the relatively low heat that all these systems generate, even under the most taxing circumstances. Records show that the *Corvis* can simultaneously use all of its weapons and jump its maximum distance even with up to 40 percent of its engine shielding compromised.

Deployment

The *Corvis* is almost exclusively deployed by Clan Hell's Horses, and functions as a "sentry 'Mech" near low-priority targets, allowing heavier units to be deployed elsewhere. The *Corvis* is also used as escort for infantry and slow-moving vehicular units. The greatest concentration of these 'Mechs appears in the Ninety-first Mechanized Assault Cluster of Clan Hell's Horses' Epsilon Galaxy (the Stonewall Brigade).

CORVIS

Type: **Corvis**
Technology Base: Clan
Tonnage: 40
Battle Value: 1,366

Equipment		**Mass**
Internal Structure:	Endo Steel	2
Engine:	160	6
Walking MP:	4	
Running MP:	6	
Jumping MP:	4	
Heat Sinks:	10 [20]	0
Gyro:		2
Cockpit:		3
Armor Factor:	134	7

	Internal Structure	*Armor Value*
Head	3	8
Center Torso	12	18
Center Torso (rear)		6
R/L Torso	10	16
R/L Torso (rear)		4
R/L Arm	6	12
R/L Leg	10	19

Weapons and Ammo	**Location**	**Critical**	**Tonnage**
Ultra AC/10	RA	4	10
Ammo (Ultra) 40	RA	4	4
2 Med. Pulse Lasers	LA	2	4
Jump Jets	LT	2	1
Jump Jets	RT	2	1

BATTLEFORCE 2

MP	**Damage PB/M/L**	**Overheat**	**Class**
4J	4/3/2	—	M

Armor/Structure	**Point Value**	**Specials**
3/3	14	

GREAT WYRM

Mass: 45 tons
Chassis: Type 56-45C Modified
Power Plant: RFUM 225 Standard
Cruising Speed: 54 kph
Maximum Speed: 86 kph
Jump Jets: None
Jump Capacity: None
Armor: CerPlate Mod 2F

Armament: 1 Mk. 44 LRM-10 Launcher
2 Series GAA-22 Rapid-Fire Cannon
2 Series 1 Mk. 3 Extended Range Medium Lasers
2 Series 1 Mk. 2a Extended Range Small Lasers
Manufacturer:
Cudahy Assembly Plant Delta, Circe

Communications System:
Block 7 TRACONM
Targeting and Tracking System:
TRTTS-X Mk. I

Overview

When General Kerensky left the Inner Sphere in 2784, he took complete copies of the Star League's data cores, which included design specifications on every piece of military hardware ever proposed to the SLDF for production.

By the twenty-ninth century, Clan warriors all over the Kerensky Cluster were clamoring for newer, more capable BattleMech designs. Clan Mongoose scientists, interested in cutting development time, looked to the Star League memory cores in hopes of finding a design that would suit their needs. What they found was a BattleMech submitted for trials in 2753, one that has become nearly ubiquitous in the Inner Sphere—the *Dragon*.

The Mongoose scientists converted the design into the *Great Wyrm*, and the results were astounding. Production models entered service just over a year after the design process began. Equally interesting is the physical profile the *Great Wyrm* displays—its resemblance to the *Dragon* is uncanny, sometimes fooling even ComStar's computer identification systems.

Capabilities

Though Mongoose scientists heavily modified the chassis they selected, making the *Great Wyrm* fifteen tons lighter than the *Dragon*, they managed to keep the same speed profile while increasing the firepower. Their only sacrifice was in overall armor protection; the *Great Wyrm* mounts 30 percent less armor than its parent design, a sacrifice deemed acceptable by its designers.

The *Great Wyrm*'s first combat trial came in 2844 when Clan Star Adder assaulted the Mongoose colony on Tokasha, where a Star of the new 'Mechs had been stationed as part of the garrisoning Trinary. The Adder Quasar Keshik made short work of the defenders, but at a heavy price. The *Great Wyrms* were the last to fall, for they used their mobility to stay out of their opponents' weapon ranges while maintaining a barrage with their autocannons. The *Great Wyrm* performed even better than expected, and Mongoose scientists increased production to capacity; they churned out scores of the units to swell their own ranks and hundreds more to trade with other Clans. Clan Cloud Cobra even retooled two of their own production lines to build the 'Mech, and both ran for nearly a decade.

The remainder of the Golden Century was not so kind to the *Great Wyrm*. With the introduction of the OmniMech, many Clans quickly relegated the *Wyrm* to solahma units. Main production halted in 2869 after the Smoke Jaguars absorbed Clan Mongoose. Clan Burrock made several limited production runs in 2871 and 2872 after they captured a former Mongoose assembly plant on Foster, but Clan Fire Mandrill subsequently seized and retooled that facility. Since then, no new *Great Wyrms* have been built.

Deployment

Every Clan includes some of these BattleMechs in their second-line Clusters. Clans Cloud Cobra, Coyote, Fire Mandrill, Steel Viper and Star Adder (through their absorption of Clan Burrock) field the most, approximately half a dozen Stars each. The remaining Clans field no more than one to two Stars each.

GREAT WYRM

Type: **Great Wyrm**
Technology Base: Clan
Tonnage: 45
Battle Value: 1,139

Equipment		**Mass**
Internal Structure:		4.5
Engine:	225	10
Walking MP:	5	
Running MP:	8	
Jumping MP:	0	
Heat Sinks:	10 [20]	0
Gyro:		3
Cockpit:		3
Armor Factor:	112	7

	Internal Structure	*Armor Value*
Head	3	7
Center Torso	14	16
Center Torso (rear)		5
R/L Torso	11	12
R/L Torso (rear)		4
R/L Arm	7	10
R/L Leg	11	16

Weapons and Ammo	**Location**	**Critical**	**Tonnage**
2 Ultra AC/2	RA	4	10
Ammo (Ultra) 45	RT	1	1
LRM 10	CT	1	2.5
Ammo (LRM) 12	RT	1	1
ER Medium Laser	RT	1	1
ER Small Laser	RT	1	.5
ER Medium Laser	LT	1	1
ER Small Laser	LT	1	.5

BATTLEFORCE 2

MP	**Damage PB/M/L**	**Overheat**	**Class**
5	4/3/1	—	M

Armor/Structure	**Point Value**	**Specials**
3/4	11	if

WYVERN IIC

Mass: 45 tons
Chassis: Type OES-45 Light Modified
Power Plant: Fusion Standard 180
Cruising Speed: 43 kph
Maximum Speed: 65 kph
Jump Jets: SL-150 Mod. V
Jump Capacity: 120 meters
Armor: Mix IIIc Composite
Armament:
1 Mk. 46 Type II LRM-10 Launcher
1 Mk. 22 Type III SRM-6 Launcher
1 Series 6b Extended Range Large Laser
2 Series 2a Mk. 5 Extended Range Medium Lasers
2 Series 1 Extended Range Small Lasers
2 Type VII Rotary Cannon
1 "Hellfire" Series II Flamer
Manufacturer: Manzikert Fabrication and Assembly Plant Gamma, Dagda
Communications System: Consolidated BMR3-CC
Targeting and Tracking System: Series I GDS

Overview

In the years following the colonization of the Pentagon in 2786, thousands upon thousands of BattleMechs were mothballed in Brian Caches across Clan space, including every surviving Star League 'Mech design. Even components salvaged from the battlefields of the Reunification War and Operation Klondike were put into storage.

Nearly two decades after the conclusion of Operation Klondike, Clan Burrock warriors stumbled across one of the many Brian Caches lost in the Pentagon War. This well-stocked cache contained a small number of BattleMechs and vehicles, but the far greater prize was the huge supply of BattleMech parts. Clan Burrock successfully defended their claim to the cache, and their scientists immediately turned the cache into a small factory for assembling and refitting BattleMechs, primarily the *Wyvern*.

Capabilities

The *Wyvern* IIC bears more than a passing resemblance to its Star League predecessor, both visually and mechanically; even its primary mission as a city fighter has remained unchanged. Only the observant will notice the extra weapons ports in the left arm and both torsos. The inclusion of Clan weapons and a new endo steel chassis allows the *Wyvern* IIC to mount a pair each of extended-range lasers and machine guns plus a flamer in addition to its traditional weapon load.

When Clan Burrock began heavily colonizing nearby worlds in the Kerensky Cluster, its Khans assigned a Star of these 'Mechs to each new settlement. Though the *Wyvern* cannot stand up to the heavy and assault OmniMechs that soon dominated the Clans' toumans, the 'Mech does offer considerable speed and a respectable long-range punch. The *Wyvern* IIC shines as a garrison 'Mech. Its hands allow it to assist in construction and other heavy lifting projects, while its machine guns and flamer are suited to handling crowds.

Deployment

Clan Star Adder fields the great majority of these BattleMech refits, having inherited Clan Burrock's complement in its Absorption bid. The Manzikert facility is reportedly gearing up for a new production run of *Wyvern* IICs, undoubtedly to fill the holes left in the Adders' second-line Galaxies in the wake of the Absorption War. As it has been in production on and off for some two hundred years, the *Wyvern* IIC has found a place in nearly every Clan's touman. The Blood Spirits and Fire Mandrills, after years of raiding the Burrocks, have a higher percentage than most others.

Type: **Wyvern IIC**
Technology Base: Clan
Tonnage: 45
Battle Value: 1,426

Equipment		**Mass**
Internal Structure:	Endo Steel	2.5
Engine:	180	7
Walking MP:	4	
Running MP:	6	
Jumping MP:	4	
Heat Sinks:	12 [24]	2
Gyro:		2
Cockpit:		3
Armor Factor:	152	9.5

	Internal Structure	*Armor Value*
Head	3	9
Center Torso	14	21
Center Torso (rear)		6
R/L Torso	11	17
R/L Torso (rear)		5
R/L Arm	7	14
R/L Leg	11	22

Weapons and Ammo	**Location**	**Critical**	**Tonnage**
ER Large Laser	RA	1	4
2 ER Small Lasers	RA	2	1
2 ER Med. Lasers	LA	2	2
Flamer	CT	1	.5
2 Machine Guns	LT	1	.5
Ammo (MG) 200	LT	1	1
LRM 10	CT	1	2.5
Ammo (LRM) 24	LT	2	2
SRM 6	RT	1	1.5
Ammo (SRM) 30	RT	2	2
Jump Jet	LT	1	.5
Jump Jet	RT	1	.5
Jump Jet	LL	1	.5
Jump Jet	RL	1	.5

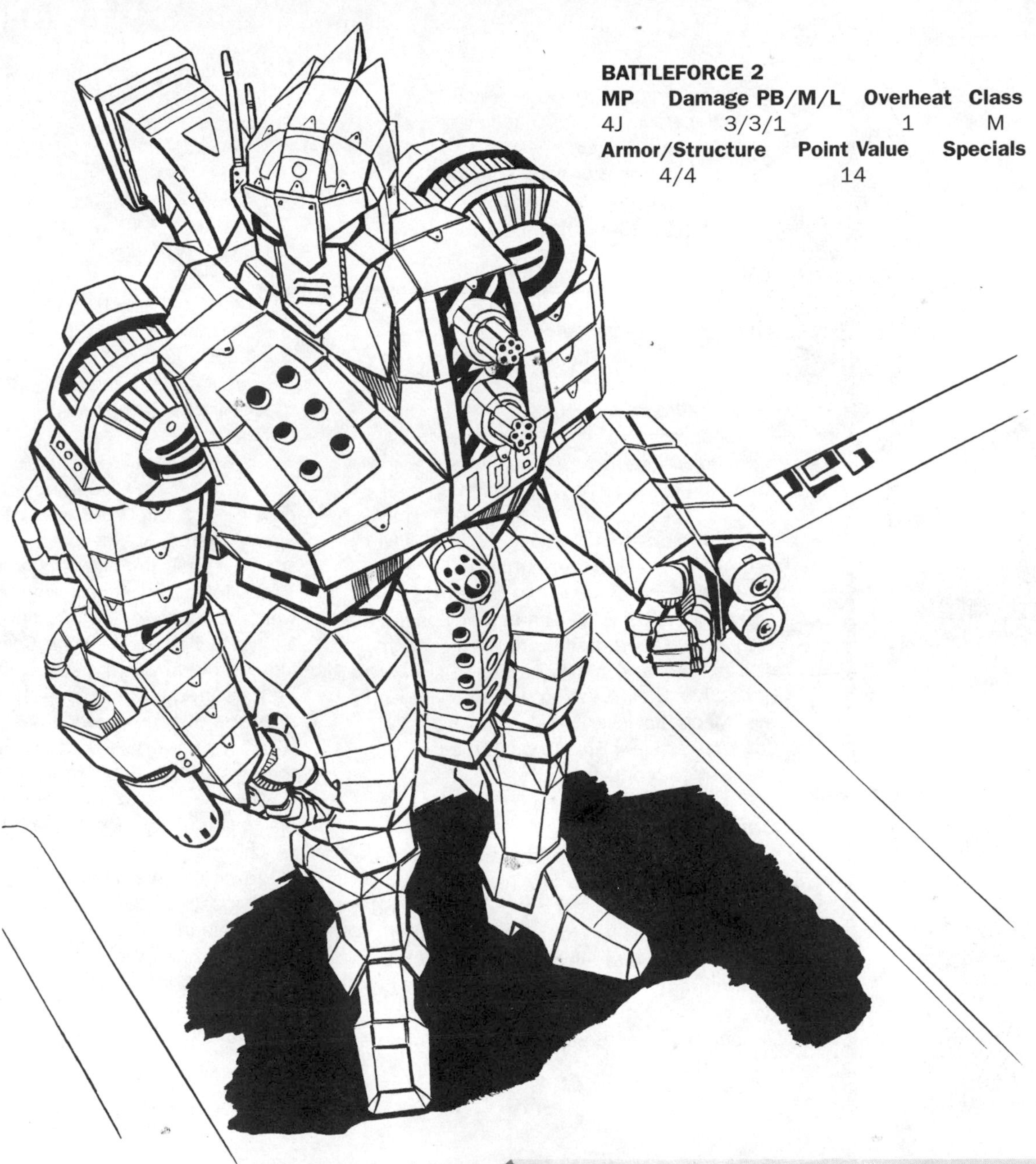

BATTLEFORCE 2

MP	**Damage PB/M/L**	**Overheat**	**Class**
4J	3/3/1	1	M

Armor/Structure	**Point Value**	**Specials**
4/4	14	

STALKING SPIDE

Mass: 50 tons
Chassis: Type QX745-50 Mod. III
Power Plant: Fusion Standard 250 Mk. IX
Cruising Speed: 54 kph
Maximum Speed: 86 kph, 119 kph w/MASC
Jump Jets: BMP Series XXI Mod. 12
Jump Capacity: 150 meters
Armor: Compound RSH5 Ferro-Fibrous
Armament:
1 Type DDS "Kingston" Extended Range PPC
2 CCWP-14 SRM-4 Launchers
2 Series PPS-XIX Medium Pulse Lasers
Manufacturer: Constantin Assembly Plant M27A-E, Homer
Communications System: Build 1700/1 Tacticom
Targeting and Tracking System: Series XXXII Multitrack

Overview

Though four-legged BattleMechs have proven to be far sturdier and more maneuverable than any two-legged 'Mech, pilot prejudice guaranteed that they were never widely produced. Even the appearance of apparently successful Clan quad designs like the *Fire Scorpion* and *Thunder Stallion* seemed unlikely to break that tradition.

Then Clan Cloud Cobra scientists acquired the remains of an Inner Sphere *Tarantula*. Based on their studies of the design, they eventually developed their own quad unit. Their greatest achievement with the 'Mech, however, was convincing Loremaster Eleni Riaz to push their new design into production.

Capabilities

The *Stalking Spider* suffers the same lack of internal space that hampers all quad 'Mech designs, but uses the available room quite efficiently. Its weapons complement is diverse enough to allow it to function in a number of different missions, but not so diverse that it suffers from being under-gunned. Its speed, augmented by jump jets and an enhanced MASC musculature and combined with its standard engine, give it the survivability a medium BattleMech requires on a battlefield dominated by OmniMechs.

The *Stalking Spider*'s greatest asset is its stability. Clan Cloud Cobra tactical doctrine teams a BattleMech Trinary with several aerospace fighter Binaries or Trinaries to form Fang Clusters. These 'Mech forces often perform combat drops, which can turn deadly for conventional BattleMechs. The *Stalking Spider*'s built-in jump jets and quadrupedal frame make it far better suited for absorbing the shocks and stresses of such operations.

The choice to mount the jump jets in the legs produces an interesting side effect. During a jump, the pilot constantly adjusts his trajectory by moving the 'Mech's legs, which creates the impression that the 'Mech is crawling through the air. Combined with the 'Mech's unique appearance, the effect can be unnerving. Commanders who may encounter Clan Cloud Cobra forces should review the briefing holos of this 'Mech with their units in order to become familiar with this unusual movement.

Deployment

The first *Stalking Spiders* were delivered to the Clan Cloud Cobra military in March of 3059. In contrast to standard Clan procedure, a majority of these 'Mechs were first distributed to front-line Clusters, including the four Delta Galaxy Clusters and both the 121st and 214th Cobra Fangs.

Unconfirmed rumors place a single *Stalking Spider* each among Clan Blood Spirit's Omega Galaxy and Clan Jade Falcon's Sigma Galaxy. Considering how recently the 'Mech was developed, we consider those rumors unreliable.

Variants

Information on the one known variant of the *Stalking Spider* is sketchy at best. It reportedly replaces the ER PPC and missiles with a single heavy laser and a dedicated targeting computer, presumably to help compensate for that weapon's inherent inaccuracy. Additional profiles also indicate that the variant mounts a TAG, an active probe and one extra heat sink, leading credence to that version's purported mission as a hunter-killer.

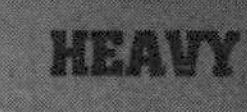

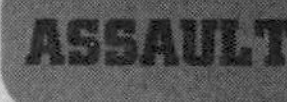

STALKING SPIDER

Type: **Stalking Spider**
Technology Base: Clan
Tonnage: 50
Battle Value: 1,884

Equipment		**Mass**
Internal Structure:		5
Engine:	250	12.5
Walking MP:	5	
Running MP:	8 (10)	
Jumping MP:	5	
Heat Sinks:	11 [22]	1
Gyro:		3
Cockpit:		3
Armor Factor:	154	8

	Internal Structure	*Armor Value*
Head	3	9
Center Torso	16	21
Center Torso (rear)		6
R/L Torso	12	15
R/L Torso (rear)		4
R/L Front Leg	12	20
R/L Rear Leg	12	20

Weapons and Ammo	**Location**	**Critical**	**Tonnage**
2 Medium Pulse Lasers	LT	2	4
2 SRM 4	LT	2	2
Ammo (SRM) 25	LT	1	1
ER PPC	RT	2	6
MASC	RT	2	2
Jump Jet	LFL	1	.5
Jump Jet	LRL	1	.5
Jump Jet	RFL	1	.5
Jump Jet	RRL	1	.5
Jump Jet	CT	1	.5

BATTLEFORCE 2

MP	**Damage PB/M/L**	**Overheat**	**Class**
5J	4/3/1	1	M

Armor/Structure	**Point Value**	**Specials**
4/4	19	

URSUS

Mass: 50 tons
Chassis: Bergan XIV
Power Plant: 200 Standard
Cruising Speed: 43 kph
Maximum Speed: 65 kph
Jump Jets: None
Jump Capacity: None
Armor: Compound A2F Ferro-Fibrous
Armament:
1 Series 7K Extended Range Large Laser
2 Series 2a Extended Range Medium Lasers
2 Kolibri Delta Series Medium Pulse Lasers
1 Type X LRM-10 Launcher
1 Type VI SRM-6 Launcher
Manufacturer: Bergan Industries, Alshain
Communications System: Garret T10B
Targeting and Tracking System: RCA Instatrac Mark VI

Overview

The Clans quickly discovered that the hardest part of waging war in the Inner Sphere was logistics. Transporting men and materiel across the vast distance between the Kerensky Cluster and the Inner Sphere posed a monumental task.

Ghost Bear Khan Bjorn Jorgensson set in motion a plan for his Clan to overcome this challenge. Shortly after capturing the planet Alshain in December of 3051, Ghost Bear technicians began bringing the Bergan Industries plant there back on line. The factory soon began producing the light 'Mechs for which it was tooled, but these antiquated machines were pathetic by Ghost Bear standards. In the lull after the Truce of Tukayyid, Khan Jorgensson ordered the Bergan plant reconfigured to produce a new second-line 'Mech. This 'Mech would combine Inner Sphere components manufactured in the Ghost Bear occupation zone with advanced weapons shipped from factories in Clan space.

The process took much longer than anticipated, mainly because of the basic incompatibility of most Clan and Inner Sphere systems. After more than seven years of work, Clan Ghost Bear solved these challenges and the revamped Bergan factory began producing the first Clan BattleMech entirely designed and manufactured in the Inner Sphere: the *Ursus*.

Capabilities

The first in a planned series of Ghost Bear 'Mechs to be built in the Inner Sphere, the *Ursus* was designed to fulfill the Clan's most pressing need: defense. The fall of the Smoke Jaguars left the Ghost Bears with a sizable border facing the Draconis Combine, and they needed a strong, flexible defensive unit to garrison a border that could turn hostile at any moment.

The *Ursus* fulfills its mission with a variety of weapon systems designed to engage a target at multiple ranges with accurate and massive firepower. As a defensive 'Mech, speed is secondary, and so the *Ursus* carries only a standard 200-rated engine, readily available in the Inner Sphere. Though this limits the 'Mech to a maximum speed of 65 kph, this was deemed a necessary sacrifice in order to mount the desired weapon systems on the 50-ton chassis.

Its highlight an extended-range large laser, the arsenal of the *Ursus* is impressive for a 'Mech of its size. Its only real weakness is a shortage of significant long-range firepower, with only an LRM-10 rack to supplement the large laser. A relatively maneuverable enemy can stay out of effective range of the majority of the 'Mech's weapons, but because the *Ursus* is expected to face inferior Inner Sphere machines, this is not as much of a flaw as it might seem.

Deployment

The first *Ursus* rolled off the Bergan assembly lines in late 3059. Already, most worlds bordering the Draconis Combine have received at least a Star of the new machines to bolster their defenses, with more on the way. The 'Mech's design purpose makes it highly unlikely that Clan Ghost Bear will ever deploy the *Ursus* in Clan space. Khan Jorgensson is so far quite pleased with his brainchild, which is the equal of Inner Sphere 'Mechs twice its size and many times its cost.

Type: **Ursus**
Technology Base: Clan
Tonnage: 50
Battle Value: 1,509

Equipment		**Mass**
Internal Structure:		5
Engine:	200	8.5
Walking MP:	4	
Running MP:	6	
Jumping MP:	0	
Heat Sinks:	16 [32]	6
Gyro:		2
Cockpit:		3
Armor Factor:	163	8.5
	Internal Structure	*Armor Value*
Head	3	9
Center Torso	16	25
Center Torso (rear)		7
R/L Torso	12	18
R/L Torso (rear)		5
R/L Arm	8	15
R/L Leg	12	23

Weapons and Ammo	**Location**	**Critical**	**Tonnage**
ER Large Laser	RA	1	4
2 Med. Pulse Lasers	RA	2	4
ER Medium Laser	RT	1	1
ER Medium Laser	LT	1	1
SRM 6	CT	1	1.5
Ammo (SRM) 15	LT	1	1
LRM 10	LA	1	2.5
Ammo (LRM) 12	LT	1	1
ECM Suite	RT	1	1

BATTLEFORCE 2

MP	**Damage PB/M/L**	**Overheat**	**Class**
4	5/4/1	1	M

Armor/Structure	**Point Value**	**Specials**
4/4	15	ecm

STOOPING HAWK

Mass: 55 tons
Chassis: York YT
Power Plant: 275 Standard
Cruising Speed: 54 kph
Maximum Speed: 86 kph
Jump Jets: None
Jump Capacity: None

Armor: Compound Alpha Ferro-Fibrous
Armament:
21.5 tons of pod space available
Manufacturer: York OmniMech Y1 Facility
Communications System: York Y2-Com
Targeting and Tracking System:
York Y2-T&T

Overview

When the OmniMech was introduced in 2854, Clan Blood Spirit simply assumed its perennial lack of resources with which to bargain or fight would prevent it from obtaining this superior technology. However, Clan Fire Mandrill, seeking to increase its land holdings, offered the Blood Spirits the new technology in exchange for territory.

Clan Blood Spirit scientists were eager to design their own OmniMech, and got their chance when Clan Ghost Bear phased out its OmniMech Prototype A in favor of the *Mad Dog*. The Blood Spirits won the Bear prototype in a Trial of Possession, developed it to its fullest and christened it the *Stooping Hawk*.

Capabilities

The frame of the *Stooping Hawk* is constructed with an extralight endo steel skeleton, advanced Compound Alpha ferro-fibrous armor and double heat sinks. The Blood Spirit scientists caste recognized that Khan Boques would not approve of the extralight engine, and used a standard engine for the *Stooping Hawk*. The XL power plant, with its comparative lack of durability on the battlefield, would have defied Khan Boques' order for low-cost, rugged 'Mech designs.

The materials used in the *Stooping Hawk* were considered excessive by Blood Spirit standards, and the weaponry the designers managed to load into its four initial configurations was likewise extreme. Massive autocannons, particle projector cannons, advanced missile tracking systems and an advanced targeting computer appear in versions of this design. Other Clans mount these systems in their Omnis as a matter of course, but the Blood Spirit Khans regularly review the *Stooping Hawk* performance records to determine if the results continue to justify the cost. If not for its ongoing battlefield success, this atypical Spirit 'Mech would have been decommissioned long ago.

Deployment

The *Stooping Hawk* is fairly rare even among Blood Spirit forces. However, this design took on new life when elements from the Fifty-fifth Red Vanguard Cluster of the Blood Spirit's Alpha Galaxy successfully raided Clan Star Adder for their new heavy lasers. This advanced weaponry was quickly installed on a new configuration of this venerable OmniMech.

Type: **Stooping Hawk**
Technology Base: Clan OmniMech
Tonnage: 55
Battle Value: 1,881

Equipment		**Mass**
Internal Structure:	Endo Steel	3
Engine:	275	15.5
Walking MP:	5	
Running MP:	8	
Jumping MP:	0	
Heat Sinks:	10 [20]	0
Gyro:		3
Cockpit:		3
Armor Factor:	173	9
	Internal Structure	*Armor Value*
Head	3	9
Center Torso	18	29
Center Torso (rear)		7
R/L Torso	13	21
R/L Torso (rear)		5
R/L Arm	9	18
R/L Leg	13	20

Weight and Space Allocation

Location	*Fixed*	*Spaces Remaining*
Head		2
Center Torso		2
Right Torso	2 Endo Steel	10
Left Torso	2 Ferro-Fibrous	10
Right Arm	3 Endo Steel	5
Left Arm	3 Ferro-Fibrous	5
Right Leg	2 Endo Steel	0
Left Leg	2 Ferro-Fibrous	0

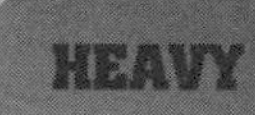

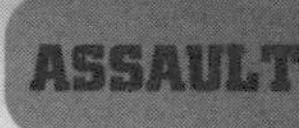

Weapons and Ammo	Location	Critical	Tonnage
Primary Weapons Configuration			
ER Medium Laser	LA	1	1
Medium Pulse Laser	LA	1	2
Ultra AC/10	RT	4	10
Ammo (Ultra) 30	RT	3	3
ER Med. Laser	RA	1	1
Med. Pulse Laser	RA	1	2
Jump Jets	LT	2	1
Jump Jet	CT	1	.5
Jump Jets	RT	2	1
Alternate Configuration A			
Double Heat Sink	LA	2	1
ER PPC	LT	2	6
3 Double Heat Sinks	LT	6	3
ER PPC	RT	2	6
3 Double Heat Sinks	RT	6	3
Jump Jets	LT	2	1
Jump Jet	CT	1	.5
Jump Jets	RT	2	1
Battle Value: 2,333			
Alternate Configuration B			
ER Large Laser	H	1	4
LRM 15	LT	2	3.5
Artemis IV FCS	LT	1	1
Ammo (LRM) 16	LT	2	2
LRM 15	RT	2	3.5
Artemis IV FCS	RT	1	1
Ammo (LRM) 16	RT	2	2
LRM 15	RA	2	3.5
Artemis IV FCS	RA	1	1
Battle Value: 1,709			
Alternate Configuration C			
ER Large Laser	H	1	4
ER Med. Laser	LA	1	1
Targeting Computer	LT	2	2
3 Double Heat Sinks	LT	6	3
ER Large Laser	CT	1	4
ER Med. Laser	RT	1	1
3 Double Heat Sinks	RT	6	3
Double Heat Sink	RA	2	1
Jump Jets	LT	2	1
Jump Jet	CT	1	.5
Jump Jets	RT	2	1
Battle Value: 2,286			
Alternate Configuration D			
ER Large Laser	H	1	4
2 ER Med. Lasers	LA	2	2
ER Small Laser	LA	1	.5
Double Heat Sink	LA	2	1
5 Double Heat Sinks	LT	10	5
Double Heat Sink	CT	2	1
5 Double Heat Sinks	RT	10	5
3 Heavy Med. Lasers	RA	6	3
Battle Value: 1,639			

BATTLEFORCE 2

Type: Stooping Hawk

MP	**Damage PB/M/L**	**Overheat**	**Class**
5J	4/3/1	1	M
Armor/Structure	**Point Value**	**Specials**	
4/5	19	omni	

Alternate Configuration A

MP	**Damage PB/M/L**	**Overheat**	**Class**
5J	4/3/3	—	M
Armor/Structure	**Point Value**	**Specials**	
4/5	23	omni	

Alternate Configuration B

MP	**Damage PB/M/L**	**Overheat**	**Class**
5	4/3/3	2	M
Armor/Structure	**Point Value**	**Specials**	
4/5	17	omni, if	

Alternate Configuration C

MP	**Damage PB/M/L**	**Overheat**	**Class**
5J	4/3/2	1	M
Armor/Structure	**Point Value**	**Specials**	
4/5	23	omni	

Alternate Configuration D

MP	**Damage PB/M/L**	**Overheat**	**Class**
5	7/6/1	—	M
Armor/Structure	**Point Value**	**Specials**	
4/5	16	omni	

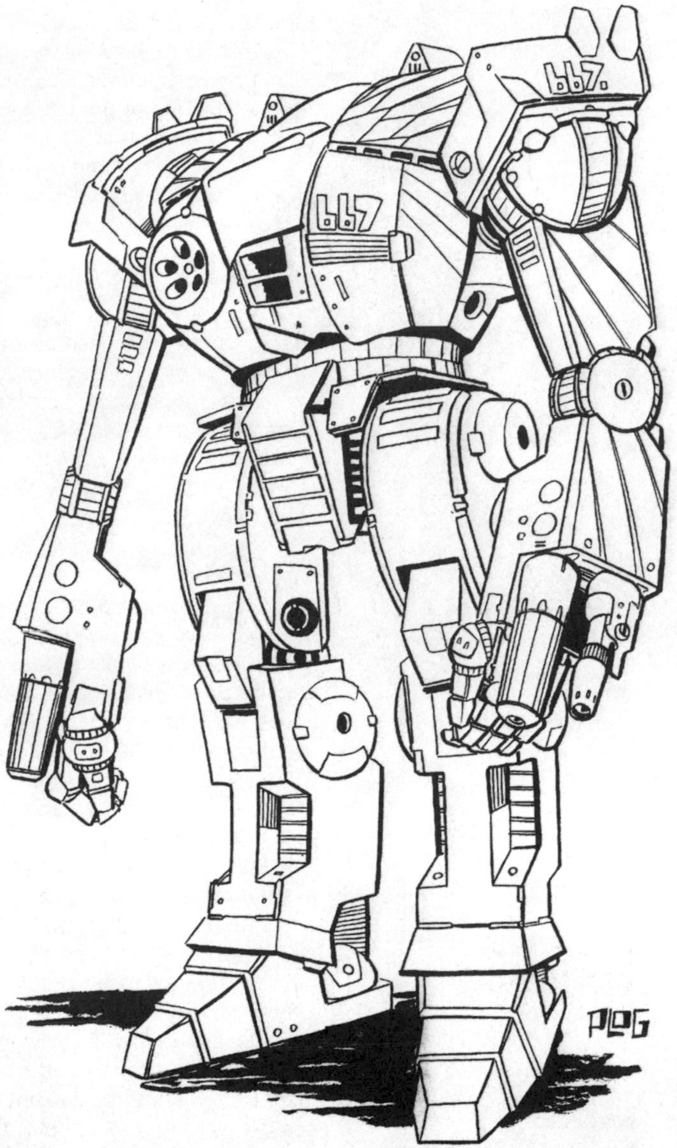

MATADOR

Mass: 60
Chassis: Viper NK7
Power Plant: New Kent Type 91 Fusion 240
Cruising Speed: 43.2 kph
Maximum Speed: 64.8 kph
Jump Jets: Pryzhok WM 10
Jump Capacity: 120 meters
Armor: Forging C629/j

Armament:
4 Series XII Rotary Machine Guns
1 Pattern J6 Streak SRM-6 Launcher
1 Pattern JX Streak SRM-4 Launcher
2 Series 2b Extended Range Medium Lasers
2 Chi Series Small Pulse Lasers
3 Lambda Medium Pulse Lasers

Manufacturer: Novy Minsk Armaments Plant
Communications System: Mercer 971
Targeting and Tracking System: GEG Pattern 491/6

Overview

The Steel Vipers, in their quest to become the ultimate warriors, have honed the skills of their troops and also developed their martial assets. The *Matador,* one pre-OmniMech development, was designed to duke it out with enemy 'Mechs at close range.

Capabilities

Like the *Atlas* and *Gargoyle*, the *Matador*'s appearance is meant to serve as a psychological weapon. Massive slabs of angular armor plates give it a look of solid power while offering the pilot and weapon systems protection unrivaled in any other 60-ton 'Mech. The placement of the *Matador*'s extensive weapon systems further enhances its formidable appearance.

Each shoulder carries paired rotary machine cannons that provide devastating anti-infantry firepower, while the right torso and head sport short-range missile packs. A pair of extended-range medium lasers located in the left torso provides the *Matador*'s principal long-range weaponry. Twin center-torso-mounted small pulse lasers are mounted just above the face-like cockpit assembly. A trio of medium pulse lasers mounted in a triangular pattern in the 'Mech's heavily armored left arm complete the load-out. Mounted in special shock-resistant housings, these three lasers remain operational even after a punch with that arm.

Though it appears slow and cumbersome, the *Matador* can reach speeds of up to 65 kph, respectable for a heavy 'Mech but slightly slower than comparable Clan 'Mechs. Jump jets in the legs, however, give the 'Mech a significant advantage in maneuverability.

Deployment

The *Matador* has seen extensive combat over the years but is now relegated to a second-line role. This pattern may change, however. In the Harvest Wars, Wolf Khan Vladimir Ward targeted several Steel Viper units equipped with the design, and those units easily held their own against the Wolf aggressors. Elements of the Steel Vipers Sixty-first Striker Cluster issued a preemptive batchall to the Wolf forces which led to the defection of almost a full Trinary of Steel Vipers to Clan Wolf. Though nominally a front-line unit, the Sixty-first, like much of the Homeworlds-based Steel Coil (Delta) Galaxy, makes extensive use of second-line BattleMechs. A *Matador* piloted by MechWarrior Shaznay was responsible for disabling two Wolf 'Mechs before a shot into the weak rear armor tore into the ammunition bins, causing a catastrophic explosion that destroyed the 'Mech.

Additional examples of the design can be found in the Jade Falcon, Star Adder and Fire Mandrill Clans, captured in numerous Trials throughout the centuries. However, because the Steel Vipers have never actively traded the design, there are fewer than two dozen *Matador*s outside that Clan.

MATADOR

Type: **Matador**
Technology Base: Clan
Tonnage: 60
Battle Value: 1,830

Equipment		**Mass**
Internal Structure:		6
Engine:	240	11.5
Walking MP:	4	
Running MP:	6	
Jumping MP:	4	
Heat Sinks:	12 [24]	2
Gyro:		3
Cockpit:		3
Armor Factor:	192	12
	Internal Structure	*Armor Value*
Head	3	9
Center Torso	20	30
Center Torso (rear)		9
R/L Torso	14	21
R/L Torso (rear)		6
R/L Arm	10	19
R/L Leg	14	26

Weapons and Ammo	**Location**	**Critical**	**Tonnage**
2 Machine Guns	RA	2	0.5
2 Machine Guns	LA	2	0.5
Ammo (MG) 100	RT	1	0.5
Streak SRM 6	RT	2	3
Ammo (Streak) 15	RT	1	1
Streak SRM 4	H	1	2
Ammo (Streak) 25	RT	1	1
2 ER Med. Lasers	LT	2	2
2 Small Pulse Lasers	CT	2	2
3 Med. Pulse Lasers	LA	3	6
Jump Jets	LL	2	2
Jump Jets	RL	2	2

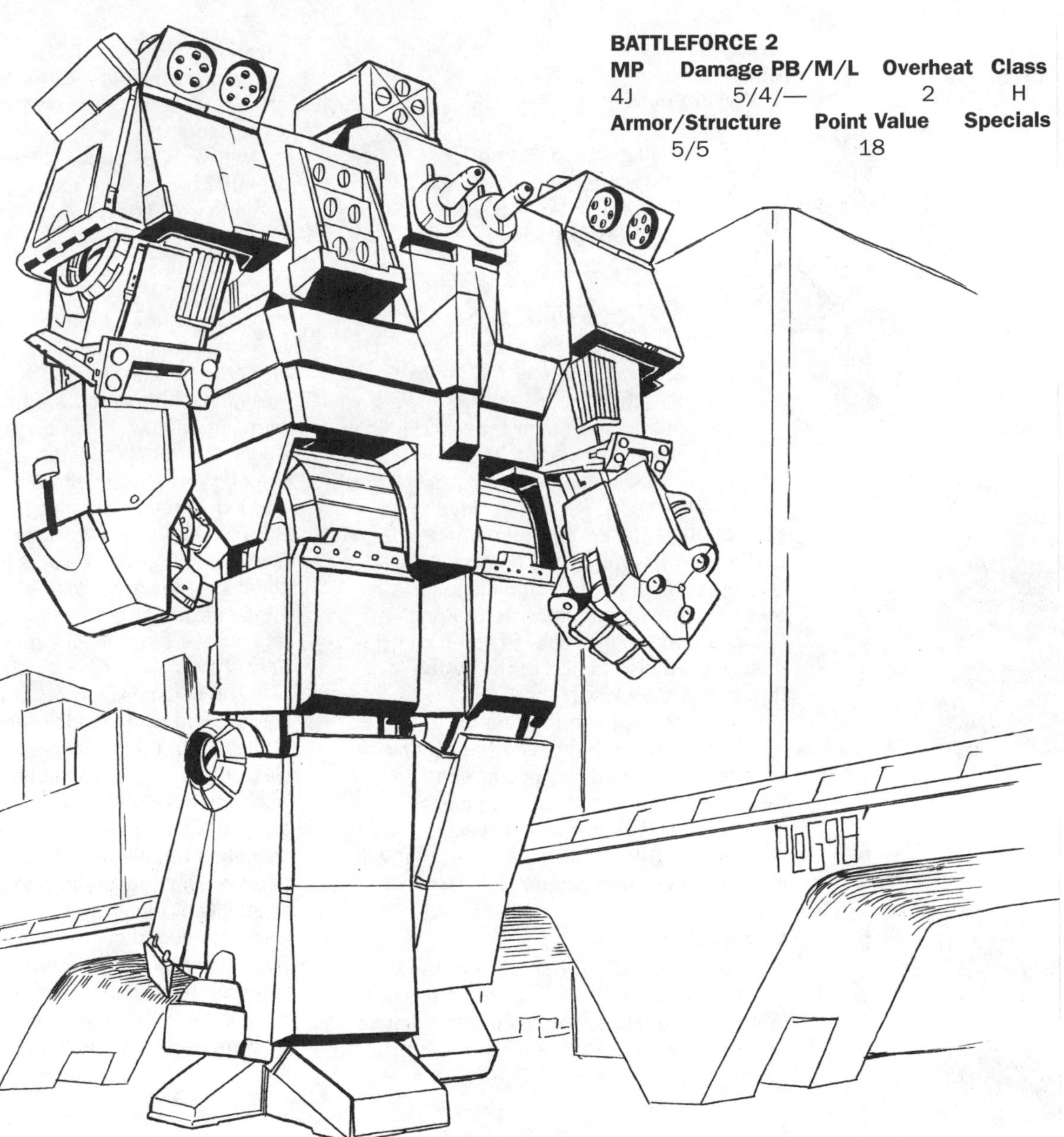

BATTLEFORCE 2

MP	**Damage PB/M/L**	**Overheat**	**Class**
4J	5/4/—	2	H

Armor/Structure	**Point Value**	**Specials**
5/5	18	

PREDATOR

Mass: 60 tons
Chassis: Process 3 Standard
Power Plant: Dagda-Production Series A 300 XL
Cruising Speed: 54 kph
Maximum Speed: 86 kph
Jump Jets: None
Jump Capacity: None
Armor: 17-J Standard
Armament: 2 Faraday LB-10X Autocannon
2 Series 2FM Extended Range Medium Lasers
2 Series 1 Extended Range Small Lasers
Manufacturer:
Kindraa Faraday-Tanaga Tertiary Facility
Communications System: KP-3 "Screamer"
Targeting and Tracking System:
Series VI TTS

Overview

The *Predator* is a testament to the new level of cooperation among the Clan Fire Mandrill Kindraa under the leadership of Khan Carrol. Produced on Atreus by Kindraa Faraday-Tanaga, this design incorporates an XL engine provided by Kindraa Kline, lasers from Kindraa Sainze and a comm system from Kindraa Payne. Two other Kindraa are responsible for shipping. The merchant caste of Khan Carrol's own Kindraa acts as the broker to ensure even distribution of the 'Mech throughout Clan Fire Mandrill.

Initial testing showed that the twin autocannon tended to shake the cockpit excessively, spoiling the pilots' aim and frequently causing radical equipment failures. The *Predator* was redesigned with a lowered cockpit, a satisfying result that was relatively easy to engineer.

Capabilities

For a second-line BattleMech, the *Predator* is well-matched against other heavy 'Mechs. It carries an impressive amount of armor, and is admirably suited to the fast-paced action of a Clan battlefield. In a Trial of Possession for the *Predator* design fought just prior to Clan Burrock's Absorbtion, Clan Fire Mandrill deployed *Predators* in a formation flanking their main front-line units. Under fire from a counterassault, five *Predators* re-formed into a Star of their own and led a charge that decimated the Burrock line. Every *Predator* walked off the field under its own power, each having claimed at least two kills. One Star Captain (since moved to a front-line force) claimed an impressive three kills (one of them a *Timber Wolf* Prime).

The take-down power of the *Predator* comes from twin Faraday-designed LB-X autocannon. Often supplied with both cluster and slug ammunition, these weapons have the power to quickly sand away armor and penetrate deep into the delicate internals of a 'Mech. Extended-range medium lasers add to the penetration capability of the *Predator*, with the smaller lasers an added bonus at pointblank range. This 'Mech design also provides well-balanced heat dissipation and almost completely avoids the common Clan problems with overheating.

Deployment

Despite some business quarrels among the Kindraa, the *Predator* continues to walk off the production line on Atreus and into the ranks of every Fire Mandrill Kindraa. Kindraa Mattila-Carrol is reconditioning a second factory on the Clan world of Shadow to increase production of this successful design.

Though the *Predator* has caught the attention of nearly every other Clan, no rivals have yet declared Trials of Possession to obtain the design. Many Clans refuse to even consider fighting for a second-line BattleMech, and apparently no Clan wants to be the first to admit that they want this design. Only Clans Blood Spirit and Diamond Shark field a few Stars' worth of this design, having traded some of their more prestigious designs to the Fire Mandrills. These few exchanges will allow those Clans to evaluate these new 'Mechs and choose whether or not to pursue further trade alliances.

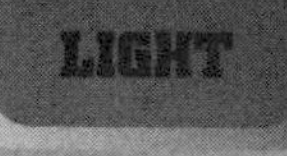

Type: **Predator**
Technology Base: Clan
Tonnage: 60
Battle Value: 1,592

Equipment		**Mass**
Internal Structure:		6
Engine:	300 XL	9.5
Walking MP:	5	
Running MP:	8	
Jumping MP:	0	
Heat Sinks:	10 [20]	0
Gyro:		3
Cockpit:		3
Armor Factor:	184	11.5

	Internal Structure	*Armor Value*
Head	3	9
Center Torso	20	28
Center Torso (rear)		9
R/L Torso	14	20
R/L Torso (rear)		6
R/L Arm	10	18
R/L Leg	14	25

Weapons and Ammo	**Location**	**Critical**	**Tonnage**
LB 10-X AC	LT	5	10
Ammo (LB-X) 20	LT	2	2
LB 10-X AC	RT	5	10
Ammo (LB-X) 20	RT	2	2
ER Medium Laser	LA	1	1
ER Small Laser	LL	1	.5
ER Medium Laser	RA	1	1
ER Small Laser	RL	1	.5

BATTLEFORCE 2

MP	**Damage PB/M/L**	**Overheat**	**Class**
5	6/5/2	—	H

Armor/Structure	**Point Value**	**Specials**
5/5	16	

FIRE SCORPION

Mass: 65 tons
Chassis: Coriolis Class VI
Endo Steel QuadFrame
Power Plant: Fusion 260 Standard
Cruising Speed: 43 kph
Maximum Speed: 65 kph
Jump Jets: None
Jump Capacity: None
Armor: Forging SA722 with CASE
Armament: 1 Type KOV LB-10X Autocannon
1 Irrlicht Gamma Series Ultra-10 Autocannon
Manufacturer: Roche QuadPlex Alpha
Communications System: JNE Integrated
Targeting and Tracking System: TRTTS Mark II

Overview

Four-legged 'Mechs offer increased stability and maneuverability over conventional two-legged 'Mechs, yet no military ever fields more than a very few such designs. MechWarriors dislike the rough ride such 'Mechs commonly provide, and resist adapting to the unique piloting style the four-leggers require.

Despite these factors, Clan Goliath Scorpion turned to a four-legged design to produce their totem 'Mech. Strongly resembling a scorpion, the *Fire Scorpion* incorporates a structure resembling a scorpion's tail raised to attack. The claw-like devices near the cockpit are actually armored guards, placed on either side of the head to keep ground troops from sniping at the unusually low cockpit.

During the brutal absorption of Clan Widowmaker on Roche, the *Fire Scorpion* developed a reputation as a resilient and deadly urban fighter.

Capabilities

The *Fire Scorpion* combines two of the most efficient weapons in the Clans' arsenal to fill a wide variety of combat roles. Equally at home providing cover from attacking fighters or supporting infantry on the ground, the 'Mech is hampered only by its relatively slow speed and lack of jump capability.

As one of the two genuine totem 'Mechs (along with the *Mandrill*), deployment of the *Fire Scorpion* is controversial. Many Goliath Scorpion leaders believe it belongs in front-line units as a symbol of Clan pride. However, most MechWarriors and commanders feel the 'Mech to have limited tactical use and decry its non-intuitive piloting style. The *Fire Scorpion*'s low cost and rugged design have made it a mainstay of Clan Goliath Scorpion's second-line forces; they are more likely to engage in urban combat, where the *Fire Scorpion* excels.

Deployment

The *Fire Scorpion* is a common sight among the garrison troops of Clan Goliath Scorpion. The Scorpions usually deploy the 'Mech together with Elemental forces, allowing its combination of heavy armor and sustainable firepower to facilitate infantry operations in close quarters.

Variants

One modification of note was adopted by Star Commander Temujin of the Twentieth Scorpion Cuirassiers. Temujin upgraded his *Fire Scorpion* to support an Ultra AC-20, two LRM-10s and five machine guns in place of the standard weaponry. With four tons of ammo to support the massive cannon, two tons of LRMs, and 200 rounds for the five miniguns, the design is a dangerous urban opponent. Rounding out the arsenal is a Beagle probe to uncover enemy ambush points, a useful addition given the possibility of action against Inner Sphere forces in the near future.

FIRE SCORPION

Type: **Fire Scorpion**
Technology Base: Clan
Tonnage: 65
Battle Value: 1,379

Equipment		**Mass**
Internal Structure:	Endo Steel	3.5
Engine:	260	13.5
Walking MP:	4	
Running MP:	6	
Jumping MP:	0	
Heat Sinks:	10	0
Gyro:		3
Cockpit:		3
Armor Factor:	224	14

	Internal Structure	*Armor Value*
Head	3	9
Center Torso	21	31
Center Torso (rear)		10
R/L Torso	15	22
R/L Torso (rear)		7
R/L Front Leg	15	29
R/L Rear Leg	15	29

Weapons and Ammo	**Location**	**Critical**	**Tonnage**
LB 10-X AC	RT	5	10
Ammo (LB-X) 30	RT	3	3
Ultra AC/10	LT	4	10
Ammo (Ultra) 30	LT	3	3
A-Pod	LFL	1	.5
A-Pod	RFL	1	.5
A-Pod	LRL	1	.5
A-Pod	RRL	1	.5

BATTLEFORCE 2

MP	**Damage PB/M/L**	**Overheat**	**Class**
4	4/3/3	—	H

Armor/Structure	**Point Value**	**Specials**
6/5	14	

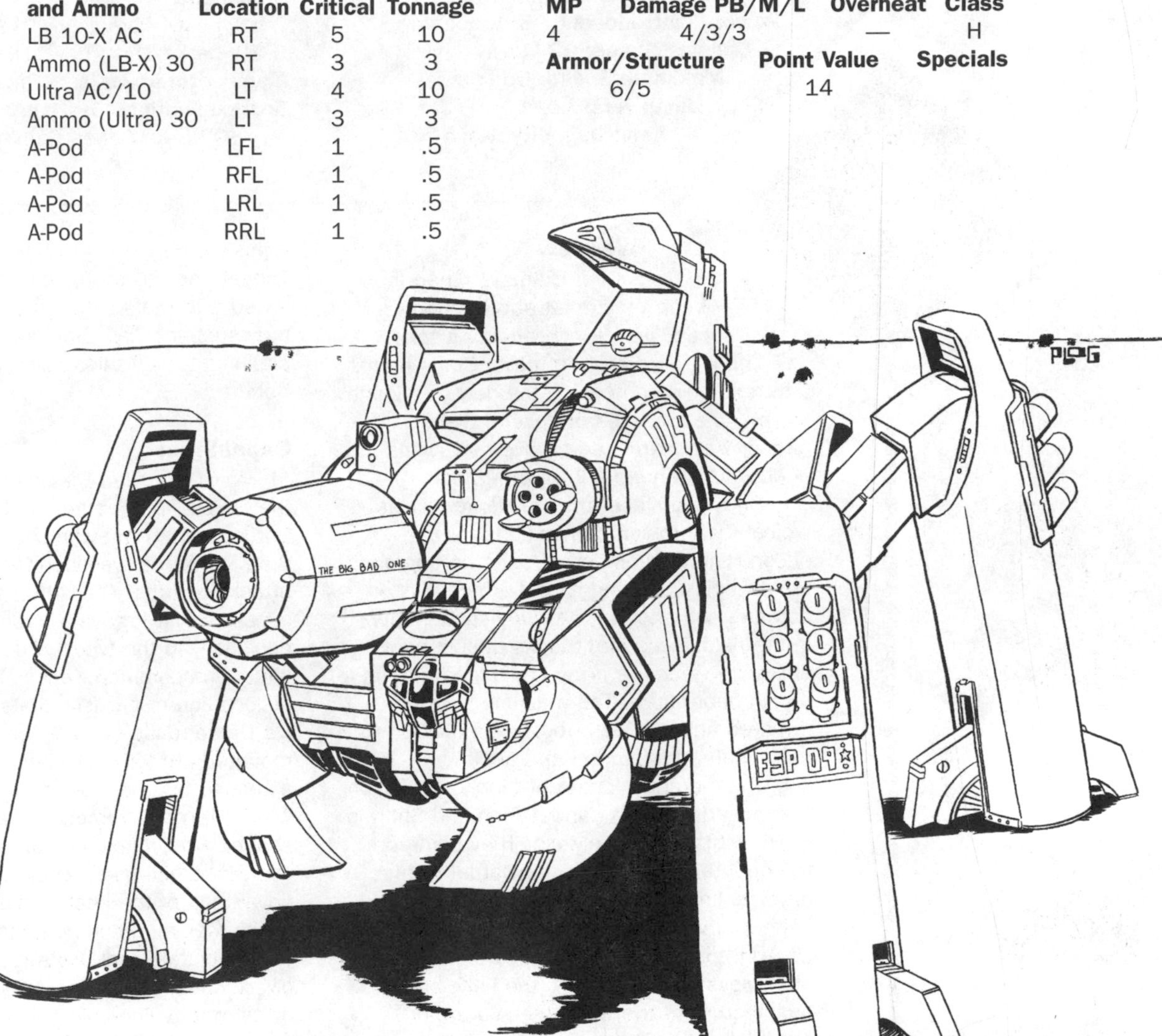

HA OTOKO

Mass: 65 tons
Chassis: Beta Manufactured Standard
Power Plant: Model SF-3 (Standard)
Cruising Speed: 43 kph
Maximum Speed: 65 kph
Jump Jets: None
Jump Capacity: None

Armor: Forging ZK11 Standard
Armament:
2 Type XX "Great Bow" LRM-20 Launchers
2 Type X "Short Bow" LRM-10 Launchers
Manufacturer: Auxiliary Production Site #4
Communications System:
S9R Beta Series Communications

Targeting and Tracking System:
Able-Seven Sensor Suite

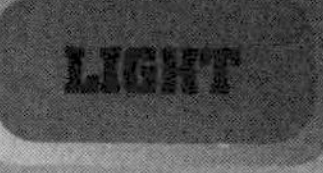

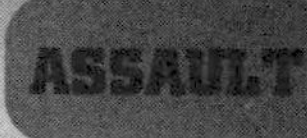

Overview

Clan Diamond Shark has been very quiet about its newest second-line 'Mech, the *Ha Otoko*. The warriors of most other Clans prefer to reserve judgment on the design, though the merchant castes of several Clans already have expressed grave misgivings about the intended use of the 'Mech.

On the surface, the *Ha Otoko* follows typical Clan design conventions for a second-line BattleMech. It uses no upgraded technologies, making it cost-effective and durable, and allowing easy logistical support in the field. Because it lacks double heat sinks, its weapons array is planned around a high heat curve. The machine is well-armored and carries enough ammunition to participate in extended operations.

The merchant caste of Clan Jade Falcon first raised concerns about Diamond Shark's intent with this BattleMech. They pointed to the oriental influence in the BattleMech's physical lines and the Japanese name, neither of which is typical of the Clans. (*Ha Otoko* translates very roughly as the Bladed Man, possibly referring to the knife-blade architecture of the BattleMech's armor.) Finally, the *Ha Otoko* would fit the Inner Sphere style of combat very well, working as a missile support 'Mech within a lance. Though the Falcon merchants have not levied a formal charge, it seems clear that they suspect Clan Diamond Shark of planning to sell this design within the Inner Sphere.

Capabilities

In 3060, Clan Diamond Shark fielded the *Ha Otoko* in battles on the planet Barcella where they helped to defend the Clan Nova Cat evacuation efforts against attacks by other Clans in return for territory concessions. It gave a strong performance, especially in the types of defensive situations commonly encountered by second-line or garrison units. In combat, the *Ha Otoko* relies primarily on its torso-mounted LRM-20 launchers, switching to the extended firing arc of an arm-mounted LRM-10 if a target attempts to flank it. Warriors piloting *Ha Otoko*s take up positions in rivers or small lakes when possible to take advantage of the heat dissipation potential of their leg-mounted heat sinks. Battlefield tactics dictate that pilots reserve a full salvo of sixty missiles to use against the enemy at its most vulnerable point—and the shot is as close to being a guaranteed success as possible.

Deployment

So far, the *Ha Otoko* has appeared in several Diamond Shark second-line units. Clans Blood Spirit and Fire Mandrill have also received a limited number of the design in a trade for technology to be designated later.

Though there is no proof that Clan Diamond Shark intends to offer the *Ha Otoko* to the Inner Sphere, merchants of the Jade Falcons and other Clans continue to disparage the 'Mech. Their latest evaluations demonstrate how the Draconis Combine could easily alter the design for use without the Clan-tech LRM launchers. Switching to an Inner Sphere XL engine with double heat sinks, which the design apparently can support, would make up for the weight differential, turning the *Ha Otoko* into an above-average Inner Sphere front-line machine.

HA OTOKO

Type: **Ha Otoko**
Technology Base: Clan
Tonnage: 65
Battle Value: 1,466

Equipment		**Mass**
Internal Structure:		6.5
Engine:	260	13.5
Walking MP:	4	
Running MP:	6	
Jumping MP:	0	
Heat Sinks:	13	3
Gyro:		3
Cockpit:		3
Armor Factor:	208	13
	Internal Structure	*Armor Value*
Head	3	9
Center Torso	21	31
Center Torso (rear)		10
R/L Torso	15	23
R/L Torso (rear)		7
R/L Arm	10	20
R/L Leg	15	29

Weapons and Ammo	**Location**	**Critical**	**Tonnage**
LRM 20	LT	4	5
Ammo (LRM) 18	LT	3	3
LRM 20	RT	4	5
Ammo (LRM) 18	RT	3	3
LRM 10	LA	1	2.5
Ammo (LRM) 12	LA	1	1
LRM 10	RA	1	2.5
Ammo (LRM) 12	RA	1	1

BATTLEFORCE 2

MP	**Damage PB/M/L**	**Overheat**	**Class**
4	3/2/2	2	H

Armor/Structure	**Point Value**	**Specials**
5/5	15	if

GUILLOTINE IIC

Mass: 70
Chassis: Clan Modified Heavy Type X (Endo)
Power Plant: Clan Standard 280 series
Cruising Speed: 43 kph
Maximum Speed: 65 kph
Jump Jets: Clan Series Type 4 Heavy
Jump Capacity: 120 meters

Armor: Forging OTR17b (Standard)
Armament:
1 Clan Mk. XVII Extended Range PPC
2 Kolibri Delta Series Large Pulse Lasers
2 Series 2f Extended Range Medium Lasers
1 Clan Series 4d Standard SRM-6 Launcher

Manufacturer: Omega Orbital Production Plant
Communications System: JNE Integrated
Targeting and Tracking System: Series VI KITT

Overview

The Exodus fleet carried large numbers of the *Guillotine*, a rugged Star League Defense Force design, away from the Inner Sphere to Kerensky's followers' new home beyond the Periphery. When Nicholas Kerensky had established his new society and retaken the Pentagon worlds with those disciplined forces, the newly formed Clans set about building 'Mech units, relying on existing designs for their blueprints. A large number of *Guillotine*s found in storage on the Pentagon worlds of Eden and Circe were distributed among the Clans who maintained enclaves on these worlds. This sturdy, dependable design served in the front lines until the advent of OmniMechs, when the *Guillotine* was relegated to second-line and solahma units.

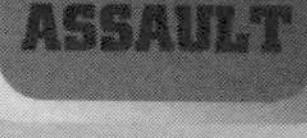

Capabilities

When the time came to produce new second-line 'Mechs, Clan Coyote engineers reworked the venerable *Guillotine* into a newer, more powerful design rather than inventing an all-new unit. Replacing the old Inner Sphere chassis with a Clan endo-steel chassis, the engineers freed up more space inside the 'Mech for weapons. Already satisfied with the 'Mech's armor protection, speed and jump capability, the engineers concentrated on giving the *Guillotine* better firepower.

The *Guillotine*'s main weapon was changed from a large laser to an ER PPC, and the arm-mounted medium lasers were replaced with two large pulse lasers. Two extended-range medium lasers and a Clan standard SRM-6 rack round out the *Guillotine* IIC's new weapons suite. To help the 'Mech dissipate heat from this load, standard heat sinks were replaced with sixteen Clan double heat sinks.

The *Guillotine* IIC was officially unveiled in 2889. Clan Star Adder won several of them in a Trial of Possession, and was the first Clan to take the upgraded 'Mech into battle. The Adders used the new 'Mechs in 2892 against a raiding force from Clan Mongoose seeking genetic material on the Adders' homeworld. The Star Adder warriors fought a grueling five-hour battle against the determined Mongoose warriors, and only the timely arrival of two Stars made up entirely of the *Guillotine* IIC turned the battle in favor of the Star Adders.

Deployment

Currently Clans Star Adder, Cloud Cobra and Coyote field the largest number of *Guillotine* IICs, and most of the other Clans employ small numbers of the 'Mechs. All *Guillotine* IICs are assigned to second-line and solahma units. In Clan Coyote, a Star Captain or Trinary Commander would pilot this unit.

CLAN

GUILLOTINE IIC

Type: **Guillotine IIC**
Technology Base: Clan
Tonnage: 70
Battle Value: 2,187

Equipment		**Mass**
Internal Structure:	Endo Steel	3.5
Engine:	280	16
Walking MP:	4	
Running MP:	6	
Jumping MP:	4	
Heat Sinks:	16 [32]	6
Gyro:		3
Cockpit:		3
Armor Factor:	192	12

	Internal Structure	*Armor Value*
Head	3	9
Center Torso	22	27
Center Torso (rear)		12
R/L Torso	15	22
R/L Torso (rear)		8
R/L Arm	11	20
R/L Leg	15	22

Weapons and Ammo	**Location**	**Critical**	**Tonnage**
ER PPC	LA	2	6
2 Large Pulse Lasers	RA	4	12
ER Med. Laser	LT	1	1
ER Med. Laser	RT	1	1
SRM 6	CT	1	1.5
Ammo (SRM) 15	CT	1	1
Jump Jet	RT	1	1
Jump Jet	LT	1	1
Jump Jet	RL	1	1
Jump Jet	LL	1	1

BATTLEFORCE 2

MP	**Damage PB/M/L**	**Overheat**	**Class**
4J	4/4/2	2	H

Armor/Structure	**Point Value**	**Specials**
5/5	22	

NOVA CAT

Mass: 70 tons
Chassis: Mynx Type Heavy
Power Plant: Consolidated Fusion 280 Extralight
Cruising Speed: 43 kph
Maximum Speed: 65 kph
Jump Jets: None
Jump Capacity: None
Armor: Alpha Compound Plate
Armament:
38 tons of pod space available
Manufacturer: Barcella Alpha, Irece Alpha
Communications System: JNE Integrated
Targeting and Tracking System: Build 2 CAT TTS

Overview

Following Clan Nova Cat's defeat at Tukayyid, that Clan began talks with the Draconis Combine. Khan Severen Leroux at the same time ordered the construction of a new heavy OmniMech. Built to protect the Clan both militarily and spiritually, the design was christened *Nova Cat*, imbuing it with the spirit of the Clan.

In 3059, when the Inner Sphere launched its counterattack on the Smoke Jaguar Occupation Zone, Clan Nova Cat's decision was at hand. The Smoke Jaguars suddenly found themselves facing Clan Nova Cat forces as part of the new Star League Army. At the forefront of the Nova Cat units was their new *Nova Cat* 'Mech.

Capabilities

Impressed by Clan Jade Falcon's *Night Gyr*, Nova Cat scientists reduced the speed of the *Nova Cat* to free a massive amount of pod space for weapons allocation, giving the *Nova Cat* its unique look.

The standard configuration has awesome long-range firepower. However, to help contol heat, the pilot must alternate his weapons fire. Relying on beam weapons allows this configuration to operate away from support for extended periods.

The A configuration is similar to the *Summoner* D, while configuration B is a missile platform similar to the *Night Gyr* D.

The C configuration is meant for urban combat, not extended campaigns. Configuration D mounts the new heavy lasers invented by Clan Star Adder, combined with an LB-X/10 autocannon. This configuration has incredible short-range firepower, but at the cost of excessive overheating problems.

Deployment

The *Nova Cat* was first produced on the Nova Cat capital of Barcella, in Clan space. In early 3059, production began in the new Irece Alpha plant in the Inner Sphere.

First seeing service with Clan Nova Cat during Operation Bulldog, several *Nova Cats* were seized by the Smoke Jaguars when they captured a malfunctioning Nova Cat DropShip. Sources in the Periphery persistently report an odd-looking 'Mech resembling the *Nova Cat*. It is possible that one or more of these machines may have become part of the arsenals of other Clans that accepted Smoke Jaguar refugees.

Type: **Nova Cat**
Technology Base: Clan OmniMech
Tonnage: 70
Battle Value: 2,165

Equipment		**Mass**
Internal Structure:	Endo Steel	3.5
Engine:	280 XL	8
Walking MP:	4	
Running MP:	6	
Jumping MP:	0	
Heat Sinks:	11 [22]	1
Gyro:		3
Cockpit:		3
Armor Factor:	216	13.5
	Internal Structure	*Armor Value*
Head	3	9
Center Torso	22	35
Center Torso (rear)		8
R/L Torso	15	23
R/L Torso (rear)		7
R/L Arm	11	22
R/L Leg	15	30

Weight and Space Allocation

Location	*Fixed*	*Spaces Remaining*
Head	Endo Steel	0
Center Torso	2 Endo Steel	0
Right Torso	2 Engine	10
Left Torso	2 Engine	10
Right Arm		8
Left Arm		8
Right Leg	2 Endo Steel	0
Left Leg	2 Endo Steel	0

Weapons and Ammo	**Location**	**Critical**	**Tonnage**
Primary Weapons Configuration			
3 ER Large Lasers	LA	3	12
2 Double Heat Sinks	LA	4	2
5 Double Heat Sinks	LT	10	5
5 Double Heat Sinks	RT	10	5
2 ER PPC	RA	4	12
2 Double Heat Sinks	RA	4	2

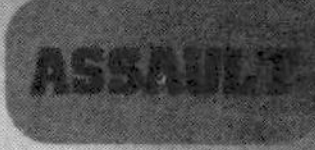

CLAN

Alternate Configuration A

2 ER Large Lasers	LA	2	8
4 Double Heat Sinks	LA	8	4
Jump Jets	LT	2	2
4 Double Heat Sinks	LT	8	4
Jump Jets	RT	2	2
Targeting Computer	RT	4	4
2 Double Heat Sinks	RT	4	2
2 ER Large Lasers	RA	2	8
4 Double Heat Sinks	RA	8	4

Battle Value: 2,646

Alternate Configuration B

3 LRM 15	LA	6	10.5
Ammo (LRM) 40	LT	5	5
ER Med. Laser	LT	1	1
2 Double Heat Sinks	LT	4	2
Ammo (LRM) 40	RT	5	5
ER Med. Laser	RT	1	1
2 Double Heat Sinks	RT	4	2
3 LRM 15	RA	6	10.5
Double Heat Sink	RA	2	1

Battle Value: 2,078

Alternate Configuration C

2 Large Pulse Lasers	LA	4	12
Ammo (Ultra) 40	RT	2	2
Ammo (LB-X) 40	RT	2	2
Double Heat Sink	RT	2	1
2 Ultra AC/5	RA	6	14
LB 5-X AC	RA	4	7

Battle Value: 1,705

Alternate Configuration D

LB 10-X AC	LA	5	10
Heavy Large Laser	LA	3	4
Double Heat Sink	LA	2	1
Ammo (LB-X) 10	LT	2	2
Targeting Computer	LT	5	5
Double Heat Sink	LT	2	1
5 Double Heat Sinks	RT	10	5
2 Heavy Large Lasers	RA	6	8
2 Double Heat Sinks	RA	4	2

Battle Value: 1,671

BATTLEFORCE 2

Type: **Nova Cat**

MP	Damage PB/M/L	Overheat	Class	Armor/Structure	Point Value	Specials
4	6/5/5	1	H	5/4	22	omni

Alternate Configuration A

MP	Damage PB/M/L	Overheat	Class	Armor/Structure	Point Value	Specials
4J	6/4/4	—	H	5/4	26	omni

Alternate Configuration B

MP	Damage PB/M/L	Overheat	Class	Armor/Structure	Point Value	Specials
4	6/5/4	2	H	5/4	21	omni, if

Alternate Configuration C

MP	Damage PB/M/L	Overheat	Class	Armor/Structure	Point Value	Specials
4	5/4/4	—	H	5/4	17	omni

Alternate Configuration D

MP	Damage PB/M/L	Overheat	Class	Armor/Structure	Point Value	Specials
4	5/4/1	2	H	5/4	17	omni

ORION IIC

Mass: 75 tons
Chassis: Type W2 Endo Steel
Power Plant: Heavy Force 300 (Standard)
Cruising Speed: 43 kph
Maximum Speed: 65 kph
Jump Jets: None
Jump Capacity: None

Armor: Composite A-4 Ferro-Fibrous
Armament: 1 Omega 12-Coil Gauss Rifle
1 Type XX "Great Bow" LRM-20 Launcher
1 Series 6W Extended Range Large Laser
1 Series 7W Extended Range Large Laser
1 Offset Pattern K4 SRM Launcher
Manufacturer: WC Aux Site #2

Communications System:
Khan series (Type 1)
Targeting and Tracking System:
Series III OPT

Overview

As Aleksandr Kerensky's chosen BattleMech, the original *Orion* held a special place within the Clans, especially Clan Wolf. Out of respect for the Great Father, the Clans maintained the design for several decades despite the invention of newer technologies. Behind the scenes, however, Clan Wolf was designing an updated version. As they saw it, neither of the great Kerenskys who had founded the Clans would have approved of blindly following tradition at the expense of military progress. The *Orion* IIC debuted early in the Golden Century, but did not garner much attention when set alongside the OmniMechs that were fast becoming the standard front-line machines.

Clan Wolf has jealously guarded the *Orion* IIC design, defending their exclusive right to it in Trials of Possession and refusing all proposed trades for other technologies despite some generous offers. Like the Kerensky bloodheritages, Clan Wolf sees the *Orion* IIC as tied to their honor, as the guardians of Kerensky's legacy.

Capabilities

Produced before the advent of OmniMechs, the *Orion* IIC features many of the technological advancements preserved or developed by the Clans. Endo-steel and ferro-fibrous construction materials lighten the design, allowing for a heavier weapons configuration, and double heat sinks allay heat build-up.

The IIC design upgrades the original Mech's medium lasers to extended-range large lasers. The *Orion* IIC is armed with two different large lasers, apparently the result of a design change late in the production cycle in which a pulse laser was upgraded to an extended-range weapon. These two different lasers remained despite the problems they posed for upkeep because the older Series 6W laser was more in keeping with the original design's architecture. Clan Wolf also exchanged the old *Orion*'s autocannon for a newer Gauss rifle that packed a harder punch, and upgraded the original 'Mech's missile launchers.

Deployment

Clan Wolf produces the *Orion* IIC in limited numbers, and uses them to reward officers in second-line Galaxies who are expected to advance soon to front-line units. This BattleMech is always sent to its recipients "with the compliments of" Clan Wolf's Khan or saKhan. No officer has ever refused such a gift, even if it meant trading in an assault-class BattleMech, and no Wolf warrior has ever challenged anyone for the right to an *Orion* IIC.

A few *Orion* IIC BattleMechs traveled to the Inner Sphere with Phelan Kell's Wolves, and remain part of the Clan-Wolf-in-Exile's second-line forces. However, no one seems to have plans to produce this 'Mech—a possible gesture of reconciliation by Phelan Kell toward the Wolf Clan.

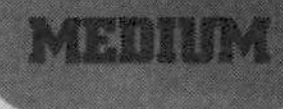

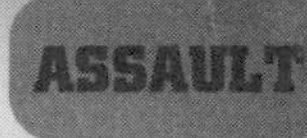

CLAN

Type: **Orion IIC**
Technology Base: Clan
Tonnage: 75
Battle Value: 1,923

Equipment		**Mass**
Internal Structure:	Endo Steel	4
Engine:	300	19
Walking MP:	4	
Running MP:	6	
Jumping MP:	0	
Heat Sinks:	12 [24]	2
Gyro:		3
Cockpit:		3
Armor Factor:	230	12

	Internal Structure	*Armor Value*
Head	3	9
Center Torso	23	34
Center Torso (rear)		11
R/L Torso	16	22
R/L Torso (rear)		10
R/L Arm	12	24
R/L Leg	16	32

Weapons and Ammo	**Location**	**Critical**	**Tonnage**
Gauss Rifle	RT	6	12
Ammo (Gauss) 16	RT	2	2
LRM 20	LA	4	5
Ammo (LRM) 18	LT	3	3
SRM 4	LT	1	1
Ammo (SRM) 25	LT	1	1
ER Large Laser	LA	1	4
ER Large Laser	RA	1	4

BATTLEFORCE 2

MP	**Damage PB/M/L**	**Overheat**	**Class**
4	5/4/3	1	H

Armor/Structure	**Point Value**	**Specials**
6/6	19	

Mass: 80 tons
Chassis: Clan Series Assault SXC (Endo)
Power Plant: Clan Type 240 XL series
Cruising Speed: 32 kph
Maximum Speed: 54 kph
Jump Jets:
Clan Standard 14X series
Jump Capacity: 90 meters
Armor: Forging ZK11 (Standard)
Armament:
4 Series 7Ja Extended Range Large Lasers
2 Type 9 Ultra-10 Autocannons
Manufacturer:
Ashton 'Mech Production Complex
Communications System: TJ6 "Bell" Integrated Communications System
Targeting and Tracking System:
TRTTS Mark II CWS

Overview

As continuing battle reports from the Inner Sphere filtered back to the Clan homeworlds, one glaring deficiency appeared again and again. Battles against Inner Sphere forces lasted longer than typical Clan engagements, and consequently Clan OmniMechs configured primarily with ballistic weapons suffered ammunition depletion. To counteract this problem, Clan Coyote scientists immediately began developing a new second-line 'Mech that would rely more on energy weapons.

Capabilities

Using an extra-light steel chassis and an advanced XL engine, the *Canis* has ample tonnage remaining for armor protection. A powerful array of weapons compensates for a speed slower than most 'Mechs of the same weight class. The *Canis* carries four extended-range large lasers, with two Type 9 Ultra-10 autocannons rounding out the weapons complement. All that firepower comes at a price, however. Despite its sixteen double heat sinks, the *Canis* frequently suffers heat problems that hamper its effectiveness.

The *Canis* received its baptism of fire in 3058, during the Harvest Trials against Clan Jade Falcon. Though the battles were short, and the Coyotes lost several *Canis* 'Mechs to the Jade Falcons, Khan Koga was pleased that the *Canis* held up so well against other Clan 'Mechs.

Deployment

Currently, Clan Coyote is the only Clan to field the *Canis* in any significant numbers. However, three of the 'Mechs fell into Jade Falcon hands during the Harvest Trials.

Type: **Canis**
Technology Base: Clan
Tonnage: 80
Battle Value: 2,223

Equipment		**Mass**
Internal Structure:	Endo Steel	4
Engine:	240 XL	6
Walking MP:	3	
Running MP:	5	
Jumping MP:	3	
Heat Sinks:	16 [32]	6
Gyro:		3
Cockpit:		3
Armor Factor:	240	15

	Internal Structure	*Armor Value*
Head	3	9
Center Torso	25	37
Center Torso (rear)		12
R/L Torso	17	23
R/L Torso (rear)		10
R/L Arm	13	25
R/L Leg	17	33

Weapons and Ammo	**Location**	**Critical**	**Tonnage**
2 ER Large Lasers	RA	2	8
2 ER Large Lasers	LA	2	8
Ultra AC/10	RT	4	10
Ammo (Ultra) 20	RT	2	2
Ultra AC/10	LT	4	10
Ammo (Ultra) 20	LT	2	2
Jump Jet	LT	1	1
Jump Jet	CT	1	1
Jump Jet	RT	1	1

BATTLEFORCE 2

MP	**Damage PB/M/L**	**Overheat**	**Class**
3J	4/4/4	3	A

Armor/Structure	**Point Value**	**Specials**
6/5	22	

THUNDER STALLION

Mass: 85 tons
Chassis: Type QMA Standard (Quad)
Power Plant: Fusion 255 Standard
Cruising Speed: 32.4 kph
Maximum Speed: 54 kph
Jump Jets: None
Jump Capacity: None

Armor: Forged Type HH32 with CASE
Armament: 1 Type Mu LB-20X Autocannon
4 Type XV LRM-15 Launchers
Manufacturer: Kirin MechWorks I
Communications System:
CH3V Series Integrated
Targeting and Tracking System:
Version Kappa-III TTS

Overview

The *Thunder Stallion* was originally planned as a totem 'Mech, along the lines of the *Mandrill* or *Fire Scorpion*. Upon learning of the less-than-ideal performance of those 'Mechs, Clan Hell's Horses de-emphasized the totem aspect in favor of more combat effectiveness; only the back legs of the 'Mech still suggest the original equine styling. Despite the changes in design emphasis, however, Hell's Horses MechWarriors still dislike this 'Mech. The *Thunder Stallion* epitomizes support, in keeping with the Horses' preference for placing infantry and conventional forces on a more even footing with MechWarriors. The *Thunder Stallion* works so well supporting non-'Mech forces that MechWarriors assigned to it feel humiliated in comparison to their colleagues in other Clans where MechWarriors dominate.

Capabilities

Designed for support, the *Thunder Stallion* has a standard 255-rated fusion plant that allows it to move just fast enough to keep up with dismounted Elementals and other support units. To make up for its lack of speed, the 'Mech mounts two paired LRM-15 launchers in each side torso, with enough ammunition to allow almost three minutes of continuous firing. Working together with spotter units, the *Thunder Stallion* can saturate enemy installations and units from the safety of covering terrain.

As a secondary weapons system, the *Stallion* mounts a massive LB-20X autocannon for close-in work. Usually employed against armor or infantry units, this weapon typically carries a ton each of cluster and standard rounds, in case the warrior should need a heavy punch against a larger opponent. Unfortunately, the arrangement of this weapon and its ammunition stores is of great concern to *Stallion* pilots. With internal room at a premium, the designers of the *Thunder Stallion* chose to run the ammo feeds for the massive gun through the 'Mech's head, just beneath the cockpit assembly, and the central torso section. Should either of these locations suffer a breach while still loaded with even a single round, death for both 'Mech and warrior is practically guaranteed. Though the 'Mech's heavy armor makes such explosion a rare event, many *Stallion* pilots refuse to reload the autocannon, preferring to risk getting caught without their largest gun rather than die ignominiously in this "quad coffin."

Deployment

The *Thunder Stallion* is unique to the Hell's Horses Clan, and is deployed fairly evenly throughout all Horse Galaxies. The greatest number of these 'Mechs, however, appear in Eta and Iota Galaxies.

Variants

The most common *Thunder Stallion* variant known to exist, nicknamed the "Fire Stallion," replaces the LB-20 and its ammo with twin large pulse lasers, solving some of the 'Mech's ammo-dependence problem and eliminating the concern about ammunition explosion. Two more double heat sinks are added to deal with the increased heat levels this model generates.

Type: **Thunder Stallion**
Technology Base: Clan
Tonnage: 85
Battle Value: 2,099

Equipment		**Mass**
Internal Structure:		8.5
Engine:	255	13
Walking MP:	3	
Running MP:	5	
Jumping MP:	0	
Heat Sinks:	14 [28]	4
Gyro:		3
Cockpit:		3
Armor Factor:	279	17.5

	Internal Structure	*Armor Value*
Head	3	9
Center Torso	27	34
Center Torso (rear)		20
R/L Torso	18	20
R/L Torso (rear)		16
R/L Front Leg	18	36
R/L Rear Leg	18	36

Weapons and Ammo	**Location**	**Critical**	**Tonnage**
LB 20-X AC	RT/CT	9	12
Ammo (LB-X) 5	CT	1	1
Ammo (LB-X) 5	H	1	1
2 LRM 15	RT	4	7
2 LRM 15	LT	4	7
Ammo (LRM) 64	LT	8	8

BATTLEFORCE 2

MP	**Damage PB/M/L**	**Overheat**	**Class**
3	7/6/4	—	A

Armor/Structure	**Point Value**	**Specials**
7/7	21	if

BLOOD ASP

Mass: 90 tons
Chassis: Type MAES-90 Light
Power Plant: Consolidated Fusion 360 XL
Cruising Speed: 43 kph
Maximum Speed: 65 kph
Jump Jets: None
Jump Capacity: None

Armor: Forging ZZ7 Ceramic Plate
Armament:
42 tons of pod space available
Manufacturer: Sheridan LM-TA 8-10
Communications System:
Series D8 CC-25X
Targeting and Tracking System:
"Hermes" CT-42 Mk. II

Overview

Clan Star Adder scientists based this 'Mech on the *Kingfisher.* Installing an extralight engine nearly doubled the amount of available pod space, though structural constraints forced them to replace the *Kingfisher*'s ferro-fibrous armor with standard plate. This 'Mech entered service as the *Blood Asp*, an insult aimed at the Star Adders' longtime rivals, Clan Blood Spirit.

Capabilities

Five variants of the *Blood Asp* have already appeared. The primary configuration mounts a pair of Gauss rifles, a Streak SRM rack and a trio of lasers in each arm.

The most common variant is an assault design, configured to deliver maximum firepower with the greatest possible accuracy. This configuration is well suited for any type of terrain. The B configuration is outfitted for sustained fire-support missions.

The C variant relies almost exclusively on ammunition-based weapons, and is therefore best suited for the short and deadly Trials preferred by Clan warriors. The final variant is configured for long-range suppression fire. Its lasers give it excellent defensive capabilities even after its ammunition stores run dry.

Deployment

Blood Asps are being assigned to Clan Star Adder's front-line Galaxies. Alpha Galaxy has received the majority of these new 'Mechs, while the two Keshiks, Delta, Gamma and Kappa Galaxies have received only a few each.

Type: **Blood Asp**
Technology Base: Clan OmniMech
Tonnage: 90
Battle Value: 2,295

Equipment		**Mass**
Internal Structure:	Endo Steel	4.5
Engine:	360 XL	16.5
Walking MP:	4	
Running MP:	6	
Jumping MP:	0	
Heat Sinks:	14 [28]	4
Gyro:		4
Cockpit:		3
Armor Factor:	256	16

	Internal Structure	*Armor Value*
Head	3	9
Center Torso	29	40
Center Torso (rear)		13
R/L Torso	19	24
R/L Torso (rear)		11
R/L Arm	15	28
R/L Leg	19	34

Weight and Space Allocation

Location	*Fixed*	*Spaces Remaining*
Head	Endo Steel	0
Center Torso		2
Right Torso	2 Engine Endo Steel	9
Left Torso	2 Engine Endo Steel	9
Right Arm	Endo Steel	7
Left Arm	3 Endo Steel	5
Right Leg		0
Left Leg		0

Weapons and Ammo	**Location**	**Critical**	**Tonnage**
Primary Weapons Configuration			
2 Heavy Medium Lasers	LA	4	2
Medium Pulse Laser	LA	1	2
Gauss Rifle	LT	6	12
Ammo (Gauss) 8	LT	1	1
Double Heat Sink	LT	2	1
Double Heat Sink	LL	2	1
Streak SRM 6	CT	2	3
Ammo (Streak) 15	RT	1	1
Gauss Rifle	RT	6	12
Ammo (Gauss) 8	RT	1	1
Double Heat Sink	RL	2	1
2 Heavy Medium Lasers	RA	4	2
Medium Pulse Laser	RA	1	2
Double Heat Sink	RA	2	1
Alternate Configuration A			
ER PPC	LA	2	6
Heavy Large Laser	LA	3	4
Double Heat Sink	LA	2	1
4 Double Heat Sinks	LT	8	4
Double Heat Sink	LL	2	1
ECM Suite	CT	1	1
Targeting Computer	RT	4	4
2 Double Heat Sinks	RT	4	2
Double Heat Sink	RL	2	1
ER PPC	RA	2	6

LIGHT
MEDIUM
HEAVY
ASSAULT
OMNI

Heavy Large Laser	RA	3	4
2 Double Heat Sinks	RA	4	2
Jump Jet	LT	1	2
Jump Jet	CT	1	2
Jump Jet	RT	1	2
Battle Value: 2,901			

Alternate Configuration B

LRM-20	LA	4	5
Artemis IV FCS	LA	1	1
Ammo (LRM) 12	LA	2	2
4 Med. Pulse Lasers	LT	4	8
Ammo (Gauss) 8	LL	1	1
ECM Suite	CT	1	1
Ammo (Gauss) 8	CT	1	1
LRM-20	RA	4	5
Artemis IV FCS	RA	1	1
Ammo (LRM) 12	RA	2	2
Double Heat Sink	RA	2	1
Gauss Rifle	RT	6	12
Double Heat Sink	RT	2	1
Ammo (Gauss) 8	RL	1	1
Battle Value: 2,662			

Alternate Configuration C

Ultra AC/10	LA	4	10
Ultra AC/10	LT	4	10
Ammo (Ultra) 40	LT	4	4
Ammo (LB-X) 10	CT	2	2
ER Large Laser	RA	1	4
LB 20-X AC	RT	9	12
Battle Value: 1,969			

Alternate Configuration D

ER Large Laser	LA	1	4
Heavy Med. Laser	LA	2	1
Gauss Rifle	LT	6	12
Ammo (Gauss) 16	LT	2	2
Double Heat Sink	CT	2	1
ER Large Laser	RA	1	4
Heavy Med. Laser	RA	2	1
3 Ultra AC/2	RT	6	15
Ammo (Ultra) 45	RT	1	1
Double Heat Sink	RT	2	1
Battle Value: 1,977			

BATTLEFORCE 2

Type: Blood Asp

MP	**Damage PB/M/L**	**Overheat**	**Class**
4	9/7/2	2	A

Armor/Structure	**Point Value**	**Specials**
6/5	23	omni

Alternate Configuration A

MP	**Damage PB/M/L**	**Overheat**	**Class**
4J	6/5/2	2	A

Armor/Structure	**Point Value**	**Specials**
6/5	29	omni, ecm

Alternate Configuration B

MP	**Damage PB/M/L**	**Overheat**	**Class**
4	10/8/5	—	A

Armor/Structure	**Point Value**	**Specials**
6/5	27	omni, ecm, if

Alternate Configuration C

MP	**Damage PB/M/L**	**Overheat**	**Class**
4	8/6/4	—	A

Armor/Structure	**Point Value**	**Specials**
6/5	20	omni

Alternate Configuration D

MP	**Damage PB/M/L**	**Overheat**	**Class**
4	5/4/3	2	A

Armor/Structure	**Point Value**	**Specials**
6/5	20	omni

HIGHLANDER IIC

Mass: 90 tons
Chassis: SL-XT Modified
Power Plant: Fusion 270 Standard
Cruising Speed: 32 kph
Maximum Speed: 54 kph
Jump Jets: Prentiss-IIIA
Jump Capacity: 90 meters

Armor:
Arcadia Compound Delta VII Ferro-Fibrous
Armament:
1 EMRG "Captain" Series Gauss Rifle
1 Type XXVI "Great Bow" LRM-20 Launcher
2 MPA-14 Mod. 12a Streak SRM-6 Launchers
3 Series PPS-VIII Medium Pulse Lasers
Manufacturer:
Arcadia BattleMech Plant CM-T15
Communications System:
C-XII Series B4 GDS
Targeting and Tracking System:
C-12 Mk. III with Artemis IV FCS

Overview

One of the most successful designs of the Star League era, thousands of *Highlanders* traveled away from the Inner Sphere with Aleksandr Kerensky and the Exodus Fleet. Though a large percentage of those were mothballed in Brian Caches, many later served in the toumans of the nascent Clans. As each Clan grew, they took more equipment from the caches to fill their expanding ranks, including the venerable *Highlander*.

The *Highlander* initially served as the mobile-assault backbone of many Clan militaries. Even after the emergence of new Clan designs, cornerstone BattleMechs like the *Highlander* continued to serve faithfully. No new *Highlanders* have been produced in more than a century, however, though an occasional few are upgraded from those left in the oldest Brian Caches.

Capabilities

Despite its IIC designation, little has changed in the *Highlander* design since the original 'Mech's introduction in 2592. As Clan technology advanced, newer and lighter equipment replaced outmoded components. As a result, though the IIC version retains the same basic configuration, the *Highlander's* firepower has significantly improved. The 'Mech's damage potential has almost doubled, and its weapons systems carry sufficient ammunition for nearly four minutes of constant fire.

The shakedown trials of the first few *Highlander* IICs made it clear that minor changes were required. The second short-range missile system in the left arm meant running another ammunition feed mechanism through the arm and into the torso. During heavy combat, missiles would frequently jam in the feed mechanism, which was routed awkwardly around the LRM launcher. Though the pilot could generally dislodge the missiles by moving his 'Mech, this tactic did not always work. In one instance of failure, the ordnance exploded with catastrophic effects. Clan engineers eventually solved the problem by relocating the LRM in the right torso and moving the three medium pulse lasers into the left.

Almost 1,500 *Highlander* IICs have been either upgraded or newly constructed in the two hundred years since the design overhaul. Though many of those units have been destroyed or scrapped over the years, several hundred still serve in the toumans of the remaining fifteen Clans. Few Clan refits enjoy the popularity of this rugged design.

Deployment

Though every Clan fields this 'Mech in second-line Galaxies, Clan Star Adder deploys the most, largely due to the recent Absorption of Clan Burrock and its forces. Some *Highlanders* serve as command 'Mechs in a few Adder front-line units, notably the Fifth Assault and 73rd Cavaliers Clusters.

Clans Blood Spirit and Wolf also field a significant number of *Highlanders*, mostly to recoup the heavy losses each Clan recently incurred. Clan Blood Spirit salvaged several frm the battlefields of the Absorption War, while Clan Wolf opened one of their last remaining Brian Caches to recommission several Stars' worth. Recent information also indicates that Wolf's Dragoons had several *Highlanders* when they traveled to the Inner Sphere.

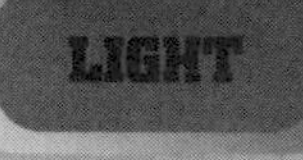

HIGHLANDER IIC

Type: **Highlander IIC**
Technology Base: Clan
Tonnage: 90
Battle Value: 2,827

Equipment		**Mass**
Internal Structure:		9
Engine:	270	14.5
Walking MP:	3	
Running MP:	5	
Jumping MP:	3	
Heat Sinks:	12 [24]	2
Gyro:		3
Cockpit:		3
Armor Factor:	278	14.5

	Internal Structure	*Armor Value*
Head	3	9
Center Torso	29	40
Center Torso (rear)		17
R/L Torso	19	28
R/L Torso (rear)		10
R/L Arm	15	30
R/L Leg	19	38

Weapons and Ammo	**Location**	**Critical**	**Tonnage**
Gauss Rifle	RA	6	12
2 Streak SRM 6	LA	4	6
3 Med. Pulse Lasers	LT	3	6
Ammo (Gauss) 24	RT	3	3
LRM 20	RT	4	5
Artemis IV FCS	RT	1	1
Ammo (LRM) 24	LT	4	4
Ammo (SRM) 15	LT	1	1
Jump Jet	RT	1	2
Jump Jet	LT	1	2
Jump Jet	CT	1	2

BATTLEFORCE 2

MP	**Damage PB/M/L**	**Overheat**	**Class**
3J	7/6/2	1	A

Armor/Structure	**Point Value**	**Specials**
7/7	28	if

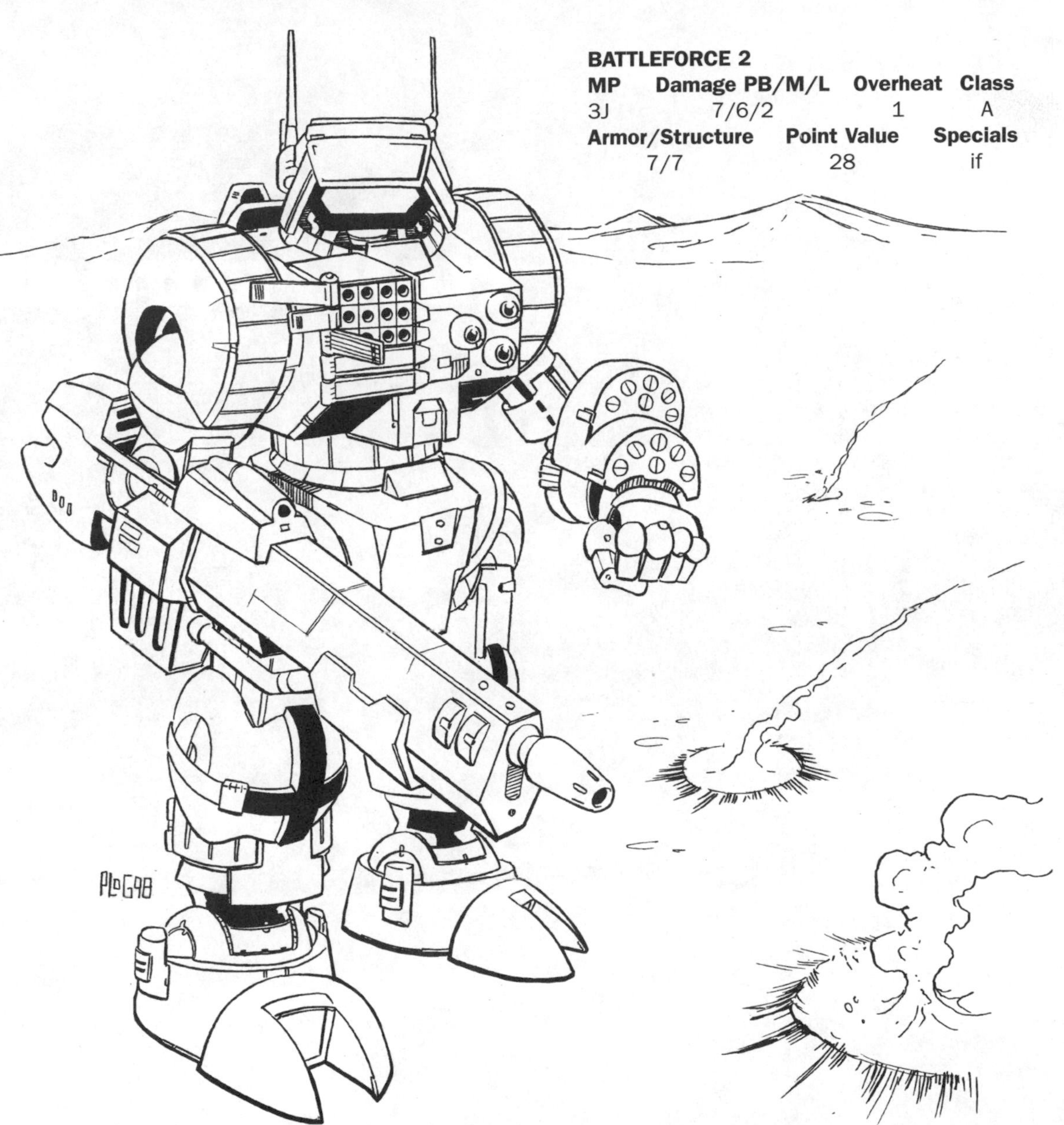

CLAN PROTOMECHS

Of all the sections in this report, I fear that this debriefing has the most long reaching consequences. For the past few months my team and I have feverishly poured over the Smoke Jaguar military files that Task Force Serpent liberated from Huntress. Although we gleaned valuable information about Clan production of 'Mechs and vehicles, we failed in the area of the Clan military unit called the ProtoMech—so much about them is still unknown. Most of the information we obtained was from first-hand accounts of MechWarriors who faced them in the field, as well as from a handful of actual ProtoMechs recovered by the Northwind Highlanders. What little information we recovered from the Jaguar files aided us in answering many of the questions being asked, but the Jaguar scientist caste was very thorough in their destruction of all military data pertaining to the ProtoMech project. Only through sheer luck and the quick thinking of Task Force Serpent personnel were we able to salvage the information we have. The largest section we decoded, almost intact, was the history. I can only assume that the scientist caste, realizing time was short, felt that keeping the history and progress of the project from us was not as vital as destroying the component information. In this crucial area, we have no information whatsoever. What materials are used in their construction, what type of communication gear and targeting and tracking do they use, what type of power plants drive them? None of that information was recoverable.

Regardless, this debriefing contains all currently available information on this new and deadly unit. As I mentioned previously, I fear this new unit for what it heralds. Although the Inner Sphere has only recently fielded Battle Armor and OmniMechs, the Clans first fielded these two technological marvels in the mid-twenty-ninth century. For almost 200 years they have been relatively stagnant in new weapon and equipment development—until now. Combined with the new heavy lasers, the ProtoMechs demonstrate what the Clan scientist caste, when properly motivated, can accomplish.

—Jared Pascal
Adept XVI-Omega
Deep Periphery
27 November 3060

In the steaming jungles of Huntress, the troops of Task Force Serpent ran afoul of a new and completely unexpected piece of Clan technology: the lightweight, agile 'Mech predators that Inner Sphere troops later learned were called ProtoMechs. Darting in and out of cover, these half-size 'Mechs made short work of their surprised opponents before fading into the jungle.

The defeat of Clan Smoke Jaguar has given the Inner Sphere a chance to analyze captured data and learn some of the history and capabilities of these unfamiliar machines. Soon enough, the armies of the other Clans will obtain ProtoMech technology, and the Inner Sphere must be prepared to fight them.

HISTORY OF THE PROTOMECH

In the months following the battle of Tukayyid, Clan Smoke Jaguar faced a serious problem. They had carved their entire Inner Sphere occupation zone from the Draconis Combine, a nation of fierce warriors whose doctrine of bushido (the way of the warrior) made them tough, resilient enemies. The Jaguars found themselves constantly harassed by civilians and by Combine troops, whose complex system of honor prevented them from accepting defeat. Guerrilla uprisings and raids left the Jaguars stretched to the limit in BattleMech resources.

This was not the first time the Jaguars had been so hard-pressed for materiel. Many times in the past, the Jaguars had been left with few resources with which to defend themselves, and each time they prevailed and rebuilt. In the latter part of the thirtieth century, Smoke Jaguar scientists admitted that their Clan worlds would soon be barren of the ores needed to produce new BattleMechs, and the imminent invasion of the Inner Sphere meant they needed to find an innovative solution or be left behind.

THE SECRET PLAN

The Clan's top scientists began working on a bold new battlefield unit design that would combine aspects of the BattleMech with the highly successful Elemental battle armor. Standing only half the height of a BattleMech, these new units would mass roughly one-tenth the weight of the larger machines, and so use one-tenth the carbon alloy, myomer and other rare construction materials. Their tiny engines would further slash the production cost, allowing the Clan to make more of them while using less material. The goal was for a Point of five of these so-called ProtoMechs, working in unison like a Point of battle armor, to be as effective as a single BattleMech, while requiring less than half the amount of construction material.

Sario (Bullfinch), one of the head scientists working on the ProtoMech development project, also studied ancient Terran mythology, and assigned names from mythology as codenames for the different ProtoMech proposals. As the work proceeded, the designers incorporated these mythological themes into the look of the ProtoMechs. They thought the fearsome designs would give the Protos' pilots an edge by terrifying their enemies.

At the same time the new machines were being developed, Jaguar geneticists began the task of creating suitable pilots. Quite the opposite of the massive Elementals, this new breed would need to be smaller even than aerospace pilots, in order to fit in the cramped confines of a ProtoMech's torso.

Acknowledging the radical nature of their research, the scientists began working on their concept without informing their Khans of their plan. The scientists knew that the new units would have to be proven in battle before the Khans would even consider them for full-scale production. That meant years of secret work before the plan could be revealed.

Indeed, decades of research and dozens of prototypes later, the scientists still lacked proven results. The machines were too small for a proper cockpit, and the genetic engineering experimentation proved unable to produce a viable new breed suitable for piloting the ProtoMechs.

THE BREAKTHROUGH

The technological advance that finally made the ProtoMech viable was the advent of enhanced imaging (EI). Around the time of Operation Revival, Clan scientists had developed the EI system to enhance the link between a MechWarrior or Elemental and his machine, improving reaction time and firing accuracy. This advance came with a steep price. To make full use of the system, the pilot had to be surgically fitted with an extensive array of electronic implants, visible near the surface of the skin as softly luminous "tattoos." These implants have a gradually degenerative effect on the nervous system of the subject, so that after an extended period of time, usually one to five years, the subject becomes unstable, often paranoid. The implants can even cause death or catatonia, though such cases remain rare.

Because of the dangers involved, only the most aggressive Crusader warriors make use of EI technology, and most of these quickly become addicted to the drugs administered to fight off the debilitating effects of the EI tattoos. Despite these drawbacks, none can dispute the awesome battlefield prowess of these warriors, and so the practice continues with the silent approval of the Grand Council, which normally frowns on artificial enhancements.

Further refinement on the system was necessary, but the basic concept of EI was the groundwork the Jaguar scientists needed for controlling the ProtoMechs. Giving the pilot direct neural control of the Proto eliminated the need for a gyroscope and full-sized cockpit. This created all the space necessary to place the pilot in the torso with room enough for weapon systems as well.

ProtoMech Pilots

Though enhanced imaging successfully defeated the mechanical challenges of the ProtoMech, the genetic challenges were less easy to overcome. Unable to create a viable new breed of warriors, Clan Smoke Jaguar was left with no pilots for their new machines except for volunteer aerospace pilots who had failed to test into the warrior caste. This temporary compromise proved also to be the solution to the problem.

Though few Clans will admit it, the Clans' attempt to breed aerospace pilots has basically failed to achieve its goal. Bred for sharp senses, increased reaction times and a natural resistance to high-G maneuvers, aerospace pilots are perhaps the most extreme example of Clan genetic engineering. The breeding for these traits has resulted in a people who are almost comically small and thin, but with enlarged heads and eyes as a side effect of their positive traits. In fact, despite all the effort put into selective breeding and intensive training, Clan pilots have proven inferior to their Inner Sphere counterparts.

This sad fact was not lost on the ProtoMech designers, who saw an opportunity in the increasing numbers of washed-up aerospace pilots who were relegated to lower castes. For several years, pilots who tested out of the Jaguar warrior caste were "appropriated" by the ProtoMech project, under the cover story of testing new fighters. These pilots were then given the chance to serve their Clan as warriors.

Aerospace pilots have many characteristics that suit them to the task of piloting ProtoMechs: they are small and wiry, allowing them to fit into the cramped ProtoMech cockpit. Their brains and circulatory systems are bred to withstand the pressure of high-G maneuvering which, coincidentally, gives them increased resistance to the negative side effects of the direct neural interface that drives the ProtoMech.

When piloting the ProtoMech, the pilot feels as though the Proto is his own body. He "sees" through the ProtoMech's external sensors. When he wills his body to move, the Proto moves instead, his actual body flexing unconsciously in response to the commands. The pilot is only vaguely aware of his physical body curled in the fetal position in the chest of the 'Mech,. The muscular stress of this activity is quite high and, combined with the bumpy ride provided by the typical ProtoMech's loping gait, the pilot must withstand considerable punishment in the cockpit.

The pilots feel as though they "are" the machine, giving them unsurpassed control. However, this direct connection also means the pilot can feel the "pain" inflicted on his machine via neurological feedback not unlike that suffered by MechWarriors through their neurohelmets when an ammunition explosion occurs. For example, when the ProtoMech's arm is torn off, the pilot feels a great deal of pain, almost as though his own arm had been ripped away. Though ProtoMech pilots are specially trained to deal with this effect, such "phantom pain" can still be a debilitating weakness in combat.

The sympathetic bond between man and machine can also lead to a kind of "god complex" in which the pilot feels as though he is unstoppable. He is reluctant to leave his machine, and may even start to believe the ProtoMech is his own body. Fortunately, the members of a ProtoMech Point are a tightly knit team, and the other members of the Point can usually control this kind of behavior before it becomes a problem. In and out of the cockpit, the members of a Point stick together, and are virtually inseparable.

Pilots assigned to ProtoMech duty carry the distinctive EI tattoos all over their bodies. To condition themselves for the rigors of the ProtoMech cockpit, the pilots must exercise constantly. For this reason, they are generally quite muscular (compared to aerospace pilots) and in good health.

THE PROTOMECH

A typical ProtoMech stands four to six meters tall and masses from two to nine tons. The pilot rides in a small compartment in the upper chest of the Proto, just below the neck. The rest of the torso contains the engine, weapons and motive systems.

Larger than a battle armor suit but smaller than a BattleMech, a ProtoMech has abilities in common with both types of unit. Their small stature means they can hide where BattleMechs cannot, and they can even move through buildings without causing excessive collateral damage.

Though tiny compared to even the smallest BattleMech, each ProtoMech can carry an impressive arsenal of weapons. And, because they operate in Points of five, their coordinated fire compensates for each Proto's individual shortcomings.

A ProtoMech is also extremely durable. Though they carry little armor compared to BattleMechs, they can survive the loss of limbs and even the head and remain effective.

The pilot controls the ProtoMech through a direct neural interface as though it were his own body, therefore all ProtoMech designs are fairly humanoid. To supplement their firepower, ProtoMechs often carry large hand-held weapons called main guns. These weapons are braced to the torso but fired with both hands, allowing the pilot accurate control of the weapon, as though he were firing a large machine gun by hand. Because the weapon fires in such similar manner to standard infantry weapons, ProtoMech pilots enjoy a significant advantage in training and combat accuracy—while both BattleMech and ProtoMech pilots must learn to accurately fire weapons directly mounted on their "body," which is not a natural state of affairs, ProtoMechs wield the main gun almost as easily as a person uses a hand gun or rifle, allowing for a more flexible firing arc.

PROTOMECH DEPLOYMENT

At the time of the battle for Huntress, only Clan Smoke Jaguar had access to ProtoMech technology. IlKhan Lincoln Osis learned of their existence only after that battle, at which point his outrage at the lengthy secret project was tempered by his Clan's desperate situation, as well as the Protos' solid performance against stiff odds. In the desperate fighting on Huntress, the Jaguars used ProtoMechs to deadly effect despite the Jaguars' ultimate defeat, giving these radical new machines a stunning debut the other Clans could hardly ignore. Certainly, ProtoMech technology will eventually make its way into the hands of the other Clans. The Crusader Clans are most likely to field them first, because their warriors are more likely to submit to the enhanced imaging surgery in service to their Clan.

Analysts feel confident that the Inner Sphere will not adopt this new technology, primarily because they lack both the aerospace pilot breed and the EI technology necessary to control the machines. Even if the Inner Sphere had access to these technologies, the invasive surgery required to use the enhanced imaging makes it unlikely they would find a sufficient number of volunteers to make the effort worthwhile.

PROTOMECH RULES

While ProtoMechs share many characteristics with conventional vehicles and infantry, ProtoMech units follow all the standard rules for BattleMechs, except as specifically noted below. ProtoMechs are Level 2 units.

Deployment: ProtoMechs are always deployed in Points consisting of five units, though circumstances may leave a Point with less than five units. Each record sheet provides space for five Protos (see p. 204), but each ProtoMech is represented as an individual unit on the game board. The player may choose to make all members of a Point the same type of Proto or different types, unless otherwise dictated by the set-up of the scenario being played.

Enhanced Imaging: ProtoMechs are controlled using a form of enhanced imaging (EI) technology, but the pilots gain none of the benefits nor suffer the drawbacks of that Level 3 system.

PLAYING THE GAME

Each of the five ProtoMechs of a Point is an individual unit. However, the entire Point's fire declaration counts as a single unit's declaration, and the player resolves all attacks for a Point before moving on to another unit.

Warriors

The unique nature of a ProtoMech means that ProtoMech pilots never need to make Piloting rolls, and so the pilots have only a Gunnery Skill Rating (see **Piloting Skill Rolls**).

Damaging a MechWarrior: The pilot of a ProtoMech can sustain the same amount of damage as a 'Mech pilot, and the damage has the same effects. However, rather than taking damage in the standard way, the pilot takes a point of damage each time a shaded critical hit box is filled in (see **Damage,** p. 191). Note that the pilot does not automatically take a point of damage when an attack hits the head.

MOVEMENT

ProtoMechs move according to the same rules as BattleMechs, with the following exceptions.

Elevation Change: ProtoMechs may only change elevation by 1 level per hex moved (as for infantry and vehicles), at a cost of 1 MP per level (as for 'Mechs).

Stacking: A ProtoMech counts as a vehicle unit for stacking purposes. A ProtoMech cannot make an attack against a unit in the same hex it occupies.

Buildings: ProtoMechs enter and move through buildings according to the rules for infantry.

Piloting Skill Rolls

One of the advantages ProtoMechs have over BattleMechs is their great agility. Because they are more agile and shorter, Protos cannot fall in the same way that 'Mechs fall. Though certain attacks and other circumstances can result in a Proto losing its footing, the unit takes no damage and can regain its feet in a matter of seconds.

In game terms, this means ProtoMechs never have to make Piloting Skill rolls. They cannot fall down, drop prone or skid. Even the destruction of a ProtoMech's legs will not result in a fall, though the unit will thereafter be unable to move.

COMBAT

ProtoMechs make attacks and are targeted by attacks in the same way as BattleMechs, with the following exceptions.

Line of Sight

Treat ProtoMechs like vehicles for purposes of determining line of sight. Unlike BattleMechs, they do not rise 1 level above the terrain (though it is easy to forget this rule if the players are using BattleMech miniatures to represent Protos on the map).

Partial Cover: Because they are only the height of vehicles, ProtoMechs can never benefit from partial cover.

Weapon Attacks

All standard rules for BattleMech weapon attacks apply to ProtoMechs. They may fire each of their weapons once per turn, (though no arm-mounted weapons may be fired in the same turn that the main gun is fired) and may fire them at the same or different targets with the standard modifiers.

Firing Arcs: ProtoMechs use the firing arcs for BattleMechs and can twist their torsos according to the standard rules. If the ProtoMech is carrying a main gun, that weapon can be fired at targets in the forward, right side and left side firing arcs, and is rotated if the torso is twisted, giving it a potential 360-degree field of fire.

Missile Launchers: When firing missiles from launchers of non-standard size (such as an LRM-7), roll on the next higher column on the Missile Hits Table, p. 31 of *BattleTech Master Rules (BMR)*. If the result is a number higher than the number of tubes fired, the shot hits with the maximum number of missiles possible. If the missile launcher has only a single tube, treat it like a standard weapon (if the attack hits, the missile automatically hits and does not require a roll on the Missile Hits Table).

Prone BattleMechs: ProtoMechs can never be prone.

Hit Location

Hit location against a ProtoMech is determined by rolling on the ProtoMech Hit Location Table. This table also appears on the ProtoMech record sheet. Hits against ProtoMechs are not affected by attack direction, and there are no rear armor locations. Both legs are considered a single hit location, as is the torso.

Near Miss: ProtoMechs make difficult targets because of their small size and extreme agility. Protos are constantly in motion, and their limbs are especially narrow and difficult to hit. As a result, an attack (or part of an attack, in the case of missiles and similar weapons) that would have hit a BattleMech might miss a ProtoMech. As shown on the ProtoMech Hit Location Table, a hit location roll result of 3 or 11 is considered a near miss. This damage has no effect on the Proto, even though the to-hit roll result indicated a hit.

Targeting Computers: ProtoMechs are so small that targeting computers cannot be used to make attacks against specific hit locations on a Proto. The standard –1 to-hit modifier for a targeting computer still applies.

Damage

Damage first destroys the armor in the location hit, and then inflicts internal structure damage, in the same way as for attacks against BattleMechs. Damage transfers normally when a location is destroyed; damage from all locations transfers to the torso, including damage from the head.

Roll on the Determining Critical Hits Table whenever the internal structure is damaged. Each location has a number of critical hit boxes on the record sheet. These are marked off from left to right as critical hits are inflicted on the Proto. Each time a shaded critical hit box is crossed off, the pilot takes a point of damage.

PROTOMECH HIT LOCATION TABLE

2D6 Roll	Hit Location
2	Main Gun
3*	Near Miss
4	Right Arm
5	Legs
6–8	Torso
9	Legs
10	Left Arm
11*	Near Miss
12	Head

* A result of 3 or 11 inflicts no damage on the target.

When a location is destroyed, all of the location's critical hit boxes are automatically crossed off as well, and all equipment in the location is destroyed.

Critical hits do not transfer, and excess critical hits to a location have no further effect.

Effects for specific critical hits and location destruction appear below.

Arm: For the first critical hit, add a +1 modifier to the to-hit numbers for attacks made with that arm, for both the weapon mounted there and the main gun. The second hit destroys the arm, along with its weapon (if any). After one arm has been destroyed, add a +2 modifier to attacks with the main gun. After both arms have been destroyed, the main gun may not be fired.

Legs: The first critical hit to the legs reduces the ProtoMech's Walking MP by 1 (recalculate Running MP). The second hit reduces the Walking MP by half (round up, and recalculate Running MP). The third hit blows the legs off and makes movement impossible, though the ProtoMech still can make a single 1-hexside facing change during each Movement Phase. After the legs are destroyed, the ProtoMech can no longer torso twist, but it can fire its weapons.

Torso: The first critical hit reduces Jumping MP by 1, and may also destroy a torso-mounted weapon. To determine if a torso critical hit destroys a weapon, roll 1D6. On a result of 1–2, Torso Weapon A (as shown in the Weapons Inventory) is destroyed. On a 3–4, Torso Weapon B is destroyed. A result of 5–6 has no additional effect. If the result indicates an empty or destroyed weapon slot, do not roll again.

The second critical hit reduces Jumping MP by half (round up), and may also destroy a torso-mounted weapon. Roll as above.

The third critical hit destroys the engine and the ProtoMech, and kills the pilot.

Main Gun: The main gun cannot suffer a critical hit.

Note that all arm damage effects are cumulative when determining to-hit modifiers for firing the main gun. For example, if the right arm has been destroyed (+2) and the left arm has suffered one critical hit (+1), the total modifier for attacks with the main gun is +3.

Head: The first critical hit damages the sensors, adding a +1 to-hit modifier to all attacks (weapon and physical). The second critical hit destroys the head, resulting in a total to-hit modifier of +2 to all attacks. In addition, the ProtoMech may make no attacks against targets at long range after its head is destroyed.

Because the pilot is in the torso, a ProtoMech can survive head destruction.

Physical Attacks

A ProtoMech is too small to make effective punching or kicking attacks, and has too little mass to make pushing, charging and death-from-above attacks. However, a Proto can make a single physical attack that is a combination of punch, kick and anything else the Proto can muster. The net effect of this effort is a single attack with a damage value of 1 for ProtoMechs that weigh two to five tons, or 2 for Protos that weigh six to nine tons. The Base To-Hit Number for this attack is 4, with the standard modifiers for a kick. The attack can only be made against an adjacent target in the front firing arc, and this arc is not modified for a torso twist (as with a kick). Unlike a kick, this attack never forces the target to make a Piloting Skill roll.

If the attack hits, consult the BattleMech Kick Location Table (p. 41, *BMR*) for a target on the same level. If the target is a 'Mech one elevation level lower than the Proto, the attack uses the BattleMech Punch Location Table (p. 39, *BMR*). When making this attack against vehicles, simply use the appropriate hit location table for the attack direction.

A ProtoMech can be the target of physical attacks as though it were a vehicle (kick if on same elevation level as attacker; punch if one level higher than attacker; club/hatchet in either case). Though it cannot be charged, a ProtoMech may be the target of a death-from-above attack. The attack uses the standard ProtoMech Hit Location Table, and because the ProtoMech cannot fall, a death-from-above attack against a ProtoMech is usually a waste of effort.

HEAT

ProtoMechs never build up heat. They are specifically designed to dissipate all the energy-weapon heat they can build up, and do not generate heat for movement or for firing non-energy weapons.

SPECIAL CASE RULES

ProtoMechs are affected by special case rules in the same way as BattleMechs, with the following exceptions.

Anti-BattleMech Infantry: ProtoMechs cannot be targeted by anti-BattleMech infantry attacks.

Battle Values: Because ProtoMech pilots have no Piloting Skill, for the purpose of determining skill modifiers for non-standard troops, use the 5 column of the BV Skill Multipliers Table (p. 144, *BMR*).

Dropping Troops: ProtoMechs can be dropped into combat like BattleMechs. Because ProtoMech pilots have no Piloting Skill, however, determine safe landing and scatter in the same way as for battle armor troops, making a separate roll for each ProtoMech.

Dumping Ammunition: ProtoMechs cannot dump ammunition.

Ejecting: ProtoMechs have no ejection system.

Fire: Because they have no Heat Scale, ProtoMechs are affected by fire (and inferno missiles) like vehicles.

Four-legged BattleMechs: ProtoMechs cannot be constructed in a four-legged (quad) configuration.

Hostile Environments: ProtoMechs are affected by extreme temperatures as for vehicles. A ProtoMech's MP is not increased for low gravity, though it is reduced for high gravity. ProtoMechs cannot get stuck in swampy hexes, though they must pay the extra MP costs.

Reversing Arms: Regardless of their arm equipment, ProtoMechs cannot reverse (flip) their arms.

CONSTRUCTION

The procedure for constructing a custom ProtoMech is based on BattleMech construction as presented in the *BattleTech Master Rules*, beginning on page 109.

Note that the weight of all equipment for ProtoMechs is expressed in kilograms (kg) rather than tons.

DESIGN THE CHASSIS

This stage creates the ProtoMech's basic framework, or chassis.

Determine Technology Base

ProtoMechs can be designed with Clan technology only.

Choose Tonnage

ProtoMechs weigh between 2 and 9 tons, in increments of 1 ton. Note that each ton is 1,000 kg.

Allocate Tonnage for Internal Structure

Every ProtoMech must have an internal structure skeleton, which takes up 10 percent of its total weight. The internal structure boxes for each location appear in the ProtoMech Internal Structure Table.

Endo-Steel: Because their construction requires advanced composites, ProtoMechs cannot use endo-steel internal structure.

PROTOMECH INTERNAL STRUCTURE TABLE

Total Proto Tonnage	Internal Structure Mass (kg)	Head Boxes	Torso Boxes	Each Arm Boxes	Legs Boxes	Main Gun Boxes
2	200	1	2	1	2	1
3	300	1	3	1	2	1
4	400	1	4	1	3	1
5	500	1	5	1	3	1
6	600	2	6	2	4	1
7	700	2	7	2	4	1
8	800	2	8	2	5	1
9	900	2	9	2	5	1

Add Cockpit

A ProtoMech cockpit weighs 500 kg (this includes the weight of the pilot and associated support systems).

Because they are so small and incorporate an enhanced-imaging link with the pilot, ProtoMechs do not require a gyroscope.

ADD OTHER EQUIPMENT

After the ProtoMech's framework is designed, the player must choose and add the remaining elements of the ProtoMech. These elements include the engine, armor and jump jets.

Determine Engine Rating

To find the engine rating for the ProtoMech, multiply the desired Running MP (not Walking MP, as for BattleMechs) by the tonnage of the ProtoMech. To find the ProtoMech's Running MP, multiply the desired Walking MP by 1.5 and round up.

Running MP = Walking MP x 1.5
Tonnage x Desired Running MP = Engine Rating

The Fusion Engine Table (p. 111, *BMR*) lists the tonnage occupied by engines of various ratings. ProtoMechs have access to a wider range of engines weighing less than 1 ton than are listed on the table. For engines rated below 40, find the weight of the engine by multiplying the rating of the engine by 25 kg.

If there is no available engine with the desired rating (i.e., if the rating is higher than 39 and not divisible by 5), use the next highest rated engine instead (for example, if the desired rating is 44, use a 45-rated engine).

XL Engines: ProtoMechs are too small to mount XL engines.

Determine Jump Capability

ProtoMechs mount jump jets in the same way as BattleMechs, except the jets weigh considerably less. As with BattleMechs, the maximum Jumping MP is equal to the unit's Walking MP.

PROTOMECH JUMP JET WEIGHT TABLE

Proto Tonnage	Jump Jet Weight
2–5	50 kg/Jumping MP
6–9	100 kg/Jumping MP

Add Armor

The maximum armor each weight class of ProtoMech (and each specific location) can mount is summarized in the ProtoMech Armor Table. Each location, with the exception of the head and main gun location, may mount no more than double the amount of internal structure boxes in armor. Note that both legs are considered a single location, as is the entire torso (front and back).

Armor is allocated in single points, each of which weighs 50 kg. This mass is lower than that of BattleMech and vehicle armor because of the Proto's small size and the use of advanced materials. The player can choose any amount of armor up to the maximum the Proto can mount and the tonnage available.

Divide the armor among the six available locations: Head, Torso, Right Arm, Left Arm, Legs and Main Gun (if available). Note that both legs together constitute a single armor/damage location. Note also that ProtoMechs have no rear facing for armor/damage purposes.

Ferro-Fibrous Armor: Because ProtoMechs use an integral advanced alloy armor, they cannot mount ferro-fibrous armor.

ADD WEAPONS, AMMUNITION, HEAT SINKS AND OTHER EQUIPMENT

Weapons are added to a ProtoMech in much the same way as for BattleMechs, but there are important differences. Only certain locations on a ProtoMech can mount weapons, and each location has a strict weight limitation. There are also special rules regarding missile launchers, ammunition and heat sinks.

ProtoMechs cannot use special construction materials (endo-steel, ferro-fibrous), nor can they use MASC. They have no need of CASE or A-Pods, and cannot mount targeting computers. Aside from these restrictions, ProtoMechs have access to all the equipment available to Clan BattleMechs, as described on pages 122-135 of the *BattleTech Master Rules*.

PROTOMECH ARMOR TABLE

Total Proto Tonnage	Maximum Total Armor*	Maximum Armor Per Location: Head	Torso	Each Arm	Legs	Main Gun
2	18	3	4	2	4	3
3	20	3	6	2	4	3
4	25	4	8	2	6	3
5	27	4	10	2	6	3
6	36	5	12	4	8	3
7	38	5	14	4	8	3
8	43	6	16	4	10	3
9	45	6	18	4	10	3

* This maximum assumes the ProtoMech in question mounts a main gun. If not, the maximum will be 3 points less.

Location Restrictions

The amount of equipment space in each body location is strictly limited as follows.

Arms: Each arm can mount one weapon weighing no more than 500 kg (0.5 ton).

Torso: The torso may mount up to two weapons or pieces of equipment. The total weight of both items may be no more than 2,000 kg (2 tons). Weapons in the torso can be mounted to the rear.

Main Gun: Each ProtoMech may also carry a single main gun. This weapon is attached to the Proto's torso, though it is aimed and fired with both hands. The main gun may be a single weapon or piece of equipment of any weight. A missile launcher consisting of multiple tubes (see below) is considered a single weapon for this purpose.

Heat Sinks

All energy weapons (listed as Energy Weapons on the Weapons and Equipment Table, p. 116, *BMR*) that generate heat must have heat sinks assigned to them during construction. As on conventional vehicles, ballistic and missile weapons do not require heat sinks when mounted on ProtoMechs.

ProtoMechs use compact and highly efficient heat sinks to dissipate the excess heat generated by energy weapons fire. To determine the weight of the heat sinks required for a weapon, multiply the heat generated by the weapon by 250 kg. These heat sinks do not count as part of the weapon for purposes of location restrictions.

Double Heat Sinks: ProtoMechs use unique advanced heat sinks, and so they cannot mount double heat sinks.

Missile Launchers

Rather than mounting standard-issue missile launchers, ProtoMechs mount missile launchers in groups of tubes. Each tube launches a single missile per attack, so that an SRM launcher consisting of 2 tubes is fired in the same way as a standard SRM-2. Each group of missile tubes can consist of any number of tubes up to the maximum normally available for that type of launcher, and counts as a single weapon for purposes of location restrictions. Note that the weights of standard-sized launchers will not always match the weight of a similar launcher built from individual tubes for a ProtoMech. This discrepancy is intentional for ease of use and maximum flexibility.

See **Weapon Attacks** in **Combat,** p. 190, for rules for using non-standard configurations of launchers.

LRM: Each LRM tube weighs 200 kg.
SRM: Each SRM tube weighs 250 kg.
Streak SRM: Each Streak SRM tube weighs 500 kg.
Artemis IV: ProtoMechs cannot mount Artemis IV.

Ammunition

ProtoMechs can carry any size ammo bins; they are not limited to full-ton or half-ton lots. Each weapon that uses ammunition must have an ammo bin. The weight of the ammo does not count for the purposes of location restrictions.

For missile launchers, a weight is listed per missile, not per shot. The number of shots available must be evenly divisible by the number of tubes in the group. For example, an SRM-3 launcher that can fire 5 times would need to have an ammo bin holding a total of 15 missiles (SRM 3 x 5 = 15), for a total weight of 150 kg (15 x 10 = 150). The ammo would be listed on the record sheet simply as SRM-3 (5), because each time the weapon is fired, it automatically launches three missiles.

The ProtoMech Ammunition Weights Table lists weapon types and the weight in kilograms per shot. Note that the weights of ammunition listed will not always match exactly with the weights of the same ammo for other units. This is intentional, to provide round numbers that are fairly easy to use.

PROTOMECH AMMUNITION WEIGHTS

Ammo Type	Kg/Shot
AC/2	20/1
AC/5	50/1
Anti-Missile System	40/1
Heavy MG	10/1
Light MG	5/1
LRM*	25/3
MG	5/1
Narc Pods	150/1
SRM*	10/1

* This weight is per missile, not per salvo.

COSTS

The cost in C-bills for a custom-designed ProtoMech is the sum of the cost of all components according to the formulas listed below, multiplied by the Final ProtoMech Cost Multiplier. When formulas refer to tonnage, use the tonnage of the ProtoMech. As shown on the table below, the Structural Cost of a ProtoMech includes everything but its weapons and equipment.

PROTOMECH COST TABLE

Structural Cost	Formula or Cost (in C-bills)
Cockpit	500,000
Life Support	75,000
Sensors	Tonnage x 2,000
Musculature	Tonnage x 2,000
Internal Structure Skeleton	Tonnage x 400
Arm Actuators (per arm)	Tonnage x 180
Leg Actuators	Tonnage x 540
Engine	(5,000 x Rating x Tonnage)/75
Jump Jets	Tonnage x (Number of Jets $)^2$ x 200
Heat Sinks	2,000 each
Armor	625 x Armor Factor

Other Costs

Weapons and Equipment

See Weapon and Equipment Prices, p. 138, *BMR*

LRM*	10,000 x Tubes
SRM*	10,000 x Tubes
Streak SRM*	15,000 x Tubes

Final ProtoMech Cost Multiplier:
(Structural Cost + Weapons and Equipment Cost) x [1 + (Tonnage ÷ 100)]

* Costs for non-standard launcher sizes only.

PROTOMECH COSTS

ProtoMech Type	Cost (in C-bills)
Harpy	614,559
Siren	635,974
Satyr	812,188
Centaur	727,020
Hydra	757,927
Roc	839,388
Gorgon	871,902
Minotaur	946,556

Note that Clan units, including ProtoMechs, are not generally available for sale, so these prices are for purposes of comparison only.

BATTLE VALUES

The process for calculating the Battle Value (BV) of a ProtoMech is virtually the same as that for a conventional vehicle. Use those rules (p. 139, *BMR*) with the following changes.

Defensive Battle Rating

Add ProtoMech Tonnage to Base Defensive Battle Rating.

There is no Vehicle Type Modifier for ProtoMechs.

ProtoMechs add 0.1 to their Defensive Movement Factor.

Offensive Battle Rating

The BV of missile launchers that have a non-standard number of tubes are listed on the ProtoMech Missile Weapons BV Table.

If the ProtoMech carries a quantity of ammo other than a full ton, follow these steps to find the ammo BV: divide the kilograms of ammo carried by 1,000 and multiply the result by the BV of the ammo per ton. The result is the BV for the amount of ammo carried. Keep any fractional results.

For example, a Centaur has 8 shots of LRM-3 ammo weighing 200 kilograms. First, divide the kilograms of ammo carried by 1,000, resulting in 0.2 (200 ÷ 1000 = 0.2). Then, multiply 0.2 by the BV of the ammo per ton (5), to get the actual BV of the ammo carried, which is 1.2 (0.2 x 5 = 1).

PROTOMECH MISSILE WEAPONS BV

Item	Item BV	Ammo BV (per ton)
LRM 1	17	2
LRM 2	25	3
LRM 3	35	5
LRM 4	46	6
LRM 6	69	9
LRM 7	92	12
LRM 8	93	12
LRM 9	95	12
LRM 11	139	18
LRM 12	141	18
LRM 13	161	20
LRM 14	163	21
LRM 16	214	27
LRM 17	215	27
LRM 18	217	27
LRM 19	218	28
SRM 1	15	2
SRM 3	30	4
SRM 5	47	6
Streak SRM 1	20	3
Streak SRM 3	59	8
Streak SRM 5	99	13

HARPY

Mass: 2 tons
Chassis: Standard
Power Plant: 10
Cruising Speed: 32 kph
Maximum Speed: 54 kph
Jump Jets: 3
  Jump Capacity: 90 meters
Armor: Standard
Armament:
  1 Machine Gun
Manufacturer: Unknown
Communications System: Unknown
Targeting and Tracking System:
  Unknown

Overview

The first attempt to build a ProtoMech, the *Harpy* proved a disappointment. Barely larger than a standard battle armor suit, the *Harpy* shares many characteristics with its smaller cousin. In standard battlefield exercises, the *Harpy* generally fared poorly compared to armored Elementals. However, this ProtoMech is more than adequate for anti-infantry operations, where its light armor gives it sufficient protection and its larger size compared to battle armor offers a significant psychological advantage.

Type: **Harpy**
Technology Base: Clan ProtoMech
Tonnage: 2
Battle Value: 28

Equipment		**Mass (kg)**
Internal Structure:		200
Engine:	10	250
Walking MP:	3	
Running MP:	5	
Jumping MP:	3	150
Heat Sinks:	0	0
Cockpit:		500
Armor Factor:	11	550
	Internal Structure	*Armor Value*
Head	1	2
Torso	2	4
Main Gun	—	—
R/L Arm	1/1	1/1
Legs	2	3

Weapons and Ammo	**Location**	**Mass (kg)**
Machine Gun	T	250
Ammo (MG) 20	T	100

BATTLEFORCE 2
Name: Harpy Point

MP	**Damage PB/M/L**	**Overheat**	**Class**
3J	1/—/—	—	P

Armor/Structure	**Point Value**	**Specials**
3/—	1	

CLAN

SIREN

Mass: 3 tons
Chassis: Standard
Power Plant: 45
Cruising Speed: 108 kph
Maximum Speed: 162 kph
Jump Jets: None
Jump Capacity: None
Armor: Standard
Armament:
2 Light Machine Guns
Manufacturer: Unknown
Communications System: Unknown
Targeting and Tracking System: Unknown

Overview

The *Siren* was designed as an ultra-fast scout. Its large engine, accounting for a third of the machine's total mass, allowed space for only minimal armor protection and a pair of light machine guns. However, it performs admirably in its intended role as a forward spotter and scout for its Point.

Type: **Siren**
Technology Base: Clan ProtoMech
Tonnage: 3
Battle Value: 52

Equipment		**Mass (kg)**
Internal Structure:		300
Engine:	45	1,000
Walking MP:	10	
Running MP:	15	
Jumping MP:	0	0
Heat Sinks:	0	0
Cockpit:		500
Armor Factor:	12	600
	Internal Structure	*Armor Value*
Head	1	2
Torso	3	5
Main Gun	—	—
R/L Arm	1/1	1/1
Legs	2	3

Weapons and Ammo	**Location**	**Mass (kg)**
Light Machine Gun	RA	250
Ammo (LMG) 10	RA	50
Light Machine Gun	LA	250
Ammo (LMG) 10	LA	50

BATTLEFORCE 2
Name: Siren Point

MP	**Damage PB/M/L**	**Overheat**	**Class**
10	1/1/—	—	P

Armor/Structure	**Point Value**	**Specials**
3/—	3	

SATYR

Mass: 4 tons
Chassis: Standard
Power Plant: 45
Cruising Speed: 76 kph
Maximum Speed: 119 kph
Jump Jets: None
Jump Capacity: None
Armor: Standard
Armament:
1 ER Small Laser
Manufacturer: Unknown
Communications System: Unknown
Targeting and Tracking System:
Unknown

Overview

The most recently developed ProtoMech, the *Satyr* is a fast and agile unit with significant firepower for so small a machine. In addition to its formidable speed, the *Satyr* features an ER small laser and the newly developed light active probe. With no need to resupply ammo, the *Satyr*'s main mission is deep-penetration reconnaissance.

Type: **Satyr**
Technology Base: Clan ProtoMech
Tonnage: 4
Battle Value: 98

Equipment		**Mass (kg)**
Internal Structure:		400
Engine:	45	1,000
Walking MP:	7	
Running MP:	11	
Jumping MP:	0	0
Heat Sinks:	2	500
Cockpit:		500
Armor Factor:	12	600

	Internal Structure	*Armor Value*
Head	1	2
Torso	4	5
Main Gun	—	—
R/L Arm	1/1	1/1
Legs	3	3

Weapons and Ammo	**Location**	**Mass (kg)**
ER Small Laser	T	500
Light Active Probe	T	500

BATTLEFORCE 2
Name: Satyr Point

MP	**Damage PB/M/L**	**Overheat**	**Class**
7	3/3/—	—	P

Armor/Structure	**Point Value**	**Specials**
4/—	5	prb

CLAN

CENTAUR

Mass: 5 tons
Chassis: Standard
Power Plant: 45
Cruising Speed: 65 kph
Maximum Speed: 97 kph
Jump Jets: None
Jump Capacity: None
Armor: Standard
Armament:
1 Extended Range Micro Laser
1 SRM-2 Launcher
1 LRM-3 Launcher
Manufacturer: Unknown
Communications System: Unknown
Targeting and Tracking System: Unknown

Overview

A fast and flexible ProtoMech, the *Centaur* is a good all-purpose unit. Its weapons reach short, medium and long ranges, making it effective in many kinds of terrain from wilderness to city streets. However, its relatively light armor and reliance on ammunition prevent it from becoming a mainstay unit.

Type: **Centaur**
Technology Base: Clan ProtoMech
Tonnage: 5
Battle Value: 140

Equipment		**Mass (kg)**
Internal Structure:		500
Engine:	45	1,000
Walking MP:	6	
Running MP:	9	
Jumping MP:	0	0
Heat Sinks:	1	250
Cockpit:		500
Armor Factor:	20	1,000

	Internal Structure	*Armor Value*
Head	1	3
Torso	5	7
Main Gun	1	2
R/L Arm	1/1	2/2
Legs	3	4

Weapons and Ammo	**Location**	**Mass (kg)**
ER Micro Laser	M	250
SRM 2	T	500
Ammo (SRM) 10	T	200
LRM 3	T	600
Ammo (LRM) 8	T	200

BATTLEFORCE 2
Name: Centaur Point

MP	**Damage PB/M/L**	**Overheat**	**Class**
6	4/2/1	—	P

Armor/Structure	**Point Value**	**Specials**
5/—	7	if

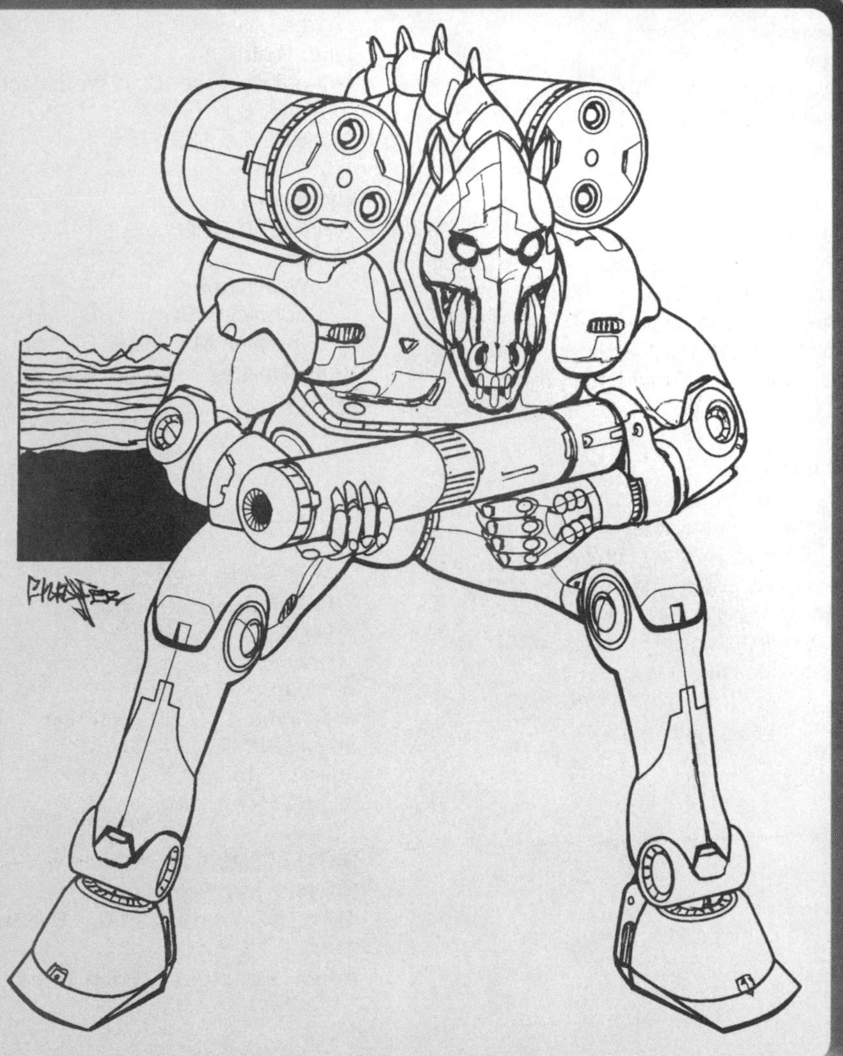

CLAN

HYDRA

Mass: 6 tons
Chassis: Standard
Power Plant: 36
Cruising Speed: 43 kph
Maximum Speed: 65 kph
Jump Jets: None
  Jump Capacity: None
Armor: Standard
Armament:
  1 Streak SRM-3 Launcher
  1 Micro Pulse Laser
Manufacturer: Unknown
Communications System: Unknown
Targeting and Tracking System:
  Unknown

Overview

The *Hydra* is designed as a medium assault unit. Its arsenal centers on a 3-tube Streak SRM launcher, giving it significant hitting power with good range. A surprisingly powerful micro pulse laser backs up the missile launcher. The *Hydra*'s only real weaknesses are its moderate speed and lack of jump jets.

Type: **Hydra**
Technology Base: Clan ProtoMech
Tonnage: 6
Battle Value: 139

Equipment		**Mass (kg)**
Internal Structure:		600
Engine:	36	900
Walking MP:	4	
Running MP:	6	
Jumping MP:	0	0
Heat Sinks:	1	250
Cockpit:		500
Armor Factor:	29	1,450

	Internal Structure	*Armor Value*
Head	2	3
Torso	6	10
Main Gun	1	3
R/L Arm	2/2	3/3
Legs	4	7

Weapons and Ammo	**Location**	**Mass (kg)**
Streak SRM 3	M	1,500
Ammo (Streak) 10	M	300
Micro Pulse Laser	T	500

BATTLEFORCE 2
Name: Hydra Point

MP	**Damage PB/M/L**	**Overheat**	**Class**
4	5/3/—	—	P

Armor/Structure	**Point Value**	**Specials**
8/—	7	

CLAN

ROC

Mass: 7 tons
Chassis: Standard
Power Plant: 60
Cruising Speed: 54 kph
Maximum Speed: 86 kph
Jump Jets: 5
Jump Capacity: 150 meters
Armor: Standard
Armament:
1 Extended Range Medium Laser
Manufacturer: Unknown
Communications System: Unknown
Targeting and Tracking System:
Unknown

Overview

The most successful ProtoMech design to date, the *Roc* combines mobility, armor and firepower effectively, and can be used in a variety of attack and defense missions. Because of its ratio of mobility to firepower, the *Roc* forms the backbone of most ProtoMech units.

Type: **Roc**
Technology Base: Clan ProtoMech
Tonnage: 7
Battle Value: 284

Equipment		**Mass (kg)**
Internal Structure:		700
Engine:	60	1,500
Walking MP:	5	
Running MP:	8	
Jumping MP:	5	500
Heat Sinks:	5	1,250
Cockpit:		500
Armor Factor:	31	1,550

	Internal Structure	*Armor Value*
Head	2	3
Torso	7	10
Main Gun	1	3
R/L Arm	2/2	4/4
Legs	4	7

Weapons and Ammo	**Location**	**Mass (kg)**
ER Medium Laser	M	1,000

BATTLEFORCE 2
Name: Roc Point

MP	**Damage PB/M/L**	**Overheat**	**Class**
5J	4/4/—	—	P

Armor/Structure	**Point Value**	**Specials**
8/—	14	

CLAN

GORGON

Mass: 8 tons
Chassis: Standard
Power Plant: 50
Cruising Speed: 43 kph
Maximum Speed: 65 kph
Jump Jets: None
Jump Capacity: None
Armor: Standard
Armament:
1 LRM-10 Launcher
1 Extended Range Micro Laser
Manufacturer: Unknown
Communications System: Unknown
Targeting and Tracking System: Unknown

Overview

The *Gorgon* is a powerful heavy support unit, often anchoring a mixed ProtoMech Point. Its main weapon is a 10-tube LRM launcher, large even by BattleMech standards. The addition of so massive a weapon prompted ProtoMech designers to develop the "main gun," a large, hand-supported weapon mount anchored to the ProtoMech's torso. The *Gorgon*'s major weakness is its lack of significant backup weapons; this tough unit must often withdraw from combat when its ammo is depleted.

Type: **Gorgon**
Technology Base: Clan ProtoMech
Tonnage: 8
Battle Value: 213

Equipment		**Mass (kg)**
Internal Structure:		800
Engine:	50	1,500
Walking MP:	4	
Running MP:	6	
Jumping MP:	0	0
Heat Sinks:	1	250
Cockpit:		500
Armor Factor:	34	1,700
	Internal Structure	*Armor Value*
Head	2	4
Torso	8	12
Main Gun	1	3
R/L Arm	2/2	4/4
Legs	5	7

Weapons and Ammo	**Location**	**Mass (kg)**
LRM 10	M	2,000
Ammo (LRM) 12	M	1,000
ER Micro Laser	T	250

BATTLEFORCE 2
Name: Gorgon Point

MP	**Damage PB/M/L**	**Overheat**	**Class**
4	5/3/3	—	P

Armor/Structure	**Point Value**	**Specials**
9/—	11	if

CLAN

MINOTAUR

Mass: 9 tons
Chassis: Standard
Power Plant: 45
Cruising Speed: 32 kph
Maximum Speed: 54 kph
Jump Jets: 3
Jump Capacity: 90 meters
Armor: Standard
Armament:
2 Extended Range Medium Lasers
Manufacturer: Unknown
Communications System: Unknown
Targeting and Tracking System: Unknown

Overview

The largest and most deadly ProtoMech, the *Minotaur* sacrifices speed for weaponry. It boasts two extended-range medium lasers—as much firepower as many light BattleMechs. This impressive hitting power is combined with enough armor to withstand a heavy autocannon attack. Slow-moving but intended for use in a defensive role, the *Minotaur* performs its function well, especially when an entire Point focuses its attacks on a single target.

Type: **Minotaur**
Technology Base: Clan ProtoMech
Tonnage: 9
Battle Value: 367

Equipment		**Mass (kg)**
Internal Structure:		900
Engine:	45	1,000
Walking MP:	3	
Running MP:	5	
Jumping MP:	3	300
Heat Sinks	10	2,500
Cockpit:		500
Armor Factor:	36	1,800

	Internal Structure	*Armor Value*
Head	2	5
Torso	9	15
Main Gun	—	—
R/L Arm	2/2	3/3
Legs	5	10

Weapons and Ammo	**Location**	**Mass (kg)**
ER Medium Laser	T	1,000
ER Medium Laser	T	1,000

BATTLEFORCE 2
Name: Minotaur Point

MP	**Damage PB/M/L**	**Overheat**	**Class**
3J	8/7/—	—	P

Armor/Structure	**Point Value**	**Specials**
9/—	18	

CLAN

BATTLETECH® PROTOMECH RECORD SHEET

Armor Diagram

Main Gun, Head, Left Arm, Right Arm, Torso, Legs

◎ = Internal Structure

Proto Type ______ **Tonnage** ______ **MP Walk/Run/Jump:** _/_/_/ **Gunnery** ______

Hit Locations and Critical Hits

2D6	LOCATION	1st HIT	2nd HIT	3rd HIT
2	Main Gun			
4	Right Arm	☐ +1 to Hit	☐ Right Arm Destroyed	
5,9	Legs	☐ –1 Walk MP	☐ 1/2 Walk MP	☐ No Move
6,7,8	Torso	☐ –1 Jump*	☐ 1/2 Jump*	☐ Proto Destroyed
10	Left Arm	☐ +1 to Hit	☐ Left Arm Destroyed	
12	Head	☐ +1 to Hit	☐ +2 to Hit; no Long range shots	

* Roll 1D6:
1–2, Torso Weapon A Destroyed; 3–4, Torso Weapon B Destroyed

Weapons Inventory

LOCATION	TYPE	DAM.	MIN.	S	M	L
Main Gun						
Right Arm						
Left Arm						
Torso A						
Torso B						
Ammo:						

Pilot Hits Taken	1	2	3	4	5	6
Conscious #	3+	5+	7+	10+	11+	Dead

Armor Diagram

Main Gun, Head, Left Arm, Right Arm, Torso, Legs

◎ = Internal Structure

Proto Type ______ **Tonnage** ______ **MP Walk/Run/Jump:** _/_/_/ **Gunnery** ______

Hit Locations and Critical Hits

2D6	LOCATION	1st HIT	2nd HIT	3rd HIT
2	Main Gun			
4	Right Arm	☐ +1 to Hit	☐ Right Arm Destroyed	
5,9	Legs	☐ –1 Walk MP	☐ 1/2 Walk MP	☐ No Move
6,7,8	Torso	☐ –1 Jump*	☐ 1/2 Jump*	☐ Proto Destroyed
10	Left Arm	☐ +1 to Hit	☐ Left Arm Destroyed	
12	Head	☐ +1 to Hit	☐ +2 to Hit; no Long range shots	

* Roll 1D6:
1–2, Torso Weapon A Destroyed; 3–4, Torso Weapon B Destroyed

Weapons Inventory

LOCATION	TYPE	DAM.	MIN.	S	M	L
Main Gun						
Right Arm						
Left Arm						
Torso A						
Torso B						
Ammo:						

Pilot Hits Taken	1	2	3	4	5	6
Conscious #	3+	5+	7+	10+	11+	Dead

Armor Diagram

Main Gun, Head, Left Arm, Right Arm, Torso, Legs

◎ = Internal Structure

Proto Type ______ **Tonnage** ______ **MP Walk/Run/Jump:** _/_/_/ **Gunnery** ______

Hit Locations and Critical Hits

2D6	LOCATION	1st HIT	2nd HIT	3rd HIT
2	Main Gun			
4	Right Arm	☐ +1 to Hit	☐ Right Arm Destroyed	
5,9	Legs	☐ –1 Walk MP	☐ 1/2 Walk MP	☐ No Move
6,7,8	Torso	☐ –1 Jump*	☐ 1/2 Jump*	☐ Proto Destroyed
10	Left Arm	☐ +1 to Hit	☐ Left Arm Destroyed	
12	Head	☐ +1 to Hit	☐ +2 to Hit; no Long range shots	

* Roll 1D6:
1–2, Torso Weapon A Destroyed; 3–4, Torso Weapon B Destroyed

Weapons Inventory

LOCATION	TYPE	DAM.	MIN.	S	M	L
Main Gun						
Right Arm						
Left Arm						
Torso A						
Torso B						
Ammo:						

Pilot Hits Taken	1	2	3	4	5	6
Conscious #	3+	5+	7+	10+	11+	Dead

Armor Diagram

Main Gun, Head, Left Arm, Right Arm, Torso, Legs

◎ = Internal Structure

Proto Type ______ **Tonnage** ______ **MP Walk/Run/Jump:** _/_/_/ **Gunnery** ______

Hit Locations and Critical Hits

2D6	LOCATION	1st HIT	2nd HIT	3rd HIT
2	Main Gun			
4	Right Arm	☐ +1 to Hit	☐ Right Arm Destroyed	
5,9	Legs	☐ –1 Walk MP	☐ 1/2 Walk MP	☐ No Move
6,7,8	Torso	☐ –1 Jump*	☐ 1/2 Jump*	☐ Proto Destroyed
10	Left Arm	☐ +1 to Hit	☐ Left Arm Destroyed	
12	Head	☐ +1 to Hit	☐ +2 to Hit; no Long range shots	

* Roll 1D6:
1–2, Torso Weapon A Destroyed; 3–4, Torso Weapon B Destroyed

Weapons Inventory

LOCATION	TYPE	DAM.	MIN.	S	M	L
Main Gun						
Right Arm						
Left Arm						
Torso A						
Torso B						
Ammo:						

Pilot Hits Taken	1	2	3	4	5	6
Conscious #	3+	5+	7+	10+	11+	Dead

Armor Diagram

Main Gun, Head, Left Arm, Right Arm, Torso, Legs

◎ = Internal Structure

Proto Type ______ **Tonnage** ______ **MP Walk/Run/Jump:** _/_/_/ **Gunnery** ______

Hit Locations and Critical Hits

2D6	LOCATION	1st HIT	2nd HIT	3rd HIT
2	Main Gun			
4	Right Arm	☐ +1 to Hit	☐ Right Arm Destroyed	
5,9	Legs	☐ –1 Walk MP	☐ 1/2 Walk MP	☐ No Move
6,7,8	Torso	☐ –1 Jump*	☐ 1/2 Jump*	☐ Proto Destroyed
10	Left Arm	☐ +1 to Hit	☐ Left Arm Destroyed	
12	Head	☐ +1 to Hit	☐ +2 to Hit; no Long range shots	

* Roll 1D6:
1–2, Torso Weapon A Destroyed; 3–4, Torso Weapon B Destroyed

Weapons Inventory

LOCATION	TYPE	DAM.	MIN.	S	M	L
Main Gun						
Right Arm						
Left Arm						
Torso A						
Torso B						
Ammo:						

Pilot Hits Taken	1	2	3	4	5	6
Conscious #	3+	5+	7+	10+	11+	Dead

BATTLETECH® PROTOMECH RECORD SHEET

Proto Type ____________ **Tonnage** ______ **MP Walk/Run/Jump:** _/_/_/ **Gunnery** ______

Hit Locations and Critical Hits

2D6	LOCATION	1st HIT	2nd HIT	3rd HIT
2	Main Gun			
4	Right Arm	☐ +1 to Hit	☐ Right Arm Destroyed	
5,9	Legs	☐ –1 Walk MP	☐ 1/2 Walk MP	☐ No Move
6,7,8	Torso	☐ –1 Jump*	☐ 1/2 Jump*	■ Proto Destroyed
10	Left Arm	☐ +1 to Hit	☐ Left Arm Destroyed	
12	Head	☐ +1 to Hit	☐ +2 to Hit; no Long range shots	

* **Roll 1D6:** **1–2, Torso Weapon A Destroyed; 3–4, Torso Weapon B Destroyed**

Weapons Inventory

LOCATION	TYPE	DAM.	MIN.	S	M	L
Main Gun						
Right Arm						
Left Arm						
Torso A						
Torso B						
Ammo:						

Pilot Hits Taken	1	2	3	4	5	6
Conscious #	3+	5+	7+	10+	11+	Dead

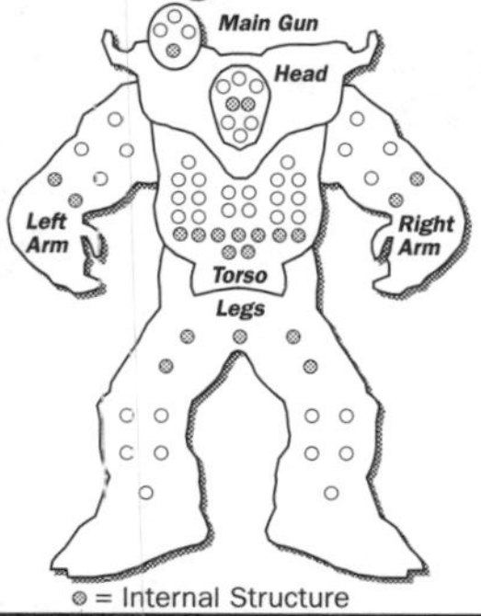

Proto Type ____________ **Tonnage** ______ **MP Walk/Run/Jump:** _/_/_/ **Gunnery** ______

Hit Locations and Critical Hits

2D6	LOCATION	1st HIT	2nd HIT	3rd HIT
2	Main Gun			
4	Right Arm	☐ +1 to Hit	☐ Right Arm Destroyed	
5,9	Legs	☐ –1 Walk MP	☐ 1/2 Walk MP	☐ No Move
6,7,8	Torso	☐ –1 Jump*	☐ 1/2 Jump*	■ Proto Destroyed
10	Left Arm	☐ +1 to Hit	☐ Left Arm Destroyed	
12	Head	☐ +1 to Hit	☐ +2 to Hit; no Long range shots	

* **Roll 1D6:** **1–2, Torso Weapon A Destroyed; 3–4, Torso Weapon B Destroyed**

Weapons Inventory

LOCATION	TYPE	DAM.	MIN.	S	M	L
Main Gun						
Right Arm						
Left Arm						
Torso A						
Torso B						
Ammo:						

Pilot Hits Taken	1	2	3	4	5	6
Conscious #	3+	5+	7+	10+	11+	Dead

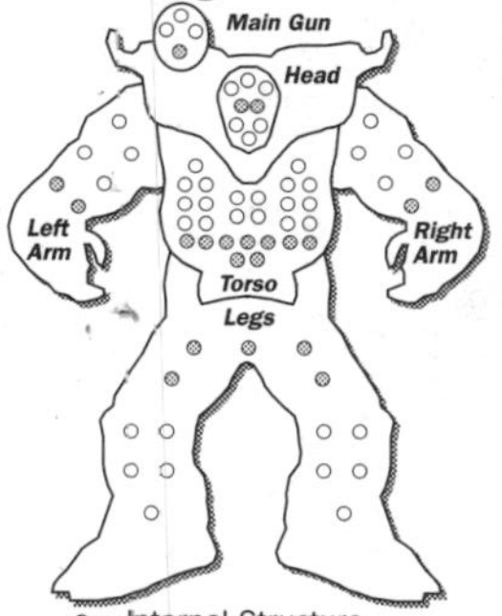

Proto Type ____________ **Tonnage** ______ **MP Walk/Run/Jump:** _/_/_/ **Gunnery** ______

Hit Locations and Critical Hits

2D6	LOCATION	1st HIT	2nd HIT	3rd HIT
2	Main Gun			
4	Right Arm	☐ +1 to Hit	☐ Right Arm Destroyed	
5,9	Legs	☐ –1 Walk MP	☐ 1/2 Walk MP	☐ No Move
6,7,8	Torso	☐ –1 Jump*	☐ 1/2 Jump*	■ Proto Destroyed
10	Left Arm	☐ +1 to Hit	☐ Left Arm Destroyed	
12	Head	☐ +1 to Hit	☐ +2 to Hit; no Long range shots	

* **Roll 1D6:** **1–2, Torso Weapon A Destroyed; 3–4, Torso Weapon B Destroyed**

Weapons Inventory

LOCATION	TYPE	DAM.	MIN.	S	M	L
Main Gun						
Right Arm						
Left Arm						
Torso A						
Torso B						
Ammo:						

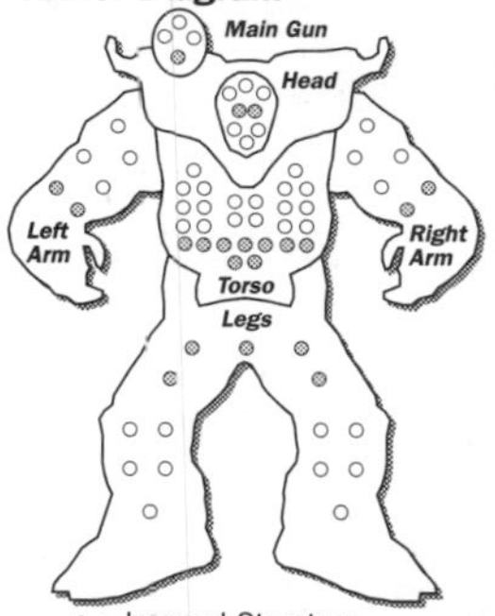

Pilot Hits Taken	1	2	3	4	5	6
Conscious #	3+	5+	7+	10+	11+	Dead

Proto Type ____________ **Tonnage** ______ **MP Walk/Run/Jump:** _/_/_/ **Gunnery** ______

Hit Locations and Critical Hits

2D6	LOCATION	1st HIT	2nd HIT	3rd HIT
2	Main Gun			
4	Right Arm	☐ +1 to Hit	☐ Right Arm Destroyed	
5,9	Legs	☐ –1 Walk MP	☐ 1/2 Walk MP	☐ No Move
6,7,8	Torso	☐ –1 Jump*	☐ 1/2 Jump*	■ Proto Destroyed
10	Left Arm	☐ +1 to Hit	☐ Left Arm Destroyed	
12	Head	☐ +1 to Hit	☐ +2 to Hit; no Long range shots	

* **Roll 1D6:** **1–2, Torso Weapon A Destroyed; 3–4, Torso Weapon B Destroyed**

Weapons Inventory

LOCATION	TYPE	DAM.	MIN.	S	M	L
Main Gun						
Right Arm						
Left Arm						
Torso A						
Torso B						
Ammo:						

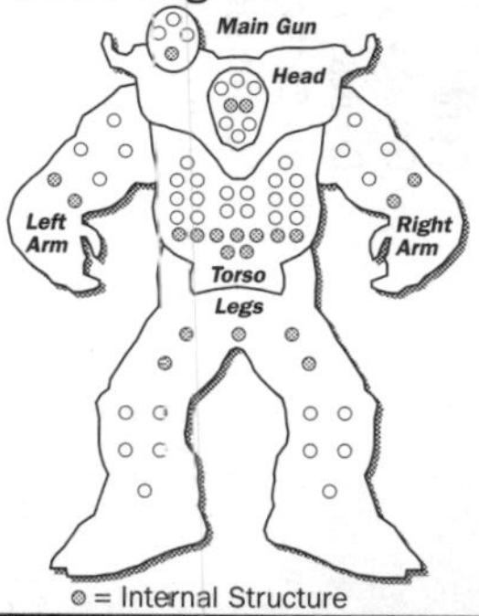

Pilot Hits Taken	1	2	3	4	5	6
Conscious #	3+	5+	7+	10+	11+	Dead

Proto Type ____________ **Tonnage** ______ **MP Walk/Run/Jump:** _/_/_/ **Gunnery** ______

Hit Locations and Critical Hits

2D6	LOCATION	1st HIT	2nd HIT	3rd HIT
2	Main Gun			
4	Right Arm	☐ +1 to Hit	☐ Right Arm Destroyed	
5,9	Legs	☐ –1 Walk MP	☐ 1/2 Walk MP	☐ No Move
6,7,8	Torso	☐ –1 Jump*	☐ 1/2 Jump*	■ Proto Destroyed
10	Left Arm	☐ +1 to Hit	☐ Left Arm Destroyed	
12	Head	☐ +1 to Hit	☐ +2 to Hit; no Long range shots	

* **Roll 1D6:** **1–2, Torso Weapon A Destroyed; 3–4, Torso Weapon B Destroyed**

Weapons Inventory

LOCATION	TYPE	DAM.	MIN.	S	M	L
Main Gun						
Right Arm						
Left Arm						
Torso A						
Torso B						
Ammo:						

Pilot Hits Taken	1	2	3	4	5	6
Conscious #	3+	5+	7+	10+	11+	Dead

BattleMechs and vehicles arranged alphabetically.

BattleMechs and vehicles listed by tons.

ProtoMechs (less than 10 tons)

10

11

15

INDEX

THE END